RAY GUY

Portrait of a Rebel

Ron Crocker

BOULDER
BOOKS

Library and Archives Canada Cataloguing in Publication

Title: Ray Guy : portrait of a rebel / Ron Crocker.
Names: Crocker, Ron (Journalist), author.
Description: Includes bibliographical references and index.
Identifiers: Canadiana 20210310669 | ISBN 9781989417430 (softcover)
Subjects: LCSH: Guy, Ray. | LCSH: Journalists—Newfoundland and Labrador—
Biography. | LCSH:
   Humorists, Canadian—Newfoundland and Labrador—Biography. |
LCSH: Satirists—Biography. | LCSH:
   Newfoundland and Labrador—Humor. | LCGFT: Biographies.
Classification: LCC PS8563.U8 Z567 2021 | DDC C817/.54—dc23

Published by Boulder Books

Portugal Cove-St. Philip's, Newfoundland and Labrador
www.boulderbooks.ca

Design and layout: Todd Manning
Editors: Jenny Higgins, Stephanie Porter
Copy editor: Iona Bulgin

Printed in Canada

We acknowledge the financial support of the Government
of Newfoundland and Labrador through the Department of
Tourism, Culture, Arts and Recreation.

Funded by the   Financé par le
Government   gouvernement
of Canada   du Canada

To Iris Brett and Sheila Fitzpatrick,
and to the memory of Katharine (Kathie) Housser.

CONTENTS

Tell all the truth, but tell it slant;
Success in Circuit lies.
Too bright for our infirm delight,
The Truth's superb surprise.
As lightning to the children eased,
With explanation kind:
The Truth must dazzle gradually,
Or every man be blind.

—*Emily Dickinson*

If one tells the truth, one is sure, sooner or later, to be found out.

—*Oscar Wilde*

It is hard for thee to kick against the pricks.

—*Acts 9:5 (King James Version)*

Bayman or bay man: One who lives on or near a bay or harbour; inhabitant of an "outport."

Out-harbour: A bay or harbour other than the chief port of St. John's; the inhabited coastal strip or settlement of such an inlet of the sea; outport.

Outport: A coastal settlement (in Newfoundland) other than the chief port of St. John's.

Townie: A native of St. John's, esp a male; usu derisive, and contrasting with bay man.

—*Dictionary of Newfoundland English*

FOREWORD

It may all come down to this—the gift that makes a great writer, and the compulsion of a great writer to write.

Ray Guy, the Newfoundland columnist, satirist, and essayist, was a gifted writer. Hard work made him better. But it was innate ability that enabled his success. His motivation to write was driven in large part by the ease with which he could.

A writer needs a core passion or subject, a subject of the heart. Dickens had London's poverty. For John Steinbeck, it was the Great Depression. Domestic relationships obsessed Jane Austen. Around such central planets, all other topics orbit.

To find that subject or subjects, a writer looks around and applies reflection to observation. From childhood, Guy looked and listened. His inclination to write about what he saw and heard became a force that could not be denied.

Guy wrote with lyrical passion about his subject of the heart—Newfoundland and Labrador.

He wrote fearlessly and defiantly about those whom he felt would mistreat or denigrate his country and his kind. He celebrated what he perceived as Newfoundland values. He satirized and ridiculed pretenders, potentates, and stuffed political shirts. He praised the best of Newfoundland's past and present. He condemned her notable defects.

Guy was fair-minded and tolerant—mostly. He could be unfair, too, and sometimes surprisingly cruel. And he was funny. Some of Guy's most serious writing was his funniest, a confection of humour and satire masking the medicine of social and political insight. If his purpose was political surgery, levity was his scalpel. In his own famous phrase, he felt he needed to "giggle the bastards to death."

As a daily newspaper columnist, Guy's top gear was satire—barbed sendups, brutal putdowns, and avenging-angel reckonings—all delivered in a clear and fluid prose. His phrasing and sentences were near perfect straight out of the typewriter, available virtually on tap. Daily and reliably, Guy afflicted the comfortable, comforted the afflicted, and, as if for a change of pace, brilliantly reprised the outport life of his childhood.

In his outport nostalgia groove, he described a receding culture deftly and often hilariously. By the time Guy wrote about it in the mid-1960s, that culture—outharbour Newfoundland of the 1940s and 1950s—already was half a generation out of step with the times.

For the decade spanning roughly the mid-1960s to the mid-1970s, Guy's daily newspaper writing, his satire, and his Encyclopedia of Juvenile Outharbour Delights were integral to Newfoundland and Labrador society and culture. By 1970, most Newfoundland high-school kids could tell you who Ray Guy was. College students adored him. More than a few could quote him.

In a sense, Guy had two careers. His 1960s and 1970s *Evening Telegram* page 3 columns were indispensable daily reading for a substantial Newfoundland and Labrador public. The name Ray Guy, in a 36-point font, enjoyed pride of place in a two-column format in the province's major newspaper, in an era when newspapers ruled. An accompanying photo, Guy once joked, "was said to be of me."

The impact of those *Telegram* columns and other Guy writings on Newfoundland political events, and on the decline and fall of former premier Joseph R. Smallwood, is indisputable. Their entertainment value was huge.

In 1967, one of Guy's *Telegram* feature stories won a National Newspaper Award and helped give him profile beyond Newfoundland. That piece, a hilarious account of a trans-island journey—both ways—on the "Newfie Bullet" passenger train, may have been the last spike in the coffin of Newfoundland's narrow-gauge railway.

In 1977, a collection of Guy's *Telegram* columns, *That Far Greater Bay*, won Canada's Stephen Leacock Memorial Medal for Humour. The purse was $15,000.

Guy continued to write extensively after 1975, of course. Indeed, he wrote until only a few months before his death in 2013. And while much of that writing was as stellar as any that had gone before, the times themselves had changed.

No longer welcome at the *Evening Telegram* after the mid-1970s, Guy's work became much more narrowly circulated. With no political windmill of Smallwood's stature at which to tilt, the drama of heretical star columnist versus omnipotent premier lost much of its torque. Other forces were at play as well. Provincial politics became more orthodox, better balanced, and, alas, less interesting. As Guy himself put it in 1972: "Now that Mr. Smallwood has gone off to write big thick books, there are no peaks or dips in Newfoundland politics—just one uniform, even, steady level of squalor."

Eventually, inevitably, the increasing homogeneity of outport and town life in Newfoundland diminished Guy's established role as tribune and keeper of the outport cultural flame. His Outharbour Delights columns reflected delights unknown to the emerging generation of post-Confederation Newfoundlanders. As Peter de Vries said, nostalgia was not what it used to be.

More pathologically, for many of those post-1970 years, Guy was a recurring prisoner of a dreaded disease, alcoholism. Not unrelated, during those years and most others, he was cursed by sporadic but profound depression, finally diagnosed in the mid-1980s as a bipolar disorder. Those afflictions would impose limitations on his career and burden his family and friends. At times, their impact was incapacitating.

In those post-*Telegram* decades, however, Guy wrote and wrote. He offered his conventional political columns and satire to any outlet that would have them. Many, such as the independent *Sunday Express* in Newfoundland, the Halifax-based *Atlantic Insight* magazine, the Newfoundland branch of the Canadian Broadcasting Corporation, and, latterly, the *Newfoundland Quarterly* and the *Northeast Avalon Times*, published Ray's work extensively and proudly.

Discovering other arrows in his quiver, Guy became a playwright and an actor. He wrote the darker-than-dark drama *Young Triffie's Been Made Away With*, which was successfully produced for the stage by Mary Walsh and later turned into a movie of indifferent quality. For Guy, it was a perennial money-maker.

Guy wrote sporadically for CBC Radio, softer-than-usual satires read by big-voiced CBC announcers. Finally, in early middle age, he defeated his acute microphone and camera phobia to play the role of Jack House, the "star boarder," in the Gordon Pinsent-inspired CBC Newfoundland comedy series, *Up at Ours*. In the 1990s, he did armchair television commentaries on CBC's suppertime newscast, *Here & Now*. He freelanced for scores of publications of all shapes and sizes, but with generally declining exposure and impact.

Guy's final newspaper columns were written for a small weekly paper, the *Northeast Avalon Times*, circulation 1,500. By comparison, his *Evening Telegram* columns would have been read daily by at least 35,000, his weekend pieces by twice that number. Still, this tiny community newspaper was important to him. Guy's wife, Kathie Housser, said it allowed him to end his career as he had begun it, by writing for a publication that he considered journalistically worthy and properly run. It also allowed him to gracefully stop writing when he felt he should. His final newspaper column ran in the March 2013 edition of the *Northeast Avalon Times*, under the inauspicious headline: "Columnist Bids Goodbye to Readers."

Part of Guy's legacy may be that in Newfoundland and Labrador the written word is far from anachronistic. The need for good writers remains undiminished. A dynamic and literate culture has obligations to those writers, not the least of which is gratitude. We owe it to them to remember and celebrate their achievements and to promote their works.

My motivation to write this book is rooted in a close friendship with Guy in the late 1960s and early 1970s when we both were reporters at the *Evening Telegram*. For nearly three years, we shared apartments in St. John's. In those years, I knew Guy at his best—affectionate, funny, and generous—and at his most troubled—sullen, silent, and dark—a hostage to innate tortures not even he could fully fathom.

We never ceased to be friends, but by the mid-1970s our educational and career roads had diverged. For subsequent decades, I followed his writing and his career with a blend of delight and worry, seeing him only sporadically. As Ron Hynes would have phrased it, I had left for Canada. Guy had not. He would have been welcomed by any major mainland newspaper. But Guy was hell-bent on survival as a freelance writer in St. John's. His determination to do so was Newfoundland and Labrador's gain.

The book aspires to two goals. Primarily, I would wish it to be read as a testament and a toast to Ray Guy's brilliant writing, and as a device to expand awareness of it.

It will be fine with me, however, if readers appreciate the book, at least secondarily, as an affectionate biography and memoir of a gifted and vulnerable friend.

Ron Crocker
Heart's Delight, NL

PART I

Newspaperman

CHAPTER 1

Adamses and Guys

The Guy family is a curious entity; the Adams family, even more so. I will save discussion of the Housser family until my meds are strengthened, or I feel stronger.
—*Kathie Housser*

It was a drama of life and death. On April 22, 1939, at the Lady Walwyn Cottage Hospital in Come by Chance, Newfoundland, a newborn baby boy struggled to survive.

Ray Guy was a blue baby, literally blue in colour, his circulation impaired, battling for each breath. A frantic and traumatic postnatal treatment, swaddled alternately in hot and cold blankets until his breathing became more certain, kept him alive.

Alice Louisa Guy was 40 years old when she gave birth that day after nearly three months of sporadic hospitalization with chronic pregnancy illnesses. She called the boy Rae David George Guy, using the R-a-e spelling usually associated with females of that name.

A year and a half earlier, Alice had brought another baby boy to term. He was the first of two of Ray's unnamed siblings who lived for only a few hours. Ray was 15 when he learned of his two lost brothers. He was profoundly upset by the news. A sense of sadness and regret remained with him always, as did profound gratitude for the one sibling who survived. Ray's sister, Iris, was born just over a year later, a thriving baby—still thriving in her mid-70s in 2021.

"Endure, endure, endure," Guy wrote half a century later, in tribute to his fellow Newfoundlanders and Labradorians.

"We should follow the example of the baymen who learned at least one thing in four centuries ... Sometimes the mute endurance of rocks, sometimes the roaring endurance of a stout bull ... sometimes the fluid endurance of the waters around us that only look soft."[1]

Endurance at birth; defiance and independence thereafter. Those forces informed and defined Guy's life and work. He came by them honestly. They were bred in the bone.

When Ray Guy was a child at home in Arnold's Cove, his southwestern gaze across the harbour had a focus. It was the old and abandoned Adams family homestead of Bordeaux, 3 kilometres away, a pastoral and cultivated parcel of land. Along with Bordeaux Island, a gunshot or two farther out the bay, the Bordeaux acreage constituted the Cove's most southerly reach.

Bordeaux was Arcadia, fertile and lush by Newfoundland standards, where Ray's mother, Alice Louisa Adams, was raised and educated, mostly without the encumbrance of day school. At Bordeaux, Alice absorbed the Victorian and Church of England verities that defined her and that helped her instill their secular equivalents in her gifted son.

> Thursday October 5, at one o'clock we landed at a little settlement called Bordeaux, to apprise the inhabitants

of my intention of holding a Confirmation tomorrow at Woody Island. This was formerly a French settlement, and the land had been cleared by the French. The present occupier is an Englishman from Sturminister, who has brought a considerable amount of land under cultivation, and grows wheat, barley and oats ... The farm is exceedingly picturesque, as well as fruitful ...[2]

The passage is from an account written in 1848 by the Church of England bishop of Newfoundland, Bishop Edward Feild. The Sturminister man who impressed Bishop Feild was Thomas Adams, Ray Guy's grandfather.

The Adamses of Bordeaux, Guy once wrote, were a distinct society. The family remained at Bordeaux and ran the farm until the 1940s. Nelson Adams, Alice's older brother, came home after World War II service and lived at Bordeaux, maintaining the farm during the summer months.

A favourite uncle who became an influence on the young Ray Guy, Nelson was the third of nine children born to James and Emily (Boutcher) Adams of Bordeaux. Their ninth and last child was Ray Guy's mother, Alice Louisa. Alice's life touched three centuries. She was born September 5, 1899. She died March 6, 2001—101 years, six months, and one day later.

Like Alice Adams, George Hynes Guy was the youngest of nine children. Ray's sister, Iris, said their paternal grandfather, Joshua Guy, was "a mediocre fisherman but an excellent boat builder. However, there was no call for that expertise as everyone built their own boats with neighbourly help. Joshua was stuck with fishing."

Joshua Guy enjoyed respect in Arnold's Cove, but with a tinge of notoriety that Ray Guy would have admired. A man of faith and a fervent Church of Englander, he rose to become a lay reader in the church, a position of some prestige. But Joshua made the mistake of straying from the sanctioned sermons prescribed for lay ministers to offer his own take on matters both spiritual and worldly. Demoted by the diocese, he enlisted in the Salvation Army, where he and his wife, Rachel Hynes Guy, worshipped for the rest of their lives. Ray Guy grew up in the Church of England faith but with an infusion of Salvation Army culture and music, instilled by Grandmother Guy.

Joshua Guy left one other mark on Arnold's Cove. He built a solid house for Rachel and their large brood of children. Under Joshua's handwritten will, which Iris still possesses, the house was left to George. Iris still lives there in 2021.

Joshua Guy died at home in 1938, a year before Ray was born. Grandmother Rachel lived in the house with the family until her death in 1949. She and Ray were close during the final decade of her life and the first decade of his.

George H. Guy followed his father into a fishing boat, gradually working his way ashore. With much help from Alice, he found himself behind the counter of the small general store that in Ray's childhood was the core of the Guy family business.

A salmon fisherman in summer and a lumberman in the fall, George Guy was still a bachelor at the advanced age of 28. He had free time in winter to indulge his favourite pastimes—reading, yarning, arguing about politics—but fewer and fewer prospects for marriage, let alone for love. For Alice, nearing 40, there were fewer prospects still.

Like the Guy family, the Adams family carried its own sheen of notoriety and stirred its share of gossip. The morality of the matriarch Emily, Ray's grandmother, was evident in her response to the mildly scandalous romantic adventures of her children, starting with the sad story of her oldest daughter, Alista Ann, and a boy named Willie.

As a very young woman, Alista Ann gave birth to Willie, a child out of wedlock. A measure of shame was inherent in unwed and unblessed sex at the turn of the last century. It varied by community, by Christian denomination, and by family standing. In Alista Ann's case, it was inflated by the Arnold's Cove gossip mill.

As one of the few comparatively well-off local families, the Adamses endured occasional village resentment, retailed through rumour and ridicule. The story got around that Alista had gone to St. John's on a pleasure trip and gotten herself pregnant on the train, the Newfie Bullet. Iris Brett believes that such a story, while not impossible, probably is fiction. Half the local girls who got pregnant, Iris joked, were "knocked up on the Bullet."

From the Adams gene pool, Willie carried forward his own measure of defiance. At 15, he fled, boarding the Bullet at Arnold's Cove Station, bound for St. John's. There he lied about his age to enlist in the Newfoundland Regiment, then recruiting for European service at the beginning of the Great War.

On November 6, 1919, a letter addressed to Mrs. Emily Adams arrived at the Arnold's Cove post office. It was from the Department of Militia in St. John's.

> Dear Madam:
> I enclose herewith cheque for $82.63, balance of estate of late Pte. W.J. Adams.
> Yours truly
> Major (Name unclear)
> Paymaster and O i/c Records

Willie Adams had been killed in action, at the Battle of Arras at Monchy-le-Preux in France in 1917. When Ray was a child in the 1940s, Cousin Willie was remembered and spoken of as a family hero.

There is no direct mention of Willie Adams in Ray Guy's writing. There is significant and empathetic mention of the common fate of "merrybegots," children born out of wedlock but taken in by the mother's family—rarely if ever the father's—and often raised as siblings of the mother. Guy's typical handling of this topic is delicate, a tribute to a more benign and generous outport attitude. He also understood that not all outports, or outport families, were equal.

> In one you would see an unmarried mother shut away with all the scorn and reproach of relatives and community turned against her until she could bear the weight no more, and died. Just as surely so if she had been in the middle of Africa and cursed by a witch doctor.
>
> In another you would see the people say it was a shocking thing but it happens, and they would call the little one no worse than a "merrybegot" (there are worse things to be called) and it would be taken in with normal joy to get a fair share of whatever a family and community gives.[3]

It was Alice's brother, Ray's Uncle Nelson, who next incurred his mother's wrath in a matter of the heart. Nelson's attentions focused on Isabella Hynes, an Arnold's Cove eligible 14 years his junior.

There was only one hurdle. In Emily Adams's mind, that hurdle was insurmountable. Isabella Hynes was Emily's niece. The audacity of such a relationship was truly beyond the pale. The message from Bordeaux was unambiguous. If Nelson married Isabella, she would not be welcome at Bordeaux, and neither would Nelson himself.

For Nelson Adams, a confident war veteran and a man not easily bullied, there was a clear course of action. He abandoned Bordeaux and built himself one of the finest houses in Arnold's Cove. One consequence of this decision was that he became a larger presence in Ray Guy's early life. In an essay written while he was a college student, Ray described a feeling of awe he had experienced at the age of nine "when my uncle told me in appropriately solemn tones, about the stars 'reaching on back for ever and ever and ever.'" That uncle was Nelson.

Nelson remained a bachelor, almost forever. Isabella Hynes married another man, with whom she departed for Canada. In 1955, aged 56, she returned to Arnold's Cove, a widow. There she soon accepted Nelson Adams, then aged 69, as her lawful wedded husband.

The story of Nelson and Isabella foreshadowed the experience two decades later of Ray Guy's parents, George and Alice. When George and Alice noticed each other in the early 1930s, the usual chilly breeze of disapproval blew in from Bordeaux. Unlike Nelson and Isabella, there was no barrier of consanguinity for George and Alice. In Emily's view, the issues now were status and class. Measured against the Adams family, George Guy was a notch below.

As it turned out, Nelson Adams was to play a minor role in bringing George and Alice together. Nelson's house in the Cove was a hangout for the local men, who gathered to chat and argue on fall and winter evenings. George Guy showed up from time to time, a lively contributor to the discourse of the day. When Alice Adams returned to the Cove, she was a frequent visitor to the home of her sociable brother.

Alice was nine years older than George, and her life had taken a remarkably different path. At 19 or 20, she had made a momentous personal decision:

> I went away to a foreign land—Canada.
>
> I don't think we had to get deloused before we could get off the Island but there were vaccinations and you had to have some money. I think it was $30 besides

your fare ... I went away and came back several times before I came home to stay.[4]

In Montreal, Alice, "with the bit of education [she] had," enrolled in a training program at the Montreal Foundling and Baby Hospital. Much of her subsequent work was with wealthy American families in New York City and Buffalo, "not as a registered nurse but as a baby nurse, looking after newborns in difficulty, premature babies in particular."

Like most Newfoundlanders and Labradorians who have left home in search of work or adventure, Alice came home as often as she could. She hoped to return to the Cove or to Bordeaux to start a business, an ambition she would realize only after she married George H. Guy and settled down for good.

At her brother Nelson's house, Alice had become reacquainted with George H. Guy, whom she had known only vaguely as a boy. What struck her about George was his knowledge of political and world events. Alice too was a reader who could hold her own in worldly chat. She was aware of another imperative—a biological clock. In her memoir, Alice wrote that she "was heading up for 40 by this time and decided if I was ever going to marry and have a family I'd better get at it. So I came home and got married."

The encounters at Nelson's house led to letters, and, if letters weren't enough, Alice played a higher card, another reliable route to the heart of an outport gentleman. As Iris tells it, Alice sat down somewhere in Canada and knit George a pair of sheep's wool socks.

At Bordeaux, the engagement was met with disdain. In Emily's stern judgment, Alice was marrying down.

In 1936, Alice and George and a small entourage of relatives and friends entrained for St. John's. They were married at the Anglican Cathedral. Forty years later, Katharine Housser and Ray Guy, with a bigger entourage, were married in the same magnificent church, following a courtship no less singular than that of George and Alice.

Beginning with Alista Ann, running through Nelson, and certainly including Alice Louisa, the children of James and Emily Adams carried forward the Sturminister Adamses' streaks of independence and defiance. In turn, Alice passed them on to Ray.

CHAPTER 2

Wise Guy:
The Making of a Writer

True ease in writing comes from art, not chance,
As those move easiest who have learn'd to dance.
—*Alexander Pope*

Ray Guy's first and most formative decade was spent in a country as different from Canada as Canada is from the United States, or Ireland is from England. It was a unique social and political world, in intriguing times.

Guy was a child in the 1940s when Newfoundland's political status was at large and Confederation with Canada was only an option. His youth and teenage years were the 1950s, the first lumpy decade of transformation from unfulfilled nation to awkward Canadian province.

Few Newfoundlanders and Labradorians became fully fledged and heartfelt Canadians overnight. Fewer still were born long enough prior to Confederation to have experienced a native Newfoundland identity. Guy was 10 in 1949 when the union was forged. His country forever would be Newfoundland and Labrador.

For the 77,869 Newfoundlanders and Labradorians who in 1948 voted to join Canada—crushing the hopes of the 71,464 who did not—Canada would be an acquired taste. Canadian identity and commitment were at least a generation away. There are Newfoundlanders dying today with their backs to the Gulf of St. Lawrence.

Comedian and writer Greg Malone has written an extreme version of the mood: "In the early 1970s, like so many of my generation I went to Toronto a Canadian and came back a Newfoundlander."[5]

Unlike Malone, Guy went to Toronto as a Newfoundlander and came back as one. Guy was not unmoved by his intense and very Canadian experience in the early 1960s as a student at the Ryerson Institute of Technology, now Ryerson University. But he was not captured by it either.

Coming of age in the 1960s, Guy joined a whipsawed generation of young Newfoundlanders. Growing up in an anti-Confederate family, Newfoundland and Labrador were seared into his soul. His was the last generation of Newfoundlanders and Labradorians haunted by the notion that an actual choice was required.

The island of Newfoundland, the physical place, changed faster than Newfoundlanders did in those transformative decades of the 1950s and 1960s. The general appearance of the outports was altered. Traditional and functional saltbox houses gave way to boxy bungalows designed by a federal agency, Central Mortgage and Housing. The fishery moved offshore into longliners and trawlers and away from coastal communities.

Many of those coastal places were abandoned as unsustainable in the 1960s and 1970s. As many as 30,000 people from 300 communities were moved through controversial displacement programs called resettlement and centralization. One of the towns changed forever was Guy's Arnold's Cove—not by people moving out, but by hundreds moving in.

During the same era, and to Canada's eternal discredit, the essential Newfoundland cod fishery was not looked after, plundered to near extinction in three decades by federal regulatory failings. By 1975, classic fishing stages and flakes with their precarious pilings and longers were becoming hard to find, even as nearly every inhabited harbour boasted a new, Ottawa-funded, and often underused breakwater.

St. John's experienced a similar dynamic, simultaneously becoming better and worse. On a good day in 1960, the growing capital got a new university, with subsidized tuition so low that almost every qualified young person could afford to attend. In a less auspicious development, the city got the Avalon Mall, satirized as the "Babylon Mall" by the 1980s music and comedy group The Wonderful Grand Band, who saw it as a temple of decline and decadence, where "parking's free but you pay to pee."[6]

It was all in stark contrast to the capital of the old colony. As a child in the mid-1940s, Guy had visited St. John's at least twice with his parents. His first bleak impressions of the pre-Confederation port were reprised more than half a century later in an essay for *Canadian Geographic*:

> I remember the coal-smoke stench of the street, the cobblestones, the small-paned shop windows, the rattling tram cars tearing along at 10 miles an hour with fearful cracks and showers of electrical sparks from the wires overhead. Dim shop interiors, wood-paneled and lit by bare 15-watt bulbs; stupefied birds called "pigeons" that you nearly trod on; much horse manure and almost as many little English motor cars as there were nags and carts. Strong smells from the shops, either tarry or

vegetable; pairs of constables, black from neck to heels in heavy great-coats, constantly glancing right and left for youthful bread thieves.

Dark, grim and suffocating was Water Street. Every building, indeed every house in the town, was painted either chopped-liver red or fungal green, old railway colors. Some said the dismal paint was to disguise the coal-smoke soot, others that the only paint used in town was pilfered from the railway depot.[7]

Ray Guy grew up in Arnold's Cove, Placentia Bay, that "Far Greater Bay" of his literary universe. As the child of a small business family, he was not deprived, but only in an outport Newfoundland context where no one was truly rich. His education was whatever was on offer, for better and for worse.

Guy did not learn to be a writer, nor did he achieve literacy, in an Arnold's Cove schoolhouse. The schoolhouse of most 1950s Newfoundland outports did not so much ignore learning as redefine it as a form of combat. School for Guy paralleled the experience of most other rural Newfoundlanders of the time, a daily challenge of discomfort, inadequacy, and frequent abuse, leavened occasionally by an able teacher who made a difference.

Especially in smaller outports, young, untrained, and underpaid teachers of the era became lone sentries in one-room, all-grade schools. They often met their match in the collective defiance of 30 or 40 charges for whom the schoolhouse often was perceived as more custodial than enlightening.

The glow of affection and bemusement Guy brought to his sporadic nostalgia columns, his Encyclopedia of Juvenile Outharbour Delights, was matched by the ferocity with which he described his Arnold's Cove school days.

In a 1968 column, St. Michael and All Angels School in Arnold's Cove, which Guy attended for 10 of his 11 years of day school, became "good old Buchenwald Elementary."

There were hundreds of these concentration camps all over Newfoundland and I guess there are still some left.

I hope so. Because I'm going to need someone to back me up when the Pepsi generation starts accusing me of telling lies.

Ah, yes, they were a bit on the rugged side. A notch above those hard knock British schools Prince Philip favors. Something of a cross between a Georgia chain gang and the Spanish Inquisition ...

The sounds of an average school day were the sounds of a continuous TV western fist-fight, the whack and crunch of flesh and bone being assaulted. We got strapped with everything but a strap.

No I tell a lie. I remember one humanitarian who tried to play it according to the Geneva Convention. With a small grant from the school board he purchased a quantity of tapping leather to fashion a regulation strap.

(For the delectation of the flagellants among us, the strap in question was three inches wide, two feet long, and a quarter of an inch thick. It didn't draw blood but it turned your hands red and made your fingers puff up like beef sausages, but it didn't leave any marks.)

By this time we had grown proud of our scars so we stole this strap and shoved it down the outhouse hole. He had to go back to making do with whatever odds and ends were handy.

Throughout the years we were strapped with a kitchen chair leg, the buckle end of a belt, a piece of driftwood, a strip of wainscot ripped from the class-room wall, a piece of the top of a desk, a broom handle, a hand-gaff handle, a heavy wooden ruler with a strip of tin down the edge, and, for variety's sake, a half fathom of manila rope.

Guy was once strapped for an offence that American jurists might consider a special type of felony—a larger, hyphenated crime committed while committing a smaller one. In his case, the offence was a farting felony.

> I remember the time the teacher gave me a strapping for (to be tasteful about it) "breaking wind."
> "You're getting this not so much for what you did," said the schoolmaster, wagging the strap back and forth to get a nice wristy action, "as for the insolent way in which you did it."[8]

Guy paused sporadically to address some obvious questions about his school days. Why were such conditions allowed to continue? And how did he and many other outport overachievers of his era survive such hostile regimes to become writers, doctors, academics, and judges? One answer may be that not enough of them did.

On the larger question of accountability for the system, Guy's views were focused and they never wavered. Nor was he inclined to understate them. In his column the following day, he returned to his school days and why they were so limiting.

> It need not have been that way. Therefore the shame and the guilt must rest on somebody's head. In our case there were a half-dozen other communities within a 20-mile radius.

They could have gotten together, built a half-decent school somewhere in between and attracted teachers worthy of the name. It seemed so obvious. Why wasn't it done?

Well, where have you been, baby? Haven't you guessed? These half-dozen communities represented three or four different denominations. Christian denominations.

So if you please—don't talk to me about the glories of denominational education. Because I may vomit.

Achievement or even survival in such a system was indeed a crapshoot. Yet certain Newfoundland outports in the 1950s and 1960s were known to have produced disproportionate numbers of high-school graduates. It was less a matter of genetics than of luck. If most rural teachers were badly cast, poorly trained, and no happier to be in the classroom than were their pupils, a select few, as Guy carefully reports, were skilled, committed, and uniquely successful.

Now let me say this ... Between kindergarten and grade eleven I must have encountered a dozen teachers. Most of them were miserable misfits who quickly turned into classroom sadists to cover their failings.

But ... there were three or four among them who—considering the circumstances—deserve to be numbered among the saints and martyrs.

They did not have university degrees and they were up against a frightful job, but they managed to show us that bashing skulls is not the only use for a book. They will have their reward.[9]

Ray Guy's progress in school was not left solely to teachers. Modesty may have kept him from mentioning another potent force enabling him and his sister, Iris, to survive high school and go on to college at a time when very few outport kids did. Their parents, Alice especially, were committed to their schooling. The year Ray turned 15 and was headed into Grade 11, Arnold's Cove failed to attract a suitable Church of England teacher for St. Michael and All Angels. Of course, neither a Catholic nor even a Methodist need apply. Threatened with losing a year of schooling, Ray was shipped off to live with cousins on Bell Island to finish high school. His teacher there, Robert Pepper, encouraged him to write.

"It was one of the few things I always got praised for in school, writing little essays and all that," Guy told the *Newfoundland Herald* for a profile piece on February 1, 1978. "I was so desperate at mathematics and that side of it. I guess most people are one way or the other."[10]

Despite the speed bumps, Guy managed to pull a respectable "pass" out of the Newfoundland Public Examinations of 1956. His best mark was for Art, 86 per cent. He was a lifelong doodler, possibly good enough to have been a newspaper cartoonist if his goal had been a shorter workday. Surprisingly, he scored 85 for Mathematics, which he always professed to hate and which he flunked in first-year university. In Guy's high-school graduating year, the separate but complementary subjects of English Language and English Literature were each marked out of 50. In those, he achieved 36 and 37 respectively.

Guy's childhood was buffeted by one other unusual and surprisingly strong current that was unique to its time and place. It was the influence of World War II and, more forcefully, the impact of a significant American military presence at Guy's doorstep.

Arnold's Cove was directly affected by American armed forces' manoeuvres in Newfoundland. In 1941, members of the US Army

3rd Infantry, a section of the 62nd Coast Artillery and the 24th Anti-Aircraft Artillery Units, arrived at Arnold's Cove Station, a few miles inland from the Cove itself. Ken Tulk, author of *Arnold's Cove: A Community History*, described their mission: "to set up anti-aircraft guns at strategic locations and to man high watch towers built at several locations in the Placentia Bay and Trinity Bay areas."

In Arnold's Cove, Tulk recounts, they built a watchtower at a point of land known as the Otter Rub, near Guy's Point, a kilometre or so from the Guy family home. At Arnold's Cove Station, the US soldiers built a barracks, a mess hall, a day room, an outside power plant, and dog kennels. The soldiers "performed continuous patrols with 'K9' dogs along the coast from Arnold's Cove to Come by Chance and along the coastline in both Placentia and Trinity Bays. Their objective was to report any sighting of German submarines or any other activity that would indicate the enemies' presence."

This level of vigilance was by no means over the top. On October 14, 1942, a German U-boat torpedoed the Newfoundland Railway passenger vessel *Caribou*, killing 137, many of them women and children. The *Caribou* was on a regular civilian run from Port aux Basques, Newfoundland, to North Sydney, Nova Scotia. Other German U-boats sank two freighters loaded with iron ore in Conception Bay, only a few miles from St. John's. In October 1943, the German submarine U-537 was photographed at anchor in Martin Bay, Labrador, where the Germans had built a weather station.[11]

In the 1940s and later, Americans populated the big US bases in Newfoundland and Labrador: Argentia in Placentia Bay (Navy), Fort Pepperrell in St. John's (Army), and the US Air Force bases in Stephenville (Ernest Harmon Air Force Base), then later as part of the Strategic Air Command in Goose Bay. The bases and their surrounding communities flourished, with the final major contingent of US airmen remaining in Goose Bay until the mid-1970s.

If the Americans were polite, they did not always behave with the humility expected of guests. During World War II, their assertive military manner and their serious mission brought the war home to Newfoundland and Labrador. The August 1941 Atlantic Charter meeting between Winston Churchill and Franklin D. Roosevelt on a ship in Placentia Bay seemed to place Newfoundland in the middle of the wartime political swirl. Except for families whose sons or brothers had already died or were injured overseas, war became exotically interesting to thousands of Newfoundlanders who were too young or too old to enlist and who were in awe of the handsome Yanks with their swagger and sparkling teeth.

World War I, for which Newfoundland raised its own regiment, had brought mostly sadness, as young men left home, communicated only sparingly with their families, and, like Willie Adams, too often never returned. It also brought home the "old-lie" paradox of war.[12]

Guy said he once asked his mother, who lived through both, which war was worse, "Great or Second?" Possibly remembering Willie, her nephew and childhood friend, Alice replied: "Oh, the Great War by a long shot. You had people over there and you could not hear from one year to another if they were dead or alive or hurt or gone mad. In the last one it seemed like every time you looked around they were home on leave."

World War II brought sorrow too. But the constant presence of smart-looking soldiers, exotic aircraft, and enemy submarines at the doorstep, delivered World War II to Newfoundland in its more benign dimension.

Guy was only six years old when the US soldiers left Arnold's Cove. But their presence, and, more likely, their legacy, made an impression on him, an impact reflected frequently in his writing. His *Telegram* column of August 14, 1973, was an endearing memoir of wartime in Arnold's Cove, from the perspective of a child.

> As I was then still in short pants, a personal recollection
> of the last Great Conflict is hazy indeed ...

I remember giving up my favorite ball toward the downfall of Adolf Hitler.

A big man-in-the moon ball it was, with a face on it ... It got taken in a rubber drive.

Someone was going around the place (Uncle Sandy, I think it was) with some brin bags collecting all the old gaiters and stuff to make tires for Spitfires ...

By and by the Americans came.

They put up some camps in at the Station, which was three miles in the road, and they sent out some people to stick up poles with wires on them going all through the place and right on across the marsh by the Salvation Army graveyard out to the Otter Rub.

I was upstairs, half under the bed, looking out the window at them, as I was timid as a child and would go under the bed whenever the doctor or the constable or anyone strange would come.

The first time I saw Americans I hardly knew what to make of them.

They all seemed to have a brownish cast to their faces (from being born in the sun, I dare say, in Ohio) and they all looked exactly alike ...

Another thing about them is they had teeth as big as horses', which looked like they were white painted.

Although my sister, Iris, being younger than myself, was always ready to have her snap taken up in their arms out in the yard, I was afraid to get too handy to them ...

School and colonial war culture were among many subcultures Ray Guy would experience in the 1940s. There were church commitments, all non-negotiable. There were Sunday School Bible instruction classes and Holy Communion boot camps. Once asked where he got his sense of humour, Guy quipped: "From the Book of Job, chapters eight through 14." Occasionally he played the organ at the Church of St. Michael and All Angels in Arnold's Cove. He would take off his shoes and socks and pump the organ with his bare feet. Church matrons were at best bemused.

Grandmother Guy, Rachel, was a Salvationist, and under her influence Guy also sampled services at the local Salvation Army Barracks, where martial hymns of the "Onward Christian Soldiers" variety, and the threat of hell's flames, enlivened Sunday evening services. Infinitely more entertaining than the vanilla evensong at St. Michael and All Angels, Sally Ann worship featured bass drums, brass instruments, and uniformed preachers, all tuned to give the great gospel hymns, and the Word of God, extra dread and purpose.

Beyond the classroom and the pew, Guy was exposed to constant storytelling of a different kind. The yarn and the cuffer were the central currencies of outport Newfoundland discourse.[13]

At the Guy family house, Alice and George H. ran the post office and a general store. Both hummed daily with community chatter and gossip. Guy absorbed it all. At Uncle Nelson's house nearby, clusters of men still gathered to chew the rag on winter evenings, an inviting haunt where young Ray needed only to hold his tongue and remain alert to hear tales of adventure and courage and the political intrigues of the day.

Guy's eclectic childhood experiences permeate his writing. His memory was elastic, harkening back at least to toddler times, occasionally even earlier. When he evoked his bucolic past, his readers remembered their own:

It is funny how the infant mind functions.

I can mind, when I was small, being lodged off down on the coats in the back of the school at dances.

This is where they put you at about two o'clock in the night when you commenced to get groggy and wanted a nap. There was a row of desks shoved in tight to the wall for all hands to put their coats on. Sometimes there would be three or four of us at once laid out heads and tails down there, some on a half-doze, more with their thumbs stuck on their gobs looking around, and others a cold junk sleeping it off.

Solid comfort.[14]

Iris Brett recalled that, as a school-aged child, Guy was a fly on the wall for all adult conversations. It developed his appetite for gossip, his obsessive interest in public affairs, and his flawless ear for dialects. He was always the designate to write skits for school concerts, just as he tended to be a ringleader in everyday childhood drama. His sense of nonsense and the ridiculous was always present.

The storytellers of Guy's youth lived again in essays written during his early career in journalism. In February 1968, he wrote a short tribute to one of the few Newfoundland politicians he admired, John T. Cheeseman of Hermitage, who had just died. His comments about Cheeseman, whom he regarded as avuncular and kind, reminded him of the influence of one of his own favourite "uncles," Uncle John Brinston. The piece provides a glimpse into the story-centred world in which Guy grew up and which shaped his own storytelling skills.

My favorite honorary uncle is also named John. He is eighty-five years old or more. He has seen many hardships and sorrows in his time and they will continue.

He is a short man who has round, rosy cheeks and smokes a pipe, but the thing he is best known for is telling "yarns."

Sometimes he can't remember things that happened a month ago but he can recall in perfect detail things that happened before this century was born.

He may start a yarn "The other year when the Boer War was on ..." or "I mind the time when the States was dry and we went down to Saint Peter's ... "

The remarkable thing is all his hundreds of stories are jolly. Having lived through what we sometimes hear were wretched and bitter times, he seems to recall only the jokes and the anecdotes and the bright parts.

"A time to laugh and a time to cry." Uncle John has discovered along the way how to subtract from the one and add to the other.[15]

Guy's Outharbour Delights essays are windows on his childhood. They are replete with mischief and mayhem, reflecting a world safely protected from such modern juvenile curses as regimented play and suburban solitude. There was no schedule for the Delights pieces in his *Evening Telegram* columns, and no obvious pattern. Typically, there were no more than a half-dozen a year. They came in handy on days when the political temperature was low. They often reflected what he had been thinking or talking about the previous evening or weekend.

The tone of Outharbour Delights is casual and pleasing, the prose more in tune with oral storytelling than with newspaper journalism. Always on display in the essays was Guy's love of pure mirth.

Tying tin cans to the tails of sheep was not benign activity. It was not without entertainment value either. Animal rights advocates may wish to move immediately to a later chapter. From Guy's Encyclopedia of Juvenile Outharbour Delights:

A hardy looking sheep with a stout tail is selected from the flock and some tin cans are secured by twine to its tail. The sheep is released and the juvenile's labors are over. He has then only to retreat to a high vantage point to observe the chain of events thus set in motion.

There is a brief pause at first until the animal takes a step forward, causing the cans to clink on the road. This serves as the starting gun, the triggering device, so to speak, in the nuclear reaction.

A vast river of lamb chops and wool then gathers momentum, bursting forth from the meadow, pouring through the lanes, spilling out onto the roads, sweeping along the beaches, flattening any of the populace which happens to be in the way.

Onward, ever onward, sweeps the wooly stampede, picking up speed at every furlong, spurred on by the noisemaker in its midst, not to stop until the string breaks or the shores of Notre Dame Bay are reached.

A sheep is the contrariest animal on the face of the earth and will not lead or drive. The outharbor juvenile spends some of the most tortuous days of his early career rounding up sheep on open country and driving them home from the winter.

This is not to say that "Tying Cans Onto Sheep's Tails" has anything to do with vengeance. Heaven forbid! But recollections of this grueling experience do help dampen any pangs of conscience.[16]

The pangs of conscience were bearable, although Guy did acknowledge that tying cans to sheep's tails was "one of many outrages that may come in for scrutiny after the seal fishery is tidied up."

The stampeding sheep piece reveals Guy in a writing mode that developed naturally and served him well throughout his career. He once suggested that his role as a comic and satiric writer earned him licence to be a more aggressive political critic. He often achieved both simultaneously. If his Arnold's Cove incubation fuelled his ability to evoke a cozier past, it also helped sharpen his fierce satirical edge.

Gifted writers can turn tsunamis and war zones into literature. If the church-based school system actually was the battleground of Ray Guy's vivid memory, the hostilities became food for his imagination and fuel for his pen.

When major public matters were at stake, Guy produced his most biting satire—essays and satirical tracts, often tinged with anger, occasionally with outright cruelty. His thinking was chisel-sharp, his wit keen as mustard, his writing always evocative. The heavier artillery of satire usually was reserved for the heavier affairs of state.

Guy's bitter day-school experiences at St. Michael and All Angels remained with him for at least three decades. His 1968 diagnosis of Newfoundland's church-run education system was widely shared even then. Still, it took another quarter of a century, plus four premiers, two referenda, and a constitutional amendment, before a fatal stake was driven through its heart.

Guy's writing may well have helped the cause.

In the early 1990s, the Newfoundland government of Clyde Wells, the province's most defiant and determined post-Joey premier, took aim at the inefficient and divisive church-based education system. A 1995 referendum on the fate of church-based education was surprisingly close, 54 per cent in favour of abolition, 46 per cent opposed. A second referendum was more decisive. Ultimately, denominational education in Newfoundland was dismantled by way of a constitutional amendment, achieved during the premiership of Wells's pugnacious successor, Brian Tobin.

In the passionate education debate of the early 1990s, politicians pronounced, priests pontificated, and professors droned on. But it was Guy who captured the absurdity of the sectarian education issue in a dozen memorable paragraphs.

Guy was in his 50s then, and his main journalistic outlet was a weekly armchair commentary for CBC Television's popular local news program *Here & Now*. It was a demanding format. Few can deliver intelligent and literate editorials straight into a television camera. His denominational education piece showed him in full satirical feather:

> Ah, some good news for a change. And about time, too. Yes, I hear by the grapevine that all of the fire departments in Newfoundland are going to be reorganized, along denominational lines.
>
> You heard it here first, folks, but wait for it on the radio. Now I think this is a wonderful thing. In a decent, Christian Godfearing province like this, we really should have decent, Christian Godfearing fire departments, according to religious denomination.
>
> Because, as any schoolboy knows, there is a proper Pentecostal way of dealing with a fat fire and there's the official Roman Catholic method of handling a chimney blaze.
>
> Come on now. Be truthful. Isn't it one of your nightmares? To be hanging out the third storey window with the flames licking at your bum? And along comes a firetruck and up comes a fireman. And with the tip of the hat he says, "Are you right with Jesus, brother? Or are you one of them satan-led secular humanists? Tough titty if you are."

Or you say, "Fireman, save my child" and he says, "that depends. Do you stand four-square behind the Holy Father regarding birth control?"[17]

Ray Guy's Grade 11 graduation on Bell Island led to Memorial University in St. John's, where he read general arts courses for two years. His pursuit of an arts degree, as opposed to a teaching certificate, which most rural students sought, was considered a tad indulgent, even pretentious, by other outport scholars. For one thing, an education degree meant lifetime employment, if no copybooks were blotted. Meanwhile, St. John's students, by far the majority, were the stuck-up townies, comprising what Guy perceived as an exclusive and unwelcoming enclave. To a pathologically shy bayman, this clique appeared impenetrable, superior by attitude and by class.

"Curse those two years at Memorial in heaps!" Guy wrote in 1982 in a brief autobiographical sketch:

> I took arts and ran head-on into the St. John's clique dominating that faculty. I was pitifully shy, had to be told where to put the money on a bus and wore a too-large secondhand suit of my uncle's.
>
> Unadulterated misery. I flunked maths and something else (French I think it was) so the two years knocked together made one good one. I chucked it up and went back to work in my father's little grocery shop at Arnold's Cove until I got sick of ramming my arms down to the elbows in the salt beef barrel.[18]

The St. John's townie-bayman division was not a joke to Guy. The townies, he told reporter Danette Dooley of the *Newfoundland Herald*, thought all baymen "were just a bunch of hicks." Among the indignities, a St. John's bus driver did make him feel stupid when Guy got on board but did not know how to pay his fare. "I was foolish and bashful back in those days," he told Dooley. "I really didn't know how to react."

> I remember the first day I got on a bus near my board-
> ing house in St. John's. I was going to the university. It
> was on Parade Street then. I had 10 cents in my hand.
> I knew that was the fare. I got in and tried to pass the
> money to the driver. He looked at me and said, "Are you
> going to put that money in the box or are you going
> to stick it up your arse." I backed right off the bus and
> walked to the university the whole winter. I was mad at
> myself for being so stupid.[19]

At Memorial, Guy attended the classes he liked, but retreated as fast as possible to his off-campus boarding house. In his first year, his lodgings were on Leslie Street in the west end of St. John's, a half-hour walk from the Memorial University campus, then on midtown Parade Street. In his second year, he and Iris, who was also attending Memorial, boarded on Bannerman Street, much closer to campus, at the home of their father's sister, Aunt Jane. Halfway through second year, Jane moved her family to distant, suburban Mount Pearl. Iris and Ray went with them. The move took them well beyond walking distance to the college, necessitating a humbling return to the buses.

Guy's writing flair was soon noticed by at least one important professor, albeit with a certain incredulity. Iris remembers that Dr. Ronald Seary, head of the Department of English, gave Ray a very good mark in an early essay, to which was added a terse and provocative note: "Excellent work, Mr. Guy. Yours?" Dr. Seary eventually became a Ray Guy fan, apparently without losing his penchant for faint praise. A couple of years later, Iris, a good writer herself, submitted one of her better essays to Dr. Seary. She remembers his marginal comment distinctly: "Good work, Miss Guy. Did Ray help you with this?"

Quick to take offence and slow to forgive, Guy attributed such comments to the bone-deep prejudice against baymen that he detected everywhere in St. John's, no less so in the hallowed halls of learning.

Guy had spent two unhappy years in St. John's, and one that was not much better back in Arnold's Cove working for his father before applying to a college with an enticing reputation, the Ryerson Institute of Technology in Toronto. The attraction of Ryerson was as a quality post-secondary school in Canada that offered specialized training in journalism. Guy had kept an early interest in journalism to himself. Ryerson offered an additional inducement—no requirement for Mathematics.

Despite his early cynicism, Seary encouraged Guy to pursue a writing career and to pursue journalism at Ryerson. Guy was readily accepted into the journalism program. He acknowledged Seary's advice and encouragement, but he continued to resent him anyway for his earlier, ill-considered innuendo.

CHAPTER 3
Ryerson Man

The Ryerson Institute of Technology, Ryerson University today, had developed one of Canada's pioneering schools of journalism, initially emphasizing craft skills—even typesetting was taught in the early years—but gradually evolving in a more academic direction.

By the time Ray Guy arrived there in 1960, the faculty had developed a distinct newspaper reporting orientation. Its practical approach to journalism, its evolving academic bias toward English Literature, and its commitment to clear and crisp Canadian Press-style writing, suited him just fine. Guy had acquired some basic writing tools as a schoolboy, spelling skills and grammar rules among them. By the time he made it to college, his grammar and syntax were much better than average. He had also acquired some attitude, a point of view, an equally essential attribute for a satirist.

Ryerson engaged Guy's interest and rewarded his writing talent in a way that Memorial University could not. He was taught the conventional inverted pyramid style of writing news stories, emphasizing facts with little embroidery. The idea of the upside-down pyramid was to write the story with the most essential information in the story's first paragraph or lead—sometimes spelled "lede." Each subsequent paragraph would be decreasingly important so editors could shorten it conveniently from the bottom up. This method emphasized discipline and economy in reporting.

In a 2003 retrospective for the *Newfoundland Quarterly*, Guy offered a sardonic twist on his Ryerson training.

> Ryerson taught us that the average mental age of a newspaper reader was 13 and a half and sinking fast.
>
> We had to learn something called the "fog index" as used by Reader's Digest to keep all our words short as a hamster's dicky, to write no paragraph more than a few lines long, to scatter around quotation marks and other punctuation marks as if from a pepper mill, to eschew solid blocks of formidable grey on the pages and to get the thing off with the snappiest lead sentence possible, i.e. "I did not shout!" Premier J.R. Smallwood shouted in the House of Assembly yesterday.

At Ryerson, Guy was coached in the Five Ws of reporting. In a 2010 piece for the *Quarterly*, he illustrated the W5 technique in jest, but pretty much accurately, adding a perfunctory "H" for How, a satirical jab at the more pious pyramid practitioners of the era.

> Almighty in those days were the "Five Ws: Who, What, Where, When and Why." The more of those you could cram in near the top the less small your bonus Christmas turkey might be.

> For example: Mrs. Beatrice Tilley found her clothes-
> line cut behind her house on Boncloddy Street at 10:30
> this morning in what the Constabulary fear may be a
> sign of city-wide vandalism. Sometimes "H" might be
> included as in: The miscreants may have gained access
> to the crime scene by way of a back fence.

None of Guy's high school or Memorial University writing survives, but several samples from his Ryerson years do. Those, and much of his early *Telegram* reporting, suggest a disposition that valued levity, but not always first and foremost.

The Ryerson pieces, mainly from his second year, are intriguing. They reveal a first-rate emerging journalist and a budding satirist barely out of his teens. At the time, Guy may not have been fully aware of his strength as a humorist, but he was clearly aware of the career path that beckoned.

The newspaper orientation of Ryerson journalism training in the 1960s also emphasized the so-called feature story. Unlike the just-the-facts-ma'am news report, the feature was meant to inform newspaper and magazine readers in some depth and to entertain them as well. In feature reports, unlike straight news pieces, detail and more stylish writing were encouraged.

One surviving sample of Guy's Ryerson work was aimed directly at mastery of the newspaper and magazine feature article. In the fall of 1961, his second year, he used an assignment in his Reporting, Feature Writing class as an opportunity to write about Toronto's busy waterfront, where hundreds of blown-away Newfoundlanders worked as longshoremen, or crewmen and wheelmen, on Great Lakes freighters. If Guy knew little about the Toronto waterfront when he dug into this assignment, he soon discovered that Toronto knew even less about some of the sizeable chunks of Canada that lie to the east of Scarborough.

I was trying hard to appear unimpressed as I stood on the Toronto waterfront and looked back at the city skyline already shimmering in the 8 a.m. sun of early September.

It was my second day in the great metropolis, fresh from one of the Newfoundland outports the travel folders always picture next to downtown Montreal or Toronto in their "land of infinite variety" bit.

"You don't build 'em like that back in New Brunswick, eh," said the taxi driver, pointing to the 30-odd story Bank of Commerce building which dominated the horizon.

"Man, what a view you get from the top of that. Well, here's your boat," he added before I could get his geography straight.

"What's she carrying?" I asked the cab driver who was eyeing a tip that probably located me in the highlands of Cape Breton.

"Beans," he said. "Don't let 'em ask you to stay for dinner."

Guy's port feature of 1962 pointed his writing in a direction that matured in his early years at the *Evening Telegram* when he wrote the solid news-feature articles that eventually earned him a daily column. Other Ryerson articles foreshadowed different qualities in his writing and his talent, humour and satire notable among them.

One example of the latter was a signed editorial in the *Ryersonian*, the student newspaper of Ryerson. The *Ryersonian* and several dozen such campus weeklies across Canada, were, at their best, informal training grounds for some of Canada's best journalists. They also traded heavily in trite and sophomoric journalism. Guy's sporadic contributions to the paper, better written than most, exhibited touches of both.

His *Ryersonian* editorial for February 16, 1962, concerned a typical campaign of the era, led by a Hogtown alderman, to crack down on campus fraternity houses. The issues, as always, were noise and ribald misconduct indulged in by fraternity members and other late-night campus revellers, fuelled by hormonal surges and unleashed by liquor.

Guy, editorialist, was at pains to take the campaign seriously, leaving behind hints of the satirist in the making. He begins solemnly enough, by quoting from "Lines Written among the Euganean Hills," by Percy Bysshe Shelley, a poet he much admired.

> Many a green isle needs must be
> In the wide deep sea of misery
> Or the mariner worn and wan
> Never thus could voyage on ...

Solemnity soon gives way to snark. Worn and wan "Rye-type mariners," observes Guy, "have habitually sought a temporary respite from the 'angst' of life on various green isles of conviviality, sometimes leaving 'three sheets to the wind,' fortified, nevertheless, to voyage on."

As a strawman for the ridicule to come, Guy strikes a half-serious note about the increasing blowback to such conviviality from Toronto's City Hall. He then turns a corner, to foreshadow the satirist he would become:

> Would they let such trifling inconveniences (loosened plaster, etc.) interfere with the mental hygiene of this nation's student body?
>
> ... In future, the mere crash of a toppling limbo dancer, the beer bottle accidentally dislodged from the apartment balcony may be expected to bring even more speedy and repressive action from the authorities.

... What can be done in the face of such near-sighted actions?

Those responsible should be informed of the stabilizing influence of these functions and the need for tolerance on such occasions ...

Quote Shelley to them. This might help.

Ray Guy's *Ryersonian* editorial is revealing. Only two years away from his unhappy time as an outsider at Memorial University, he is very much an insider as an editorialist for the newspaper at Ryerson. At that select sanctuary, a student could be introverted and shy—one could even speak Bayman—and still become part of a college elite, recognized for the skill that mattered most—smart and entertaining writing.

Guy's Ryerson writing reveals other skills that are burnished even as they are practiced. His unerring eye for political baloney and guff is very much in play, as is his remedy for it—piercing political satire. Surely a Toronto alderperson must have more to worry about than over-partying undergraduates.

Also in clear view is Guy's growing range of literary awareness and achievement. He no doubt quoted Shelley from memory, as was his wont, albeit with one small error.

An undated Guy *Ryersonian* piece, likely written in 1962 and titled "Byline ... Ray Guy," exhibits a Swiftian touch. Set in 1967, the piece conjures up a speech by a future prime minister of Canada, one John G. Fantasi, opening Canada's anticipated Centennial celebrations.

The "John G." designation was not accidental. For the benefit of readers who can't recall whether Studebaker was the prime minister and Diefenbaker the car, or the other way around, John George Diefenbaker ("Dief") was a populist Saskatchewan Progressive

Conservative politician, a renegade in the estimation of his biographer, Peter C. Newman.[20]

As prime minister from 1957 to 1963, Diefenbaker was impatient with Québec's demands for something approximating special status in Confederation. "Macdonald didn't talk about two Canadas," Dief would roar. "Laurier didn't talk about two Canadas."

As a satirist, Guy could bend both the past and the future to his will. His Centennial ceremonies open in Ottawa, not Montreal, and for good reason. In Guy's creative casting, there is no Expo 67 in the offing. Québec has long since become the Free Laurentian Republic, where, according to Prime Minister Fantasi, a supposedly distinct society now exists in peaceful contiguity beside a much-diminished Canada. Guy's future prime minister has come to regard it all as more or less normal.

> On our eastern borders the red ensign flies in peace beside the fleur de lis with frogs rampant. Further cementing the bonds between the Free Laurentian Republic and Canada (apart from the fact that President Richard and myself use the same brand of hair tonic) engineers of both countries work side by side on the huge Chaput Wall Project.
>
> When completed it will extend from James Bay to connect with the heavily defended 50-mile strip of no-man's land along the southern bank of the St. Lawrence River.
>
> Canada's share of the project is being financed by last year's auction of the North West Territories to the US and the Soviet Union.

On a photocopy of that article, which Guy sent home to his parents in Arnold's Cove, the word "Maurice" in his handwriting is inserted between the words "President" and "Richard." He wished to make it clear that he was referring to the great Montreal Canadiens hockey star, Maurice "The Rocket" Richard. The "hair tonic" reference was to a television commercial Richard did in the 1960s for a hair dye called Grecian Formula 16. Richard would point to his nearly coal black "do" and admit: "Today I still leave a little touch of gray. The wife likes it."

Prior to the October 1970 Québec separatist crisis, and excluding the Winnipeg General Strike of 1919, the closest thing to culturally rooted political violence in 20th-century Canada was a protest riot that occurred in Montreal on March 17, 1955, after National Hockey League president Clarence Campbell suspended Richard for the remainder of the season for striking an NHL linesman.

Guy might have felt that Richard, at the time, could have been elected premier, or perhaps even president, of Québec simply by putting his name on the ballot. It generally has been accepted—in Québec it never has been doubted—that an undercurrent of ethnic prejudice informed Campbell's decision to suspend Rocket Richard.

Notable in this piece is Guy's own use of the pejorative "frog" in a jesting reference to French Canada. Today, such an offhanded use of the term in a Canadian publication would draw hellfire. In fact, he used it more than once in subsequent years. At worst, this may have revealed a current of discomfort or even ill will toward Québec, not unknown in Newfoundland, especially in frontier Labrador, where the provinces share a zigzag border that Québec has long disputed. At best, it may have reflected another Guy characteristic, a refusal to flirt with the emerging dictates of political correctness.

The fantasy Centennial event is mostly fun. But it hints at future facets of the aspiring journalist. Guy was in touch with the larger political currents of the time, as well as narrower political occurrences. The piece was an early application of his satire in the service of serious social and political commentary.

It is not surprising that in 1962 a young, sensitive, and nationalistic Newfoundland writer would have imagined a future Canadian prime minister reporting the secession of Atlantic Canada with undisguised, thanks-be-to-God relish. On that front, J.G. Fantasi does not disappoint:

> Looking further east, the situation is no less hopeful. The secession of Canada's Atlantic holdings in 1964 was a tremendous boost to this country's morale, removing as it did from our confines, fog, unemployment, and Don Messer. By this one action our climatic, financial and cultural standings have been raised immeasurably.

The study of journalism is, or should be, a study of writing and of literature, ideally embracing a foreign language or two—all overlaying an intense interest in society and politics, the cardinal prerequisite for the profession. Ryerson, like most Canadian universities of the time, defined literature as English Literature, mainly as the literature of Britain itself, with all else secondary or ancillary.

One of Guy's heaviest tomes for "Journalism 1A" was a text called *English Literature and Its Backgrounds*. Belying its description as the Shorter Edition, this doorstop between hard covers runs to 1,398 pages. Its modest claim is to cover the period from Old English to the 20th century, or, as its included timeline chart illustrates, from Elizabeth I, around 1550, to George VI, around 1940. The Shorter Edition was published in 1950.[21]

Among the novels that Guy studied at Ryerson was Emily Bronte's *Wuthering Heights*. In February 1962, he submitted to his "JII" professor, Mr. Hersh, an essay entitled "Wuthering Heights: The Setting." The essay is a nuanced piece of work. Studious on balance, it contains clever writing indicative of his inability to take even Emily Bronte totally seriously.

The opening paragraph is by Guy, the serious and better-than-average student of literature at Ryerson:

> Emily Bronte's characters symbolize her concept of the main forces of life, storm and calm. She has placed them in a setting which emphasizes this symbolism and which provides a simplified background to the action. As Mr. Lockwood, one of the narrators, explains, "Wuthering Heights" is an appropriate name for Mr. Heathcliff's dwelling. Bleak and exposed, the few fir trees around it have been stunted by the north wind and gaunt thorns "crave alms of the sun" just as Heathcliff's bitter desire for revenge has stunted and withered the people who live there.

The second paragraph reveals Guy, the seemingly repressed, impatient humorist:

> The rough and desolate appearance of the house, outside and in, its stormy location and inhospitable aspects complement the characters and the inhabitants. Any environment less savage would hardly be suitable for a character like Heathcliff who could imagine such robust amusements as "flinging Joseph off the highest gable and painting the house-front with Hindley's blood."

For much of the essay, Guy offers keen observations about the actual importance of setting in the novel. They include the contrast between the rough and rugged Wuthering Heights of Heathcliff and the pacific calm of Thrushcross Grange, seat of Heathcliff's rival for Cathy's attentions, the sadly civilized Edgar Linton.

Eventually Guy finds in the novel exactly the opening he needs to indulge in much-needed levity. It is also clear that he perceives, or perhaps hopes, that Emily Bronte is laughing right along with him. The subject is the role of dogs in the novel—not precisely on topic, but too rich to resist:

> Apart from the human, architectural, geographic and atmospheric aspects of the Wuthering Heights setting there is a prevalence of dogs in the novel, none of them nice ...
>
> ... we soon find out that neither Mr. Heathcliff nor his dogs are to be trifled with. But the dogs at the Grange are no less nasty. The bulldog which grabs Cathy Earnshaw by the ankle has to be strangled until "its slavering purple tongue hangs out a foot." Before it lets go, Miss Bronte's dogs get the full pre-RSPCA treatment. They are hanged, booted, throttled and stretched; they are given such unappealing names as Gnasher, Skulker and Wolf. While this brutalization of four-footed friends complements to some extent the degradation suffered by the human characters, we cannot help but suspect that Miss Bronte didn't like dogs either.

There is no record of Mr. Hersh's response to the essay, nor of the grade awarded. There is a record of what Mr. Hersh thought of another essay, the most substantial piece of fiction of Guy's Ryerson years.

In November 1962, Guy wrote a short story for a class assignment. It is an early and rather sober iteration of his childhood, wartime memories. Entitled "The Grand Canyon," the story is biographical in thrust if not in detail. Like Ray, the hero, Ben, has a three-letter name. Ben is dispatched by his father, as Guy may well have been, to a newly established American army camp near Arnold's Cove to try and sell a crate of lobster to the mess-hall staff for 12 cents a pound, another detail perhaps not far from fact.

The dramatic tension in the story is created by the contempt in which one of the US servicemen holds Arnold's Cove and the people who live there. This attitude is mitigated by another serviceman who is kind to Ben and critical of his fellow soldier's condescending tone. Guy had seen both attitudes in his own childhood. The US military had maintained a small surveillance base near Arnold's Cove during World War II. He also had good reasons from his own experience not to tar all American servicemen with the same brush.

Guy's vibrant imagination is at play in the piece when his young protagonist, Ben, imagines the surrounding local cliffs and shrubbery as resembling images his teacher had described of how the Grand Canyon might look from the moon. The "one giant leap for mankind" was years away, but US president John F. Kennedy's moon-landing objective had been assigned to NASA in May 1961. One consequence was that there was conjecture already about what moonwalkers gazing earthward actually might see.

The devil-skin kid in Guy is revealed in "The Grand Canyon" through Ben's determination to time his trip to the camp strategically to return home shortly after 9 a.m. That would make him too late to go back to school until after recess at 10:30, an hour and a half of freedom thus achieved. Ben reflects Guy's own dislike for school, "except perhaps geography." Ben's plan, again possibly reflecting young Guy's own dream, was to leave school the following year, upon reaching the age of 15, to see the world.

> Maybe the war would be over by that time and he would get a job on a merchant vessel and see Boston and Barbados and Cadiz some day and perhaps even the Grand Canyon.

In his lifetime, Guy was not an ambitious traveller. But his sense of geography, remote topography, and different cultures was well developed. He had a reader's, and a writer's, appreciation of the world.

Mr. Hersh described Ray's story as "neatly done" and gave him a grade of 75 for the four typewritten pages.

But Mr. Hersh astutely pointed out the story's key weakness, which was underdevelopment of the characters of the two US servicemen encountered by Ben. In a salute to academic discipline perhaps more common in 1962 than today, Mr. Hersh's instruction to Guy reflected this criticism: "Has possibilities for fifth page. Please revise and submit." The revision, and its rating, are lost in the past.

There is no doubt that as a student Ray Guy read widely and wrote well. He was learning to dance. His formal post-secondary education, at both Memorial and Ryerson, broadened his literary base and stoked his appetite for more. Alternately stressful and pleasant, each experience helped prepare him to write for a living and to live largely to write.

CHAPTER 4

The People's Paper

Toronto may be Canada's coldest and loneliest city and, paradoxically, its most stimulating one. Ironically, Ray Guy was happier and less lonely there than he had been while attending Memorial University in St. John's.

At Ryerson, Guy found his fellow students, a more diverse and polyglot crowd than those at Memorial, less concerned about class and status and refreshingly oblivious to the subtle divisions and resentments of his Newfoundland and Labrador world. Ryerson professors and classmates were as likely to inquire about the Old-World genesis of a Placentia Bay accent than they were to denigrate or mock it.

Despite the attractions of Toronto, Guy turned his attention to the chattering village of St. John's in the winter of 1963, as graduation from Ryerson approached. There is no evidence that he sought work in any other province. His application for work at the *Evening Telegram* included his Ryerson essay on the docks of Toronto. The paper's managing editor, Steve Herder, was impressed. Ray's starting pay was $45 a week, equalling about $387 today.

The St. John's *Evening Telegram* was founded by William James Herder in April 1879. Its masthead motto, "the People's Paper," was adopted almost immediately. The newspaper remained in the Herder family fold for 90 years, before being sold in 1970 to the Thomson newspaper chain owned by Roy, Lord Thomson of Fleet, "a great rude wind from Canada," as the *Times of London*, a newspaper he once owned, had called him.

From its earliest days, the *Evening Telegram* was more than a small-city business. A century before mission statements for all manner of businesses became the rage—even for banks, as if we didn't know their mission—the Herder *Telegram* exhibited a sense of purpose. In an editorial in 1954 celebrating the newspaper's 75th anniversary, the founder's intent was captured in aspirational language:

> ... to make available a journal which could discuss impartially and without fear or favour any matters of public concern, which provided a medium affording citizens the opportunity freely to express their opinions; which used its influence in the promotion of progress and the general welfare, and which upheld civil and religious liberty and loyalty to the Crown ...

Throughout its nine decades under the Herders, the *Evening Telegram* was never far from the centre of Newfoundland and Labrador political discourse and cultural reflection, and never closer than during the early decades of the post-Confederation era, the 1950s to the 1970s.

During those years, the paper evolved and grew. Circulation nearly doubled. On good days, the *Evening Telegram* could be a political tour de force, with star columnists such as Harold Horwood in the 1950s and Ray Guy in the 1960s and 1970s leading the way. The late 1960s and early 1970s were marked by strong editorial leadership, increasing numbers of university-educated reporters and feature writers, and reasonable newsroom travel budgets.

It was the Ray Guy era.

"Guy still has a nostalgic hankering for the late 1960s and early 1970s," journalism professor Ian Wiseman wrote in 1985, "what he ruefully calls the 'golden age of journalism.'"

> *The Evening Telegram* of those years had a large staff of writers and reporters, including novelist Harold Horwood, playwright Michael Cook, journalist John Fraser, and a host of others who became stars with CTV, CBC Radio and Television, and Canadian Press. To be a *Telegram* reporter in those days was to have a prestigious identity, and the man who kept morale the highest was Ray Guy.[22]

Harold Horwood still wrote for the paper in the 1960s, but he had abandoned his politically charged Political Notebook column of the 1950s, reinventing himself as a naturalist and environmental soothsayer. Horwood's Political Notebook had been the province's first real journalistic challenge to J.R. Smallwood, Newfoundland's domineering premier from Confederation in 1949 to 1972. In the 1960s, Horwood wrote the weekly Outside Information column for the *Telegram*, a well-researched series of essays that viewed the planet through a more expansive lens than that of parochial Smallwood politics.

The *Telegram*'s editor-in-chief when Guy arrived was Michael F. Harrington, a recognized historian, poet, anti-Confederation

Newfoundlander, and solid St. John's citizen. Harrington joined the paper in 1959 and stayed for 23 years, writing daily editorials, frequent features, and a weekly column, Offbeat History.

The newspaper that Guy joined in 1963 had strengths, but it was far from perfect. Beyond the columnists and a few of the more seasoned reporters, the *Telegram*'s news pages were often indifferently written, tedious, and under-edited. Guy was only a shade beyond the facts when he offered his satirical recollection of the newspaper of the day and his personal impact on it:

> At the time *The Telegram* was like a cross between a business letter and a legal statute. It certainly wasn't meant to be read by the deserving poor. So I stuck out a bit dressed only in journalese ... a habit which, as you see here, I can no longer break.[23]

The *Telegram*'s news and sports copy was formulaic and clichéd. Worse, it was often riddled with high-blown and clumsy prose as undertrained reporters and editors—many of us fitted that category—tried too hard to spruce it up.

A sports trophy invariably was "emblematic of senior soccer—or hockey or curling—supremacy." One acquaintance claimed to have read a *Telegram* sports report of the era that described a local hockey goalie as "the aging, side-burned, crew-cut cage-cop."

On the other side of the newsroom, general news writing had its own well-worn argot. A homeless person appearing in Magistrate's Court was "a person of no fixed address." A local house fire not obviously caused by smoking in bed or a deep fryer was "a fire of unknown origin," a cryptic phrase vaguely suggestive of arson. Even editorialists indulged: "It never ceases to amaze us that ... " Guy swore he read one editorial in either the *Telegram* or the rival *Daily News* that began this way: "In this age of moonshots and nudity on the stage, it never ceases to amaze us that ... " Some such tales were apocryphal, of course. But the truth often trumped the fiction.

Even in the late 1960s, well after Guy came on board, routine *Telegram* news reporting often meant capturing the passing parade of prominent personages, political events, and crime. Stories were at their best when they involved all three. Still, there were gradual improvements.

As the editorial effort evolved, regular beats such as Magistrate's Court, City Hall, and the House of Assembly were created to help foster journalistic expertise. For much of the 1960s, the *Telegram* maintained a one-person seasonal Ottawa bureau, manned by the dapper Bob Moss, who sported ascots, vests, and lapel pocket hankies. Moss's job, indicative of the paper's expanding editorial ambition, was to report on the activities of the seven Newfoundland and Labrador federal Members of Parliament when the House of Commons was in session.

Not all reporters achieved that relative measure of glamour. Most of us, Guy in his early *Telegram* years included, were assigned daily to cover mundane events such as speakers at Rotary or Kiwanis Club lunches, the notorious rubber-chicken circuit, and visits to the city by Members of Parliament or Senate committees on tour.

Covering speakers at service club luncheons in the late 1960s was routine and ritualistic. The premier, the mayor of St. John's, local MPs, and various captains of industry would make annual appearances. No matter who the speaker was, the meetings would start with grace and a toast to Her Majesty, after which smoking was permitted and widely enjoyed. The luncheons would end with all hands, reporters included, rising to sing the "Ode to Newfoundland." Nearly two decades after Confederation, the "Ode" remained the anthem of choice in Newfoundland and Labrador. "O Canada" had little currency at the time, although Expo 67 moved that dial noticeably. At many public events, "God Save the Queen" was commonly sung for good measure.

Ray Guy's early *Telegram* years were good years. His talent was recognized by the newspaper's publishers and editors and, more importantly, by a growing number of readers. He was writing creatively, enjoying travel around Newfoundland at his employer's expense, and earning a young bachelor's living.

As a bonus, Guy finally had St. John's friends, a pleasant change from his Memorial University days, and perhaps more companionship than he had enjoyed since childhood in Arnold's Cove. His ticket to popularity was his skill with words. It was manifested most often in his writing, but also at times in a witty and enigmatic turn of phrase, in company where he felt comfortable enough to speak.

Having friends did not mean Guy was a party man. By nature, he was a loner. At the *Telegram*, he seemed to find adequate company among his ink-stained cronies. They were a unique cast of characters.

Not always highly educated in a formal way, most of Guy's *Telegram* colleagues of the mid-1960s possessed the native cunning, street savvy, and cynicism that reporters tend to exhibit. Increasingly in the late 1960s, reporters at the *Telegram*, Guy included, had post-secondary education and training. By the end of the decade, a few boasted journalism degrees from Carleton University or some other J-school on top of their undergraduate arts or science diplomas.

A few *Telegram* luminaries, such as columnist Harold Horwood and editor-in-chief Michael Harrington, were scholarly and accomplished writers in various genres, including, in Horwood's case, prose fiction and nature writing, and, in Harrington's, poetry and history. Neither Horwood nor Harrington was close to Guy. Both appeared to maintain a bemused distance.

Awkward and at times aloof, Guy sought nobody out and he curried no favours. His friendships grew mainly from incoming overtures by more gregarious individuals who loved his humour and, in turn, found ways to make him laugh.

Guy's first important friend at the *Telegram* was David Day, a law student from St. John's who worked at the paper during summer and school vacations in 1965 and 1966. David Day, Q.C., remains, in 2021, a respected elder in the St. John's legal community, still practicing in his 70s.

A student of writing himself, with an unlawyerly affinity for journalism and newspapers, Day remembered the Ray Guy he knew in a short memoir written soon after Ray's death in 2013.

> Guy occupied a desk at the back of *The Telegram*'s newsroom, then located in the Parland Building, 271–275 Duckworth St. Typically, he commenced each matchless weekday column about 1:30 p.m. Using an Underwood, later a Remington, manual typewriter, he would continue to be engrossed in crafting a column at 6 p.m.—often, until much later.
>
> His painstaking choice of language was as precise as the wielding by a surgeon of a scalpel in an operating theatre.
>
> He teased each paragraph, slowly and cleverly, from his droll mental hard drive.
>
> Often, he consulted on this or that turn of phrase with newsroom colleagues: Mary Deanne Shears, the women's editor (later, managing editor of *The Toronto Star*), and Mary Deanne's understudy, Jane Williams; news reporters Don Morris, Ron Crocker (later, a CBC producer), Gary Callahan, George Barrett, and Frank Holden (now a playwright); sports department writers Bob Badcock, Pee Wee Crane, and Ron Rossiter; editing desk staff Bob Ennis (later, of *The Montreal Gazette*), Maurice Finn and Tommy Power, and Canadian Press correspondent David Butler.

Because he regarded Premier Smallwood as fancying himself a messiah, Guy seized on every opportunity to capitalize pronouns, within sentences, referring to the premier. Invariably, the editing desk detected and lower-cased them.

Torpid summer afternoons in *The Telegram* newsroom were memorable for Guy's arrival, barefoot, ferrying 10-pound watermelons, which he distributed to colleagues, employing a lobster knife secreted in his desk ...

Assigned to report an event in Bishop's Falls, Guy and I missed the late afternoon train from St. John's. At alarming speeds, he tooled his green coupe to Holyrood station. At first, a police stallion, then a police cycle and eventually a police car pursued him. Guy eluded all comers.

On arrival in Holyrood, he concealed his vehicle in a copse of poplars on private property and we caught the train as it chugged from the station.[24]

Guy may have been driving his prized Chevrolet Corvair that evening. Guy liked to drive, and he enjoyed cars built for car buffs. The Corvair was an early favourite: stick-shift, engine in the rear, aerodynamic, and fun to drive. Perhaps part of the thrill may have resulted from the American consumer champion Ralph Nader's description of the Corvair as "unsafe at any speed."[25]

Guy's wife, Kathie Housser, has said that he was the last Newfoundland writer influenced by the King James Version of the Bible and by the Anglican Book of Common Prayer. Day agrees:

Guy was not a fervent adherent of organized religion, but his conversation was often punctuated with brief liturgies from the Church of England's Book of Common Prayer.

And during summer lunch hours, at least twice monthly, he and I accompanied reporter John Fraser (later, Master of Massey College, Toronto) to the Anglican Cathedral in St. John's.

There we were Fraser's only audience as he performed hymns, movements and dirges on the cathedral's Robert Hope-Jones/Casavant organ ...

Another of Guy's close friends at the *Telegram*, reporter Bob Benson, had pursued advanced studies in English Literature and was, like Guy, a keen student of the 18th-century writer and London literary fixture Dr. Samuel Johnson. Between university and journalism, Benson went to sea, obtaining a second-mate's ticket. His seagoing career might have included a master's ticket but for increasing myopia.

Benson habitually devoted at least an hour a day to reading: news magazines at worst, high-minded literature most often, and in that pursuit Benson and Guy bonded. Not only could Benson quote Johnson, he and Guy occasionally adopted a mock Johnsonian and Boswellian mode of discourse, aping the formality and high-blown wordage of the sages.

Benson once read or quoted some lines from James Boswell's *Life of Johnson*, one of the great English language biographies. The full passage:

> He, I know not why, shewed upon all occasions an aversion to go to Ireland, where I proposed to him that we should make a tour.
>
> JOHNSON. "It is the last place where I should wish to travel."

BOSWELL. "Should you not like to see Dublin, Sir?"

JOHNSON. "No, Sir; Dublin is only a worse capital."

BOSWELL. "Is not the Giant's-Causeway worth seeing?"

JOHNSON. "Worth seeing, yes; but not worth going to see."[26]

This prompted an exchange between Benson as Boswell and Guy's Johnson, roughly along these lines:

Benson: "Do you not perceive, sir, that the fish will be especially vile at Marty's today, it being a Monday?"

Guy: "Vile sir, yes. But Squires [a Marty's Restaurant waitress of the time, known for her candour] will apprise us of the degree of vileness before relieving us of our Monday morning wages."

Bob Benson died too young, at 65. At the funeral in March 2006, Guy eulogized his friend. A reporter who attended recalled the occasion. Standing to one side as Guy began his speech was the presiding clergyman, solemn in his robes.

"Bob Benson was the best friend anybody could ever have," Guy began. He then turned very directly to the reverend gentleman and added, "with the notable exception, of course, of our Lord and Saviour, Jesus Christ."

While the Guy-Benson friendship lasted, it had its scratchy moments. In Guy's correspondence file at Memorial University's Newfoundland Archives, a letter from Benson to Guy dated April 20, 1976, contains an enigmatic reference to "the John Wayne incident," which remains a matter apparently known only to themselves.

"The John Wayne incident has passed into the recesses of ancient history," Benson wrote, "there to remain forgotten and interred forever." His letter apparently was in response to a previous reconciliation note from Guy. Benson apologized for what he says may have been "an overreaction on my part," caused by family stresses, "and a different time and circumstance would have produced a more rational assessment." Whatever the bones of that dispute, the letter reveals the value Benson placed on his friendship with Guy. It ends with a true Bensonian touch:

> Your letter to me clearly shows that a gentleman, in the very meaning of the word, can still survive in this rotten and decaying century. We should resume our get-togethers. Mrs. Hunter would be so pleased.

Guy was also close to the *Telegram*'s photo editor, Bill Croke, a former official Newfoundland Government photographer who later moved to Toronto to become photo editor for the Canadian Press. Croke was theatrical, an extrovert who might have been the city's first boulevardier if St. John's had had any boulevards.

Another reporter whose company Guy enjoyed was the witty and impish Gary Callahan, a pure-wool townie who endeared himself to Guy by laughing a lot and being unpretentious. Callahan reflected blue-collar Irish St. John's. He knew corner-boys and downtown winos by their first and last names.

During their joint coverage of the House of Assembly in 1966 and 1967, the Guy-Callahan friendship flourished, often fuelled by late Thursday post-production evenings—the weekend *Telegram* was published on Fridays in those days—at the all-hours Newfoundland Press Club, housed in a stone building at the corner of Springdale and Water Streets. The building was part of the old Newman premises where the company aged Newman's Port wine in barrels.

Their friendship faded, however, as Callahan exhibited too much regard for Premier J.R. Smallwood for Guy's taste, while Guy developed too little for Callahan's. One round of the quarrel took place late one night at the Press Club. Callahan, well on, accused Guy, well on, of having "a yellow streak down his back" in his dealings with the premier. It was a sad and sorry end to a friendship based on laughter and affection.

During those mid-1960s *Telegram* years, a decade from meeting his future wife, Guy enjoyed sporadic romantic relationships with at least two and possibly three young women who worked at the newspaper. In those days, such dalliances were called affairs, or "company-ink" affairs if office-based—more than one-night stands, but a long way from making the *Telegram*'s social pages. Two of the women to whom Guy was attracted were itinerate, literate journalists from the mainland on career-development sojourns in St. John's. The moxie to choose newspaper journalism, overwhelmingly a man's world, and to pursue it in Newfoundland, may have given those women the courage to pursue Guy. Given his insularity and bashfulness on this front, active solicitation would have been required.

Guy liked photography, and he loved the world of 35-millimetre black and white film processing. He would often drift into the newspaper's darkroom where the photographers, a team of four in the late 1960s, would be busy developing the day's photos and producing thumbnail or contact sheets for scrutiny by the editorial desk staff.

The darkroom and its adjacent office space were early man-caves, enclaves for all sorts of entertainment, from girly pictures to mock captions. Included among the captioned photos was one that featured a vivacious young woman in a low-cut dress dancing with Premier J.R. Smallwood at the annual Liberal Ball, circa 1968. The woman was Penelope Rowe, wife of the equally handsome Smallwood Cabinet minister Bill Rowe. So well turned out was Rowe himself that newsroom wags referred to him as the man on the wedding cake. In light of Smallwood's evident political slippage, Guy had captioned the photo "The Naked and the Dead."

Often, the last photographer to leave for the day was a gaunt and mustachioed and cheerful eccentric named Wyndham Ploughman, "Wyndy" for short. Wyndy would always close out his day, speaking in the general direction of whoever was left around, with an amended refrain rooted in Gray's "Elegy": "The Ploughman homeward plods his weary way. / And leaves the world to darkness and to thee."[27]

At the *Evening Telegram* of the late 1960s, the sports reporters constituted their own fraternity with their own rituals. Guy called them the "sportifs." He enjoyed their company. On summer evenings, the sportifs would be at soccer and softball fields until 9 p.m. or so, arriving at their desks laden with Ches's fish and chips and Pepsi. Guy and the evening-shift copyboy frequently placed orders.

The Sports Department was a republic. It enjoyed its own staff of four or five, its own newsroom geography, and its own editor. Sports was under the ultimate authority of managing editor Robert J. Ennis. However, the department benefited hugely from the fact that Ennis, a confirmed political junkie, had little interest in any sport not requiring a starched collar and tie.

The sports editor was Bob Badcock, a lanky and angular athlete. While sports editor, Badcock also served a stint as playing coach of the St. John's Capitals senior hockey team, in an era when senior hockey in Newfoundland packed local arenas. No conflict was perceived.

The closest the *Telegram*'s sports department ever came to controversy in the 1960s may have been after a young and personable sports reporter, Albert "Pee Wee" Crane, died in an accident on his way home from work late one night, plunging his Rambler sedan into a street excavation that had not been properly marked.

Smitten with grief, Badcock, Crane's friend and boss, wrote a moving obituary that contained one awkward but memorable sentence expressing his despair. "Why, at the age of 23," Badcock wrote, "could the Great Umpire not have given him a walk?"

The line had consequences, reflecting both its time and its place. It prompted a stern letter to the editor from a local senior cleric of the Salvation Army faith, of which Crane's family were adherents. The complaint was not about sentence structure or a misplaced modifier. It criticized both Badcock and the newspaper for the heretical audacity of questioning the Great Umpire's call.

If Guy was covering the House of Assembly, and sometimes when he was not, his workday began around 11 a.m. and frequently ended well after midnight. As his years at the *Telegram* rolled on, he worked later and later into the night, whether or not the House was sitting.

In those pre-internet days, a local newsroom such as the *Telegram*'s had few windows on the world. A key one was the Canadian Press newswire, a teletype delivery service that rattled all day, delivering national and international news. The Canadian Press in turn subscribed to international news services such as Reuters and the Associated Press, culling those services for stories of consequence to Canada.

The core Canadian Press domestic service was delivered by staff correspondents. There was at least one in most provinces, Newfoundland and Labrador included. CP foreign bureaus in the 1960s were located in the major Cold War capitals: Washington, Moscow, and London.

Guy would stand around the CP wire and read "feeds" of news, or he would collect sheaves of it from the horseshoe-shaped news desk where the copyboys had separated and neatly stacked it. Copy*boys* ruled in those mid-1960s years. It would be the early 1970s before there were copygirls, and the positions became known more neutrally as communications clerks.

Guy would riffle through the copy to stay on top of national and international news. A separate feed would be emitted from a teletype machine connected to the *Western Star*, the *Evening Telegram*'s sister daily in Corner Brook. Guy would consume that feed for west coast and northern Newfoundland news. Labrador news was especially scarce. As the last reporter standing almost every day, Guy would read all the locally produced copy as it had emerged from the reporters' typewriters and before any of it was edited. Often his columns would be drawn from those local stories, his page 3 commentary triggered by page 1 local news.

Guy usually monitored letters to the editor prior to their publication. More than one correspondent was mentioned in his column, sometimes positively, sometimes not. Seldom would he strike back directly at criticism aimed at himself. He did on one occasion, when a letter cast aspersions on family relatives residing on Bell Island, and on another, when a businessman in Arnold's Cove questioned the accuracy of a column Guy had written about the household resettlement program.

More than any other local reporter of his time, Guy mined all available sources of information. The *Telegram*'s library contained fat manila file folders of articles clipped from the paper on every imaginable topic. The indexing system was maintained by librarian Evelyn Power, which made her indispensable. Files contained labels such as Crime, Crime St. John's, Crime St. John's (Violent), Crime St. John's (Rape), Churchill Falls, Fish Plants (Gaultois), and so on. During the two midsummer weeks when Evelyn drove her Consul Cortina to the west coast of the island for her annual vacation, file research would slow to a trickle.

The library also housed hundreds of full editions of the *Telegram*, going back months. Much more valuable to Guy were daily editions of major mainland papers such as the *Toronto Star*, the *Toronto Telegram*, and the *Toronto Globe and Mail*, as it was then called. All arrived by mail, and so were out of date. It didn't matter to Guy. He devoured them. As a night owl, he would also borrow the latest newsmagazines—*Time, Newsweek*, and *Maclean's*—from Mike Harrington's in-basket, where they arrived for the editor's initial scrutiny before being moved to the library. Guy would scan every page, shake off the ashes, and return them to their place.

In those days, only the editor and the managing editor had private offices adjacent to the newsroom. Neither office was all that private, especially when Guy, an inveterate snoop, was around.

Once the sportifs had called it a night, Guy and the overnight copyboy usually were the last people remaining in the newsroom. Soon Guy would be at his desk hammering away at his Underwood, pausing only to light an Export A from the butt of the previous one.

For Ray Guy, the shortest part of writing the column was typing it. Kathie Housser said Ray wrote nothing until he had composed it just about completely in his head. The neat copy Guy usually produced straight from his typewriter lends credence to Housser's comment. Guy recognized early in his career that the cleaner the copy out of the typewriter, the cleaner it would be in the paper after running the dangerous gauntlet of copy editors, reperforation tape typists, linotype machines, and proofreaders.

If Guy composed full paragraphs or even full columns in his head before typing them, it could account for his disconcerting habit of chortling out loud and talking to himself while writing. He frequently laughed at his own lines, not just because they were his, but because they usually were funny. The *Telegram*'s copy editors did not tamper extensively with Guy's work. And there is little history of the Herders or their editors censoring it.

Little history, but not none. Journalist Bob Wakeman of St. John's, whose time at the *Telegram* overlapped Guy's, recalls one exception which involved the late Bill Kelly, a former *Telegram* reporter who also worked with Guy.

Kelly, whose political sentiments were reputed to have aligned with Joey Smallwood's Liberal Party, and reporter Pat Doyle, sometimes thought to have harboured Tory leanings because of family connections, were sent out together to cover a Progressive Conservative convention in Gander. Guy wrote a rather nasty column supposedly revealing an unseemly newsroom strategy, that Kelly's and Doyle's alleged political leanings were designed to offset each other in the coverage.

The piece never saw the light of day. According to Wakeham, "Bill dug the column out of Ray's garbage bucket, showed me the section that had incensed him, and proceeded to tear the whole column into tiny pieces, cursing on Ray the whole while." There is no doubt that any suggestion that either would have injected partisan political views into their coverage would have driven both of those seasoned journalists to distraction. And with good reason—it would not have been true.

The *Telegram*'s editorial improvements that coincided with the Ray Guy era—better writing, better editing, more in-depth treatment of stories, and significant travel by reporters—were all supported by the Herders. But they were not designed by them.

A young newspaper ace, Robert J. (Bob) Ennis, was the main catalyst behind those improvements, which would define the paper in the mid- to late 1960s and early 1970s, bolstering its circulation, its reputation, and its advertising revenue.

If Guy's early career had a salutary impact on the overall quality of the *Evening Telegram*, Bob Ennis, supported by the Herders, had a salutary impact on Guy's early career.

Ennis was tall, thin, and uncommonly tidy, the only man in the newsroom whose suits seemed to fit him. He was Guy's age, mid-20s. He appeared out of nowhere. Hired as a copyboy in 1961, Ennis rose in about a year to acting city editor, and by 1964 to city editor, the paper's third-ranked editorial position. In that role, he ran the editorial department, all except the editorial page itself, which was the exclusive domain of editor Michael Harrington. He subsequently became assistant managing editor and then managing editor in 1969, by which time he had been running the show for about five years.

Ennis had attended one of the best schools in Newfoundland, St. Bonaventure's College in St. John's. He studied science for one year at Memorial University, with medicine as a distant goal. Academic science did not agree with him. He claims to have dissected one frog, mistaking its lungs for its heart, and he gagged on the smell of formaldehyde. He worked briefly for the US Army in a clerical position at Fort Pepperrell in St. John's before finding his natural niche at the newspaper.

Ennis understood the newspaper business innately, and journalism with political edge and a public service purpose appealed to him, as it did to the Herders. By his own admission, he was not cut out to be a reporter, and he was not a confident writer. Instead, he saw the newspaper as a social force, and he understood his own role as one of leadership.

When Guy arrived in 1963, Steve Herder was managing editor and technically his boss, but Ennis was rising fast. Soon Steve moved from the newsroom on the third floor to the executive fourth, there to join his cousin Hubert Herder, vice-president, his uncle Jim, publisher, and Cindy Post, their cheerful secretary and factotum.

One of Ennis's early morning duties would be to read Guy's feature report or column written the night before. This chore could affect his disposition, usually for the better but occasionally not. It was the little things in Guy's columns that tended to cause problems. Those could trigger what one journalist, Randy Joyce, called "The Committee on UnHerder Activities."

One day, Ennis recalled, Guy used the word *bugger* in a column:

J.M. [publisher James M. Herder] had a fit. But I explained that while we were aware of the literal definition, there was a somewhat more colloquial use of the word. When a fellow wanted someone to get out of his face, it was not unusual to hear him say "bugger off." Sometimes it was used in the context of sleeveen: "ah you bugger you." I told him about a close relative whose pet name for his wife was "buggers." Anyway ... J.M. just scowled ...

Ennis recalled another occasion "when Ray got into his juvenile outharbour delights thing and wrote about the 15/16 clapboard condition. Again, J.M. was upset. I'm sure that it was Steve who calmed him down on that one, telling him that the record was 22." The "15/16 clapboard condition" referred to the once common outharbour juvenile (boys only) competition to determine who could pee the highest up the side of a house, measured in clapboards and adjusted for the varying heights of competitors.

Ennis encouraged original reporting at the *Telegram* and introduced the novel and moderately expensive strategy of sending reporters on road trips in search of stories, rather than merely covering static and staged St. John's news events and photo opportunities.

Guy was a regular traveller. He could take flight within the province almost whenever he felt like it, a measure of his rising favour with Ennis and the Herders, and his popularity with readers. He was one of only a few St. John's reporters ever to visit Labrador. He travelled there as often as he could, both to report from there and to visit his sister, Iris, and her husband, Herb Brett, who lived in Happy Valley-Goose Bay. Guy wrote extensively and eloquently about the Big Land, whether travelling on *Telegram* business or on his own dime.

In 1968, Guy did something else that no other reporter could ever contemplate. Consulting nobody at the newspaper in advance, he announced through his column a high school essay competition the subject of which was "Why I Would Like to Visit Labrador," the declared prize for which was a free trip there.

To Guy's astonishment, businesses in Labrador fell over each other with offers to the winner of free flights, free accommodation, and helicopter side trips to view and fish the bountiful lakes hidden among the Mealy Mountains. The contest was a big to-do. After months of delay and indecision, the prize was awarded to Laurie Bartle of Grand Falls.

As it turned out, the trip did not happen. Iris Brett said she understood that the winner was unable to make the travel at the most opportune time and that Guy had awarded a cash prize instead.

Years later, Guy wrote about the contest himself, perhaps with clouded recollection:

> I once got all melancholy and nostalgic about Labrador. So I scratched together $500 of my newspaper pay and a relative matched it ... a prize of $1,000 to the high school student who writes the best essay on "Why I Want to Visit Labrador." The winning submission was by far the best and most convincing effort; the young winner accepted the prize and bought a really good set of golf clubs with it.[28]

A letter from Laurie Bartle to Ray Guy in February 1969 acknowledged a prize of $250, not $1,000.

Within a year or so of his arrival at the *Telegram*, Guy had become its star reporter. Ennis deliberately expanded Guy's reporting opportunities, offering him choice assignments that tapped his talent and drew attention to his byline. Ennis credits the Herders with supporting this strategy, though nervously, with Steve, the youngest executive Herder, his strongest ally.

Increasingly under Ennis's direction, the news feature of substance emerged as Guy's principal stock in trade. With Guy's writing flair and Ennis's editorial savvy, the staid *Evening Telegram* was becoming more readable, more exciting, and more user-friendly.

CHAPTER 5

Colouring outside the Lines

A Ray Guy news story in 1963 would not have read much differently from one by any other reasonably competent *Telegram* reporter. Unlike most of us, however, Guy paid only brief dues as a general assignment reporter, confined by the limitations of the genre with its five Ws, inverted pyramid construction, and mundane events.

While Guy was a good reporter who worked the phones and knocked on doors, it was feature writing that soon set him apart. In short order, he was being noticed for more substantial articles and a flirtatious inclination toward commentary.

On October 25, 1963, only months after joining the staff, Guy wrote about a young East German seaman who defected from his ship and sought political asylum in St. John's.

This was a good story by any measure. But it was Guy's in-depth treatment and fine writing that won it the entire front page of the newspaper's weekend edition, illustrated with photos by Pat Mahoney. The red banner headline was in a 60-point font: "Cold War Drama Unfolds on Pier 3—RCMP Help Young East German Defect to the West." Guy's byline itself was 14 point or bigger, accented by a two-column box.

The story reflected its Cold War context and Ray Guy's awareness of the day's East-West ideological divisions. It demonstrated the impact and importance of the *Evening Telegram* in its St. John's milieu.

The lights of Water Street may not be the brightest in the free world nor its shop windows the most luxurious, but to Hans Joachim Dost, a 19-year-old ship's engineer, they looked good enough to risk breaking through the Iron Curtain.

Dost, a stocky blond crewman of the 2,900-ton East German factory ship *Bertolt Brecht*, is now in the custody of immigration officials here after being taken off the ship by the R.C.M.P. yesterday afternoon.

He made a dash for freedom late Monday night but was brutally beaten by four other crewmen and dragged back aboard the ship when local police refused to help him.

Early yesterday afternoon, eight carloads of R.C.M.P. and immigration officials, including senior officer H.H. Bragg of the Department of Immigration and Inspector H.A. Russell of the R.C.M.P., drew up to the pier and began a search of the *Bertolt Brecht*.

Hans Joachim Dost would get his second chance for freedom. The R.C.M.P. would escort him off the ship, and if force was necessary to find him they were prepared to use it.

Guy's research and his attention to the requirements of professional reporting were displayed throughout the Dost defection piece. Importantly, he brushed up on Canadian immigration law.

> Under the Immigration Act, an R.C.M.P. officer or an official of the immigration department may muster the crew of a foreign ship docked in a Canadian port.
>
> This provision in the act is implemented whenever authorities feel they have a good reason to take the step. After the crew has been gathered on deck any member may make representations for political asylum to the Canadian authorities.

Guy's sense of journalistic drama was at play in this piece, as he recounted the important moment of discovery. He reported that the Mounties searched the ship for two hours before locating Dost.

> ... A sturdy young crewman in a black and white sweater was brought into the cabin. He had a large bruise over his right eye ...
>
> "Are you Hans Joachim Dost," asked Inspector Bragg through an interpreter, and Dost replied that he was.
>
> "Do you wish to seek political asylum in Canada?" When Dost replied "Ja" the search was over and he was escorted down the gangplank and into one of the police cars ...
>
> As Dost walked away from his ship and from his homeland the crew of the *Bertolt Brecht*, including six or

seven women, lined the rails and watched him go. Some of them took pictures.

The final three paragraphs of the story had their own poignancy and a distinctive Ray Guy touch.

> At the center of yesterday's drama on the St. John's waterfront was a ship that carries the name of a famous German playwright who lashed out against the oppression that crept over Germany during the 1930s.
>
> Bertolt Brecht was forced into exile by the Nazi regime in 1933 after denouncing Hitler and Fascism. He fled to the US where he continued to write of the terror and injustice of dictatorship.
>
> He was converted to Marxism and after the war returned to East Berlin where he died in 1956. One of his most famous plays, which has been translated into a dozen languages, he called "Mother Courage and Her Children."

Guy had no help from internet search engines in 1963. The *Evening Telegram*'s library did not have an encyclopedia. It is entirely possible that when he left for work that morning, already aware of the name of the vessel he would write about that day, he tucked one of his big Ryerson drama texts under his arm. It would have confirmed for him the details of Bertolt Brecht's life.

For Guy, and for many of his grateful readers, those details were worth the trouble. The piece was exemplary for a reporter six months out of college and 24 years old.

An equally defining news feature of Ray Guy's early career appeared in the *Telegram* on December 18, 1964. It was based on a sad event.

Whitbourne is a sleepy, landlocked community 75 kilometres west of St. John's. Once an active transfer station for the Newfoundland Railway, a waystation for bus services to and from Trinity and Placentia Bays, and a fuel stop for traffic headed in several directions, today even the Trans-Canada Highway passes Whitbourne by.

It was a different place on December 17, 1964, a day of dread for Whitbourne: the scene of a standoff between two RCMP officers and four violent men who earlier that morning had broken out of Her Majesty's Penitentiary in St. John's. When the standoff ended, Constable Bob Amey, a 24-year-old Mountie from Nova Scotia, lay dead in the snow on a Whitbourne street.

The escapees had stolen two vehicles in succession that morning, run a police blockade, and were finally cornered and confronted by the Mounties on Whitbourne's main street.

This was a big local story. To the surprise of a few newsroom veterans, the *Evening Telegram* dispatched one of its youngest and least experienced reporters, alone. Guy's report of the tragedy that cost a young Mountie his life was a detailed and descriptive piece.

Newfoundlanders, always avid radio news junkies, would have heard the spare details of the young Mountie's death in brief radio reports on December 17. They also would have known that they would have to wait 24 hours to get the detailed story from one or both St. John's daily newspapers.

Guy's piece was a news feature of substance and clarity. More than gathering the facts, Guy gathered their meaning. He did not stop at the five Ws, or even at the H. If letters are to be assigned, perhaps he introduced a C for context and an E to represent the emotional dimension that such a tragedy carries with it, especially in a small provincial town. More than anything else, Guy listened hard that day. Newfoundlanders already had the raw facts. He provided the story, in depth and detail, in 2,500 plain words, fluidly arranged.

Guy started his story the way Whitbourne had started its previous day. He noted sunrise had been at 7:42, and the weather—a bright winter morning with "still, frosty air." Suddenly a reader was in Whitbourne with him, bearing witness and feeling the tension in the air.

> Bob Amey, the 24-year-old RCMP constable everybody liked was soon to be shot and killed in front of a Whitbourne store by a young man he had never seen before.

This economical paragraph is a study of how a good reporter engages a reader, or a listener or viewer, and builds empathy for the victim's family and friends. Every reporter who covered the shooting would have reported Constable Amey's age. It is less likely that anyone else would have bothered to establish, as Guy did, that Amey was a well-liked, churchgoing young man. Guy may not have asked anyone those questions directly. He would have absorbed much of the information by listening to others talk about the victim, who had lived in Whitbourne only briefly but clearly had connected with many residents.

The words "shot and killed in front of a Whitbourne store" are different from "shot at Whitbourne." More critically, the words "shot by a young man he had never seen before" are a world away from a more predictable treatment such as "shot by an escaped convict." Guy's deliberate choice of words evokes the random and senseless nature of the crime. To write it, a reporter must feel it.

The report has many such examples, among them Guy's reconstruction of the bizarre jailbreak. Even the perspicacious Mr. Hersh of Ryerson might have given an A-minus for these paragraphs:

Seven hours earlier and 50 miles away in St. John's four small-time crooks serving time in her Majesty's Penitentiary for break, entry and theft hacked feverishly at the wooden floor in their dungeon cell.

They squirmed out through half frozen earth, smashed a lock on a prison door and scuttled over the walls, beginning a flight which ended in tragic gun-battle in the streets of Whitbourne.

How they managed to escape, for the second time in less than a month—must be left for another story.

In subsequent days, Guy picked up those aspects of the story. Before leaving them on December 18, however, he raised the obvious questions surrounding the escape. In effect, he invited readers to stay tuned.

Guy named the four escapees without identifying the probable killer. He also noted their ages, which compounded the pathos of the tragedy. One was 21. Two were 19. One was 17. Guy reported that all four also had broken out of the nearby Salmonier prison camp twice in the previous month:

Why, on recapture, were all four put together in one cell? Why were they confined to a cell in the prison's abandoned dungeon? Is a wooden-floored room to be considered a maximum-security cell?

How did the four cut their way out and, if with a knife, how did they manage to smuggle it into their cell?

These are some of the questions which may be answered after the investigation but which now remain a mystery.

In the convention-bound world of 1960s print journalism, the subtle differences between a straight news story and a news feature, and the difference between those forms and editorial or column-writing, can all be noted in the various potential treatments of this story. Guy's feature approach gave him licence, but not carte blanche.

In a news story, a reporter would need to have quoted someone else—a corrections expert perhaps—asking whether a jail with a wooden floor could be considered secure. A feature writer can raise such a question, but not answer it. An editorial writer or columnist might condemn the authorities for putting the four convicts in a common cell with a wooden floor. All of these conventions have changed, of course. Television, "talk radio," and torrential social media have reinvented them or repealed them altogether.

Returning to the central story, Guy reflected the drama of that morning in Whitbourne as he felt it from talking with witnesses. It was a graphic picture:

> Barrett's store, owned by 43-year-old Fred Barrett, is separated by only a lane from a smaller shop owned by William Drover.
>
> The two-story Drover house is attached to the store and from an upstairs window Mrs. Drover and her two daughters watched in horror the scene below in her driveway.
>
> They watched as Constables Amey and Keith backed the four convicts off the road and up against the front of Barrett's store.
>
> Here, Constable Keith attempted to keep them covered with his revolver while Amey ran back down the road to the police car to radio for help from the two other officers of the Whitbourne detachment.
>
> Then the four jumped Keith. "They knocked him down and started pounding him," says Mrs. Drover.

"They grabbed him by the hair and banged his head again and again on the ground ... then they took his gun."

Young, the smallest of the four, had the gun. There are houses on either side of the two stores and others facing them across the road.

On the still morning air the shouts of the four convicts could be heard throughout the neighborhood. There were savage threats, curses, and obscene warnings directed at anyone who would try to stop them.

Constable Amey rushed back from the car. In her terror, Mrs. Drover does not remember if he had his gun drawn nor did she see the convict shoot.

But she saw him stagger when the bullet hit him in the left side of the chest. He fell against a car parked in the lane and crumpled slowly to the ground ...

One of the strengths of this report, and of many others by Guy, is its extensive collection of direct quotes from individuals at the scene. It is unlikely that Guy would have used a tape recorder that day. By 1967, *Telegram* reporters were issued recorders for major stories. But this was 1964. And even that first generation of record-ers would have required a pocketful of batteries for a day of reliable service.

If not so equipped that day, Guy's capture of the actual words that were spoken was impressive. Guy was a good note taker, his cursive writing large and legible. A young person's steel-trap mem-ory did not hurt either.

The words of witnesses would have taken readers as close to the frightening event as they could get without having been there. Those words can still bring a chill. Guy quotes Mrs. Drover:

> "He [Constable Amey as he fell] seemed to reach out his gun to Constable Keith, who took it from his hand. My husband saw he was wounded from a downstairs window and went out a side door into the lane to try and help him."
>
> Constable Keith shouted, "Get back in the house, Bill. You may get shot." Mr. Drover dashed back inside. Young sent a bullet crashing into the side of the store as Drover slammed the door behind him.

That paragraph alone may suggest an artifact of small-town policing half a century ago. Today, as reflected regularly on television newscasts and police dramas, an agitated policeman would scream, "get the f——k back in!" Constable Keith had a different relationship with Bill Drover, because he knew him.

As Constable Amey lay dying or dead, an extraordinary second chapter of the drama developed next door in Fred Barrett's store. Fred had not heard the shots nearby, was unaware of events, and was in his shop around 8:30 to open up for the day. Suddenly he was a hostage, as Melvin Young, 19, came up behind him with a chilling greeting.

> "I don't want to have to shoot you," he said. "And I won't unless I got to."

Another reporter might have written this quote slightly differently, perhaps as "but I will if I have to." Guy wrote it as it was reported to him by Fred Barrett—"and I won't unless I got to"—more likely as Melvin Young would have said it.

The drama continued:

> Young stood in the doorway with Mr. Barrett, the gun held against his chest. Meanwhile, Constable Keith had

come around behind the store through the back yard and taken cover behind a small shed next to the Barrett house.

Keith shouted to Young to give himself up. Then he started talking to him. He said, "We'll do the best we can to help you. That's the only chance you've got. Give the gun to Mr. Barrett and let him go."

"Who is Mr. Barrett?" shouted Young. "He's the man you're pointing the gun at," said Keith. "Let him go and give yourself up."

In an impressive piece of police work, Constable Keith continued to talk Young down. Eventually, Young did surrender the gun to Barrett. Barrett went outside, and for the first time he saw Constable Bob Amey, lying still in the snow.

"I got a sheet from the house and put over him," Barrett told Guy. "The doctor was there and said he was dead. He probably died right away."

Aware of his duty as a journalist, Guy did not ignore the questions and controversy that immediately erupted in Whitbourne around Amey's death:

Why hadn't the RCMP constables used their guns when the three convicts resisted arrest? And why didn't Constable Keith shoot Young after the convict had his revolver, some were asking.

RCMP inspector Russell said in a statement later the RCMP wanted to make the arrest without violence and would refrain from shooting unless absolutely necessary.

"I thought they could have shot to wound them when they got out of the car and were backing away down the road," said Mrs. Drover.

"I suppose they didn't want to hurt them. They took an awful lot of abuse from them ... but even when they had them rounded up the Mounties didn't lay a hand on them."

Equally aware of his duty as a human being, Guy realized that the immediate story was about Constable Amey, and about a town experiencing a crime of terror for the first and only time in its history to date.

A Memorial Service will be held in the Anglican Church at Whitbourne at the same time Constable Amey's burial takes place in his Nova Scotia hometown.

For Mrs. Drover, who watched in unbelief the incredible scene below her window, memories of the bad day at Whitbourne will remain a long time.

"I hope they'll let me have his mother's address," she said. "I got to write to her. She'd want to know how it was and that her son had friends here."

Ray Guy's report ended there. The story of the Whitbourne police murder, however, had a remarkable dénouement. Guy's achievement on the story notwithstanding, it was left to another Newfoundland reporter, Jack Fitzgerald, to complete the story of Constable Amey's death years later. He did so in his book *Crimes That Shocked Newfoundland*, published in 2008.[29]

Melvin Peter Young of Stephenville Crossing, Newfoundland, was convicted of the capital murder of Constable Bob Amey. Fitzgerald reported that Young, who was 19 at the time of the shooting, had lost his father as an infant and became a classic victim of parental tragedy, neglect, and foster family instability.

Justice was swift in Young's case. Three months less a day from the date of the crime, Young's trial began in St. John's before a judge and jury. A week later, the jury convicted him after deliberating for under three hours. Justice Robert Furlong imposed the stipulated sentence of the day for capital murder: hanging.

Young's lawyer, Fintan Aylward, a future minister of Justice for Newfoundland and Labrador, appealed the verdict. His strategy was to inject the requisite reasonable doubt in the minds of the judges by arguing that more than one shot had been fired and it had not been proven that the single bullet fired by Young had killed Amey.

On the evidence, the appeal failed. Inadvertently, it may have saved Young's life.

At trial, the execution date had been set for July 15, 1965, less than four months hence. The appeal was set for May 3, 1965, and to accommodate it, Furlong set the new death date for October 15. Then, as part of their own decision, the appeal judges revised that date to November 18.

As Fitzgerald records it, on November 14, 1965, four days before Melvin Young was to have been hanged, the Canadian Federal Cabinet commuted death sentences for the 11 remaining convicted capital murderers on death row in Canada, Young included, to life imprisonment.

Capital punishment had ended in Canada. Melvin Young lived to spend most of his life in a federal jail, eventually earning parole.

CHAPTER 6

A Small, Wooded Trail

On October 25, 1963, the same day that his in-depth German defector report dominated the *Telegram*'s front page, page 2 revealed a different Ray Guy.

On display was an example of the occasional opinion pieces Guy was writing long before the launch of his page 3 daily column two years later. The topic was a federal announcement about the 1967 Canadian Centennial plans, four years in advance of the event. Ottawa revealed that every Canadian would be entitled to receive $1 as part of the celebrations.

Unlike his *Ryersonian* Centennial satire of the previous year, Guy did not have to make this stuff up. There was a dash of satire in this piece, however, one of his earliest displays of the form in the newspaper. He professed astonishment that Newfoundlanders had exhibited little joy or even much awareness of the fact that half a million free federal dollars were up for grabs.

> This type of behavior is against every established principle that Newfoundlanders hold dear. All it takes is a little ingenuity and the half million smackers are ours ...
>
> As things stand, this is indeed a crucial moment in the island's history. Our hitherto unsullied reputation as the nation's champion freeloaders hangs in the balance.

At this point in the piece, Guy was just having fun. Further along, he would reveal more consequential content—early if oblique references to Premier J.R. Smallwood, minor jibes but still potentially irritating to the thin-skinned premier. The hints were indicative of Guy's tendency to regard the premier as only an occasional object of mirth. The column displayed levity but fell far short of the devastating ridicule eventually to be deployed as Guy became immersed in Newfoundland and Labrador political issues and increasingly appalled by Smallwood's personal bombast.

Flying closer to the sun, Guy recommended that Newfoundland's half million Centennial dollars be pooled to fund a lobby to ensure that "at least one symbolic bow-tie" and "that distinct species of Newfoundland fauna, the bison" would be represented on the proposed new Canadian flag.

The bow-tie reference was of course to Joey's enduring affection for that notice-me piece of haberdashery. The bison reference was a mild mockery of Smallwood's maniacal notion to have a herd of Manitoba bison installed on Brunette Island in Fortune Bay.

That really happened by the premier's *ex cathedra* decree. In June of the following year, 24 of the hairy prairie mammoths arrived—five bulls and 19 cows. Sadly, none survived for long. Many were said to have run headlong over steep cliffs. Folk tales, gleefully published by Guy and others, had it that some Burin Peninsula residents had sampled a lighter and less gamey local meat that was not exactly as they recalled the taste of moose.

Those contrasting articles in a single edition of the *Telegram* testified to Ray Guy's range and productivity.

Bob Ennis assigned Guy increasingly to political event coverage, which often meant covering Smallwood, usually as he announced new industries, or cut ribbons for causeways, highways, byways, and slipways.

As a daily news reporter indulging in sporadic satirical pieces, Guy showed little inclination to criticize the premier directly, and no hint of the latent animus toward him that would flare before too long. Years later, Guy recalled this early, gentler phase:

> When I came with the *Telegram* nine years ago this May coming, Smallwood was no more to me than Malcolm Hollett or Tommy Toe or the man in the moon ...[30]

By the middle of 1964, however, it was possible to detect an increasing edge and a cheekier disposition in Guy's references to the premier.

On August 20 of that year, Guy found himself in Boyd's Cove, Notre Dame Bay, executing typical feature coverage of a typical Joey Smallwood production. A new causeway was being opened across Dildo Run, linking New World Island, where 5,000 people lived, to the mainland of Newfoundland. The causeway cost $3 million to construct. Guy reported that 3,000 people attended the opening:

> The main speaker was Premier Smallwood, whose hour-long address was an elaboration of the theme that

"Newfoundland is the one place in the world where miracles still happen."

He listed these "modern miracles," all of which have occurred within the past 15 years, reaching from the wilderness of Labrador even unto the wave-lashed shores of Baie d'Espoir.

The premier stressed that unless these developments and improvements are continued, the youth of the province will seek greener fields: "Fish have tails and can swim away; our young people will swim away too if we don't give them good reason to stay."

A tangential reference in his report from Boyd's Cove suggested an ambivalent view about outports and outport life that Guy may have been nurturing at the time. The delicate balance between small-town tranquility versus "progress" is acknowledged in the report. It is a subject to which he would return throughout his career.

The new road is narrow and winding over haystack-shaped hills and through tall stands of black spruce and aspen, through the small communities of Summerford, Carter's Cove, Virgin Arm, Hillgrade, and connects with most other villages on the island.

New service stations and gas pumps are going up, many houses already have a car parked in front of them, but the blight of the mainland, the automobile graveyard, has not appeared.

The settlements still have the tranquil look of a small island, which will soon give way to a faster, four-wheeled tempo.

A number of cars have been operated on the island for years, but crossing to the island was only across sea ice in winter and was often dangerous. The latest such fatality occurred last winter when a car broke through the ice and its driver drowned.

Other references reflected the enormous standing that Smallwood enjoyed in 1964, especially in communities on the traditionally Liberal northeast coast of the province.

> Small groups of residents greeted the official party along the way as it passed under lines of flags and evergreen arches.
>
> Some of the children waved hand-lettered signs: "Thank you Mr. Smallwood for all you have done for us" and "New World Island liberated by the Liberals."

Guy made no direct comment on the political nature and photo-opportunity extravagance of the event. Indirectly, he made it plain that no self-respecting Liberal politician with any hope of re-nomination would be caught dead anywhere but in the premier's Boyd's Cove chorus on that important day. Nor should any local contractor expect a future cost-plus government contract without saluting the occasion.

> A crowd, estimated at more than 3,000, waited on the flag-bedecked bridge as the premier and party assembled on the platform.
>
> Premier J.R. Smallwood; Attorney General L.R. Curtis; Finance Minister E.S. Spencer; Municipal Affairs Minister B.J. Abbott; Public Works Minister J.R. Chalker; Highways Minister Dr. F.W. Rowe; Speaker George Clark, MHA Carbonear; Gerald Hill, MHA Labrador South; William Smallwood, Green Bay; Harold Starkes, MHA Lewisporte; Ross Barbour, MHA Bonavista South; Eric Dawe, MHA Port de

Grave; Steve Neary, MHA Bell Island; and Val Earle, MHA Fortune.

Transport Minister J.W. Pickersgill (L-Bonavista-Twillingate) flew down from Ottawa especially for the occasion and rejoiced that with the exception of Fogo Island he was now able to cover all of his district by car.

Federal MP Charles Granger (L-Grand Falls-White Bay-Labrador) also attended.

The mayors of surrounding towns, representatives of the clergy and officials of contracting and construction firms were among those who rounded out the impressive gathering.

Guy's closing observation made it clear that in Newfoundland in 1964 not all the queen's Newfoundland and Labrador ministers were equal.

Premier Smallwood left Twillingate by helicopter at 7:30 p.m. yesterday, while the rest of the party left for Gander by car.

In 1966, Joseph R. Smallwood, aged 65 and 16 years into his career as Newfoundland's first premier, won his biggest election victory ever. Of the 42 seats in the House of Assembly, Smallwood's Liberals captured 39.

Joey had led the Confederation with Canada forces to their narrow run-off referendum victory on July 22, 1948. Thus ended forever the dream of Joey's nationalistic opponents to re-establish the "Responsible Government" the poverty-stricken British colony of Newfoundland had surrendered in 1934.

Thereafter, and prior to 1966, Smallwood as premier had won five provincial elections, all by landslides, leading a Liberal Party closely aligned with its federal Canadian counterpart. With his near rout of his political opponents in that year, Joey was at the peak of his popularity and power.

The three good men elected for the Progressive Conservative Party in 1966 faced a juggernaut. Briefly, the three stalwarts were led by a young and scholarly Progressive Conservative, Gerald Ottenheimer. Unfortunately, Ottenheimer was forced to quit in 1970 following a sex scandal in which he was the only apparent victim. He had been arrested and charged with being illegally "found in" a Montreal brothel. Ottenheimer resigned immediately, a lamentable loss for Newfoundland and Labrador Tories and more good news for Smallwood.

With a few notable exceptions, the new government was comprised of individuals beholden to and completely dominated by Smallwood. From the day of the election onward, the new government, though activist and ambitious in the Smallwood way, was personified by its leader. It also was characterized by growing arrogance and by contempt for all detractors, once more in the Smallwood manner. Increasingly, especially on the industrial development front, the government was marked by ineptitude. With Smallwood's close connections to perfidious characters such as John C. Doyle and Oliver L. Vardy, it was soon shadowed by corruption.[31]

Despite its dominance, a surprising fact about the 1966 Smallwood government was that the seeds of its demise were evident almost from the beginning. Despite the durability of the Smallwood brand, by 1968 a viable if unorthodox opposition to Joey was gaining momentum.

That opposition only incidentally included the official Progressive Conservative caucus. The emerging opposition to Smallwood included a small cluster of independent-minded ministers in his own Cabinet, most notably John Crosbie and Clyde Wells, both of whom defected from the Cabinet in 1968. Less obvious, but significant, was increasing discomfort on the part of Liberal Party grandees such as the principled Aiden Maloney, who left the Cabinet in 1970, and Ed Roberts, Smallwood's brightest minister and closest political confidant, who stayed on to bristle in growing discomfort.

Guy's growing anti-Smallwoodism tapped two major currents of political sentiment at play in Newfoundland and Labrador in the late 1960s.

An acknowledged hangover of anti-Confederation emotion was still shared in the mid-1960s by thousands of Newfoundlanders, especially in St. John's. This was especially true among the St. John's historic business class—old Newfoundland money—whose numbers, if not their means, were in decline.

There was also a fresher and colder opposition emerging, a new generation of Newfoundlanders and Labradorians, rising in reaction to Smallwood himself and to his increasingly impaired ideas of both development and democracy. Those newer components of the unofficial opposition were more amorphous, harder to name, and their impact difficult to quantify. But they were on the move, and they would multiply.

On another major front, Newfoundland fishermen, the province's most essential workforce, were restless. The slow and rocky transformation of the fishery from indigenous inshore to international competition for midshore and offshore stocks was not going well. Major fish species were threatened by the rapacity of both Canadian, including Newfoundland, and foreign fleets, and by the inadequate federal resolve to protect them. For the first time in more than half a century, Newfoundland and Labrador fishermen, often accompanied by their wives who worked in the processing plants, joined unions. They were led by a new breed of populist politicians and reformers.

Most prominent among those union leaders was the peripatetic Richard Cashin. A former federal MP and Liberal gadfly, Cashin had begun, and could have continued, a successful career as a mainstream politician. He opted for more challenging social and industrial reform. In the same reform-minded mould was Cashin's friend from their St. Francis Xavier University days, Father Desmond McGrath. In 1969, McGrath founded Newfoundland's first modern-day fishermen's union, the Newfoundland Fishermen, Food and Allied Workers, in Port aux Choix, launching a movement as significant as any political party of the era.

Cashin and McGrath, with increasing national and international trade union support, gradually built a collective power structure in Newfoundland, independent of Smallwood and his Cabinet and increasingly at odds with industry owners and with governments at all levels.

Fishery organizing activities harkened back to two auspicious events in Newfoundland union and political history. One was the Fishermen's Protective Union founded by William F. Coaker in 1908, which transformed Newfoundland's northeast coast fishery over two subsequent decades. Coaker, the FPU's only significant leader, had been Smallwood's earliest mentor and political hero.

The FPU and its successful business adjunct, The Fishermen's Union Trading Company—co-operative movements more than unions—played a large part in liberating inshore fishermen from the servitude of the truck system. Under that nearly cashless construct, fishermen for a century or more had been grub-staked to all supplies by fish buyers each spring, then obliged to "square up" each fall at the buyers' reckoning, usually with little or nothing left over for themselves.

The other and more relevant historical event was the 1958 International Woodworkers of America loggers' strike against the Anglo-Newfoundland Development Company's woods operations in Central Newfoundland.

That strike, led by a fearless British Columbia union man, H. Landon Ladd, turned into a debacle that culminated in a riot in Badger in 1958 in which a St. John's policeman, Constable William Moss, was killed. It also cast Smallwood, Coaker's erstwhile acolyte, in a new and very different role: union-buster. The premier had the IWA union decertified, literally running Ladd out of town on a narrow-gauge rail and a ferry across Cabot Strait.

Smallwood's biographer Richard Gwyn reported that Smallwood once "brought an audience of businessmen to its feet" at the Empire Club in Toronto by describing the IWA as "the barracuda of the trade union movement ... a savage shark, extremely clever and experienced. They did a better job of brainwashing than anything this side of Moscow."[32]

But not better than Smallwood. In place of the legitimate and powerful IWA, Smallwood established his own government-promoted loggers' association, the Newfoundland Brotherhood of Woodworkers, led by a provincial Cabinet minister, Max Lane. "Pick up your axe and follow Max," Smallwood entreated loggers in a province-wide radio broadcast. Many loggers did. Many others have gone to their graves resenting Smallwood's action. A few considered themselves to have been lucky enough to have lived to witness Smallwood's own reckoning in 1971 at the hands of Newfoundland and Labrador voters.

Another component of the evolving opposition to Smallwood was of his own creation, the massive expansion of Memorial University on a sprawling new campus, opened in 1961. This virtual revolution in post-secondary learning potential in Newfoundland and Labrador was a Smallwood brainchild and his most profound achievement. Smallwood's own words portray his genuine excitement about the new university, along with his usual pathological worship of pomp, title, and station:

> Can there have been many university functions to equal the one that we had to launch Memorial's new campus in 1961? I invited Mrs. Eleanor Roosevelt to come and open it. She was the special personal representative of President John F. Kennedy for the occasion, and arrived in a stylish American Government jet. The Prime Minister of Canada, Mr. Diefenbaker, was there for the Government of Canada, and the Duke of Devonshire came for the British Government. I invited the president of every university in Canada to attend, and chartered a large plane to pick them up at airports all the way from British Columbia to Halifax.[33]

By the late 1960s, along with random gusts of student rebellion—Guy once referred to Newfoundland at the time as "the elephant graveyard of radical chic"—platoons of young community workers from Memorial University's Extension Service swarmed around the province on random missions of social and political intervention. Those bright and benevolent busybodies involved themselves with communities in mostly positive and creative ways, promoting social and economic reform in places such as Fogo Island and Burin. Usually, and especially in Fogo, their initiatives were in defiance of conventional power structures, the Smallwood government included.

At Memorial University itself, there was significant academic activity that represented new and uniquely independent challenges to Smallwood's development theology.

Economists and historians such as David Alexander and Keith Matthews were challenging both the conventional wisdom of how the fishery had been and should be run and the Smallwood industrial development model for Newfoundland. Sociologists

Noel Iverson and Ralph Matthews examined the various household resettlement programs and found them misguided in concept and malignant in execution. More gradually, but importantly, Memorial's Department of Education was turning out teachers and school administrators with an ever-declining commitment to the province's church-based education system.

Loosely connected, and at times even suspicious of each other, all of those forces contributed to the emerging and unofficial opposition to Premier Smallwood.

And then there was Ray Guy.

Chapter 7
Rae David George Guy and Goliath

Somewhere early on I decided that the only course was, perhaps, to giggle the bastards to death. That too, I soon found, was slow and steady work, like the tomcat eating the grindstone ...
—*Ray Guy, 2008*

About the only weapon available was what has been euphemistically called "humor" which is to say scurrility, innuendo, rumor-mongering, character-assassination and, generally, jolly old spit-disturbing.
—*Ray Guy, 2008*

A lone ranger by nature and by choice, Ray Guy often rode in the same direction as other Smallwood detractors, sometimes ahead of them, sometimes behind. But he was never with them, and he was never of them.

It is not possible to quantify Guy's role in destabilizing Smallwood. But few of the forces arrayed against the premier in the late 1960s were as present and pervasive as Guy's pen.

Even before the 1966 Liberal triumph, Guy had his everyday bully pulpit on page 3 of the *Evening Telegram*. From there, he could express his mounting contempt for Smallwood, connecting with tens of thousands of readers. Guy also possessed weapons that most Smallwood antagonists or Smallwood supporters lacked or rarely used—wit and humour.

Guy's daily *Telegram* column was launched in January 1965 when the House of Assembly opened for its winter-spring session. It was headed Ray Guy—In the House, and, as a daily column, it was initially meant to be confined to House sittings. Once started, however, it ran almost uninterrupted for a decade, with Guy's occasionally mild digs at Smallwood gradually gusting to ridicule, on a path to total contempt.

The *Telegram*'s editorial and executive chieftain, Steve Herder, never doubted the value of Guy's work. The other Herders, Steve's cousin Hubert, vice-president, and his uncle Jim, publisher, while officially neutral, were by disposition anti-Smallwood, as were most St. John's business elders. More importantly, they generally were on side with the escalating political content of Guy's daily columns and his mounting antipathy to the premier.

Following Confederation in 1949, Smallwood declared he had established "Her Majesty's Outport Government." By the late 1960s, Guy had become the outport people's tribune, an entertaining but serious columnist writing in a homegrown vein of humour, spiked with exaggeration and mockery.

Guy's columns were read hungrily by politicians, business barons, and public servants. Political junkies also got their fix. Edward Roberts, Smallwood's closest political confidant, recalled that as soon as the *Evening Telegram* came off the presses each day, he and other politicians would spend their lunch hours devouring Guy's column. Guy, Roberts said, "became an effective opposition."

Young and old alike read Guy. Urban Newfoundlanders with outport roots could zone into Guy's childhood reminiscences. The younger crowd, with grievances of their own, enjoyed the daily treat of seeing their fresh ideas fully baked and brilliantly expressed in the newspaper.

John C. Crosbie was another prominent Guy reader. Then in his 30s, Crosbie had entered politics as deputy mayor of St. John's before being recruited by Smallwood as the unelected Minister of Municipal Affairs just prior to the 1966 election.

"I became a devoted reader of Guy's columns in *The Telegram*," Crosbie wrote in an introduction to *The Smallwood Years*, a collection of Guy's columns published by Boulder Publications (now Boulder Books) of St. John's in 2008. He continued:

> To write as he did during those years Guy had to have great courage, a strong independent streak, and a great gift for satirical writing—holding up to folly and ridicule and lampooning individuals who have great power but come to misuse it and get carried away with it.

Crosbie said he read some 400 pages of Guy's commentary written during the 1960s and 1970s before writing that introduction: "I remember vividly and can testify that the events and incidents he wrote about in fact occurred."

By mid-1968, Guy had become the Smallwood-baiter who mattered most. Smallwood's Achilles heel was his government's spotty and expensive record of industrial development and his personal obsession with land-based wage jobs of questionable value and often ridiculous cost.

Guy gradually created a picture of Smallwood's develop-or-perish policy as a mad-hatter carnival, and its champion as more or less demented. His August 28, 1968, column was prototypical, the anti-Smallwood satirist in full feather. According to Guy that day, the latest Smallwood announcement of yet another natural resources jackpot had left the entire Newfoundland and Labrador populace in paroxysms of delight:

> A long-time observer of Newfoundland affairs says he has never seen such a display of public joy and enthusiasm on the island.

These celebrations, he says, even exceed the general jubilation when the news was flashed to Newfoundland that John C. Doyle had skipped safely across the border to escape a US jail term.

John C. Doyle is forgotten today. Smallwood made Doyle a household name in Newfoundland and Labrador in the mid-1960s. Doyle was Smallwood's industrial developer of choice. They remained loyal to each other long after few others did.

Doyle was an American promoter who helped develop the western Labrador iron ore fields, a qualified Smallwood success story. Hundreds of mining and pelletizing plant jobs were created in Labrador West for Newfoundlanders and Labradorians. Hundreds more were exported downstream for manufacturing enterprises in Sept-Îles, Québec, and in the US. Doyle also promoted a brewery and a paper mill at Stephenville, the former simply not needed, and the latter without a reliable wood supply. Both became develop-or-perish failures. In 1969, Memorial University students marched on Confederation Building chanting, "Hey, hey, John C. Doyle. How many palms did you have to oil?"

Doyle eventually was charged in the US with stock manipulation and in Canada with fraud and income tax evasion. Neither country could extradite him on those charges from Panama City, to which he had fled and where he lived out his years in luxury and without a court reckoning.

"The important thing to remember about John C. Doyle," John Crosbie wrote in his autobiography, *No Holds Barred*, "was not that he was charming and personable, brilliant and cultured, a linguist and oenophile, and a concert-calibre pianist and organist—he was all of those things, I suppose—but that he was a crook."[34]

Guy's "report" of the public reaction to the latest Smallwood announcements continued, still quoting his "long-time observer":

Even that memorable occasion of 15 years ago when the government predicted that Newfoundland would become the world's foremost mink breeder can't match it, he says.

In fact, he is of the opinion that it far surpasses the dancing in the streets on that fateful day when Premier Smallwood announced that the cowboy would replace the fisherman in Newfoundland.

Our observer tells us that he has run down the long catalogue of Great and Momentous Announcements made by the premier but can find nothing to equal the frenzied excitement that now grips the province.

"When the premier announced that Dr. Valdmanis was worth his weight in gold to the Newfoundland people, there was a great outpouring of public joy and gratitude," he continues, "but nothing to match this."

Alfred Valdmanis is another story. A multilingual and diabolically brainy Latvian economist with a spy-novel résumé, Valdmanis was hired by Smallwood in 1950 to promote relatively small-scale manufacturing industries in the first wave of post-Confederation economic development.

Dozens of small plants making shoes, rubber boots, cement, and eyeglasses were created, with substantial public contributions. Virtually all were failures. Their extravagant promotion, mainly by Valdmanis himself, plus start-up subsidies, cleaned out much of the $40 million budget surplus Newfoundland brought into Confederation in 1949.

In 1954, Valdmanis, foreshadowing the conduct of his successor, Doyle, was charged with defrauding European companies investing in Newfoundland of $470,000. Unlike Doyle, who fled, Valdmanis pleaded guilty and was sentenced to four years in prison.

Richard Gwyn captured the succession from Valdmanis to Doyle with efficient and colourful accuracy. "In 1953," Gwyn wrote, "Doyle's rising star passed Valdmanis' in descent."

The celebrations of success, Guy's "source" continued, did not end there. Guy was on a roll:

> "When the premier announced that only over his dead body would a certain iron ore plant be built outside Newfoundland in Quebec, there was bell-ringing and flag-weaving," he says, "but there's no comparison to what we are seeing today. "When the premier announced that Newfoundland had 'escaped the clutches of Quebec' and Churchill Falls power would flow through the island on its way to the New York subways, people wept openly and perfect strangers hugged each other in the streets.
>
> "But that was only small stuff," he says, "compared to this. As were other Great Announcements—chocolate bar factories, rubber plants, battery plants, at least five Third Mills, the great Fisheries Conference."
>
> Thanking our observer for his observations I went down into the teeming streets and was swept along by the jubilant throng. Car horns blew. Women held babes in arms alive with confetti and paper streamers.
>
> "Haven't you heard the Great Announcement?" screamed one overjoyed citizen who wore a party hat and swigged from a hip flask. "Salt! Salt discovered on the west coast! Vast amounts of salt!"
>
> "And potash," interjected his companion. "Vast, vast amounts of potash. Beautiful, wonderful potash. Just think, until yesterday we didn't even have ash, let alone a pot to put it in."

"One of the greatest discoveries of minerals in the long history of this province," added yet another. "No doubt about it. Have you heard that the Long Range Mountains are 86 per cent Limburger cheese?"

The great minerals announcement of the previous day was a rare opportunity to bundle the entire catalogue of Smallwood fantasies, with a few apocryphal additions thrown in. The result may have been Guy's most devastating anti-Smallwood satire, recasting Smallwood, the great development guru, as a figure of absurdity, pomposity, and ultimately of pathos.

Ironically, Ray Guy became one of the few Newfoundlanders since Smallwood to establish a strong and direct media rapport with outport people. Smallwood had achieved this in the 1940s as "The Barrelman," a radio grab bag of yarns, information, and trivia, all obsessively related to Newfoundland and Labrador, delivered with professional verve by Smallwood himself.

A few other Newfoundland broadcasters and writers had comparable achievements. In the 1950s and 1960s, Don Jamieson, broadcaster and future federal Cabinet minister, hosted two land-mark programs. His Sunday morning *Chapel for Shut-Ins*, a collage of hymns and spiritual stories on CJON Radio, connected mainly with the elderly and was hugely popular. Jamieson's nightly *News Cavalcade* on CJON Television, on which he would pause during the newscast and light up a Rothman cigarette to promote his sponsor, was the leading local TV newscast before CBC invaded the television news field in the late 1960s and swiftly conquered the local supper-hour market with its *Here & Now* show.

In the same era, Ted Russell, a man of sweet temperament who, as a former politician first supported but later defriended Smallwood, wrote and read the weekly CBC Radio feature, *The Chronicles of Uncle Mose*. The Chronicles were brilliantly crafted yarns, fictional but laden with truth, especially in the outports on which they were based. They were set in a fictional village, Pigeon Inlet.

All of those storytellers and broadcasters shared common skills with Guy. But there were critical differences. Smallwood and Jamieson were both building political bases. For them, broadcasting was preliminary and convenient. Russell, when writing *The Chronicles of Uncle Mose*, had forsaken political life as a Smallwood partisan and appeared to be seeking redemption. Guy's political contribution was large and real, but it flowed from his calling as a writer and satirist, not the other way around.

It was not until the Confederation campaign in the late 1940s that Smallwood adapted his *Barrelman* radio skills exclusively to political ends. He spoke convincingly to Newfoundlanders about their compromised social and economic status, and the income bonanza that could be theirs through Canada's advanced social safety net of old-age pensions and the "baby bonus."

Two decades later, Guy used his own connection with his readers, based partly on humour and outport nostalgia, to deliver serious political content. Much of it was aimed directly at what he saw as Smallwood's growing megalomania and arrogance, chip-chipping away at the premier's vaunted invulnerability.

At the height of his power, Smallwood talked to Newfoundlanders and Labradorians incessantly about his philosophy of big-scale industrial development, designed to reduce the instability that plagued the province's economy and was endemic in the foundation industry of fishing.

By contrast, Guy wrote about outport strengths and values. In those columns, he was more Barrelman than political analyst. His Encyclopedia of Juvenile Outharbour Delights made baymen and townies alike laugh out loud. The Encyclopedia was a sideshow among his daily columns, but it was an essential component of his rapport with Newfoundlanders. Guy pretended that its pages were numbered in the hundreds, citing entries such as "Tying Cans onto Sheep Tails," which he said could be found at page 867.

Through the Encyclopedia, Guy spoke more movingly to the hearts of Newfoundlanders than the post-Confederation Smallwood could speak to their pocketbooks. Smallwood traded in dollars and cents. Guy's words evoked emotions: literary emoticons. Only weeks before his August 28, 1968, desecration of the Smallwood industrial development theology, Guy had been writing his way into the Newfoundland psyche by way of the Encyclopedia, demonstrating impressive range:

> Today's Juvenile Outharbor Delight is just as widely known as Catching Connors. It is none other than "Walking Around Shore," a noble pursuit if ever there was one.
>
> ("Walking Around Shore": General directions and also incorporating that associated delight, "Picking Up Stuff.") You will need a shore for walking around and since you are lucky enough to be in Newfoundland, you have 6,000 miles.
>
> An excuse to do it is not necessary, although if you are over 10 years old and below 65 an excuse will come in handy in case you are accused of wasting time.
>
> Picking up wood is a good excuse. All you have to do is haul a few likely looking pieces of firewood above high-water mark and pile it. Or bring back a nice piece of BC var (Fir)—always appreciated.
>
> Or you can say you're going to have an eye out for the family horse put out on the country for the summer. Or you can even take a brin bag and say you are going to pick up some blue mussel shells and white rocks— greatly favored by the old folks for doing up graves.

These few little duties are quickly done and you can get down to the real business of "Walking Around Shore" and "Picking Up Stuff."

You may find, once a summer, a bottle with a note in it. That's something, I tell you. Because you can send it away and they'll send you back a fifty-cent piece. Not many can have that to say ...

There are all kinds of caps. People on vessels are always losing their caps. If you keep at it, you can make up a collection of sailors' caps from foreign lands.

Hoares egg shells (sea urchins) are good for looking at the sky through when you sit down to take a spell. They're light green on the outside and full of pin holes like lace curtains.

There is a scattered doll washed ashore. Pitiful, they are, like drowned little people and likely to give you a start if you come across one suddenly.[35]

Unusually for an Encyclopedia entry, Guy indulges another interest in "Walking Around Shore." Two-thirds of the way through the column, he turns a hairpin corner from nostalgia to environmental concern. Even in 1968, it was easy to observe drastic changes in the Newfoundland beachscapes of Guy's childhood. The childhood beaches were far from pristine, but their trash was different, more amenable to natural degeneration:

Walking Around Shore, sad to say, is not what it used to be. The plastic, you see, has nearly ruined it. Before now the wood used to rot, the bottles got smashed and ground up and the tin cans rusted away.

The landwash was always being cleared away for the next lot of good stuff to wash ashore. But plastic. It will never rot in the walls of hell.

A few of the sources of Ray Guy's contempt for Smallwood are easy to discern. Others are more obscure, and those may be more interesting. Guy offered his own reasons as well, and those can be considered valid, if incomplete.

Guy's detractors, especially around Placentia Bay where his family was well known, speculated that he had been influenced by his father, George H. Guy, an anti-Confederate Tory. In fact, Ray was much more influenced by his mother, Alice, and by his grandmother, Rachel Guy.

Alice's Newfoundland patriotism, anti-Confederate but perhaps more reasoned than George's, may have had a mild impact. Grandma Rachel offered him warmth and comfort but little in the way of political guidance. Overall, it is safe to say that family influence was not a decisive force. Even as a child, Ray was independent-minded and autonomous, literally to a fault.

One indisputable influence was Guy's growing revulsion in the 1960s and 1970s to Newfoundland's household resettlement programs. The programs often have been cited, validly, as a source of his contempt for Smallwood. It is true that the resettlement phenomenon rankled him in a dramatic and personal way. It inspired many of his finest columns. But resettlement alone is an incomplete explanation of Guy's reaction to the premier.

Guy's own declared reasons for his disregard are on the record, set out neatly in a column he wrote a year after the former premier was finally defeated.

"Whether it is the heights of biggery or no," Guy wrote on January 22, 1972, deploying the colloquial turn of phrase he occasionally used when he felt the need to look his readers in the eye, "I must mention myself in connection with Joey Smallwood."

"'How come you were always wonderful down on Mr. Smallwood?' is what I had put to me the other day. 'Isn't you ashamed of yourself now that the poor man is gone?'" Joey was not dead, of course. In early 1972, he was "gone" only politically, following a wild and disputed election in October 1971 and the eventual transfer of power to Frank Moores's Progressive Conservatives in January 1972.

In October 1971, disaffected by a variety of stresses, including a brief strike at the paper, Guy had taken an unscheduled three-month break from the *Telegram*. It gave him time to think. His return in late January 1972 coincided with Smallwood's departure as premier. It struck Guy as a good time to explain his antipathy to Smallwood. Neither contrition nor atonement was on the menu that day. But defiance was.

"Down on him is damn right," Guy wrote:

> Nights and nights when I should have been home in my bed I was cooking up names to call Joey Smallwood and his clique and twisting it up in every way, shape, and form possible.
>
> He's out of it now and some of the ones around him are dead and in their graves. Ashamed? The only shame on my head, sir, is that my laziness and lack of talent prevented me from laying it on 10 times as hot and 10 times as heavy.
>
> If I hurt any of them (which, please God, I did), it was only because I believed the whole noxious bunch of them were hurting thousands of other people every day that passed over their heads.
>
> There were two main things that turned my blood against Joey Smallwood ...
>
> ... One day we were all called in for a news conference in Confederation Building. He was going to announce that Ottawa had a new insurance scheme for lobster pots. The fishermen would pay 10 cents a pot and get $8 or $10 if it was wrecked.

After the thing was finished and the cameras and tape recorders turned off, one of the reporters said to Mr. Smallwood, off the record, "What's the big deal about this scheme? There's not that many pots wrecked in Newfoundland each year, is there?"

"Ah, ha," says Smallwood. "If I know our Newfoundland fishermen, they'll find ways to make the most of it. Who can prove what goes on all those back beaches?"

It went through me like a shot.[36]

As a second reason for reviling Smallwood, Guy cited the premier's bullying and belittling of his opponents and sometimes his own colleagues in the House of Assembly and elsewhere.

Guy's explanations have a tidy appeal, but even the words from the horse's mouth are not completely satisfying. That is not because they aren't true—Guy, on such matters, can be taken at his word—but because they are incomplete. It is hard to credit that one narrow incident, as he suggested, along with a general impression of Smallwood as a bully, could generate the intensity of his disaffection or crank up the energy required for a focused anti-Smallwood campaign that lasted nearly a decade.

St. John's journalist Kathryn Welbourn, the editor and publisher of the *Northeast Avalon Times*, became a close friend of Kathie Housser and Ray Guy in the final few years of his life. Welbourn said she believed that everything anyone ever wanted to know about Guy could be discovered readily in his writing. There is much truth to that, but there are times when important truths about him must be extrapolated from his writing and combined with other information about the man behind it.

An important influence was inherent in his character. Guy was a moralist, as many of the best journalists are. He had an old-fashioned and fierce commitment to truth and free expression, or at least to his own versions of those values. He was a self-appointed avenging angel who loved to smite the enemies of justice, especially the bullying kind. If Guy could read those characterizations, he might cringe. But the truth is that anyone fortunate enough to have known Guy personally was aware of that streak of rectitude. Occasionally, the streak could gust to piety. Occasionally, it could be unbearable.

As Welbourn suggested, many of Guy's influences can indeed be found in his own writing. One notorious Smallwood gambit stoked Guy's righteousness like no other. As political dissent gained momentum by 1968, the Smallwood government announced an anti-democratic initiative that struck a nerve with many and drove Guy to distraction.

Fed up with growing media criticism, even from the traditionally adoring Mainland media, Smallwood decided to publish his own newspaper, the *Newfoundland Bulletin*. Guy usually referred to it in print as the Bull-etin. On July 10, 1968, the first edition of the *Bulletin* had just been sent out, supposedly to every Newfoundland and Labrador home.

Guy had received several copies in advance. He responded creatively, with controlled fury and a devastating blend of sermonizing and satire.

The first thing dictators do is start newspapers, Guy wrote. He cited Russia's *Pravda*, the largest newspaper in the world, explaining its role in the Soviet autocracy:

> When a dictator overthrows a democracy the very first thing he does is padlock the newspaper offices and either shoot the newspaper owners or dump them in jail.
>
> This is what any dictator does first, be it the Communist type such as we see in Russia or China or the fascist type such as reigned in Nazi Germany and in Mussolini's Italy.

> The dictators know instinctively that their greatest enemies are newspapers. They know they'll never be safe until the newspapers are strangled. So they do that first.
>
> Then they start to print their own newspapers. Official government newspapers. Dictators know that free newspapers are their greatest enemies. They also know that newspapers they can control are their most valuable tools ...

At one level, this column reflected Guy's professional manifesto, his free-press statement, a salute to a modern value, well before the Canadian Charter of Rights and Freedoms existed. In its unusually serious and somewhat preachy tone, the column revealed the depth of Guy's commitment to media freedom and his sensitivity to the perils of government-controlled information.

Having set the table with a general declaration against instruments of distortion and repression, Guy turned to the *Bulletin* itself, volume 1, number 1. He reviewed the contents and found them all fair game for ridicule. First came a droll heads-up in which he telegraphed to his readers the magnitude of the matter at hand.

> OK. I know it is summer, but we can't have fun and games every day ...
>
> ... The very first thing Premier Smallwood has done in his vigorous drive to put himself back on top (or as he terms it, to put the Liberal party back on top) is to start an official government newspaper ...
>
> Printed by a government which claimed for years that Hansard (a report of what was said on both sides of the House) was too expensive ...

The first issue of this government-controlled news-paper is already out. Let's see what the premier means by the right kind of news.

Starting at the back we see that all the "news" is favorable to the government. Very favorable. "New-foundland is fourth in Mineral Production." Good show. Quota maintained under five-year plan?

"Motor vehicle sales indication of affluence."

"Soft drink and beer sales striking example of prosperity."

"Increase in personal income; agreeable and encouraging."

We learn what a splendid chap John C. Doyle is as he "pioneers again in Labrador." What a splendid job the government is doing at Come by Chance, Baie d'Espoir and in centralization. Everywhere.

This splendid and apparently perfect government tells you how great it really is—gives you all the news the premier thinks you should read.

And on the front page ... there is a huge picture. It takes up half the front page. And who is that picture of? Come now? Need you ask? The man himself, the Only Living Father—Premier J.R. Smallwood.

That was his very first step. What will be his second?

Ray Guy's first evisceration of the *Newfoundland Bulletin* in July 1968 humbly ignores a salient fact. The very existence of the *Bulletin* was Smallwood's unintentional but ultimate tribute to Guy's column and to the growing anti-Smallwood influence of the independent *Evening Telegram* newspaper. The Bull-etin was a gift from God to Guy in another important way. It provided endless grist for the satirical mill in which Guy ground Joey into ever diminishing grains.

Guy's March 6, 1969, column reported on a remarkable House of Assembly debate the previous day. The *Newfoundland Bulletin* had come up for discussion. What a piece of luck!

> Premier Smallwood ran off a superb comic skit yesterday wherein he played the role of an infant megalomaniac. He rattled the bars of his play-pen and shook his rattlebox at the bestial, partisan and biased world outside ...
>
> As usual, Premier Smallwood got all the best lines—the real rib-ticklers. He carried the running gag. It's an old joke but still good for a laugh: "The Newfoundland Bulletin is unbiased, non-partisan, unslanted and carries all the news you need to know."

With those extraordinary Smallwood remarks placed on the public record, Guy was unleashed. A newsroom observer would have seen billows of smoke rising from his cigarette, or perhaps from his typewriter:

> Taking this piece of merry nonsense to the ultimate, we can imagine what the other news media in Newfoundland might be like if they took (or were forced to take) the premier's little joke seriously.

According to Guy, the *Daily News*, the city's second daily newspaper, would offer its own version of the truth. One probable headline:

> Unemployment can be fun, says father of 12.

Guy then imagines a front-page photo of a worst-for-wear Newfoundland mother:

> Miss Sylvia Knucks, a grand old Newfoundland lady who celebrates her 27th birthday tomorrow, says she'll be buried with a photograph of Premier Smallwood clasped to her bosom ...

In Guy's version of the new media world, CBC Television, as befits the public broadcaster, would take a more analytical and contextualized approach to its information services.

> Ladies and gentlemen. Tonight "Here & Now" takes a look at the fishery. Our special guest is Premier J.R. Smallwood.
> ... Here's our panel. On our left, Ed Roberts, Dr. F.W. Rowe, Aiden Maloney, and our special guest expert tonight, Mrs. J.R. Smallwood. I'm your moderator, Bill Callahan.

Readers at the time would have recognized all but Mrs. Smallwood as powerful members of Smallwood's Cabinet. Mrs. Smallwood, renowned for her lack of involvement in public affairs, was known as a gentle, family-oriented woman. But Guy was hunting elephants that day. He would not be distracted by smaller footprints.

Guy's *Here & Now*—then as now the actual name of CBC's supper-hour newscast—continues:

> Here is the CBC news. Premier Smallwood in a logical and well-reasoned announcement, today expressed grave concern over the obviously growing tide of poison, character assassination, trash and dirty Tory lies

being spread in a great, foul, dirty conspiracy that has its tentacles in every corner of the province.

The leader of the dirty Tories replied to the premier's charges in a press release today. We'll have the leader of the dirty Tories' comment in our 3:30 a.m. news bulletin sometime early next summer.

And now the weather. Premier Smallwood announced today that the low pressure system stationed just east of St. Anthony for the past several days will move off slowly during the night and ...

After working his way down Grub Street, Guy finally makes it to his own newspaper. It is now known as The Premier's Paper, Guy reports, after having been inappropriately characterized as The People's Paper since its founding in 1879.

Headline:

Still another success for Smallwood government— burning rectal itch relieved in minutes.

Editorials:

Don't go, Joe.
Who Owns Our Everlasting Gratitude?

Guy column:

Great news, my duckies! Premier Smallwood struck another blow for truth and common sense today when he defended to the hilt that most estimable example of journalistic excellence. Oh, yes!

EDITOR'S NOTE:

Sorry folks, but we're afraid Mr. Guy has just lost his cool again. A moment ago he started to turn green around the gills and was then seized with the dry heaves. Something he wrote must have disagreed with him. With the help of the proper physic we hope to have him revived and on deck again tomorrow.

Satire aside, Ray Guy's aversion to the *Newfoundland Bulletin* and the anti-democratic impulse it represented was a barometer of the values and character he brought to his vocation.

A more direct statement of those values came in a column two years later when the forces for political reform were consolidating. With a certain wariness, those forces were gradually getting behind the mainstream opposition, the Newfoundland and Labrador Progressive Conservative Party. In May 1970, Harbour Grace fish merchant Frank Duff Moores was handily elected to lead them.

For Guy, it was all too handily. After half a decade of tilting at the Smallwood windmill, there was little doubt that Guy regarded Joey's impending defeat as devoutly to be wished. Moores's resounding leadership victory, however, left him less than joyous. Most of us in the local media saw the outcome as nothing more consequential than bad news for Smallwood. Only Guy had detected an odour that made him quiver.

Guy remained moody all that weekend. On Monday, May 18, 1970, his tone was dour and his prose unusually grave:

After more than 20 years of that sort of thing, those short hairs on the backs of our necks tend to crawl whenever we hear of anyone winning any sort of an election by a "landslide victory."

Burned children dreading the fire is what we are, and we flinch instinctively whenever any crowd gives its "overwhelming support" to any one of its number.

Moore's [sic] grossly lopsided victory on Friday carried a faint reminder of singed flesh with it. Those who will cry out about unfair comparisons must remember that we have our scars.

Perhaps we react this way because we have been conditioned for the past two decades by one "landslide victory" after another. More hopefully, it is because we have learned at least something from past mistakes ...

In the normal state of politics—if there is such a thing—no one is that good. And no one is that bad. No one will become that bad unless enough think, at the start, he's that good.

The column reflected consistencies in Guy's views of society and politics. One of those was an innate fear of demagoguery. Guy's detestation of Smallwood reflected his perception of a Smallwood dictatorship. By 1970, Smallwood had become for Guy something closer to what psychologists call a trigger, in this case for convictions at the core of his character.

Where did such proclivities come from?

That may be a question for psychologists. But along with his own writings, helpful sources should include the works of a few great satirists. Swift, certainly. Perhaps, as Guy's friend David Day believed, the writings of the American humorist, S.J. Perelman ("I've got Bright's Disease and he's got mine"), and those of Mark Twain. Indeed, Twain's Tom Sawyer and Huck Finn are a bit like outharbour juveniles, lovers of life and incidental mischief. As both Day and Housser noted, moral influences on Guy would include the major Biblical testaments and prayer books with their parables and metaphoric wealth. The literature-laden Ryerson journalism program of the early 1960s had an impact, as did Alice, née Adams, Guy's mother.

In 2008, Guy was asked to write a foreword for a new collection of his columns, *The Smallwood Years*. He obliged. The result was a cogent and elaborate reflection, written just five years before his death, on Smallwood and his times.

There's no escaping Joey Smallwood. By then he'd been rock-solid King of the Rock for over a decade with no more than three or four huddled members in opposition and despite little pin-pricks from some sections of the press, floated higher than ever on a cloud of triumphalism ...

Smallwood was caught up in what one editorial writer called "a tide of rising expectations." Here's where his phrase "Great New Industries" cut in. At first they were merely bizarre, like the proposed orange juice factory, the herd of 20 buffalo on Brunette Island, or the 1,000 head of cattle imported to the Burin Peninsula, heralded by the immortal words: "The cowboy looms larger in Newfoundland's future than the fisherman ..."

"But at least he tried!" say some of Smallwood's apologists to this day. What did he try, must be our reply. He tried with every megalomaniacal fibre of his being to hold onto power is my own answer.

They were interesting times, but frustrating, too. Especially for a journalist. All public records were either destroyed or under lock and key. Somewhere early on I decided that the only course was, perhaps, to giggle the bastards to death.

That too, I soon found, was slow and steady work, like the tomcat eating the grindstone ...

Looking back from 40 years on I'm astonished by what riotous, incredible, disastrous, pell-mell, interesting times those were. False modesty to one side, I'm amazed at how savage I was ... and how funny.

Two lieutenant governors, at last one chief justice, and other current mucky mucks all benefited from my gentle chastisements of so long ago. But what of some lesser fry? I worried for about five seconds that my sucker punches of 40 years past should come back to bite them in peaceful retirement now. Was this fair?

They said and did it then. I wrote about then. Let it stand now.[37]

CHAPTER 8
Unsettling News

If there was ever a time when I knew Ray that he emitted a bitter
emotive bearing, it was when he talked of resettlement.

—*David Day*

David Day's choice of the words is appropriate. Other subjects,
from Smallwood's great new industries to the *Newfoundland Bulletin*, could annoy and enrage Ray Guy. The response usually was
wicked satire, not unbridled rage.

This was different. The infamous Newfoundland centralization
and household resettlement programs, which ran in various waves
and phases from the mid-1950s to the mid-1970s, engendered
intense fury in Guy. At times, his anger simply became too hot,
obscuring his usual laser vision. Too often it fostered a despair that
hurt him personally and occasionally impaired his journalism.

Guy's discomfort with the resettlement process also intensified
his detestation of the man he considered its principal architect, Premier Smallwood.

Guy's reaction to the resettlement programs revealed different aspects of his makeup as a writer and a person. It measured his deep and gnarled roots in Newfoundland culture and history and his genuine love of the place. It stirred his contempt for anyone who would ever suggest that he might grind an axe in print for his father's business interests. It plumbed the depths of his humanity.

"I applied myself to the subject of centralization with such an intensity that even now I get slightly stomach-sick whenever I have to look back and review the situation," Guy wrote in 1981.

> There was a haste and tumult and a fever to "centraliza-tion" that battered people's souls and grievously wound-ed their minds. Why this cruel haste? A neat pins-in-a-map scheme was sold to the federal government in quick return for the instant cash to carry it out.
>
> The blitzkrieg destruction of communities and frantic movement of people created a bogus air of prog-ress, produced an eve-of-war excitement, temporarily convinced many people that "something," at least, was happening.[38]

If the nearby Placentia Bay islands intrigued Guy as a child, their place in his psyche grew larger as he grew older. The resettlement programs, sponsored by both provincial and federal levels of government, were mass migrations of people from those islands and many other isolated Newfoundland communities to designated "growth centres," among them Guy's hometown, Arnold's Cove.

A movement of historic infamy now, the centralization process—voluntary in principle, high-pressured in fact—was a displacement of human beings with enormous consequences. At least 30,000 people and 300 settlements were dislodged.

As a growth centre at the receiving end of resettlement, Arnold's Cove was typical: three decades or more of social upheaval during which a village of 180 souls became a town of nearly 2,000. Arnold's Cove would never be the same.

Those displaced from the Placentia Bay island communities, no fault of their own, invaded the not-always-welcoming established settlers of the Cove. Into this delicate cauldron rushed various commercial opportunists and political brokers whose mission was to enable and in some cases profit from the process.

Huge barges were built, big enough to float two-storey houses from the islands to the mainland. Building lots were cleared and mini homes offered for rent and purchase. New houses went up in days and were sold to arriving families, all of whom got government subsidies to buy them. Many migrants left decent houses behind, to rot and eventual ruin. Many others landed in a new development area that remained a muddy swamp for years.

During the early resettlement period, Guy visited Arnold's Cove regularly and had a bird's-eye view of it all. George and Alice Guy's shop and post office, both operating in the Guy family home, were nerve centres of local information and resentments. Guy soon discovered that he could not ignore as a journalist what he knew as a son of the Cove. Ray Guy of Arnold's Cove took the consequences of this upheaval personally. He carried his resentment like a locked and loaded shotgun.

Guy's most graphic reporting on resettlement was displayed in two columns written a week apart in June 1968, when the flow of inbound traffic from the Placentia Bay islands to Arnold's Cove was constant. His column of June 3, 1968, focused on "a middle-aged outport housewife" who finally faced the day she "prayed desperately would never come." He gave the woman a name, Mrs. John Dare. It was a pseudonym to protect her identity.

Until last fall, Mrs. Dare lived in a small community on an island in Placentia Bay. Her husband was a fisherman and made no better and no worse a living than his neighbors.

Mr. Dare and the oldest of their three sons caught enough fish even in bad years to support the family. They kept gardens and grew enough vegetables for their own use. In winter they cut and brought home wood for heat.

Their proudest boast was one that used to be almost universal in Newfoundland—that they "never owed no man nothing."

Then last summer a strange thing happened in the small island community. Almost overnight a rumor swept the harbor that the place was to be abandoned. Nobody quite knew why, just that "moving fever" was on the bay.

Some said a government feller came around and started it; others said that there'd be no clergy and no teacher next year; nobody wanted to be left behind in the winter. There were frantic preparations.

On the last day before they left, Mrs. Dare went up to the graveyard on the hill. There were several other women there. Then they went back down to finish packing all the belongings they thought would be useful in the new home.

What they could not take they piled in a heap on the beach and burned, because they knew that soon after they left gangs of young men in motorboats would arrive to smash and pillage the deserted houses ...

At the mainland relocation center, they found an earlier influx of people from the islands had taken up all the available houses and land. They were told the only place was a small plot in a government-approved subdivision on the outskirts of the community.

They had about $3,000 in moving money from the government, but found this was hardly enough to cover the price of the piece of land. As the government grants increased, so had the land prices.

They found that even a small house would cost more than $10,000. There was much confusing talk about bank loans and mortgages and financing which they only half understood. They do know they can no longer say the "owe no man nothing ..."

Last Saturday there was nothing left in the house to eat, and no money. Some neighbors gave her enough to make dinner yesterday. Today ...

As it turned out, the pseudonym was not well chosen. A letter to the editor a few days later carried its own remarkable freight, demonstrating, among other themes, the distance between two men closely connected to Arnold's Cove when it came to resettlement. It also demonstrated how ugly the polarized interests and opinions could become.

A businessman wrote to the *Telegram* to advise that there was no one in Arnold's Cove by the name of Dare. To his credit, Kevin A. Wadman of Arnold's Cove signed his letter, which ran on June 10, 1968, under the headline "Not So, Mr. Guy." Wadman was up for a fight, and he was not intimidated by Guy's erudition. Wadman, too, had read some classics. He launched his letter with a quote from Alexander Pope: "Some truth there was but dashed and brewed with lies."

Wadman attacked Guy's most vulnerable flank when it came to resettlement reporting: numbers and statistics. While hardly opposed to facts, Guy was an evocative writer who worked best in observations and impressions and emotions. For Wadman, statistics, proven or otherwise, were the weapons of choice.

"The truth," Wadman wrote, "is that only two of the more than 160 families who have relocated at Arnold's Cove, have, for short periods, received able-bodied relief. Nearly all except the sick or elderly have jobs or are fishing and 99 per cent prefer their new home to their old one ... Of the approximately 90 homes located in the subdivision only four were built new; all the rest were moved in from settlements in Placentia Bay at a cost to their owners of between $1,000 and $2,000."

Reliance on statistics may have given Wadman the pole position, but it did not determine the outcome. If Guy had fewer numbers, it did not mean he had less truth. For one thing, every $1,000 or $2,000 spent to move a house became revenue for contractors moving it, Wadman prominent among them. The reality was that Wadman wanted something more satisfying out of his encounter with Guy than victory on debating points. He wanted to kick some sand into the face of his tormentor.

Wadman ended his letter by throwing down a gauntlet at the feet of the *Telegram*'s editor: "Mr. Editor, I challenge you to publish this letter in its entirety in your paper. This would certainly be the least you could do to counteract the effect of a malicious, lying article."

Mr. Editor was up for that challenge. Unfortunately, the newspaper placed a thumb on the scales in Guy's favour by allowing him to respond to Wadman's letter the same day that it was published.

As was his habit, Guy would have read the next day's letters to the editor sometime the previous evening. The result was that most *Telegram* readers on June 10, 1968, would have seen his response to Wadman's letter before they saw the letter. In his letter, Wadman said there was no Mrs. John Dare in Arnold's Cove, implying deceit and fabrication on Guy's part.

Following some levity about the thrill of receiving a nasty letter, Guy threw off his jacket and lunged. "The harder you pinch 'em," he began, "the louder they squeal."

Good old Kevin let out a yelp you could hear from Come by Chance to Chapeau Rouge ... Finding civilized language unequal to expressing the frustration within his bosom, Mr. Wadman has dipped his pen into rattlesnake venom ...

Mr. Wadman took it for granted that that piece was about Arnold's Cove. Maybe it was. Maybe it wasn't. There's nobody in Arnold's Cove by the name of "Mrs. John Dare," says Kevin.

That's true. There isn't. Did he really expect me to plaster her real name in print? She has enough trouble already. I took pains to keep her identity secret. "Mrs. John Dare" is a name I made up—but I can assure Mr. Wadman her plight is all too real.

Unfortunately, I found out later there are several new families in Arnold's Cove with a name that sounds something like "Dare." I understand they've been getting embarrassing phone calls from certain parties.

I don't know these people, have never seen them, have never spoken to them. I'm sorry the fictitious name I used turned out to be so close to theirs.

One likely homonym is Deir. Resettled families named Deir came from Port Anne, a community located in Nonsuch Arm on the western side of Placentia Bay. The community of 126 resettled in 1966, some families to Baine Harbour on the Burin Peninsula and others to Arnold's Cove.

That fact itself leaves a minor mystery and certain journalistic misgivings about Guy's column. It is hard to imagine that he was not aware of a relatively common Placentia Bay surname, by then well known in Arnold's Cove. It is equally hard to imagine that he would have wished to draw attention to a Deir family by using the name Dare.

One explanation may lie in the perils and pitfalls of writing a thousand or more words a day, five days a week. Guy's column of June 3, 1968, published on a Monday with references to last Saturday and even to "this morning," was based on a weekend visit to the Cove. The real "Mrs. Dare's" welfare note might well have been taken up at the Guys' general store.

Another explanation may have been the torrents of outrage and anger that Guy could not effectively harness. Righteous indignation may have inspired much of his best work. But even when driven by anger, Guy's writing usually was created in cold blood. His column on Kevin Wadman was not.

During the entire Wadman entanglement, Guy surely displayed what Day called a "bitter emotive bearing," playing the game at a low and personal level:

> But who in the world, you may well ask, is Kevin A. Wadman? Mr. Wadman comes to us from Bar Haven, an island community (now deserted) in Placentia Bay.
>
> Unlike some other island merchants, Mr. Wadman had the great foresight to move off the island before his customers did. He set up shop on the mainland (Arnold's Cove) some years before the exodus began. When the other people on the islands got caught up in centralization, good old Kevin was ready to welcome them with open arms ...
>
> Good old Kevin has been loud in his praise of the way centralization has been carried out. He says it has been of great benefit to many people. No doubt it has.
>
> But I venture to say that few people have benefited as much from centralization as has the enterprising Kevin A. Wadman.

Within a year, Guy again crossed pens with the new Arnold's Cove establishment. In January 1969, he reacted to one of a series of government announcements about the Come by Chance petrochemical complex that never seemed to produce either petrochemicals or jobs. His January 31, 1969, column had various targets, including provincial and local politicians and bureaucrats.

> Probably their biggest job is dealing with the hundreds of unemployed who turn up at Come by Chance after every great announcement from Confederation Building.
>
> Some of these men seeking work come from as far away as the other side of the Island. They learn the hard way that you mustn't believe all you hear.
>
> Nearby is poor old Arnold's Cove, the shining star in the government's centralization crown, the miraculous "growth centre" that was distorted and misrepresented recently in the government's propaganda rag, *The Newfoundland Bulletin*.
>
> People were herded into Arnold's Cove by the government from the islands of Placentia Bay. Many of them were forced to huddle together on the official subdivision (sometimes referred to as a slubdivision because of the mud) which lacks an adequate water supply and sewerage system.
>
> The latest calamity to hit these unfortunate and ill-used people is disease. The department of health reports that last week alone there were 13 new cases of German measles at Arnold's Cove (compared with one at St. John's); eight cases of chicken pox (one at St. John's); and 16 cases of infectious hepatitis (two for St. John's) ...
>
> What other troubles must these people endure?

Within days, the Board of Trustees of the Local Improvement District of Arnold's Cove responded to Guy. Theirs was an even more bitingly personal tirade than that of Wadman's the year before.

> The facts which Mr. Guy and *The Telegram* did not care to publish are that the district nurse located at Arnold's Cove reports statistics for six other settlements located from five to twenty miles from Arnold's Cove and that the cases referred to were located in other settlements and had nothing to do with Arnold's Cove ...
>
> When Ray Guy refers to residents of the subdivision who are without sewer facilities, no doubt he is referring to the persons who purchased building lots from his father, George H. Guy. About three or four years ago Mr. Guy sold some residents building lots, which were really crown land to which he held no title, and to date these lots only are not served by a sewer main. Possibly your readers would like to know that Mr. Guy also attempted to claim and sell other crown land, until prevented from doing so by officials of the provincial office.[39]

Journalistically, the situation was unstable. Both Guy and his newspaper were skating on sish ice, and the Arnold's Cove Trustees, among others, saw opportunity. Guy's journalism was informed, legitimately, by his proximity to a resettlement nerve centre. In journalism, however, perceived conflicts of interests have impacts similar to those that are real. Guy was perceived as opposing resettlement to help protect George H. Guy's business interests in Arnold's Cove. George's business interests were not Ray's, but their existence gave aid and comfort to his critics.

As for the *Telegram*, the usual licence granted a columnist, even a satirist, required close scrutiny during the resettlement wars. A satirist is never under oath. But a columnist writing seriously about the hottest social and political topic of the day must be held to at least the baseline journalistic standard of citing convincing sources.

Among other missteps, the *Telegram's* editorial handlers should have avoided such red flags as the Guy column on communicable diseases appearing prominently in his page 3 space—the paper's most widely read corner—with the Board of Trustees' rebuttal buried on page 28. On the other hand, the Trustees' letter should not have been printed at all without a signature and without a shakedown of the facts. The Trustees' statements about George Guy's alleged Crown land deals, published without evidence, were potentially defamatory, and indefensible if not true.

Beyond his mud-fights with Kevin Wadman and his supporters, Guy was criticized by more detached parties for singling out Arnold's Cove in his resettlement columns. Among the more challenging feedback was a letter from a local high-school class expressing concern about the impact of his writing on the town's reputation.

In the introduction to his 1981 book *Beneficial Vapors*, Guy recalled the high-school incident with understanding. But he did not equivocate, nor did he express regret. As always on the resettlement topic, he wrote with passion:

> It [resettlement] was a nasty, criminal business that killed many of the older people and drove others mad. At the height of it, the provincial minister responsible declared that "the old must suffer for the sake of the young."[40]

> Suffer they did, but what their great emotional and mental distress gained for the young is far from clear.
> ... So Arnold's Cove got mentioned because I couldn't go home for the weekend without hearing the

church bell toll for another victim or talking to people who sat around in a daze, dispirited, fearful and without hope.

A high school class in the new Arnold's Cove wrote me an angry letter for making these things public and so giving their new home a bad image. Perhaps they were right. I saw Arnold's Cove only on weekends while they had to face their own grandparents very day of the week ... a burden better borne in private.

Yet I found that "centralization" time so sad and outrageous that I couldn't help myself mentioning by name the place I belong to. Perhaps it wasn't fair to Arnold's Cove to be named only in connection with misery. Look you here then at all the times no names were mentioned, when the nearest I got to it was "That Far Greater Bay," but when it was a cove and not a bay that I was really talking about.[41]

Studies by sociologists Noel Iverson and Ralph Matthews indicated that many of the displaced were miserable or no better off than they had been on the islands. On the receiving end, many long-standing growth centre residents felt set upon and confused.

Political elders in Newfoundland today, including Ed Roberts and William Callahan, both members of the Smallwood Cabinet during several years of intense resettlement activity, point to dynamics and realities of resettlement that, in their view, were either ignored or understated by critics such as Guy.

They assert, correctly, that resettlement had been a natural phenomenon in Newfoundland and Labrador in the 1940s and 1950s and to some degree even earlier. The government incentive programs merely assisted people who wished to move anyway. At the same time, they offered the universal public benefit of consolidating and augmenting services such as education and health, improving those services, and reducing the taxpayers' burden.

Key differences in the past may have been that pre-subsidy resettlement was more gradual, more natural, and less frenzied. It was neither a money-making enterprise for select local businesses nor a provincial government grab for poorly targeted federal funding, the latter perhaps a by-product of federal fisheries mismanagement.

In interviews, both Roberts and Callahan made oblique suggestions that Guy's perspective may have reflected threats to the business interests of his father, George H. Guy. For George H., resettlement cut both ways. He made some money. But the Guys' thriving little store and related businesses experienced not just opportunities but unaccustomed competition from established firms that moved from the islands to the Cove.

Guy's sister, Iris, remains adamant that her brother's revulsion to resettlement had nothing to do with family business. The very notion that he opposed resettlement because new business traders such as Kevin Wadman might eat his father's lunch drove Guy to distraction, and rightly so.

In truth, Guy had too many other reasons to oppose resettlement. Those were reasons totally in keeping with his character and his journalistic values. He saw the heart-breaking impact on hundreds of people, especially elderly people, who were terrified to move away from their houses and communities, or who felt they must follow younger and more resilient family members.

Younger family members usually were the first to be swept up in what was dubbed by academics as moving fever, and by artists and musicians as "the government game."[42] Many of those younger migrants became victims too, of years of unemployment and promises unfulfilled.

Guy's fury about the human consequences of resettlement was genuine and based on the realities he had witnessed. Although he occasionally was sucked into the vortex of local division and gossip, his contempt for the politics of local privilege and vengeance was genuine. The early growth centre living conditions he observed first-hand in Arnold's Cove were difficult to portray as progress, for either the old town or the new.

Guy's writing on resettlement was acute and often brilliant. It remains an important perspective on the issue. By conventional journalistic standards, it exhibited flaws. By the standards of personal journalism, a recognized genre championed by major modern writers such as Tom Wolfe, it could be considered triumphal. Ernest Hemingway encouraged writers to write the truest sentence they know. Guy admired Hemingway and followed his advice.

A generation and a half later, Arnold's Cove appears to have found a blended, collaborative peace. Resettlement wounds have mostly healed. The current stable and viable community exhibits an accommodating mix of Guys and Hyneses from the Cove and Warehams and Wadmans from the islands. There are several families of Deirs.

Arnold's Cove now looks uptown and prosperous, a merger of old and new. Many houses display proud signs such as "moved from Tack's Beach" or "moved from Merasheen." A blending of the names of resettled islands and of old Arnold's Cove town names marks the roads and streets, tributes to peace and harmony at last.

Tack's Beach Place, Harbour Buffett Road, Bar Haven Heights, and Merasheen Crescent are all named for abandoned island settlements whose former families, in third generation, now make up a majority of Arnold's Cove residents.

In the older section of town, one of the oldest Arnold's Cove homes dates from 1887. It is a square-box-frame structure with an attached adjunct that looks like the single-storey shop it once was. The shop portion has been renovated into a lovely apartment where Iris Brett lives with her two dogs and a cat.

A minor irony that only a small community can foster is that one of the most energetic and respected leaders of the "new" Arnold's Cove was a local councillor and one-time mayor, the late Herb Brett—Iris's husband and Ray Guy's brother-in-law.

Today a small, pretty roadside park welcomes visitors to Arnold's Cove. Among the park displays is a plaque "Dedicated to the Memory of Herbert D. Brett (1940 to 2007)":

> Herb was that rare individual who every municipal council and volunteer organization would have to have ... He was a tireless, caring individual interested in all aspects of social and economic development in the community ...
>
> The Town remembers Herb with gratitude and fondness.

Herb Brett's passing in 2007 inspired Guy to write a moving short note to his sister. He invoked the old custom of sending telegrams of condolences, simply called messages, to be read aloud at wakes and funerals. Only a day or so after Herb's funeral, Iris opened the letter:

> Hi Iris:
>
> I forgot about this fashion of writing "messages" and perhaps having them read out. Shame on me. Maybe I would have written:
>
> Three of our grandparents died over in the old house. Our mother died there. And now my brother-in-law, Herb, has died in that old house.
>
> Death is a fraud. Death is a pitiful little bogey man. Death is a muddy pot-hole compared to the great and wide bay of life.
>
> It is the lives lived that are so much the greater.

Herb brought splendid life of a certain kind to the old house. A hustle and bustle, a coming and going, phones ringing, letters in and out, serious and worthy public business discussed, a steady flow of, as Joey Smallwood called them, "the greats and the near greats." No moment was allowed to be dull.

And it strikes me now with great certainty that the sort of great and constant life Herb brought to the house was exactly the sort that our father would have greatly admired, approved of, relished and certainly boasted of to all and sundry had he lived to see it all.

They were surprisingly alike in this. I say this wistfully because Herb's dynamo and whirlwind effect and method and resulting public affairs is something I could never have hoped to present for our father's approval.

I wish I had told Herb all this. Perhaps he already knew. Anyway I must tell it to you now.

Guy ended his message with "30"—the traditional mark to end a newspaper story. Then, postscript, he added:

Something like that, you see. I would not have added that to get Dad to say all that out loud I expect Mom would have to pinch him really hard.

So it really struck me strongly when we got back so I had to write it down ... Love. Catch ya later. Rae.

CHAPTER 9
Lions' Den

An unhappy but devastatingly funny columnist.
—*Harold Horwood*

Whale me no whales.
—*Farley Mowat*

Even at the peak of his popularity in the 1960s and 1970s, Ray Guy was not a recognized "Canadian" writer, either in his everyday world of journalism, or in the realm Canadian literature to which many of his readers and some academics felt he should aspire. Nor did he seek to join that loose chain of writers who in the early 1970s banded together in the Writers' Union of Canada.

Until the turn of the current century, when Newfoundland fiction writers such as Wayne Johnston, Michael Crummey, and Lisa Moore gained national notice and international regard, English Canadian writing that did not reflect a more pan-Canadian sensibility got shorter shrift. That included Newfoundland and Labrador writing, fiction and non-fiction, along with *pure laine* Québec writers whose work could be as deliberately regional as Guy's.

Language localized Québec. Newfoundland and Labrador writers were isolated by geography, by lack of exposure and, it is fair to say, by limited literary output.

Quality journalism with regional roots and sensibilities was not treated much differently. By literary and reader impact measures, Guy's writing soared beyond most mainstream Canadian journalism. But it continued to be read almost exclusively by Newfoundlanders and Labradorians.

Not only was Guy only briefly a national columnist and almost unknown in Canadian literary circles, he remained relatively isolated from his fellow Newfoundland writers and emerging local academics and intellectuals of his time. An irony was that by the mid-1960s many of those opinion leaders sang from the same hymnal. Their tune, one of increasing anti-Smallwood sentiment and defiance, was not so different from Guy's.

When it came to Newfoundland literary luminaries, Guy's wary circling of his fellow *Evening Telegram* columnist Harold Horwood was typical. Horwood's and Guy's careers overlapped briefly at the *Telegram*. But by the late 1960s, Horwood had become Newfoundland's most prominent novelist and nature writer. Unusually for his time, both Horwood and much of his writing successfully crossed the Gulf of St. Lawrence. After moving to Nova Scotia in the 1980s, Horwood also became a founder and long-standing promoter of the Writers' Union of Canada.

During the Confederation campaign of the late 1940s, Horwood and Smallwood had been joined at the brain. Along with another poet-politician, Greg Power, they were known by their political rivals as the Three Bolsheviks.

After a brief stint as a member of Smallwood's first government representing Labrador, Horwood left politics in boredom and disgust. Soon he launched Political Notebook, the *Telegram*'s and Newfoundland's second most celebrated and powerful newspaper column—second only to Guy's. Notebook became increasingly critical of the premier in the 1950s, getting under Joey's skin as only a former friend can, and blazing a trail for Guy's ascendancy in the 1960s.

When Horwood tormented him, Smallwood declared both treason and war, counterattacking bitterly from the defamation-free sanctuary of the House of Assembly. In June 1954, in full rant, Joey referred to Horwood as "this dastardly clown, this loathsome literary scavenger, this cut-throat, this rat who has been using the columns of *The Telegram* to carry out his own personal vendetta. He hates me like the devil hates holy water."[43]

Smallwood hinted darkly that Horwood had communist affiliations, popular condemnation in those early Cold War and Senator McCarthy years. Elsewhere, he called Horwood a snake and a crocodile and dismissed any critical *Telegram* story as "a Horwood lie." He subsequently suggested that Horwood might be a degenerate, and, horror of horrors, a card cheat. "Degenerate" was code for homosexual, the 1950s being as profoundly homophobic as it was communist averse.

The Horwood-Smallwood falling out was much like a divorce, where each party becomes the least reliable source as to the other's virtues. If he was not as Joey described him, Horwood was a true rebel, brilliant, lonely, arrogant, and a journalist of courage and skill—all qualities, except for arrogance, he would have shared with Guy.

Importantly, the Herder family, owners of the *Evening Telegram*, supported Horwood, stood by his journalism, and held firm in the face of Smallwood's fits and rages and threats to withdraw government advertising. Richard Gwyn reported that the *Telegram* at one point was offered "$60,000 of government job printing if it would drop Horwood as a political columnist." The Herders politely declined.

This defiance of Smallwood and defence of their writers was a Herder characteristic. The Herders remained stolidly behind Guy in the 1960s as their new star columnist became more and more acerbic in his anti-Smallwood attacks.

Smallwood's anti-journalist trash-talk, emanating under cover of privilege from the Legislature, spilled well into the 1960s, with a milder version of it saved for Guy.

Joey called Guy impolite names, although Guy may have started it by dubbing Joey "an infant megalomaniac" and the Only Living Millstone. This latter moniker parodied Smallwood's self-designation as the Only Living Father of Confederation. Guy's favourite Smallwood riposte came on January 6, 1969, when Smallwood, prompted by a question from a child on a local television program, took a satirical tack himself, declaring Guy a personal trophy to be compared with Confederation and Churchill Falls. "Ray Guy? I love him," Smallwood declared. "He's my third greatest asset!"

In response, Guy could do no other than to reach back in time to his organ-playing days at St. Michael and All Angels Church in Arnold's Cove, or possibly to his childhood attendance at Salvation Army gospel hymn sings. "In keeping with the solemn circumstances," Guy wrote, "the work is set to the same tune as that of a familiar Sunday school song."

(Immoderately, with foam-flecked feeling):

> Joey loves me? Way to go!
> Why was I the last to know?
> Emily Post, tell me one thing,
> Who's supposed to buy the ring?
>
> Chorus
> (Bear down and clap)
>
> Yes Joey loves me!
> Cold sober, was he?
> Plants kisses does he?
> On asset number three.[44]

Despite his apparent ambivalence toward Horwood, ultimately Guy respected him. He also regarded him as a figure of entertainment and fun, especially in the late 1960s when Horwood suddenly donned countercultural, hippie robes, despite being closer to 50 than to 20.

Horwood had left the *Evening Telegram* in 1958, repairing to a writer's hermitage in Beachy Cove, Conception Bay. He had deliberately sacrificed a full-time job and a decent income for an uncertain literary calling, at which he eventually succeeded, while never getting rich. For many years following his *Telegram* tenure, Horwood continued to freelance *Outside Information,* his impressive weekly nature and environmental column for the paper.

In 1971, having by then written two successful books, the novel *Tomorrow Will Be Sunday* and the outstanding nature study *The Foxes of Beachy Cove,* Horwood suddenly announced that he was decamping for points west, perhaps forever. By then, a hippie in full, his sojourn included a stay in stoned Vancouver where he wrote essays with such titles as "The Acid Is Shitty in Van."[45]

In his April 28, 1971, *Telegram* column, Guy lamented Horwood's departure. The piece is intriguing, exhibiting measured cynicism toward Horwood, as well as genuine admiration.

Guy first declared, not quite truthfully, that he did not know Horwood well, having learned about him mostly through his published writing. He did not acknowledge that he had other sources too, including a private journal that Horwood accidently left in a *Telegram* office one night, into which Guy indiscreetly pried. He learned, among other gossipy tidbits, of a torrid romantic affair in which Harold was then engaged with a St. John's society woman.

In praise of Horwood, Guy wrote:

> It doesn't take much imagination to realize what a remarkable thing that column [Horwood's Political Notebook] was. It must have been like backing off 10

paces every day and running your head full butt into a brick wall.

In those days there was not the slightest crack in that monolithic wall and those smug people could mock and jeer from the top of their impregnable fortress and go their merry way without a care.

Then, as if to keep Horwood humble, Guy added:

He turned out a few books among which was the famous (or infamous) "Tomorrow Will be Sunday" ... There's not a single human character in it who bears the slightest resemblance to life ...

But ...

... the rocks and the trees ... Ah, he has put them on paper to perfection.

For no obvious reason, Guy then turns to ridicule, with a drizzle of venom—amusing, if uncalled for:

But there's precious need for anyone else praising Horwood's work. He's not exactly bashful about doing that himself. Never the one, was our Harold, to stick his finger in his mouth, cock his head to one side with eyes downcast, and blush modestly. In fact his series on "The Birth of the Universe" sounded more like a first-hand account than anything else.

And lastly, a significant tip of his hat:

Horwood is leaving us in the spring. The birds wait til fall. Even so, he leaves with a little less to be ashamed of than most of us.

Horwood returned to Newfoundland, but soon left again for the Annapolis Valley in Nova Scotia, where he married and lived the last two decades of his life, writing prolifically, a fully established charter member of CanLit. He died of cancer in Nova Scotia in 2006, at 82.

What Horwood thought of Guy's writing remained a mystery for more than three decades. Nor do we know whether Guy's well-recorded ambivalence toward him had any impact. We do know what Horwood thought of himself—Guy's "Birth of the Universe" reference was not all satire—and especially what he thought of Political Notebook and its legacy.

"Political Notebook" started as a miscellany of political chit-chat (at Joey's own suggestion) but soon developed into the principal organ of government criticism. From 1953 to 1958 I published a long series of revelations about backstairs politics, uncovered a number of minor scandals, and shaped the course of many public attacks on the government.[46]

Horwood legitimately could have written something similar about Guy. For years he wrote nothing. The omission was most acute when, in 1989, Horwood published *Joey: The Life and Political Times of Joey Smallwood*. By then, Guy had written more words about Smallwood than anyone else on the planet, certainly more damaging words. Few Newfoundlanders would have denied the obvious impact of Guy's writing on the political and cultural changes in Newfoundland during Smallwood's final years in power. But Horwood's 348-page life of Smallwood is a Guy-free zone.

Then, finally, in 2000, perhaps in redemption, Horwood finally gave the Arnold's Cove devil his due. The belated recognition arrived on page 240 of his 242-page memoir, *A Walk in the Dreamtime.*

Horwood's general theme was the positive changes at the *Telegram* in the 1960s and 1970s under Ennis's leadership. His single-paragraph tribute to Guy was magnanimous, and vintage Horwood:

> Ray Guy, an unhappy but devastatingly funny columnist, had been added as frosting to the daily cake. He was consistently funny at the government's expense, but he did not probe into their secret affairs and drag the skeletons out of their closets as I had done ten years earlier. His was in many ways a better, cleverer, more literary column than mine had ever been, but not nearly so damaging to those in power. Later he was to win the Leacock Award for a collection of his columns, and to add playwriting and acting to his repertoire.

Ray Guy and Harold Horwood were not friends. Ironically, and surprisingly, they had an important friend in common, the writer and adventurer Farley Mowat, from Ontario. Mowat won the respect of both Horwood and Guy by exhibiting a remarkable knowledge of and affection for Newfoundland and Labrador, an affection rivalling their own.

If Guy maintained a wary distance between himself and his fellow Newfoundland writers and sages, he developed, in contrast, a significant friendship with the gregarious Mowat.

The fact that Mowat was himself only grudgingly welcomed by the mainstream Canadian literary-political-media axis may have enhanced that friendship. More likely it was the fact that Mowat,

Newfoundland-obsessed since the mid-1950s and Burgeo-based from 1962 to 1968, recognized the power and honesty of Guy's daily depictions of Newfoundland political and outport life.

Jolly and jocular, Mowat penetrated Guy's insularity and shyness and won his friendship and regard. Perhaps St. John's in the 1960s did not have room for both Horwood and Guy and their overlapping local fame. But there was plenty of room for Mowat and Guy, who essentially plied complementary trades; and, perhaps more significantly, only one of whom was a Newfoundlander.

For Guy, the Smallwood antagonist, this was tricky terrain. Until at least 1967, Mowat was a friend and fan of Smallwood, having ingratiated himself to him for years, allegedly using the allure of a biography of the Only Living Father that Mowat later said he had had no intention of writing.

Sociologist James Overton has reported that around the same time Mowat and Horwood wrote a proposal for a creative and expensive cultural project aimed at preserving the oral history of Newfoundland. It was humbly titled "Outline for a Historical Reclamation Project in Newfoundland."[47]

In his search of the Smallwood papers, Overton also came across a note from Mowat to Smallwood, the subject of which was Horwood and the oral history project:

> Because of his long feud with you, Harold is somewhat distrait about participating in this project. However, I know him well, and can assure you that he is deeply involved in the idea. Furthermore, and between ourselves, he is much less intractable than of yore and, I suspect, would welcome an end to a long and fruitless conflict.

That significant passage, and the Mowat-Smallwood affair in general, invites speculation about the dynamics of relations among the three most prominent writers in Newfoundland in the 1960s and 1970s—Horwood, Mowat, and Guy.

Differences of character, between Guy on the one hand, and Horwood and Mowat on the other, certainly existed. One was Guy's near religious commitment to journalistic independence, a virtue not always saluted by either Horwood or Mowat. Relations with Smallwood by both Horwood and Mowat waxed and waned over time. By contrast, the notion that there could ever be a reversal of Guy's disdain for Smallwood would have been absurd. Guy was not the forgiving type.

The reciprocal attraction between Smallwood and Mowat, meanwhile, was such that in 1966 the premier organized a banquet for the Mowats in St. John's, to which the couple was helicoptered from Burgeo to St. John's at government expense and put up in a room at the Newfoundland Hotel. Normally, one would expect such Smallwood profligacy to repulse Guy. There is no evidence he even noticed.

As it turned out, the Guy-Mowat alliance was at its most focused and friendly during an infamous event that eventually converted Mowat from outport curiosity to one of the most reviled individuals in Newfoundland and Labrador.

For six years, 1962 to 1968, Mowat and his wife, Claire, lived in Messers, near Burgeo. For most of that time, their stay was a remarkably successful integration of two outsiders as acceptable Burgeo residents.

The complex tale of the Mowats' rise, fall, condemnation, and at least partial redemption in Burgeo and in Newfoundland was widely publicized. Guy's role in it is less well known but was surprisingly large. His relationship with Mowat, like much else about his adult life, is best discovered through his writing.

"Moby Joe in Burgeo Going on Relief," screamed a page 1 headline in the *Evening Telegram* on February 1, 1967, over Guy's byline and, one suspects, under Ray's suggested title.

A 60-foot, 70- or 80-ton fin whale had grounded itself in Aldridge's Pond, a sizeable body of salt water near Burgeo. The pond was accessible only by a narrow inlet deep enough for shoal draft fishing boats, and deep enough on a full moon spring tide to float a fin whale. An imperial mammal, the fin, or "finner," is the second largest whale species, which was, and remains, endangered. With strategic planning, the whale could have been liberated by moonlight in time to save its life. Alas, in Burgeo, it was not to be.

Alarms and outrage spread far and wide when local men pumped hundreds, possibly thousands, of bullets and loadings of shot into Moby Joe, poked and prodded it with sticks and boat hooks, and eventually, and inevitably, put the creature to death.

Confronted with this confounding barbarism by the very people he had long celebrated as brave and stoic, a people abiding commendably in harmony with nature, Mowat became a wild man with a mission. Luckily, he now had friends in high places, or at least one friend, Joey Smallwood, in a very high place.

Smallwood offered immediate aid to the whale—hence Moby Joe—assigning a small platoon of government officials and experts to diagnose and treat the injured beast and to rescue and free it if possible. He committed $1,000 up front for herring—whalefare presumably. The whale had a fierce appetite. Upon close inspection, Moby Joe turned out to be Moby Josephine, who, in Mowat's confident opinion, needed to eat for two.

Despite heroic efforts to herd live herring into the pond and keep them there long enough for the whale to devour them, Moby Josephine could not be saved. On February 8, 1967, the great beast perished.

Guy's February 1, 1967, piece, a big local story about the unfortunate whale in Burgeo, already on the dole, had been a comparatively straightforward news feature. He had reported on the efforts to feed Moby Josephine, and on the whale's apparent recovery from the "barrage of 500 bullets fired into its back." In the week that followed, the Burgeo whale chronicles were all over the local and national media.

On February 8, 1967, Guy returned to the story from his vantage point in the House of Assembly press gallery, reporting on Moby Josephine's unfortunate demise. His piece that day was less journalism than commentary, betraying whale fatigue and a dash of cynicism about the entire Burgeo incident. But the columnist was conflicted.

> Premier J.R. Smallwood, manfully masking his emotions rose in a subdued House of Assembly on Tuesday to read a distressing dispatch from Farley "Ahab" Mowat, Keeper of the Whale (Ret.) ...
>
> After an anxious vigil on the shores of Aldridge's Pond Tuesday, the Keeper concluded that the beloved behemoth had either succumbed and sunk or else (and the chance is pitifully slight) had managed to escape from the barrisway by lunging across a sandbar at the entrance ...
>
> Kindness is what killed "M.J.," Mr. Mowat concludes. Newfoundland's "hospitality" in the form of a riddling with some 500 .303 bullets and a rallying by motorboats and small aircraft.
>
> Several members nodded gravely and those on Opposition benches appeared on the verge of delivering something suitable from Tennyson ...

Still, this was a more typical Guy piece, betraying an essential truth about his approach to his work and, not incidentally, to life. Guy was not indifferent to the suffering of a whale, anymore than he would have been to the misfortunes of a cat, a dog, or a person. He at times seemed capable of hugging a pine tree. Nor was he unimpressed by Mowat's humanitarian efforts and his justifiable rage.

But central to Guy's being was the soul of a satirist, a near pathological inability to shut down for long his sense of the ridiculous and the absurd. The debacle in Burgeo was tragic, sickening, pathetic, and pointless. It was also surreal, even slightly zany. Where there is absurdity there is potential for levity. It is the job of the satirist to identify and mine that vein.

On February 1, Guy had demonstrated that he could write about a stranded whale with all the sobriety and solemnity of a "capital J" journalist. But he could not do so for long without suppressing, even damaging, the fundamental talent that made him tick. In his February 8 follow-up piece, that talent emerged.

Far from ending with her death, the great Moby Josephine fiasco was only getting started. As round two, the post-mortem, began, Guy's pen remained red hot.

On February 10, he was at it again, reverting to what appeared to be straight reportage, but perhaps not straight enough. This time his principal and perhaps only informant was Mowat, always a risky source on matters pertaining to whales.

> Doctors ruled Thursday the whale died of septicemia, a blood poisoning caused by massive infection of wounds suffered January 21–22 when "a handful" of the 1600 residents of Burgeo blasted away at the helpless creature with ex-army rifles.

The reference to "a handful" of residents clearly is information from Mowat. It is also an early foreshadowing of what would be Mowat's official version of what transpired in Burgeo. The emerging Mowat mantra was that it was a cluster of rogue CBFAs—Come Back From Aways—corrupted by their exposure to Mainland Canada, and in turn Canadian exposure to the font of all evil, the USA, which perpetrated the crime. In no way could such brutality have been the work of the majority of the noble and pure-worsted fish-erfolk of Burgeo.

Guy's piece continues:

> Mr. Mowat, admittedly hurt by the mammal's death, said it could have been kept alive if residents hadn't fired at it. He explained yesterday that "the whole of Burgeo shouldn't be blamed for killing the whale as it was just a minority group ..."
>
> The author said he will probably write a book about the whale and "it won't be pleasant; it will describe the conditions here at the time."

Five years later, in 1972, Mowat's *A Whale for the Killing* was published. Its central thesis had been revealed long before, in Guy's columns.

In death, Moby Josephine was more famous than ever. Unfortunately, it made Burgeo, and Mowat, notorious. It drove a bitter wedge between a large and shrill faction of Newfoundlanders who instantly cursed all things Mowat and a much smaller faction who hailed as long overdue an unsettling truth about Newfoundland: the noble outport male could be as cruel as he was noble.

Well before the Moby Josephine saga, Guy and Mowat had bonded. In Guy, Mowat recognized a fellow writer of talent and a kindred spirit whose sacred themes related to outport life, outport verities, and outports in decline. In Mowat, Guy acknowledged a consequential writer. Guy tended to speak of Mowat, however, less in reverence of a great writer than as an avuncular fat elf—comedic and devil-may-care. Guy liked people who made him laugh, and Mowat did.

Guy once recounted a rum-fuelled soiree with Mowat and Horwood—possibly including broadcaster Geoff Stirling—where there was half-serious chatter about forming some sort of political movement to hasten Joey Smallwood's demise. There even was talk of one or another of them running for office. In the early 1950s, Horwood had been elected to the Newfoundland Legislature from Labrador on Smallwood's Confederation coattails. Perhaps Horwood could win on his own. But the notion of either Guy or Mowat "offering" would have reduced them both to paroxysms of laughter the minute they drew their next sober breath.

Guy's respect for Mowat's writing is plain in his review of Mowat's 1969 book *The Boat Who Wouldn't Float*. Guy makes a fine distinction in his review between writers and others who would look down superior snouts at Newfoundland, and those, like Mowat, who acknowledge the province's oddities and defects but revel in the differences and perceived strengths. Mowat, Guy reported with unusual enthusiasm, found a way to laugh with Newfoundlanders, not at them:

> It is the funniest piece of literature about Newfoundland that I have ever read (discounting the unintentional humour in certain political speeches) ...
>
> I've been waiting for someone to get wind of the book and again carry the "what THEY are going to think of us" obsession to ridiculous extremes. But the fact is that Mowat is making fun with us, not at us, and anyone who tries to make out differently should be blacklisted.
>
> True, the locals of "Muddy Hole" on the southern shore where this remarkable scow, the "Happy Adventure," originated are caricatured unmercifully, but the same treatment is also given to one Jack McClelland of Toronto.
>
> McClelland, one of Canada's largest book publishers and Mowat's also, was Farley's partner on the boat deal. A classic confrontation results.

Into Muddy Hole rolls Jack, the Toronto executive, radiating optimism and efficiency, clad in yachting cap, sharkskin slacks and hopsack sports jacket, and driving a massive automobile.

The twain meet at last. The west comes face to face with the inscrutable east. It's the best sociological report on the subject yet written.[48]

The Boat Who Wouldn't Float sold well, both in Newfoundland and elsewhere. Guy, read daily by tens of thousands of Newfoundlanders, likely did Mowat a significant commercial favour with his unqualified celebration of the book.

It may not have been Guy's finest hour. Nor was it the only time that reflections of the Guy-Mowat friendship showed up in his column. Guy wrote extensively, and often generously, about Moby Josephine, about Mowat, and about the grand and disturbing issues that swirled around the Burgeo event. The subjects, however, conflicted him.

Guy's February 10, 1967, piece betrayed this unusual tendency to employ something approximating spin on behalf of a friend. Guy was running the risk of out-Mowating Mowat. Fortunately, he recognized almost immediately that he needed to get back to basics, to journalistic detachment.

To achieve it he would be forced to unfurl his own whaling colours and nail them to the mast. How better to do so than to draw on his juvenile outport experience?

I can only add a whale experience of my own. One day when I was 16 or 17 a bunch of pothead whales appeared in the harbor. Something new. Pandemonium broke loose all at once.

Every available motorboat cast off, carrying every able-bodied man and youth in the community. For a whole afternoon in mid-September they rallied the potheads back and forth, pumping shot-gun shells, bullets and slugs into everything that broke water.

They speared and hacked the potheads with every makeshift harpoon they could get their hands on, and before long there was hardly a whale that did not trail a cloud of blood.

All the while, a federal fisheries boat, which happened to be there, scurried back and forth in the mouth of the harbor to keep the potheads from escaping ...

I didn't have a gun or a harpoon, but I had a ringside seat at the head of one of the motorboats and, as I recall, I had a whale of a time. I found it all tremendously exciting and can't remember having any qualms about it.

But Farley has an answer for that, too. He has said earlier that there are no real outports on the Avalon Peninsula. In that case our trouble is the Isthmus of Avalon (so that) we missed being a real outport by about five miles.

The convoluted Guy-Mowat whale exchange did not end there, but eventually it took a more discreet tack. Mowat again showed up again in the October 20, 1969, column in which Guy wrote glowingly about *The Boat Who Wouldn't Float*. Thereafter, whales were left astern and Mowat largely disappears from Ray's writing. But correspondence between them continued; at least Mowat wrote letters to Guy. Two of his letters were among materials gathered over the years by Guy's mother, Alice, and stored at Arnold's Cove.

The Mowat letters are spirited, amusing, essentially frivolous, and very badly typed. In her own worthy Burgeo book *Outport People*, Claire Mowat complained about Farley's abominable typing, which was left to her to correct. Each of Mowat's letters to Guy exudes friendship. Each is the same length, a page and a half, double spaced. Neither reveals the year in which it was written.

In one, Mowat carries on at length about two of his dogs, Victoria and Albert, who are meant to breed but can't seem to agree on a position for sex. That letter is dated "Jan. or Feb." The second was dated March 20.

Various clues suggest the year of both was 1970. There is a reference in the "Jan. or Feb." letter to Harold Horwood's Animal Farm, the free-school project of Horwood's hippie days, and another to an edgy novel Horwood was working on at the time, allegedly entitled *Blow Me, Jesus*. The novel never saw the light of day, no doubt hobbled by its limited chances of making the high-school curriculum in Green Bay. Those gossipy nuggets almost certainly would have been supplied to Mowat by Guy, who would have delighted in them.

The March 20 letter begins: "Mon ami. Which is NOT the same as Bon Ami. I bloody well can't stand it anymore. Your selections from Hansard are choking me up to the suffocation point." Guy had quoted extensively from the newly restored House of Assembly Hansard in his March 1970 columns, including some seemingly unhinged posturing by Smallwood.

Smallwood was teetering at this point, despite having kept the Liberal leadership out of John Crosbie's "wrong hands" the previous September. After mentioning that he hoped to finish his latest book, *Siber*, Mowat ended his letter with a pile-on reference to his former friend, Joey:

> Will the little old bastard wait that long? If not I'll have
> to drop everything and hustle down to help administer
> the coup de grace. Cheers chum. F.

In his January or February letter, Mowat addresses Guy as "El Raymondo." He signs off, "Cheers. You fakir." Fakir is variously defined as a Muslim or Hindu religious ascetic or medicant monk commonly considered a wonder-worker; a dervish, and as one who is self-sufficient and only possesses the spiritual need for God.

Fakir doesn't sound that much like Guy. Could this have been another display of Mowat's fat-fingered typing? In any case, Guy had been called worse things, perhaps by better people.

CHAPTER 10

Ray Guy Up Close: Veering South

Arnold's Cove looks optimistically south. The horseshoe-shaped outport where Ray Guy grew up faces the broad and windy fetches of Placentia Bay. Its back turns to the icy bays and harbours of the island's more hostile northeast coast.

In the middle distance southward, on a rare sunny day, loom Placentia Bay's great islands: Long Island, Red Island, and, prominently, Merasheen, with its "hard and rocky rocks."

They were and are lands of story and song, destinations as evocative to an Arnold's Cove schoolboy in the late 1940s as Madagascar might have been to a lad in London or Paris.

Out of sight to the south, 100 kilometres distant, the raw Atlantic rolls. Far beyond those great waters are the exotic southern lands and countries of the Caribbean, distant dreams only to most Arnold's Cove residents of the 1940s and 1950s.

For Guy, whose school days spanned the decade from the end of World War II to the mid-1950s, south was always a seductive compass cardinal. Even in childhood, the subtropical US south and the West Indies represented an enticing, if unattainable, goal. As a teenager, merely dreaming about sun and sand became an afford-able diversion from the damp fogs of Placentia Bay and St. John's and their companions in misery, the northeast wind and rain.

As a young reporter, with the means to travel at last, the Florida of Canadian snowbirds became a sporadic welcome escape for Guy from the grind of daily journalism, and, as the 1960s ripened, from the dead weight of Newfoundland and Labrador politics in the darkest Smallwood days.

One such escape was a six-week motoring marathon that Ray Guy and I shared in 1979: St. John's to Key West, Florida, to Toronto to St. John's.

Guy was an established Newfoundland newspaper columnist during that particular journey. I was a young student of English Literature at Memorial University and a summer and weekend re-porter at the *Evening Telegram*. The college term had ended. Guy took six weeks off. It was May and June, Newfoundland's most hopeful months—more hopeful than ever in the sunny long ago.

Guy had his vacation pay and a few extra dollars that his moth-er, Alice, stuffed into an envelope when we stopped at Arnold's Cove en route to Port aux Basques. As a weekend and summer wage earner, I still had most of the past year's student loan in my pocket and a summer job at the *Telegram* to come back to. I had converted my own cash into a currency of the day known as travellers' cheques, determined to break no more than one $10 cheque for each day on the road.

To save money, we slept many nights in a tent. This fact will astonish even some who knew Guy well: the renowned indoorsman was a relatively happy camper, at least when he was south of the Mason-Dixon Line.

A sunset arrival at a rest stop just south of St. Augustine inspired him to near rapture. After the torrid three-day drive in Guy's new Datsun 510—four-on-the-floor, no air conditioning—we climbed a sand dune to survey the strand, and a sea much gentler than had ever washed the rocks of Merasheen.

Those subtropical surroundings fuelled many of Guy's more personal obsessions and interests, especially those to do with flora and fauna. An emerging horticulturist himself—anyone, he said, could be a gardener—Guy always joked that February was his favourite gardening month, representing the armchair planning phase rather than the rubber-boot execution phase.

Guy's horticultural pursuits, and his depth of gardening knowledge, grew hugely with the years, as did his hands-on cultivation. The subject occupied dozens of columns. At least one complete essay examined the relative fertilizing virtues of manure from various animals.

His admiration for and curiosity about the wild and varied vegetation and creatures of the south was genuine. In Florida, he would stop to admire palm trees and orange orchards, exotic birds such as peacocks and parrots, and the snakes and alligators along Alligator Alley. He welcomed the brief vacation flirtation with fresh unprocessed foods, whole pineapples, real orange juice, especially with vodka, and, then, only a day or so distant, fresh oysters amid the Hemingway culture of Key West.

On that crazy journey, Guy claimed to have first discovered his primary appeal to the bronzed young women who swarmed the southern sands. His ace of hearts was his uncanny Newfoundland ability to light cigarettes in wind of any velocity. He had mastered the open-boat fisherman's knack of quickly sheltering matches from the gale with tightly cupped hands. If needed, a half-dozen Salems or Belvederes could be lit with a single match.

Unfortunately, what we gained on the cigarettes we generally lost on the pipes. Back then we both smoked pipes. Guy smoked to get his requisite nicotine fix. I liked the sweet smell of Erinmore pipe tobacco. More important, in my own case, pipe-puffing was an important badge of insufferable sophomoric pretension.

If the pipes failed to repel every prospect, Guy's pith helmet took care of the rest. Some distant great-uncle, perhaps his honorary Uncle John, must have delivered it back from Johannesburg at the end of the Boar War. Guy wore it regularly on the beach, surely the only tourist in Florida ever shaded by such exotic millinery. There we were: two vertically challenged weirdos, one in a pith helmet, one a long-haired geek smoking a pipe. Sadder still, we both sported hides of winter-in-Canada alabaster, except for sunbaked shoulders, where leprosy appeared to have set in.

I remember those Florida beach days as long and tedious. In the half-century since, I have not sat on sand for more than five minutes at a stretch. But Guy loved the beach, where he would sit and read for hours, oblivious to the curse of sand and sunblock glued to the pages of his *Esquire* or *New Yorker*.

One sultry evening on the return leg, following a roundabout route road back to Newfoundland that would wind through Buffalo, Niagara Falls, and Toronto, torrential rain overtook us near Bowling Green, Kentucky. It had been 1,000 kilometres that day from somewhere south of Tallahassee, Florida. We were tired and we could have used a not-too-pricey motel. At one reception desk, we were told there probably would not be a vacant room for at least 100 miles. The kindly clerk did offer to make one call on our behalf. We overheard only a snippet of the conversation: "yeah, de'ah why-at."

Time to shove on north.

Despite such unappealing encounters, Guy exhibited considerable regard and affection for Americans we met on that trip. As revealed in his Ryerson short story "The Grand Canyon," Guy was not unaware of the potential of Americans to look down their noses at Newfoundlanders. However, like many Newfoundlanders whose wider awareness of the world was rooted in the 1940s, his more positive view of the "Yanks" reflected the generally polite comportment of US servicemen who came to Newfoundland in thousands during World War II.

On the Florida frolic, return trip, and comfortably north of the border via Buffalo and Niagara Falls, Guy remained in top spirits, endlessly informative and entertaining. I saw the majestic falls for the first time, but Guy had been there before. As usual, he knew all the important trivia—the skipper on the tour boat, *Maid of the Mist*, was a Newfoundlander, and so on. Guy quoted—actually misquoted—Oscar Wilde's alleged description of Niagara Falls as a new bride's second greatest disappointment.

Guy's tendency to quote English literary figures amounted to a minor talent, with Oscar Wilde, Percy Bysshe Shelley, and especially Dr. Samuel Johnson, always favourites. David Day remembers him quoting S.J. Perelman at length. Impressive as well was Guy's detailed knowledge of unusual matters, details that left one wondering where he had consumed it all.

One such example occurred in Toronto. There we strolled around the Ryerson campus to assuage Guy's moderately nostalgic regard for his old stomping ground. In truth, he seemed more interested in re-visiting his favourite nearby Orange Julius outlet on Yonge Street than any campus haunts. This was followed by a turn around the Queen's Quay section of the waterfront. It was only my second visit to Toronto, and I was surprised about the scale of port activities and waterfront infrastructure.

"Fifth largest port in Canada," Guy observed. "People within 100 miles of us consume about a third of everything sold in Canada."

How the hell did he know that? Half a century later I found out. Guy's Ryerson feature on the port of Toronto, noted in Chapter 3, was a model of the fact-driven, detached journalism of the age, and of Ryerson reporting values:

> Here, in Canada's fifth largest port, ocean going ships from every corner of the world as well as the homely lake boats take on and discharge 70,000 boxcar loads and over 1,500,000 truck loads of cargo a year. With total tonnage of more than 4,500,000 annually, inland Toronto surpasses many saltier ports such as Marseilles, Oslo and Seattle. Ships from 114 ports and 54 countries service, through the port of Toronto, the 100-mile radius that contains one-third of Canada's purchasing power.

In the same report, there are more acute observations, and evidence of a good reporter's patience for the tedium of less accessible but more interesting research, all pre-Google of course.

> Looking out over the lake I could see the two-mile long crescent-shaped group of islands which form the natural foundations of Toronto harbor. The islands are composed of silt brought down by the Niagara River and deposited by the current 30 miles from its mouth on the opposite side of Lake Ontario.

Among the features of US business culture that Guy most admired during our Florida tour were their customer-focused service stations. He was amused by and approving of the young station attendants who would bound out of their shops and kiosks, armed to the teeth with squeegees and rags, to yes-sir and no-sir their way around the car, ministering to its every need and blemish, all for two ill-clad northern lummoxes in a Japanese compact—not promising tippers.

May bled into June, and as it did, a more ominous aspect of Guy's being presented itself, unheralded and unwelcome.

For context, it should be recorded during the few years that Guy and I worked together, hung out together, or shared domestic digs, we generally got along well. Guy, in his late 20s, was funny, considerate, mentoring, generous, and often outrageous. At 19 or 20, I was far less grown up than he was, and significantly less well informed. But our sense of the ridiculous was similar and our common interests genuine. I was proud to be Guy's friend, appreciated the charm of his company, and occasionally could augment his wit, in a certain you-had-to-be-there way.

Pastimes included collecting in a spiral notebook words and phrases used by our parents and grandparents that we considered unique to Newfoundland but no longer in common use. We also compiled a minor collection of newspaper typos. The winner was from an October front page story in our own *Evening Telegram*: "A freak fall snow-storm overnight left two inches of snot on the Trans-Canada Highway." A snow-covered TCH in October has rarely been better described. A runner-up in the typo wars was a sentence from a story about a government report that had just been completed. "The report," it was revealed, "has been submitted to the Department of Municipal Affairs where it will be analized."

Other minor collections included favourite curses. Guy once had one of his recurring outport characters, Skipper Abe, utter a fine specimen: "You lord lifting, hopped-up, reeving, dying, merciful, blood of a flaming, sawed-off, mortalizing, son of an ever-lasting, terrified, jumping, cross-eyed, slimy, snot-faced jack-a-bon!"

The Newfoundland words and phrases collection would have been a pale shadow of the *Dictionary of Newfoundland English*, although a few of our words can be found in that masterpiece. Ray Guy and Dr. George Story, one of the editors of the *Dictionary*, admired each other. Guy once recalled having been invited with some other guests to Story's home on Southside Road in St. John's. There he was regaled not only with Story's engaging tales but with piano pieces by Story's talented wife, Alice, including what Guy reported as a superb rendition of "Jesu, Joy of Man's Desiring."

The spiral notebook no doubt found its way to the St. John's landfill at Robin Hood Bay. The few words I can recall included *anighst* (for near); *dumbledores* (West Country English for busy bees, but still in use in Arnold's Cove in Ray's childhood); and *cod o'misery*, a favourite of my father, that roughly translates as hangashore, which in turn roughly translates as ne'er-do-well.

And that's the way it was. But despite such whimsy, good cheer did not always rule. Driving east through Ontario, a dark and ominous cloud descended upon Guy, the like of which I had witnessed only once before. There was no obvious trigger. No cross words were spoken. But for three or four stone-cold days, Guy spoke scarcely a word. Offers to relieve him at the wheel were ignored. Suggestions for pit stops were silently rebuffed, ideas for sightseeing sneered at. The tent had been stowed for good, apparently as was all joy.

New Brunswick, the drive-through province, had never taken longer to drive through. The Trans-Canada Highway in Nova Scotia was interminable, Cabot Strait never so wide. Not a word, civil or otherwise.

Then, as suddenly as it had befallen him, the cloud lifted. Arriving at Port aux Basques, the ill-used Datsun overheated. We pulled in at the nearest service station. No sign of life. This was not the I-95. Guy leaned on the horn. No response. He honked again, short annoying beeps this time, in rapid succession. A door opened a crack, widened a little more, and out marled a youth in a goofy cap and sneaker boots.

"We don't wish to impose, sir," Guy said in a burlesque of a well-mannered gentleman. "But would you consider looking under the hood. This sonofabitch is boiling over."

The young man did as he was bidden, shuffled around for a brief moment, and strolled back to Guy's window. He had checked the radiator.

"H'empty to the Jesus world," he announced.

Guy began to titter, then squirm with muffled laughter, then lapse into his patented convulsive giggle.

He had returned from somewhere dark and distant. I was chuffed to have him back. He would go again, of course. But for that good moment, St. John's, 1,000 kilometres eastward, did not seem far at all, the company unfailingly cheerful.

CHAPTER 11
Friends of My Enemy

Guy is to Newfoundland what the Fool was to King Lear—a cranky, disconcerting, insistent reminder of a previous dignity, now violated.
—*Patrick O'Flaherty*

A coddled Arnold's Cove snot.
—*Patrick O'Flaherty*

Ray Guy's disrespect for J.R. Smallwood splashed beyond the premier himself to dampen his associates, followers, even his relatives. Guy's greatest concern was that Smallwood possessed autocratic tendencies coupled with messianic powers. Guy reserved a special loathing for politicians in whom he detected cult leadership tendencies.

He could turn on those individuals for reasons that were at times mysterious, or at best appeared too flimsy. Guy's attitudes toward, and treatment of, certain events and people sometimes had dimensions that were difficult to fathom.

So-called charismatic leaders made him cringe. As one example, he was not a fan of Pierre Elliott Trudeau, even in the Trudeaumania phase when almost everyone else was.

The War Measures Act declared by Trudeau in response to the *Front de liberation du Quebec* (FLQ) crisis of October 1970 left Guy apoplectic. Under that oppressive instrument, designed for the urgencies of war, due process of law was suspended, replaced by wanton search and seizure and crude presumptions of guilt. Some 300 people, most of them going about lawful occasions and with no involvement with the violent FLQ, were rounded up and held without ever being charged.

The event focused Guy's attention on national affairs with uncharacteristic gravity. He waited a few weeks to write about it, which he did, no doubt with the calendar in mind, on November 11:

> If Ottawa admits that it takes the suspension of civil rights all across Canada and half the Canadian army to control three or 300 criminals, they admit there is something greatly wrong with Canada's regular laws and police.
>
> Or if they acted on the belief that conditions are such in Canada that a tiny minority could arouse a large part of the population of the country behind them in civil war, then they admit that they have been sadly out of touch with reality.
>
> While admittedly the man lacked sleep and was under much tension, Mr. Trudeau showed an unexpected side of his nature over the past weeks.
>
> During the election campaign and thereafter, he gave the impression of some sort of Hindu holy man in Mod Squad regalia, bobbing about the country sniffing daisies. Now it seems that flower power has given way to a hint of the jackboot.
>
> ... "Just watch me!" he muttered when a reporter asked him what other steps the government might take.

Not "us" mind you, but "me." It would be a pity if Pierre got carried away. There's no need for him to prove how tough, tough, tough he is deep down. Anyone who skindives, practices judo and invites the formidable Barbra Streisand up to the house for cookies can't be all soft.

The War Measures Act, a highhanded state intervention defended by a rhetorically powerful prime minister and saluted by millions of Canadians, offended Guy's libertarian streak. So did many other activities that bore no resemblance to the War Measures Act.

Guy's attitude toward unions was always one of ambivalence. Never a joiner of organizations and clubs—the Press Club except-ed—he was skeptical of minor clusters and cliques, let alone mass movements.

There was something about the dynamic of unions, of collec-tive worker action against management, that caused Guy discom-fort. While his sympathy for underpaid workers was genuine—he considered himself among them—he had difficulty distinguishing legitimate worker demands, and collective action to achieve them, from an ingrained fear of authoritarian leadership and unruly crowds bearing placards.

At the *Evening Telegram* in 1971, printers briefly went on strike in a wage dispute. Guy winced and squirmed. He wanted no part of it really, despite his own mounting discomfort about how the newspaper was being run by its new owners, Thomson Newspapers. Guy was hardly a shill for management either, although in earlier days at the paper he had found more mirth than menace in the benign paternalistic culture of the Herder family owners. As late as 1970, many employees still referred to the Herders as Mister Jim, Mister Hubert, and Mister Steve.

Increasingly agitated by the 1970 sale of the paper, Guy refused to cross the printers' picket line. Wrongly assuming he would be fired as a consequence, he simply left town.

Bob Ennis recalled this episode with amusement. "Years later, long after I had left, he wrote a column for some other publication and, employing his selective memory, he recalled taking great pleasure telling me during a 1975 strike that he was quitting. One of my brothers or sisters had sent the column along to me with a chuckle … I had left two years earlier in '73." The only two strikes of the decade at the *Telegram* were in 1971 and 1979.

In 1971, Guy's silent sympathies in fact were with the wage earners, as they were much more assertively in 1979. That year, when he no longer worked for the paper, his former colleagues, 35 reporters and printers, by then members of a single union, again went on strike.

During that tense fight, Guy was more overt in his sympathies. He had not been working full-time for the paper since 1974, and his distaste for the Thomson organization had curdled into something even more fierce, sweeping up the Herders themselves in its path.

Drinking hard at the time, Guy met for beers almost daily with the strikers at the old Welcome Hotel, roughly across Duckworth Street from the *Telegram*, or at Dirty Dick's, now the Ship Pub, directly across Solomon's Lane from the main *Telegram* building. Booze bolstered his rapport with key strike leaders. Guy commiserated with them, entertained them, and wrote for the *Signal*, the alternative tabloid they published during the strike.

A characteristic Guy anecdote came out of those beery sessions, often retailed by former *Telegram* and CBC journalist Bob Wakeham, who was there. The 1979 *Telegram* strike was a nasty one, with acts of vandalism and violence that at one point saw the windows smashed on the street-level floor of newspaper's Duckworth Street offices.

Steve Herder had become the paper's publisher, the last of the founding Herder family still involved. He reported, uncomfortably, to the Thomson Newspaper command in Toronto.

Steve Herder's St. John's home was a lovely residence that backed on Rennie's River, the rattling waterway that flows through the heart of the old city. The house was largely concealed by a high wooden fence from a pedestrian trail that runs by the eastern riverbank.

The fence was tagged with spray paint. The strikers, of course, were suspects. A specific word displayed on the fence was one of the seven words that the American comedian George Carlin said could never be uttered on television. It was, in fact, the only Carlin unmentionable that to this day, and to my knowledge, has never been uttered on the CBC.

The pub gathering that afternoon was rife with speculation about who might have committed such a heinous offence against Mister Steve, as the strikers now mockingly called him. Guy had remained silent; but suddenly he spoke up: "It was the proofreaders," he declared with confidence.

"How do you know?" The question was asked in unison.

"They spelled it with a *k*."

One result of Ray Guy's ambivalence toward collective action was that he paid too little attention to some of the substantial social and community development movements of the late 1960s and early 1970s, and at times too much attention to their leadership.

One pivotal front was the fishery, where local labour and management skirmishes had become frequent, and where a showdown in 1971, the Battle for Burgeo, became iconic, symbolizing a stagehead and sou'wester revolution.

Plant workers struck at a major enterprise that in various company guises controlled much of the south coast fishing industry. That control expanded in the 1950s when Spencer Lake of Burgeo, head of the sprawling Lake family fishing enterprises, married Margaret Penny of Ramea, heiress to a large fishing company long dominant on Ramea island.

The Newfoundland Fishermen, Food and Allied Workers Union (NFFAWU) won several battles in Burgeo, for certification and for subsequent contracts, propelling the union to organization and bargaining successes throughout Newfoundland and to durable status as the collective bargaining voice and lobbying force for most Newfoundland and Labrador fishery workers. Burgeo itself was riven by these battles. The Lake family soon left the community and their multiple local business interests behind.

Intriguing development movements also were occurring in places such as Fogo Island, where a different but remarkable social change experiment took place.

The Fogo transformation was powered by a collaboration between the Extension Service of Memorial University and the National Film Board of Canada. Residents of the Fogo Island communities were interviewed extensively and then invited to watch themselves in a series of short films. Revelations and understanding fostered by the films helped break down parochial barriers and promoted island-wide co-operation.

The ultimate achievement of the so-called Fogo Process was that Fogo became one of the very few islands around the Newfoundland coast whose communities did not succumb to the allure—or the coercion—of the government-subsidized resettlement schemes.

For that reason alone, it should have attracted the attention of Guy. There is little evidence that he was either smitten by or even very much aware of the Fogo developments, despite their contribution to thwarting "moving fever" in several remote and vulnerable Newfoundland settlements.

Guy's writing about the union movement in the fishery focused disproportionately on leadership rather than issues. It often imposed guilt by association, especially on those whose principal vice was association with Smallwood.

Guy paid particular attention to Cashin, who was at the centre of the early fish-front battles, serving as union president from 1971 to 1993. To Guy's thinking, Cashin had two strikes against him. He was an erstwhile Smallwood disciple, and he became one of Newfoundland's most powerful union leaders. Despite being two years his junior, Guy referred to Cashin as Young Dickie, and occasionally as Red Ricky or the Scarlet Pimpernel.

Guy also made dismissive references to Father Desmond Mc-Grath, the activist Roman Catholic priest, Cashin's friend and associate, who in 1969 founded the Northern Fishermen's Union (NFU) with a small cluster of fishers in Port aux Choix. He wrote of the pair derisively as "Cashin and his clerical squire."

As a young man, Cashin had been a political gadfly. His first real job was Member of Parliament. As a Liberal with Smallwood's blessing, he captured the traditionally Tory St. John's West federal seat in 1962. He held it only until 1968, when Newfoundlanders, defying the Trudeaumania of the day, and telegraphing rough sledding ahead for Smallwood, sent six Tories to Ottawa out of seven seats available. Future premier Frank Moores was one of the new MPs. Red Ricky was out.

In 1969, McGrath's NFU was the progenitor of Cashin's NF-FAWU and of its modern offspring, the Fish, Food and Allied Workers. In recent years, and as of 2021, the FFAW is affiliated with Unifor, Canada's biggest private sector union.

Along with the fish companies and governments, the union of Newfoundland and Labrador fishery workers has been the powerful third player in fishing industry development for half a century. The emergence and rapid growth of a union of fishery workers (mostly men) and plant workers (mostly women) rivalled the downfall of Smallwood and the resettlement program as pivotal socio-economic shifts in Newfoundland and Labrador in the early 1970s. All such dynamics seemed to demand Guy's attention. Only the fishery phenomenon was covered sparingly.

Cashin's talents—notably those of persuasion and a take-no-prisoners rhetoric—were not unrelated to those frequently exhibited in Guy's prose. One big difference was Cashin's apparent lack of levity, or at least any public displays of it.

A minor irony is that the Cashin name had considerable cachet among the many remaining Newfoundland anti-Confederates and Canada skeptics, Guy's parents, Alice and George, among them. This was owing to the leadership role played by Peter Cashin, Richard's uncle, in the anti-Confederate campaign.

In Newfoundland and Labrador, Peter Cashin was commonly known as The Major, a World War I veteran and leader. The Major headed the anti-Confederate forces during the bitter referendum campaigns that eventually brought Newfoundland into Confederation in 1949. Smallwood led the pro-Canada campaigns, of course, but Peter Cashin was more than Joey's nemesis. He came close to ruining Joey's Canadian dream. The referendum result was a squeaker.

Peter Cashin's status as the man who championed Newfoundland independence against the Smallwood Confederates, whom he considered opportunists and traitors, was not lost on Guy. Nor was there ambiguity in Guy's own regard for The Major. On the back cover of volume 1 of Cashin's memoirs is an extraordinary endorsement. "Any child of mine will be told that one of his father's proudest boasts is to have lived in the time of Major Peter Cashin ..." It is signed, Ray Guy.

An additional minor irony was that during Guy's two years at Memorial University, one of his few townie friends was Laurie

Cashin, Richard's younger brother. Laurie Cashin became a leader too, one of Canada's strongest advocates for the rights of the hearing impaired.

The paths of Richard Cashin and Ray Guy crossed, or at least they ran for a while on narrow-gauge parallel tracks. For a short period in 1969, Guy and Cashin were joined in an unspoken and unacknowledged alliance that helped solidify the standing of both men among Placentia Bay fishing families. It was one fishery story that received Guy's undivided attention.

Early that year Placentia Bay fishermen noticed that herring in the bay were turning a curious colour of red. The closer to Long Harbour the fishermen were, the more scarlet herring they saw. The Electric Reduction Company (ERCO) had recently established a phosphorous plant in Long Harbour, lured by cheap electricity and the notoriously low environmental safety standards of Newfoundland and Labrador industrial strategy in Smallwood's develop or perish era.

The herring were dying in schools. Tales of the toxic phenomenon reached Guy on his frequent trips to Arnold's Cove. A trenchant account of this tragedy appeared in his column of March 26, 1969:

> Nearly two months have passed since the first of the mysterious red herring began to appear in Placentia Bay. Nobody is any the wiser yet—or if they are they're not talking ...
>
> When the malady struck, herring were seen to rise to the surface and twist and spin crazily about the top of the water, darting beneath and rising to the surface again, skittering and shuddering about as if in a frenzied agony.
>
> Gradually their struggles against the sickness that gripped them became more feeble. They became weaker

and weaker until, one by one, they turned belly-up on the surface. Waves brought them nearer to shore. Most of them were dead by the time the sea washed them up on the beaches in their thousands.

Their eyes were red and bulged from their heads like ugly clots of blood. Their silver bellies and white fins were startlingly changed to a bright scarlet. The dead red herring.

Guy reported that the federal Department of Fisheries was investigating but no results had been released. He posed the questions that were on the minds of every Placentia Bay fisherman:

Why? Why the delay? Why the silence? It could be just another natural phenomenon, or it could be a matter of greatest urgency. Who knows? But why is it taking so long?

Guy left no doubt about where both he and the fishermen believed the problem originated:

Until there are some answers, most of the fishermen directly concerned are pointing to the Long Harbour plant as a potential monster.

This belief, whether justified or not, is founded mainly on a frightening "accident" that occurred late last year, just after the $40 million phosphorous plant began operation.

The "accident" turned the waters of Long Harbour a milky grey. The stench that came from the polluted harbor was at times intolerable. It was a sharp acrid smell like brimstone or the stink caused when a box of matches exploded.

After a time the water cleared to reveal the bottom of the harbor littered by dead fish. Flounder, smelt, eels, and other varieties. All dead.

Guy had done some fieldwork. His own observations became the best evidence in his report:

> I saw the pollution first-hand late last week. Two waste pipes of two or three feet in diameter empty directly into Long Harbour waters. The continuous discharge through these pipes turns the water a milky grey and makes the sea cloudy within an area of several hundred feet of the outlets.

With the arrival of red herring in Placentia Bay, Richard Cashin's mundane St. John's law practice suddenly became exciting. On behalf of a group of Placentia Bay fishermen, some of whom had been constituents in his St. John's West federal riding, Cashin took a class-action case on a contingency basis.

Guy and Cashin played complementary roles in the red herring debacle, each powerful in its own way. Like Cashin, each time Guy declared decisively for or against an issue that enhanced the standing of outport people—against resettlement, for example—he advanced his own status and credibility. In Guy's case, those assets then could be applied to other causes, most notably his determined discrediting of Smallwood and the Smallwood industrial creed.

Whether Cashin's Placentia Bay work impressed Guy or not is not clear from his columns. If it did, the harmony was short-lived.

Never fully in Smallwood's pocket but never fully out of it either, Richard Cashin decided to attend the 1968 Newfoundland Liberal

Party convention organized by Smallwood as a Hail Mary pass to give the party a veneer of democratic legitimacy. There, again with Smallwood's backing, he was elected party president. Smallwood admitted that before then he had personally picked 99 per cent of the Liberal candidates for provincial elections.

Cashin lasted less than a year in the president's role, declaring the Liberal Party aimless, while scouting more aspirational career paths for himself. Soon he would be not just a union leader but an avowed supporter of the New Democratic Party.

It is reasonable speculation that Guy's wariness of and general negativity toward Richard Cashin had much to do with Cashin's tolerance of and flirtations with Smallwood and the Newfoundland Liberal Party. Those flirtations, coupled with his privileged childhood and his provocative personality, made Cashin a tempting target for the satirist. The 1968 Liberal convention offered a golden moment.

Guy's *Telegram* column of October 1, 1968, opened with a characteristically catchy lead:

> At 3 a.m. Saturday, September 28, the Holiday Inn in Gander rocked like a Brazil Square boarding house on the night after VE Day.

Guy first mocked Smallwood's absurd boast that the Liberal delegates, many of whom had overnighted in Gander en route to the convention in Grand Falls, represented the grassroots of a newly regenerated political movement:

> But who made up most of the 1400 in Grand Falls? Where did they come from? Their faces seemed vaguely familiar. They appear to have cropped up at other Liberal gatherings of this sort.

Are they taken out of storage like stage scenery when needed, dusted off and arranged in rows? You get the creepy feeling that they have electrodes planted deep in their brains and are wired to a master control button backstage.

When the button is pressed, does it cause their hands to rise from their laps and slap rapidly together?

One can only imagine the revulsion toward Guy bestirred in the 1,400 delegates, Cashin included, by those depictions. And, by contrast, the sheer joy to be found in such writing by the increasing numbers of anti-Smallwood rebels and politically transitioning Newfoundlanders.

Having dealt with the grassroots, the columnist got around to Cashin:

> All those tired old faces. And, much more depressing, some tired young faces. How fitting that the most outstanding specimen of the latter group was elected president.
>
> Mr. Cashin may be young in years but he has the attitude of a politician of 68. Who can talk more and say less than young-old Dickie? Who better gives the impression of having been left a political career in somebody's will with no choice but to make the best of it?

When Cashin was elected president of the expanded fisheries union in 1970, Guy—from out of right field, it seemed—expressed even greater personal disregard for him. Once more he harped on Cashin's alleged political and career opportunism, virtually spitting the column out:

... now we see young Dicky and his clerical squire entering the lists on the other side, fearlessly declaring that the accursed oppressors of the poor, downtrodden fishermen should be gutted, head on.

This is noble work and long, but not entirely without recompense both financial and political. There's more than one way to skin a happy peasant.[49]

Three decades would pass before Guy offered even a backhanded compliment to Cashin, and even at that the focus was narrow. In the February 2006 edition of the *Northeast Avalon Times*, he credits Cashin with summarizing the life force of Moores, the cordial playboy who unseated Smallwood in 1972 but soon became bored with the complexities of government.

Wrote Guy: "Frank Moores I leave once again to Dicky Cashin's observation: his daddy left him five or six million, but when he became premier he found himself rubbing elbows with people worth twenty or thirty million. Dissatisfaction set in."

In context, Cashin's role in the dead, red herring episode may have intensified Guy's resentment of him. After all, the red herring phenomenon occurred exclusively within Guy's very own Far Greater Bay. Moreover, Cashin's role in it was easier to measure.

Guy's reasons for calling down damnation on any individual or event rarely are simple. Cashin certainly bore the stigma of a sometime Smallwood acolyte. But in the red herring crisis, Cashin, unlike Guy, won his victory in the currency the mattered most: actual dollars in the pockets of fishermen. Guy's contributions to the episode through his excellent columns were potent but more abstract. Like Guy's larger impact on the Newfoundland and Labrador psyche, they resided in the realm of emerging political awareness and growing cultural confidence. It is possible too that he resented Cashin's new-found standing in Guy's own Placentia Bay.

On a very different front, Ray Guy jousted with a contemporaneous local leader who proved to be a good match for him in the world of words and rhetoric. This happened when Guy crossed pens with Dr. Patrick O'Flaherty, a respected writer and professor at Memorial University, and a persistent political player.

O'Flaherty was not a union leader, but he checked other boxes on Guy's *non grata* list. As well as being an excellent teacher of English Literature at Memorial University,[50] O'Flaherty was a partisan Liberal, in Joey Smallwood's contrail. A familiar dynamic was at play: a Smallwood friend is perforce a Guy foe.

As an active academic and critic, O'Flaherty was inclined to measure Guy with detachment and even oblique praise. "Guy is to Newfoundland what the Fool was to King Lear," O'Flaherty wrote, "a cranky, disconcerting, insistent reminder of a previous dignity, now violated."[51]

In other ways, on top of being unduly admiring of Smallwood, O'Flaherty could be provocative. Whip-smart, confident as a peacock, and a first-rate writer himself, O'Flaherty at times invaded Guy's journalistic turf.

Guy and O'Flaherty both were born in 1939 in Newfoundland outports. In Arnold's Cove, Guy grew up in the cold thrall of Book-of-Common-Prayer Anglicanism, better known then as the Church of England. O'Flaherty was raised in Northern Bay, Conception Bay, in a confessional religious culture more Irish than the Irish and more Catholic than the pope. Guy's childhood world is well surveyed in his Juvenile Outharbour Delights columns. O'Flaherty's is chronicled in his equally pleasing memoir, *Paddy Boy: Growing Up Irish in a Newfoundland Outport*. Combined, the works comprise a defining record of outport Newfoundland boyhood life in the 1940s and 1950s.

Like Richard Cashin, Guy and O'Flaherty were overachievers in their respective callings and realms. They also shared an interest, bordering on obsession, in Newfoundland political affairs.

Neither the O'Flaherty nor the Guy family was wealthy, but neither were they bereft. Both boys exhibited obvious intelligence and talent in their school days. O'Flaherty was sent as a boarder to the prestigious St. Bonaventure's College in St. John's to complete his high-school education. Less grandly, but for essentially the same reasons, Guy was sent to Bell Island to complete Grade 11 where he lived with cousins to attend a better school.

Both young men attended the old Memorial University on Parade Street in St. John's, and in that experience their important differences loomed large. In St. John's and at Memorial, Guy, whose shyness and lack of confidence were handicapping, tugged at his forelocks. O'Flaherty, brash and much more secure, walked taller than his height.

Guy hated Memorial, and during his two years there he also cultivated a lifelong disregard for St. John's. His academic standing was up and down. By contrast, O'Flaherty thrived at Memorial and in St. John's. He loved the capital—"a marvelous old slut of a city." He waltzed through an undergraduate degree, headed for England for graduate work, and was back in St. John's at age 23 with a PhD in English Literature from London University. He was soon welcomed by Memorial, which even then was aware of the shortage of native Newfoundland faculty members and the abundance of blown-away Brits. "Oh, to be in England," opined one faculty wit, "now that England's here."

In the late 1960s, O'Flaherty's academic reputation evolved almost on a parallel path to Guy's journalism and satire. By age 30, O'Flaherty was one of Newfoundland's leading critics, historians, and public-minded intellectuals, while Guy was, by a mile, Newfoundland and Labrador's leading political columnist and satirist. O'Flaherty clearly took note and became the first serious scholar to declare that Guy's writing "ranks as literature."

That recognition and more came in March 1974 when the *Canadian Forum*, Canada's respected *Independent Journal of Opinion and the Arts,* devoted virtually its entire edition to a section entitled "Newfoundland: Nation and Province." The edition marked the 25th anniversary of Newfoundland and Labrador as a Canadian province.

The magazine's cover was illustrated with a Christopher Pratt drawing of a classic Newfoundland sailing punt. The *Forum's* articles featured the cream of Newfoundland intellectuals and popular writers, including economist David Alexander, literature and Newfoundland Dictionary scholar George Story, historian Peter Neary, and folklorists Neil Rosenberg and Herbert Halpert. Ray Guy wrote the opening article on relations between Newfoundlanders and Mainlanders. Next up was O'Flaherty, who assessed Newfoundland writers of the early post-Confederation period, paying particular attention to Guy.

Guy's piece, studded with enough political incorrectness to get it burned today, lamented the fact that Newfoundlanders, even after a quarter of a century of being Canadians, remained wary of Mainlanders due to certain dark memories that have survived the ages. He cited the long-ago military capture of much of the island of Newfoundland by the Montreal-born French conqueror, Le Moyne d'Iberville:

> That was in 1696. The Frenchman, d'Iberville, struck on the notion of rounding up a troop of Iroquois in Lower Canada and bringing them down here to meet the Newfoundlanders.
>
> They landed in the French capital of Placentia in hot blood and went about the good work with all the vim and vigor of federal civil servants who are transferred here from the Mainland today.
>
> St. John's was burned, its citizens deported, and the same theory of public relations put in effect on all

settlements of the Avalon Peninsula starting at Witless Bay and proceeding clockwise to Come by Chance.

A few years later another load of Mainlanders in similarly spirited mood visited Newfoundland and repeated their previous success.

So it is all a matter of having got off on the wrong foot.

Guy then reminded *Forum* readers of Newfoundland's other grievances against French Canadians. Subscribers in the salons of Rosedale and Westmount may have winced, whispering "ingratitude."

The grievances ranged from Québec's 1927 British Privy Council challenge to the Labrador-Québec boundary, which failed but left a serious scar, to the 1969 contract with Hydro-Québec for the purchase of hydro electricity from the Churchill Falls development.

To this day, Newfoundlanders and Labradorians regard that contract as a beggar-thy-neighbour display of unequal bargaining power wielded by Québec with Ottawa's indifference. Québec refused to allow Churchill Falls power to cross its provincial territory en route to US markets unless Hydro-Québec purchased it upfront at a bargain to resell south at much more lucrative prices, pocketing the profits. The contract runs until 2041.

A few pages later in the *Canadian Forum*, O'Flaherty characterizes Guy's usual response to "Newfoundland's incipient loss of identity and vulgarization" as one of "anguish and rage," contrasting it with Harold Horwood's "sullen aplomb," manifested in his reinvention of himself as "an apostle of hippiedom."

O'Flaherty reviews several post-1949 writers, declaring Horwood "the province's most distinguished writer." He then turns his attention to Guy:

He is serene only when he recreates scenes from his early life in his evocative essays entitled "Juvenile Outharbour Delights." As he looks at the province today, however, he finds little to please him. Guy's appeal derives principally from his habit of saying openly what many Newfoundlanders feel but try to keep hidden.

When O'Flaherty wrote that assessment of Ray Guy in 1974, he would not have imagined an intriguing turn of events that subsequent years would bring.

"I can't recall exactly when the Guy-O'Flaherty spat occurred," O'Flaherty said. "I had a column in *The Daily News* in 1977–8 (also 1980–1) and it was during the 77–8 period that I wrote the item Guy objected to …"

In that item, O'Flaherty flattered Steve Neary, a high-profile former labour leader and Smallwood Cabinet minister whom Guy intensely disliked. Guy then slagged O'Flaherty in a column of his own and the gloves were off:

> I recall that he wrote I had "crawled out of a garbage can on Gower Street" or words to that effect; in my retort I called him "a coddled Arnold's Cove snot," which I think is an accurate quote, plus some other choice words. I think I wrote another piece too, in much the same vein, even worse, but I'm not sure.

Despite such billing and cooing, O'Flaherty ultimately remained more generous to Guy than Guy had been to O'Flaherty. O'Flaherty questioned Guy's motivation, but never his power or impact:

... While campaigning for federal election in 1978–9 in St. John's West I ran into a voter, a woman in the vicinity of Mundy Pond, a Guy fan, who objected strongly to what I'd written and refused to vote for me on that account. It seemed to me remarkable that a columnist could have had such an impact. People read newspapers back then!

I can't say I'm now proud of my role in this affair, but I couldn't just let Guy off with his dirty smear, which I thought at the time smacked of religious bigotry. I think he was given too much of a free hand by those afraid to tackle him in print, and by his editors. I believe he abused his position at *The Telegram*, knowing few would hit back at him out of fear of being scorched.

The exchanges between O'Flaherty and Guy were more suggestive of Northern Bay and Arnold's Cove schoolboy snark than of either Ryerson or London University. Half a century later, O'Flaherty was sanguine about the episode. He believed the most biting insult from Guy reflected the fact that he (O'Flaherty) owned rental properties on Gower Street, then a rundown section of old St. John's, today gentrified and in demand.

It is entirely possible that Guy disliked O'Flaherty's standing and obvious ambition, just as he may have resented Richard Cashin's. Cashin had invaded Guy's Far Greater Bay. O'Flaherty invaded Guy's remit of journalism, which Guy considered hallowed ground and certainly no place for players such as O'Flaherty with their partisan Smallwood tattoos.

It is easier to record than to analyze Guy's attitudes toward and treatment of those early 1970s events and the personalities who drove them.

Guy could be petty and unfair, and, like all journalists whose unenviable role is to publish the rough first draft of history, he was not always fully informed. If hardly a coddled snot, there were dark demons in Ray Guy's soul.

Behind that smoking typewriter, on as many days as not, there was a coiled and angry young man.

CHAPTER 12

Dog Days of Summer '69

No life is free of speed bumps and travail. Yet Ray Guy's world from about 1960 when he entered Ryerson to 1969/70 when his *Telegram* career peaked had remarkably few external stresses. It was spiked with achievement, positive reinforcement, and popular regard. There were those dark clouds of the mind, of course. They stalked him always.

The summer of 1969 and winter of 1970 foreshadowed a bleaker period of Guy's time at the *Telegram*. There still were quality assignments and many strong columns. But there was a scent of change in the air.

When Guy returned to work in June 1969 after his five-week road trip to Florida and Ontario, he detected a mild adjustment in his status at the paper. It resulted in a measure of discomfort about his professional lot in life, possibly his personal lot as well.

In the summer of 1969, a close reader of Guy's columns could have picked up a disconcerting vibe. Most of the signs were subtle, but one was not. The traditional everyday home of Guy's column, top to bottom on the left flank of page 3, was no longer his as a matter of right. This was the choicest real estate in the newspaper, which advertisers could not buy. Page 3 left is the focal point for a newspaper reader's eye when the front page is turned to reveal the next two pages.

Guy's first column upon his return from vacation showed up on page 2. This was the so-called "floating column" approach. It bothered him, although it may have represented nothing more than an evolving newspaper practice. He worried that the change conveyed a subliminal message, to him as well as to his readers.

"Psst. Over here. I'm over here," Guy wrote on June 20, 1969, page 2.

Found myself shifted over here when I got back from my holidays. It seems a bit strange after two years but I guess I'll get used to it.

The reason, I think, is that they want the whole of page three for the real news. And ads for rum and funeral homes. From now on, I believe I'll be chasing the weather around.

I'll be on the same page as the weather—wherever that happens to be. Anywhere from page two to page 82. So you'll get two doses of bad news on the same page.

They call this shifting you around to different pages every day "floating." But I suppose floating around is not a bad pastime for the summer if you can keep out of hot water.

Publicly, Guy joked about the change and appeared to take it well, settling for wisecracks about the advertising department. Privately, he seethed.

Floating had been a common placement principle for nearly all other *Telegram* columnists who wrote weekly. Some were handled as "ROP," or Run of Paper, which meant they could show up not only on any page but on any day of the week. But Guy was the only daily columnist, and he was popular. The only other *Telegram* writer with roughly predictable daily space was the editor himself, who owned page 6 for his editorials every day, in keeping with newspaper tradition.

Beyond the floating column, the midsummer weeks of 1969 were uneventful for Guy, and the relative calm was reflected in the quality of his work and interests. In fact, late June and early July presented opportunities for him to tie off some unfinished business from earlier columns and subjects. Those were topics on which he had written with power and authority in the past and which had contributed to his reputation for acute observation and award-winning prose.

Dead and discoloured herring were turning up again in Placentia Bay, near the site of the ERCO phosphorus plant in Long Harbour. ERCO persistently denied any connection between the dead fish and their plant. Provincial and federal authorities had continued to investigate, but no conclusive information was ever shared with the public.

Meanwhile, ERCO announced that it was contributing $1 million "for social purposes" to the people of Long Harbour. Guy was not buying it. His skepticism was matched only by his mistrust of the government agencies charged with looking after both the fish and the fishermen of Placentia Bay. The dead fish phenomenon had triggered Guy's rhetorical rage earlier in the year, and it did so again in a June 30 column. Once more he asked the obvious question: who is to blame?

The company? The one fact we do know is that they would have saved $1 million by pumping their waste directly into Placentia Bay.

Federal fisheries? It was their duty to see to it that the plant would not kill fish. They apparently stamped it simon pure and allowed it to reopen.

Now, more than six months later, they tell us that less than 25 parts of phosphorus to one billion parts of water can kill herring and trout. And that the acid water pumped out by the plant could be just as dangerous. Twin streams of poison.

So who takes the blame for that little foul-up? Which expert can that be pinned on?

The ever-smilin' Jack Davis [federal Fisheries minister] is the logical target. But what satisfaction is there in trying to slam a swinging door? He's afflicted with the famous Trudeau [Prime Minister Pierre Trudeau] shrug of indifference.

Our own dear leader [Premier J.R. Smallwood] prefers to escape the stink of red herring and scuttle off to Red China.

After all, the enterprise at Long Harbour is a "great new industry" in the flesh. That Newfoundland pays them twice as much in subsidized electricity as they pay out in wages is beside the point.

For the past week a vessel appropriately named the "Ottawa" has been taking aboard thousands of tons of poisoned fish in Placentia Bay. She steams down the bay and dumps the polluted saltbulk some 50 miles off Cape St. Mary's.

Federal fisheries says things are back to normal; the company makes a gracious gesture "for social purposes;"

and the father of great new industries is in Hong Kong buying knickknacks for his mantel shelf.

July brought another golden moment when Guy revisited the Newfie Bullet story, the subject of his 1967 National Newspaper Award-winning feature that earned him respect among the national media and a modest reputation beyond Newfoundland and Labrador shores.

The Bullet as a passenger train was to make her final trans-island journey. To get the holistic experience of travelling to Newfoundland from Mainland Canada without the aid of an airplane, Guy travelled to North Sydney as a starting point for the journey home. He was accompanied by Photo Editor Bill Croke and Dave Butler, a former Canadian Press correspondent who had moved to the *Telegram*. The idea was to take a Marine Atlantic ferry across Cabot Strait, then a voyage of seven or eight hours, and join the Bullet in Port aux Basques for its final, 22-hour meander across the island.

A tsunami of words attended this historic event, before, during, and after the trip. The story was treated as both tragedy and farce, sometimes by the same writers. The *Telegram* carried pages of copy by Guy, by Butler, and by a new staff writer, Sharon McLeod, who decided to make the trip her honeymoon with her new husband, Don McLeod, the new Canadian Press reporter in Newfoundland.

What a to-do. Guy's coverage for the most part offered levity and journalism-light, until his final piece. When the long trip was over, he was seized by the poignancy and symbolism of the Bullet's demise. The resulting article was emotional. It rolled out at a graceful and poetic pace, as if to match the leisurely rolling rhythm of the old train itself.

I intended to make light of it all, my love, but I am not able.

But a wake it was. Somebody wrote a verse to the papers last week calling you "you," like you were a person or something and here I am foolish enough to be doing the same.

Don't think, you poor comical monster, that we are calling a mess of wheels and machinery "you." You are all the people you ever carried and the country you carried them across.

You were more than a machine and that's the closest we can come to it. You took us away from home and you brought us back for a long time.

You shook up our livers and our lights and you shook up our emotions at the same time whether you brought us east from Port aux Basques or west towards it ...

In September, 1966, I wrote a piece saying you should be buried. It wasn't that I had anything against you but the people who couldn't afford a sleeper and tried to get two hours sleep out of a miserable 24 frightened me.

And you were dead then. It was disgusting that your corpse had to be dragged about and squabbled over for so long ...

... Anyway, there's not much sense hashing it over anymore. We're too poor a rock to afford a train, according to the CNR. They'll sit us in plastic buses on plastic seats and have us gobble food in plastic restaurants and they'll trundle us through a 500-mile long gravel pit.

They talk about "transportation" and the passenger-mile ratio and cost factors and efficiency, not about people and trips. We are at the tender mercies of computers and the men they operate.

Do not rest in peace. Curse them with a long and howling curse like your whistle in the night.[52]

Guy's obituary for the Bullet was sublime. His coverage of the event had been a fine week's work. A brief letdown followed, but by mid-July his mood was brightened by an anti-Guy letter-writing campaign among some American ex-patriots stationed in Newfoundland. In one of his periodic references to his recent US travels, he mocked Americans' jingoism and flag-waving proclivities. In his column of July 10, 1969, he took a cheap shot at their eating habits before focusing on what he called their flag fetish.

On the flag topic he did manage some slings and arrows, but he never quite rose to the heights of ridicule of which he was capable. He professed delight about the angry letters, yet his columns on the topic betrayed an offhanded and careless tone, a sense that his heart was not fully in it. Moreover, his disposition collided with the more positive appreciations of Americans that he had written previously. The US flag rantings were Guy at his most churlish.

Gas stations, service stations, banks and restaurants, businesses are all exhorting the populace to "Fly the flag proudly." They're selling them, giving them away free, plastering them on cars and everything else that moves.

The flag is now the Queen, the Prime Minister, the President and Frank Sinatra rolled into one. With Tricky Dicky following Lyndon it must be a comfort to have something to cling to, even if it is only a piece of drygoods.

(I know. I know. There's another flag over there on the editorial page. But we don't tend to fixate—not with two flags, three "national anthems," and a half a dozen heads of state and the Queen Mum.)

The States is just about awash in flags right now. A chap pops up on some tv stations at regular intervals reminding all hands to "Fly the flag proudly."

And at sign-off time where we get two pieces of landwash with a mountain and a turnip patch in the middle they get a positive orgy of stripes, stars and M-15 rifles.

One tv station rounds out the day with a resounding prayer of thanks to "our brave boys in Vietnam and American fighting men around the world" who have held back the howling Communistic hordes long enough for it to bring still another episode of "The Beverly Hillbillies" and "As the World Turns."

The column ended with a perfunctory disclaimer—too little if not too late. His tirade against a US flag fetish and their food-porn affliction, Guy suggested, was not to be taken personally. But by that point he had become tone-deaf to the implications of his tirade.

As a nation America stinks. But take Americans one by one and they're palatable (so to speak) individuals. So that makes the US no different from any other nation in the world.

To hell with America. But God bless Joe Schlitz, 197 Peach Avenue, Atlanta, Georgia, and most of the other 199,999,999 people south of the border.

With that defiant comment, Guy was either channelling Jonathan Swift or else great satirists think alike. "Principally I hate and detest that animal called man," Swift wrote to Alexander Pope on September 19, 1725, "although I heartily love John, Peter, Thomas and so forth."[53]

Not surprisingly, the column was taken personally and seriously by many US citizens then living in St. John's, among them individuals of prominence in industrial, ecclesiastical, and minor diplomatic positions—that is, individuals inclined to write letters to the editor.

One scathing letter came from Rev. J. Stanley Bowe, S.J., who wrote from the St. Pius Rectory in St. John's. After establishing his credentials as an American citizen who had been born in St. John's but raised in the US, Bowe indulged in his own brand of ad hominem trash-talk: "This Ray Guy. Is he for real? ... He either had hashish in his pipe or acid in his soup on Thursday. The resulting caricature of Americans had little, if any, relation to reality."

Bowe then waxed Jesuitical.

> I believe it was Virgil who first coined the expression: Ab uno disce onmes. And every school-boy debater is warned against this fallacy of making generalizations from a single instance. But Ray Guy announced at the outset of his Thursday rantings that he would extrapolate precisely according to this fallacious principle ...
>
> His observation of a "flag fetish" is news to me. I admit my experience is limited to the northeast from Washington to Maine. But then by his own admission his is limited to the expressways and a few weeks in Florida. In my forty years and more the kind of chauvinism he attributes to the Yanks I have observed only in an extremist and discredited minority ...
>
> I could forgive all of this as a poor attempt at humor. But I resent the slur that "Freedom," "Justice," "Democracy" and similar ideas are mere parrotings of ritual chants by Americans. True, we have often fallen short of our ideals but we have them and it does no good to sneer at them. For an all-time in journalistic tastelessness I award the palm to two of his concluding

statements: "As a nation America stinks," and "to hell with America." This is simply vicious.

The response from Bowe and others did little to chasten Guy. Indeed, it stoked him into an even more biting attack, perhaps a more legitimate one. His counteroffensive was to mock and ridicule the more hysterical letter-writers by contrasting them with a challenging but measured response from a US Navy couple stationed at Argentia.

A letter from Elizabeth and John Smith appeared in the *Telegram* on July 14, 1969, alongside Bowe's. It damned Guy with faint praise. In his column of July 17, 1969, Guy quoted the letter in its entirety.

> Dear (?) Ray Guy:
> We thoroughly enjoy your column ... that is most of the time. We laughed heartily at your description of traffic in St. John's and your trip across our highways in the US and about Boston. Never heard a truer statement in our lives.
> Your complaints about Washington, D.C. are very justified, which we admit to our shame ...
> So far, so good. But, boy, did you put your typewriter into motion before you put your brain into gear when you wrote that blurb about our Stars and Stripes.
> My husband and I are very proud of our Flag and do not have to be told about displaying it and our Patriotism boiled over when we read your remarks ...
> Sincerely,
> Elizabeth M. Smith
> John M. Smith, HMCS, USN

Guy was fine with that response, which he used, tactically and effectively, as a stick with which to beat the more pugnacious US patriots. Meantime, there had been yet another flag-hugging missive that drew his wrath. It came from Otto Lessing and was published on July 15. Guy battled back in his July 17 column, this time managing to drag a dash of Smallwood's third-mill industrial development politics into the fray.

And another thing about Americans ...

They never display their flag fetish so clearly as when they're protesting they're obsessed with it.

Some, like Mr. and Mrs. Smith, spring to the defence of the Star Spangled Pyjamas "more in sorrow than in anger."

Others ... whip themselves into such a frenzy they're scarcely coherent ...

Tuesday's Yankee Doodle letter writer [presumably a reference to Father Bowe's] has the insolence to come into this country and give us our orders on how we must pay due reverence in all humility to the Stars and Stripes.

He is exceeded in his insolence only by one Otto Lessing who has written the US consul in St. John's seething with righteous indignation that the lesser breed is besmirching Old Glory.

Mr. Lessing is better known to us as head of the famous Shaheen "third mill" enterprise at Come by Chance—a US concern that went so far in attempts to suck the blood out of Newfoundland that even some of our cabinet ministers were revolted ...

The entire US food-flag fuss was an oddity that Guy had not expected. In fact, he had signed off his column only a week earlier, on

July 11, 1969, with a promise to head out of town and write bright summery pieces from the outports. In that piece, Guy as much as admitted that he had little else to write about on those doggish summer days.

> As you've probably guessed by now the pickings are pretty lean in the summer for a column when you're confined to an office and the boys in at Conglomeration aren't so generously providing the ammunition on the floor of the House ...
>
> ... Next week I'll get out and around a bit and see what's cooking the other side of the St. John's overpass. The columns might not appear every day but a couple of days a week.
>
> They'll be longer and decorated with appropriate photographs. So we'll see you later. If not Monday then sometime before the week is out with one of the new, blue super intensified, summer columns.

Inexplicably, Guy again changed his mind about leaving town. On Monday, July 14, he was back on page 2 with a piece about anything but the pastoral vistas he had so recently promised. He commented that day on the glorification of war as reflected in the endless summer-reruns of television documentaries reprising the two world conflicts of the 20th century.

> The way they tell it, it looks like a great lark. Apart from a few flashes of blood, gore and atrocity to keep us in mind of who the bad guys were, it looks like "a loverly war."
>
> Either the glorious British forces saved the world for democracy or the brave American boys rescued the

earth from the clutches of tyranny ... depending on which country made the film.

The next day found Guy again in breach of his promise of the previous Friday, complaining this time about the latest edition of the *Newfoundland Bulletin* and about the conduct of certain RCMP officers.

Guy, who usually expressed general respect for the Mounties, cited what he felt was total misconduct on the part of two Newfoundland-based officers. They had stopped two women, both teachers, for speeding, and insisted on tearing apart their luggage and their car. Guy hinted that this was for no obvious reason other than the vehicle's Québec licence plates. The car was owned by one of the women, a Newfoundlander teaching in Montreal. Nothing suspicious was found and no apology was offered.

Curiously, inexplicably, and maddeningly for Guy, this column had floated back to page 9. It might as well have been burned. It was one of the very few occasions that a Ray Guy column appeared anywhere except pages 3 or 2. It renewed his annoyance about floating columns. Still, this was not the sort of thing he felt he could question directly in an era when the columns of other writers floated too—less entitled writers, he secretly may have thought.

Nor did Guy offer any explanation of why he had hung around town so long in midsummer instead of heading west as he had planned. A safe inference is that he was uncertain about what he was doing that summer. This uncertainty marked the first hints of reciprocal discomfort regarding Guy's status inside the newspaper.

By mid-August, however, after finally delivering a handful of light outport travel features enhanced by Croke's photos, Guy appeared to be ready to reclaim his title as the champion satirical sage of Newfoundland and Labrador politics. This was fortunate, as Smallwood was well into his 1969 leadership campaign, apparently determined to secure his own black belt as premier in perpetuity.

Back on page 2 on August 15, Guy's political edge was as wicked as ever. He cautioned women voters not to be seduced by Joey's sudden discovery of bespoke haberdashery.

> Gone are the baggy black suits of Hong Kong manufacture. Gone are the frayed collars and dowdy neckties. Gone are the street-sweeper cuffs. The Khrushchev cut is out.
>
> In his new campaigning gear, Mr. Smallwood cuts a dashing figure. The ensemble is done in a delicate beige although it comes over as near-white on television. Some viewers took the Last Great Announcement for a fried chicken commercial.
>
> But this is only a small disadvantage. Joseph's shirt is even more stunning than Joseph's coat. Blazing, aggressive, vital vermilion. Rooster red. Altogether devastating.
>
> And topping off the whole concern is the frightfully debonair bow-tie bespeaking the continental elan of Charles Boyer or the smouldering Latin charm of a Ramon Navarro.

With similar entertaining candy, Guy wisely left the drab summer behind. On August 29, he wrote one of those columns that seemed to get better as it rolled out, not uncommon. The dynamic reflected the fact that Guy typically wrote his pieces over several hours, during which his disposition could be affected by an agreeable lunch, a jovial conversation, or even a dash of sunlight.

Guy was deep into that column before he turned his attention to the Opposition Progressive Conservatives, or the Pork Chops as he referred to them at the time:

They've just trooped back in body from a "fact-finding tour." I don't know if they realize it or not but they're breaking the law.

They've been picking facts out of season. The fact season doesn't open until Sept. 15 in most areas. They're not ripe yet.

It seems that facts will be more plentiful this year than last. Must have been the right amount of rain at the right time. There's nothing better than a nice bit of fact jam on a slice of fresh bread.

Or, for that matter, a little dish of facts with milk and sugar. What will be the price of facts a gallon this year, I wonder. The youngsters are already selling crocks of them by the highway but the price is scandalous.

Guy had drifted through an inauspicious summer, absorbing his mild demotion stoically while achieving a few landmark features and columns. As fall 1969 approached, he and the entire editorial team at the *Telegram* moved into grittier territory. For Guy, this entailed total immersion in political news and commentary leading up to the October 29, 1969, Liberal leadership convention in St. John's.

The convention was the first direct personal challenge to Smallwood and the post-Confederation Liberals. It split the Liberal Party but was a welcome opportunity for politically disheartened Newfoundlanders.

The Liberal leadership convention should not have been as divisive as it was. But this was not a traditional political fight. It was a generational and cultural shift in Newfoundland society and politics, personified by Smallwood on behalf of the old ways and by John C. Crosbie for the new.

The political fate of the province was the recurring theme in Guy's work. He editorialized often and with vigour, but some of

Guy's best work that autumn was closer to straight-up reportage than to sermonettes or satire.

Despite his contempt for Smallwood, Guy was remarkably measured in his coverage. He followed his now familiar pattern, rising to the occasion on serious political matters, but never overlooking the laughable and the loony. When Joey announced a hockey stick factory for Stephenville, Guy could see no reason why such an industry could not be expanded in a vertically integrated way, eventually to manufacture blue lines and second and third periods.

Down to business on October 22, Guy wrote a long and revealing inside report on the machinations of the Smallwood leadership campaign. It demonstrated the ground-war method behind the Smallwood victory, a strategy replicated in scores of Newfoundland and Labrador communities in the lead-up to the convention.

The event Guy described took place in Cartwright, an isolated community of about 600 people on the southern coast of Labrador at the entrance to Sandwich Bay. Cartwright was readily reachable only by boat or aircraft. Guy reported the names of all the individuals involved. One such key player was Gerald I. Hill, then a Smallwood Cabinet minister and the representative for the district of Labrador South.

Labrador South warranted 20 delegates to the leadership convention, and it was Hill's job to deliver them all to Smallwood. Hill believed that he could do so by the simple expedient of flying into Cartwright and hand-picking them. This would avoid the inconvenience of an open meeting where supporters of other candidates might show up—John Crosbie supporters especially.

All that was required was the purchase of 20 Party memberships at $1 each in the names of 20 loyal Smallwood supporters. Hill knew everybody in Cartwright and could name both the Smallwood and the Crosbie loyalists. The Smallwood membership cards would all go to folks Ray Guy called the "classic Smallwood core—clergy, merchants and government agents." The assumption,

Guy wrote, was that Cartwright's isolation would mean that "no disagreeable rumors would pass beyond the boundaries. Word doesn't get into and word doesn't get out of Cartwright that easily."

Hill and another Liberal Party Association operative flew into Cartwright, were met by a prominent local merchant, took lodgings with a provincial government official, and essentially associated exclusively with the town's elite, including the clergyman and his wife. All were Smallwood loyalists, and all were taken-for-granted delegates at the convention of October 29.

All could have gone according to plan, or plot as the case may have been. However, and not coincidently, a Crosbie campaign chieftain, the well-known Labrador coast man, Joe Harvey, arrived in Cartwright the same day and spread the word of a Crosbie campaign meeting that very night.

As Guy reported, some 80 Cartwright residents showed up at the Crosbie meeting and complained that they were never given an opportunity to obtain Liberal Party membership cards or vote on a delegate slate for the convention. They then crashed a nearby hall where Hill and his 20 or so card-carrying members were assembled to vote for themselves as delegates.

The lone RCMP constable in Cartwright was summoned. The Mountie ordered non-Association members to leave the hall, declaring the meeting to be private. He was ignored. He left, wisely concluding that he could not arrest all 80 gatecrashers. An attempt by Hill to pacify the situation failed, and the meeting simply dissolved.

"It was, you might say, civil disobedience," Guy reported on October 22. "It was, you might say, defiance not only of an arm of the law and a Minister of the Crown but of a representative of the man who, as he tells us, stands next to the Queen herself!"

Guy reported that the party representative "was not tame. He called the meeting off. He and Hill went off through the crowd to (the merchant's) house with part of the crowd following some distance behind."

Guy did not report the ultimate outcome of the delegate selection process, which presumably was that the Liberal Association's first choices as delegates prevailed. He did, however, report the outcome of Hill's and his colleague's journey home that evening.

A group of mischievous Cartwright children gave them directions at a fork in the road. Hill and company wound up in pitch darkness at a local henhouse.

Guy sought comment about the Cartwright events. He quoted a community councillor who revealed that the town had been threatened with the loss of a small government grant and with the potential loss of jobs due to the misconduct of its citizens the night before. He also sought input from Hill and from the local clergyman. Hill declined comment. The clergyman denied involvement.

The significance of Guy's Cartwright report is worth noting. Even with rapidly expanding dissent and opposition, the premier still could achieve a substantial victory over Crosbie, based overwhelmingly on a ground-level roundup of remaindered 1949 Smallwood Liberals and a newer flock of the petty bourgeois beholden in the outports.

The reasons why that was possible were effectively captured by Guy in his Cartwright column and others. They included Smallwood's continuing command of his Cabinet and of the powerful levers of government, his iron rule over elected Liberal members, his control through surrogate members of the Liberal Association, and the enduring loyalty of provincial employees and small-time contractors at the community level. His was a victory rooted in a malign misuse of raw power, one increasingly at odds with emerging Newfoundland and Labrador political sentiment.

At the convention itself, Smallwood's decisive victory over Crosbie and three other candidates was less an endorsement of Smallwood than a damned-nuisance delay. If the time was not quite right, the time was nigh. Smallwood's win was a triumph of the premier's well-organized traditional base of support—the beholden and the benighted—many of them simply the elderly who recalled a very different and more deprived Newfoundland than Smallwood had sought to redeem. The convention was the last hurrah for the diminishing throng of loyal Liberal baymen, veterans of the Confederation battle, whom Smallwood had called his ragged-arsed artillery.

Smallwoodites at the convention wore Styrofoam pork-pie hats that a fire marshal might condemn today. Guy's post-mortem column on November 3, 1969, referred to the convention as the Mad Hatter's Tea Party. He saw the outcome as cause for both hope and consternation.

> It proved one basic thing but no more than has been common knowledge for some time—we have a government that has the support of much less than half the people.
>
> Smallwoodism is dead but it won't lie down. More than half the voters voted against Smallwoodism in the last federal election. And now we see that a great chunk of the Liberal party is also against Smallwoodism.

Guy was offended by the cost and the glaring extravagance of the convention itself, held in the old Memorial Stadium in St. John's with Smallwood delegates billeted in abandoned Newfie Bullet sleeper cars. He reported that $3 million had been spent and noted that the amount was $70,000 more than the cost of a national Liberal Party convention in Ottawa the previous year.

He was also struck, as he had been in the past, by what he felt were the strains of totalitarianism in Smallwood's regime. Guy pointed out the obvious: the Nazi salutes seen at the convention itself—the protest response of Crosbie supporters—were a mockery of such salutes, in condemnation of the man who had won the day:

To interpret the demonstration at the stadium as an indication that those giving the Hitler salute were admirers of Hitler is a little too brazen for even the glazed-eyed idiots to swallow.

What, in the height of emotion, the demonstrators were doing was protesting the elements of Hitlerism that exist in Smallwoodism. They were saying it was a disgrace to the memory of those who died fighting Hitler to allow any trace of it to exist in Newfoundland—and in the St. John's Memorial Stadium ...

When the victory was announced, the doors of the stadium burst open and a great and hideous thunder of drums overwhelmed the building. A blare of trumpets drowned all protest.

For anyone who had those other things in mind it was a brief moment of sick terror. But then you saw that the drums were being beaten by little girls in pretty costumes ...

Smallwood's Liberal leadership victory in October 1969 was indeed pyrrhic. Smallwood was still around and would be for more than two more years. But Smallwoodism, as Guy had observed, was running on fumes. For Guy's purposes, if Smallwood was not yet a spent force, he was no longer the omnipotent premier, the satirist's dream, that he had been as recently as 1968.

CHAPTER 13

A Great Rude Wind from Canada

Overall, 1969 had ended for Ray Guy better than it had begun. The new year, 1970, and indeed his remaining time at the *Telegram*, would be a different quintal of fish.

At the beginning of 1970, there was indeed a different wind blowing at the *Evening Telegram*, and a stronger one. It was hard to capture or define, but hyper-intuitive insiders such as Guy could smell it.

The floating column was a symptom of mutual disaffection, Guy for the *Telegram* and the *Telegram* for Guy. The tensions were real, if initially only annoying. Guy's early 1970 columns occasionally betrayed a sense of indirection. At the same time, some of his friendships were scratchier than usual and his loneliness was more pronounced.

For several years after returning to St. John's from Ryerson, Guy had lived in boarding houses. His first actual apartment mates in St. John's were *Telegram* reporters Bob Moss and me. During the fall of 1968 and spring and summer of 1969, we occupied a large space at Hillview Terrace Apartments on Torbay Road.

Hillview Terrace Apartments were neither terraced nor were there any hills in view, at least from our windows. It was the city's first big-scale apartment complex, built by an ambitious young developer named Craig Dobbin. Guy occasionally slagged those buildings in his column, and with good reason. Elephants tramped the stairwells. If the bathroom cabinet doors were simultaneously ajar in two side-by-side apartments, light from the mirror-image bathroom on the other side would shine through. If a razor blade was flicked vigorously through the disposal slot in the cabinet, it could land in the opposite apartment.

Moss was a seasoned *Telegram* reporter who frequently was assigned to Ottawa to keep an eye on the Newfoundland and Labrador MPs, a useful service that no other Newfoundland news organization ever funded. After the Thomson *Telegram* stood down the Ottawa bureau, Moss left the paper and became editor of the weekly *Gander Beacon,* a position and a community he thoroughly enjoyed.

In 1969, when Moss left for Ottawa for one of his longer stays, Everett Bishop, a student friend of mine from Heart's De-light, joined us at our new digs, Freshwater Plaza Apartments, on Freshwater Road, a 10-minute walk from Memorial. Bishop was a good fit, bright and easygoing, and more relaxed than either of his roommates.

As an inveterate reader, Guy had a weekend routine that was different from that of most young bachelors. He wrote his columns for the Friday weekend edition on Thursday nights, freeing him until Sunday evenings when he wrote his Monday dispatch. On

Friday mornings, he could sleep late, his week's work completed. For Guy, the pathological night owl, that meant noon or 1 p.m.

Commonly on Friday afternoons, Guy would cruise the magazine stands and bookstores of downtown St. John's and the Avalon Mall and return laden with bags of weekend reading material, mostly magazines. Those usually included the principal newsmags of the day—*Time, Newsweek, Maclean's*—and then possibly *Esquire* or the *New Yorker*, a gardening magazine or two, and a couple of books. He also would have stopped by the liquor store, usually to collect a 26-ouncer of Smirnoff vodka, sometimes two.

At Freshwater Plaza, Bishop and I often joined Guy in his weekend apartment retreats, supplementing the booze supplies with a half-dozen Dominion Ale or whatever our more modest student budgets would allow. While we sometimes shared them, the rituals really were Guy's. Bishop studied philosophy and he would amuse and impress Guy by quoting oracles such as Nietzsche: "There is always some madness in love. But there is always some reason in madness."

Those apartment weekends could be entertaining. There was drinking, of course, especially by Guy, but they were not flat-out drunken events. Guy at his most relaxed would read, sometimes out loud to his roommates, tell stories, play his *Beyond the Fringe* British comedy albums, drink immoderately, smoke immoderately, and laugh a lot. Occasionally, he would take up his melodica. On that humble plastic pipe, he would produce a bizarre blend of tunes ranging from Clancy Brothers and Tommy Makem ballads to lilting spirituals. He liked old hymns such as "Where He Leads Me I Will Follow," a dirge well known in Protestant outports of his childhood, and a Salvation Army staple. Guy had a vast store of such venerable pieces and remembered them fondly. He claimed to have attended a Salvation Army wedding as a kid in Arnold's Cove where one of the hymns selected was "I'd Rather Have Jesus."

Or he would read in silence, propped up on one elbow on a living room rug of near-septic deterioration. Within Guy's reach would be an overflowing ashtray, a half-full glass of vodka and orange juice with melting ice cubes, and perhaps the latest edition of *The New Yorker*. The Smirnoff supply, unless two had been purchased, would not survive the weekend.

For a period when we shared digs, Guy kept sporadic company with a smart young woman who worked at the newspaper and lived in Maddox Cove, just outside the city. For some mysterious reason, he was much more likely to spend a Tuesday or a Wednesday night at what he called the Cove of the Mad Ox than he was to avail of that retreat on weekends.

As haphazard as it was, Guy's domestic world likely would have been a welcome change from the *Telegram*, his workplace and his primary social milieu where he spent far too much time. His routine remained spare for a bachelor in his 20s. At times, the apartment set-up served to remind him that he was older than his roomies. Both Bishop and I were students. For us, the university itself offered more varied diversions than the newspaper offered Guy.

Guy valued his friends, but the constants in his world were his writing and his reading. His spare-time consumption of books and magazines was major and an ongoing influence in his life and on his writing.

Another important influence was the Far Greater Bay. Ray tended to head out for Arnold's Cove on a Saturday at least once a month, returning late on Sunday evening to write his Monday column.

Those brief visits were important to him, and even more important to his mother, Alice, who worried about him constantly. George H. was always interested and curious, but much less engaged. "Have Ray got any girlfriends in St. John's?" George asked on one occasion. I suggested, politely, that he should ask him directly. "No good," George said. "Ray don't publish much."

Six months into 1970, Guy's domestic and social issues were eclipsed by more urgent matters.

At the coalface on Duckworth Street, there was a recurrence in early 1970 of Guy's 1969 anxieties. In a perverse way, the columnist missed Joey Smallwood's commandeering presence. The premier's leadership victory in October of 1969 really had been a pit stop on a road to nowhere. If Joey was not a spent force, he had joined the walking dead. The premier was no longer the omnipotent political boss and the satirist's best friend that he had been for so long. For Guy, the game had become less fun.

The first edition of the newspaper for the new decade, on January 2, 1970, did not contain a Ray Guy column. On Monday, January 5, 1970, there was a Guy column, again on page 2, the traditional throwaway page.

Even by his crankiest standards, Guy's opening piece for the new decade was a dyspeptic rant. The column was too realistic and documentary to be fully satirical, and too satirical to be fully reliable. Its target was welfare cheats, or alleged cheats, individuals thought by many Newfoundlanders of the time to be ripping off or gaming a badly managed provincial social security system. After running down a list of for-instances, Guy settled on an individual who, he implied, was an actual case study:

> Far from us to give him away. His cheerful candor and admirable boldness in milking the department to the last drop is a joy to see. Heroes are scarce enough these days.
>
> We will say that he comes from somewhere between the northwest and southeast coast, that he is not yet 30, is married and has a couple of kids.
>
> He was first moved under the government's centralization scheme and hasn't looked back since. He was set

up in the new location with a house and furnishings, a regular check and none of the tiresome bother of work.

After a few months there he had the urge to hit the trail again and was again set up in a community 50 miles distant from the first one. A few more months and he demanded to be moved again, this time a distance of about 10 miles.

He broke the monotony between moves with trips to town by taxi, at government expense, since he understandably refused to put up with the fuss and inconvenience of the CN bus ...

Taxis deliver beer to his door, a neighbor picks up his regular check at the post office for him, and he has obtained a vehicle which by happenstance has a diesel engine. He runs it on stove oil provided free for heating by the department.

It is tempting, and not unreasonable, to speculate that the source of the details of this bitter chronicle was George H. Guy, possibly the driver of one of the taxis that ferried this putative freeloader around his new community. Guy's Christmas vacation in Arnold's Cove would have been replete with such tales of government maladministration, all with kernels of truth, few of them fully researched. If you "find of your back" and have the patience, Guy concluded uncharitably, "you too can be admitted into the circle of the blessed ..."

Guy again found himself on page 2 on January 6. But just as readers might have been thinking he had moved there for good, the same space the next day was occupied by Harold Horwood. Guy showed up on page 6, where Horwood should have been. Like the page 9 placement of his column the previous July, this mercurial treatment of his work angered and depressed him.

Guy figured only one person, managing editor Ennis, could be making those decisions. Perhaps only two people, Guy and Ennis, were giving such decisions even a second thought. Whatever the truth about column placement, by this time Guy and Ennis had become mistrustful of each other. Ennis felt Guy was journalistically careless. Guy felt that Ennis felt that Guy was journalistically careless. Still, Ennis and Guy remained important to each other. If both bristled at times, neither sought confrontation.

This pattern of no pattern continued throughout the month and into February 1970. Guy mainly occupied page 2, but increasingly his column was relegated and hidden: January 9 on page 5, January 14 on page 6, January 16 page 5 again, and on it went.

The January 16, 1970, obscurity of page 5 would have been especially galling for Guy. His traditional page 3 space that day was occupied, in effect, by none other than his nemesis, Smallwood, whose speech to a local service club the previous day was reported there in stenographic detail.

That same day Guy, pleading "a touch of this gout that's on the go and still not the best," had filled his page 5 space with a half-dozen of the most banal Newfoundland jokes then in circulation. This he did with only the slender caveat that "I asked people around *The Telegram* newsroom for their favorite 'Newfie Jokes.' You don't think I'd take the blame myself for this load, do you?" It was a new low. For this thin gruel, page 5 seemed more than adequate. With ups and downs, this trend held throughout the winter and spring of 1970.

On June 17, 1970, Guy appeared on page 2 with an innocuous column of musings about St. John's, inspired, he said, by observing the city from Signal Hill while listening to Beethoven on CBC Stereo. He apologized to the *Telegram*'s excellent music critic, Averill Baker, whose work he admired, for his limited knowledge of classical music. His understanding, he wrote, was that Harry Hibbs was an accordion man, while Beethoven was a piano man. Beethoven sounded fine on Signal Hill. Guy was unaware that the reverie would be short-lived.

The Beethoven column had been written the previous evening, Tuesday, June 16. Like all *Telegram* workers, Guy had no warning of the next day's front-page bombshell that would affect him and his colleagues so profoundly.

Below the top story, which was about the Charles Manson cult murder trial, and just below the fold, *Telegram* workers discovered the only headline that mattered: "*Telegram* Bought by Thomson Group."

Roy, Lord Thomson of Fleet, was an Anglophile Canadian capitalist in the Rupert Murdoch and William Randolph Hearst/ Citizen Kane mode, rapacious and profit obsessed. The Thomson way was to home in on profitable smaller city dailies, preferably in one-newspaper or low-competition markets, and take them over, usually in a friendly way, but otherwise if the occasion demanded.

The post-Confederation *Evening Telegram* was a prime target. The paper was lush, its full-page Water Street ads augmented by pan-Canadian franchise ads for automobile brands and retail giants such as Canadian Tire and Woolworth's. The sale included the *Telegram*'s sister daily, the Corner Brook *Western Star*.

Thomson had offered to buy the *Telegram* several times before but had been rebuffed. Now the planets were in alignment. The newspaper's restrained wages and generally thrifty management were bonuses, as was its editorial and circulation improvements of the Ennis and Guy era. The faltering competition offered by the only other St. John's daily paper, the cash-starved *Daily News*, could safely be ignored.

More importantly, the Herders were motivated to sell. Crippling federal estate taxes were the prevailing issue, and they applied to the Herder family in a dramatic and cruel way. In 1970, the paper was wholly owned by four male Herders, all middle-aged or older, all part of a family cursed congenitally with middle-aged heart failure.

The last surviving member of the great newspapering Herder family to have had hands-on *Telegram* experience is W.J. (Jim) Herder. Jim is the only son of James Milley Herder, "JM," who in 1970 was the publisher and major shareholder of both the *Telegram* and the *Western Star*.

Jim Herder is in his early 70s now (in 2021), a survivor of open heart-valve surgery performed 15 years earlier. Jim credits "the genius Doctor Tyrone David who invented the natural pig replacement valve solution" for his survival: "Hoping the 'Herder hearts' which took many of my uncles, and my Dad, are a thing of the past."

Young Jim, as he was known with some affection by his colleagues, worked at the paper during his high school summers and briefly thereafter. When the sale took place, Jim joined the broader Thomson organization and filled a series of managerial and executive roles in Toronto for half of his career.

Jim left the Thomson company abruptly after 15 years. His ambition had been to be a publisher, possibly even of the *Telegram*. "I certainly had a sense that I would one day work at the *Telegram*," he recalled. With a mid-1980s change in Thomson's senior management, he realized it was not to be. He moved to St. Andrew's College in Aurora, Ontario, his old high school, as Director of Development and president of the college's Foundation, remaining in that job from 1985 to 2008, when he retired.

The story of the sale of the *Telegram* and the *Western Star* was a taxation story, but Jim Herder says the outcome was not foreordained. The constant threat of an estate taxation raid posed by the "Herder Hearts" could have been lessened greatly by transferring the entire business to Young Jim himself. But more profound forces were at play, among them Herder family bonds and gender fairness. Publisher J.M. Herder was by far the paper's largest shareholder. Jim was his only son, but there also were three daughters, and several nieces and nephews. The story is best conveyed in Jim Herder's own words:

> Dad, Hubert and to a lesser degree Steve [because he was a lot younger] had a major problem. How to be fair to their children, and how to treat them all equally?
>
> Were my parents going to leave the majority of shares in The Evening Telegram Limited to me, the only son and the youngest child? And leave virtually nothing to my sisters? No.

If the estate taxes threat had been managed with an outright gift of all of J.M. Herder's shares to Jim, it would have largely dispossessed the Herder sisters. It was not to be. Spreading the shares evenly was deemed not feasible; "a recipe for disaster," Jim said, "perhaps like the position *The Toronto Star* now finds itself in."

With the newspapers already in Thomson's hands, the final bitter irony of the sale was only months away.

> Finance Minister Edgar Benson's changes in the tax code of Canada in its most basic terms eliminated estate tax ... in favour of a new Capital Gains tax ...
>
> Unfortunately for our small branch of the family only, estate taxes stayed in effect until December 31st, 1970. My Dad died on October 25th, 1970.
>
> My mother, my sisters and I paid nearly 50 per cent tax on his estate.
>
> Had Dad lived two and a half more months we would have paid zero ...
>
> My own reaction was simple. I loved the place. I loved when the press started up. I also loved that Dad's pressure cooker had ended and that maybe he would

have time and fun in retirement. I thought he was ancient at age 65, and he had had a pretty good run.

With the sale of the paper, J.M. Herder, the seventh and last living son of the founder, announced his retirement, effective July 31, 1970. Three months later he was dead, at 66.

"Printer's ink ran in his veins," said the October 26, 1970, editorial in the *Telegram*. "He was a working publisher, who was to be found as often in the composing room as in the board room."

Following J.M., his nephew Hubert Herder became publisher. Another nephew, Steve Herder, stayed on as general manager. Both were grandsons of the founder. Both agreed to work for the new owners, Thomson Newspapers. Hubert rarely came to the office after the sale. In 1976, Steve succeeded him as publisher, serving until his retirement in 1991.

For Steve Herder, a man of large emotions, the changes were dramatic events. He was the last Herder to be directly involved in the running of the paper. It was the newspaper his grandfather had founded; the paper that his father, Ralph, had served as publisher for two decades. In one way or another, Newfoundland's newspapering Herders had been at it for 112 years.

The emotional impact of the sale was not limited to the Herder family. Workers at both papers, the *Evening Telegram* in St. John's and the *Western Star* in Corner Brook, were upset and anxious.

Guy was devastated. On the day the sale was announced, he left town, in shock and despair. He took refuge in Arnold's Cove. His sense of an increasingly vague mandate at the paper, and of being personally less in favour than before, was exacerbated by the sale. Like most informed newspaper people, he was fully aware of the Thomson reputation for editorial attrition and frugality. He also saw the change for what it was—another nail in the coffin of Newfoundland and Labrador-owned businesses that in the past at least had operated under the scrutiny of community roots and commitment.

In 1965, Thomson had joked to Mordecai Richler of CBC Television's *This Hour Has Seven Days* that editorial content of newspapers is the stuff that separates the ads. When asked what his favourite music was, Thomson, also the owner of numerous Canadian radio stations, said it was "the sound of radio commercials at 10 bucks a whack." The *Times of London*, Lord Thomson's own newspaper, had once referred to him editorially as "a great rude wind from Canada."

Perhaps the best account of the *Telegram*'s 1970 transition was written by Horwood, who was still writing a column for the paper in June 1970. Among *Telegram* journalists, he was the only intimate of J.M. Herder, the publisher, with whom he shared a love of gardening. In his 1997 memoir, *A Walk in Dreamtime: Growing Up in Old St. John's*, Horwood described the newspaper insightfully, as it had been in 1970 and as it would become:

> The Staff had become more literate. There were university graduates in English and history, and two people on their way to doctorates. Production had been streamlined, and there were great investments in new equipment, computers, teletypes, a photo-engraving department that could produce a 48-page paper daily on zinc plates. Circulation was still rising: the paper was getting bigger, and new features were being added every year.
>
> And then the sky fell.
>
> We woke up one morning to learn that the whole operation had been sold to the Thomson organization. From now on our ultimate boss would be that grinning Philistine, the Right Honourable Lord Thomson of Fleet, who had descended upon Canadian daily

newspapers like the wolf on the fold. The Herders had expanded their two newspapers beyond the limits of their financing. It was either sell out or retrench. Thomson made them an offer they couldn't refuse, and the hundred-year-old family business was swallowed up, absorbed into the mainstream of homogenized garbage that the newspaper chains were spreading across Canada, coast to coast.[54]

On June 18, 1970, the day after the takeover was announced, there was no Ray Guy column, and no explanation for its absence. On Friday, June 19, the weekend edition of the *Telegram* carried the message that "Ray Guy is on vacation" at the bottom of page 3, left, the traditional but by then the less common location of his column. Guy in fact was on vacation by then, although he had had no plans to be away before the announcement. The *Telegram*'s managers, old and new, did not want an unexplained Guy absence to coincide with the Thomson purchase.

A week went by with no further information on when Guy would return. On the Friday of that week, June 26, the *Telegram* reported that its rival St. John's newspaper, the *Daily News*, also had been sold. Its local owner at the time, Andrew Crosbie, brother of John C. Crosbie, sold the paper to another local owner, Edsel Bonnell, who had been its most recent publisher. The article reported the *Daily News* circulation at the time to be 8,300, a distant second to the *Telegram*'s, which was around 20,000 Monday to Thursday, with its Friday weekend edition approaching twice that number.

Guy stayed away until Friday, July 10. He returned to page 2 that day in a relatively buoyant mood. He said he had been on vacation, which was technically true, but only because in those days there was no such thing as paid stress leave. Back at it, he sounded relaxed.

Hello and how's your bobber?

Might just as well strike a few taps for his Lordship, I guess. There's no difference in the color of his money. As long as he knows his place and doesn't stray too much from it there should be no problem. He may be kept on.

In fact, Guy had become bored, as well as depressed. Lord Thomson or not, he did not wish to be outside of the St. John's-centric political and media swirl. The remainder of his July 10 column was conventional political commentary. His next few pieces remained light and bright.

By Thursday, July 16, his mood had swung and his tune had changed. Out poured a creatively packaged and obscure torrent of disregard for the *Telegram*'s new owner.

The ridicule masqueraded as a lesson in Newfoundland history, delivered by Guy's half-demented fictional alter-voice, Aunt Cissy Roach. Aunt Cissy, the ancient and misanthropic witch of the Witless Bay Barrens, was Guy's most outrageous creation. He used Aunt Cissy's voice from time to time for delicate observations that were hard to make directly. Guy's Aunt Cissy pieces, eccentric and obscure, often were undervalued by readers, passed over as frivolous or even bizarre. In fact, they often revealed the writer at his most creative and his most mischievous.

A reader of the July 16, 1970, piece could safely take Aunt Cissy's words for Guy's own feelings about "lords"—peers both hereditary and appointed—and their nefarious role in Newfoundland and Labrador history, culminating, in his view, with His Lordship, the Great Rude Wind from Canada.

Guy had not set out that day to ingratiate himself to his new bosses. The unfortunate fact, however, was that the piece would have played well only to a narrow readership, an exclusive Ray Guy fan club. George Story and Bob Benson would have been delighted;

other insiders would have chuckled. Thomson himself almost certainly would never have seen it, and many in His Lordship's orbit who did might have missed the point completely.

As happened from time to time in his work, Guy's principal audience that day may have been himself and perhaps a few of his friends. He would have been entertained and relieved, enjoying a grand old time getting stuff off his chest, while spinning and sprinkling his narrative with obscure Newfoundland words and phrases—"podauger days" and "crunnick" for example.[55]

Aunt Cissy Roach kept on top of current affairs. She had heard about the Thomson takeover of the *Telegram*:

> "Ah, a fool and his money is soon parted. I don't know about the rest of the parcel but I'd say His Lordship got a poor deal when he bought you, Lantern Jaws. It'll take the whole fall to fatten you up and what'll we have then but a fat, lazy layabout."
>
> "My dear woman," I said snappishly, "I didn't come out here to listen to that kind of nonsense-talk. I took a day out of my paltry few holidays to come out here on a sociable visit, not to be insulted and made sport of in the light of recent transactions."
>
> "I thought you'd be in better trim," continued Aunt Cissy, seating herself on a crunnick in the dooryard of her humble domicile which is located some 13 miles in over the Witless Bay Barrens. "Most Newfoundlanders enjoys being bought and sold. Always have and always will. They thrives on it. Being sold is mother's milk to them.
>
> "Perhaps it is the lack of class that is galling you," continued the ancient anchorite. "The best we can get is Labor lords and Upper Canada hayseeds in satin ceremonial breeches.[56]

"God be with the good old days," sighed Aunt Cissy. "When there was enough of the genuine article to go around. The real McCoys. Title descendants of the bastards of Henry VIII and them dotty and chinless Hanoverian wonders.

"We'd generally get the black sheep but still they was the genuine article. My favorite was the one who used to run stark naked, winter and summer, through Bannerman Park whenever there was a full moon.

"Certainly, I'm prejudiced," said Aunt Cissy, taking another fearsome swig of her medicine. "My father's father had a tiff with a lord of the realm back in podauger days.

"Tied me father's father down across a hatch cover, did his Lordship, the Admiral, and lashed his back to a mummy with a cat o'nine tails. Had a little pan of strong vinegar brought up from the galley and stirred two handfuls of Cadiz rock salt into it. Dipped a piece of oakum into the pan and painted me father's father's back with it, they did."

"But you must remember, Aunt Cissy," I said to her, "this was in the good old rough and ready days when such punishments were the thing for petty criminals."

"Criminal, he was" snickered Aunt Cissy Roach. "Broke the law right and left. Bonded to one of his lordship's friends for five years and ran away. Built a house with windows and a chimney into it on the shore. Tried to make a home in Newfoundland and stay here until they catch him."

It was pleasant indeed to find the elderly lady in such fine spirits and interesting to listen to her colorful anecdotes of days gone by. So heartily did she laugh and slap her skinny flanks that two ravens the size of turkeys perched in one of the rampikes gracing her patio took fright at the uproar and battered off, croaking in terror.[57]

All told, June 1970 had turned out to be a month of action and transformation in Newfoundland's narrow world of publishing.

It had started in the Newfoundland House of Assembly on June 1, when the Smallwood Liberals quashed an opposition motion to reduce funding for the *Newfoundland Bulletin* to $1.

An Opposition member had reported that the floors of rural post offices were littered with discarded copies of the *Bulletin* at the end of every month, an outcome no doubt influenced by Guy's devastating reviews of the Smallwood rag. Another wanted it scrapped and its funding diverted to an adoption promotions program. A Cabinet minister claimed the *Bulletin* had saved the province $100,000 the previous year by carrying photos of children, or "wards," available for adoption. The loquacious John Crosbie called such efforts to justify the *Bulletin* "lame, supine and weak-kneed." The Liberal majority approved continued funding at $140,000, bravely excluding the editor's salary of $12,000.

The sales of the province's three daily newspapers in the same month were historic. The *Evening Telegram* and the *Western Star* have not been locally owned since, and almost certainly will never be again. When the Herder papers changed hands in 1970, the *Daily News* was little more than a decade from disappearing.

Guy soldiered on through 1970 on His Lordship's shilling, diverting himself as best he could. By autumn, the professional ennui he had experienced during the summer of 1970 had receded somewhat, and Guy fell into a temporary groove that kept him even-tempered, less stressed, and frequently entertaining.

By then, he had moved into new shelter, a suburban bungalow in Chamberlains, Conception Bay South. Guy called the new place Chamberpots, mimicking the habit of an older St. John's aristocracy whose summer homes in the same general area always had cute names. Chamberlains was a short commute from downtown St. John's. His father, George H., had purchased the house as an investment property, and to put a permanent roof over the head of his unworldly son.

In Chamberlains, Guy lived alone. His former roommates had scattered. Everett Bishop had graduated and left town. I had moved into a room of my own on campus, the better to pursue activities and interests there. Living with Guy was not a readily forgettable experience. But all three of us had discovered a longing for greater privacy.

During the summer and fall of 1970, Guy benefited from his continuing workplace friendship with Bob Benson, his durable friendship with Wick Collins, and an emerging friendship with reporter Robert Sinclair.

If autumn became more tranquil for Guy, it had not started out that way. Readers on September 2, 1970, were startled by his brief report following the Labour Day long weekend:

> Sorry I didn't get the regular load wheeled along to the market yesterday. The reason for the lapse this time is more unusual than usual. We had the misfortune to be involved in a fire.
>
> I left Monday in company with a colleague [Bob Benson] from the People's Paper in a trailer, intending to see something of the country outside of St. John's. A trailer would be a good compromise, I figured, between a canvas tent and a motel as a protection against slings and arrows of the great outdoors.

The thing started in the night when a heater caught fire and exploded a gallon tank of gas. It seemed no more than a few seconds before the whole thing was going up like a tinder box. Anyhow it was a nightmarish business while it lasted.

Guy was not injured in the fire, but Benson received serious hand and arm burns and was hospitalized.

Guy rounded out the autumn with a mix of political and non-political daily columns, drawing more heavily than usual on Aunt Cissy Roach and Outharbour Delights. He also produced some excellent and straightforward journalism.

There were fresh auguries of impending change at the newspaper that fall. Thomson "suits" were in greater evidence, portending nothing good. At least Ennis remained in charge of editorial matters. And Steve Herder still sauntered through the newsroom with his tall and friendly presence, his work no doubt being assessed by Thomson bean-counters half his age. But so far no one had asked Guy to do anything different and so far no jobs had been lost. If there can be a phony war, there can be phony peace. For Guy, autumn 1970 had its distractions, and the Thomson matter was not always top of mind.

Since June 1970, there had been storm clouds of a more ominous nature gathering on the distant horizon. In December, those clouds burst, and the malaise that Guy had experienced in the summer and fall 1970 received a sudden and unexpected jolt from a most unlikely source, a Canadian senator.

For a year or more, Liberal senator and power broker Keith Davey, known as the rainmaker in federal Liberal Party circles, had been leading a group of senators studying Canadian media, primarily newspapers. Davey's three-volume report, *The Uncertain Mirror*, was a detailed, provocative document. The report summarized the Newfoundland and Labrador media landscape in two terse sentences:

"In 1970 the Herder family sold two of the provinces three dailies to the Thomson group. Geoffrey Stirling controls one radio station, and one of the two TV stations in St. John's which accounts for 46.2 per cent of the province's total TV circulation."

Beyond the raw facts, it was the report's stark forecasts of the fate and future of newspapers under increasingly concentrated ownership that hit Guy and his colleagues the hardest. One widely cited paragraph was especially bitter for all Canadian newspaper journalists:

> The most insidious effect of journalistic monopolies, however, is the atmosphere they breed. Every reporter soon learns that there are only a few newspapers where excellence is encouraged. If they are lucky or clever or restless, they will gravitate to those newspapers. If not they will stay where they are, growing cynical about their work, learning to live with a kind of sour professional despair. Often you can see it in their faces. Most city-rooms are bone-yards of broken dreams.

Boneyards of broken dreams!

When Guy scanned the Davey report, he wrote that he had never read anything in his life with which he so fully agreed. His dramatic column of December 10, 1970, read like his professional obituary:

> I've come at last to the column it is impossible to write.
> For most of the day and half the night the teletype machines in The Telegram newsroom have been chattering out articles on the report of the Senate Committee on the press ...

I've read all that's come in on the teletype so far and find myself explaining at nearly every paragraph "Exactly! Exactly! Exactly!"

... Obviously this lad's role right now on the senate committee findings (is to) make reference to the local press. This is impossible. Such a column would never see the light of day.

Obviously, such a column was not impossible. Guy delivered 1,000 words or so on precisely that topic, alternately insulting his employers, who were by no means censorious, while adding a layer of uncharacteristic bathos to the effort.

To comment and give all the facts as I see them on the local press would mean that I would have to tell all the ins and outs I know about The Telegram which forms a big part of the local press.

The Telegram would never print such a column. The only possible chance I'd have of getting such an article in print would be to pass in my resignation and shuffle off with my grubby manuscript in a brown envelope and submit to some "underground" newspaper of which the only local equivalent is the university student journal, the Muse.

In that same column, Guy drew an unconvincing comparison between journalists who know where the bodies are buried and Cabinet ministers who take oaths of secrecy requiring them to conceal information that they believe the public should have. At some point, he contends, either one may have to decide to "cross the House" or not:

...To cut this rigmarole short one offers by way of illustration a personal example.

At this moment I am part of The Telegram and The Telegram is part of me; same is true of all hands here. This implies two things:

(1) to date The Telegram believes that I have done wrong by it at no more than 49 per cent of the time and that I have done right by it no less than 51 per cent of the time.

(2) To date I have been ashamed of The Telegram no more than 49 per cent of the time and I have been proud of The Telegram no less than 51 per cent of the time.

It was all too ponderous. Better placed, perhaps, was his reference to a World War I cartoon which showed two bedraggled British soldiers in the same foxhole.

There's mud and shrapnel and bullets flying around and one of the two is obviously having a royal old bitch for himself. "Look mate," says the other, "if you knows a better hole then hop to it."

Guy was honest about his emotions and his reactions to the sale of the *Telegram* and to the Davey Committee report. But he was no longer sure of his footing, not fully confident in the reasoning with which he approached the topics.

He ignored one glaring contradiction. Once he had alluded coyly to secrets and goings-on inside the newspaper so dark that to reveal them he would have to fall on his sword, he had done at least as much damage as if he had rolled it all out in chapter and verse.

If Guy's column that day appeared to have been over the top, there may have been more to it than met the eye. Intuitive as ever, he was absorbing and reflecting the changing tone inside the newspaper. Ennis's own evolving mood was part of it, as were some of the grim truths about Guy's chosen profession that Davey had exposed, truths made grimmer than ever since by the sale of the *Evening Telegram*.

The words of the Davey report echoed in Guy's ear. Davey could find very few places of refuge for good print journalists. The number of quality newspapers was declining.

"If they (journalists) are lucky or clever or restless, they will gravitate to those newspapers," Davey had written. Guy was clever and restless enough, but in 1970 he did not feel lucky. Where might be those tolerant and independent publications that would share his commitment to Newfoundland and Labrador, that would publish his unique and uncompromising prose?

Could one of them be the *Toronto Daily Star*?

Guy wrote several good columns for the *Star* in the late 1970s, but eventually he gave it up, complaining that he had to explain too many local references. "Pretty soon it will be all footnotes and no column."

The Toronto *Globe and Mail*?

The *Globe* tended to notice Newfoundland and Labrador during provincial and federal elections, or when a prime minister visited; or, occasionally, when the colourful Premier Smallwood poked a stick in the Ottawa cage, as he did in 1959 when he declared three days of mourning and a half-masting of provincial flags in an arcane dispute with Prime Minister John Diefenbaker over Term 29 of the Newfoundland-Canada contract. The so-called national newspaper has never had a Newfoundland bureau.

And what of the CBC?

The public broadcaster would be large in Guy's future, but many years away. Despite its emerging focus on television news and current affairs, and its established respectability as a purveyor of straight-up local radio news, the CBC in 1970 appeared to Guy to be almost a foreign medium, its broadcast journalism an alien and different trade for which he had little training.

In 1970, the print man, the satirist, the established newspaper columnist could no more see himself joining "the sandal-shod minions of the CBC," as he called them, than he could see himself reporting to Geoff Stirling at CJON. Guy usually referred to Stirling's station as CJRS—the JRS for Joseph Roberts Smallwood.

Newsrooms are chronically understaffed, the Davey report observed. "The turnover in personnel is scandalous, and the best people, unless they have a penchant for personal philanthropy, frequently move to some other industry, such as advertising or public relations, where talent is recognized and rewarded."

As 1970 career choices for Guy, only advertising and public relations were further out of the question than the timorous CBC or Stirling's CJRS.

In a matter of months, Lord Thomson of Fleet and Senator Keith Davey had entered Ray Guy's world. They had changed it forever.

CHAPTER 14
The Writing on the Wall

Managing Editor Robert J. Ennis, Guy's erstwhile promoter and champion, greatly influenced the changing culture of the *Evening Telegram*. At the same time, a measure of mutual disenchantment between Ennis and Guy increased Guy's discomfort at the newspaper.

In the mid-1960s, Ennis and Guy, while not close friends, were sympatico and functional colleagues. Ennis's vision of the newspaper, strong on feature reporting and politically charged commentary, embraced and encouraged Guy's strengths.

By the end of the 1960s, Ennis was looking for something more than satire and commentary to distinguish the *Telegram*, especially in the realm of political journalism. He instigated a shift toward a different kind of political reporting, more breaking news oriented, more research oriented; more empirical, less interpretative.

Behind the scenes, an uncharacteristic decline in the traditional confidence of the Herders had set in like arthritis. It had been absent or well camouflaged prior to the Thomson deal. Soon after, it was obvious that the Herders were no longer in charge.

By 1971, Ennis, while remaining professional and outwardly supportive of Guy, harboured a more constant mistrust, an occasionally accurate but often exaggerated suspicion that Guy at times over-reported what he had under-researched.

Such suspicions were inevitable. Guy's brand of journalism was difficult to compartmentalize. As a reporter, he was expected to be as factual and neutral as possible. As a satirist, he had licence to exaggerate and create. For editors, the problem was complicated by the fact that Guy's columns and his news and feature writing were not water-tight compartments. Often there was news in his columns, and opinion in his feature stories. His straight news reporting, however, generally was as "objective" as most reporting ever is.

Objectivity, like balance, is a quaint and rather unhelpful term in journalism, implying that every opinion can be offset in an equal and opposite one. Even if two opposing views of equal weight can ever be found and set against each other, the third component in the equation, the reporter, remains a wild card. All reporters, and Guy is an excellent case study, bring personal life history and perspectives to every story. To pretend those have no impact on the product is to be naïve.

Fairness is a more achievable goal in journalism. Reporters can earn public trust and reputations for fairness by being hard-working and respectful, by demonstrating a curious and probing approach in their work, by acknowledging the limitations of their role, and by demonstrably working for their readers, listeners, and viewers.

After 1965, Guy did little routine news reporting. His writing soon became sufficiently interesting and entertaining that most readers did not fret much about the nuances of information versus opinion. But editors are paid to scrutinize content. Ennis was paid to protect the *Telegram*'s credibility and keep it out of court. As the Thomson screw tightened, not even he could be confident of management's full support, whether for his continuing tolerance of Guy or for his efforts to strengthen new journalistic approaches.

Despite his emerging misgivings, Ennis had always found plenty to admire in Guy:

> While he may have cultivated the rumpled-fellow image (joked about only changing his socks when they stuck to the wall, making wine in the bathtub) I never got the sense he was personally sloppy. There was no doubt though about how meticulous he was about his craft. He was very particular about his material. He would stop and start and re-work pieces over and over. In the end the copy that he turned in was immaculate. Three and half to four pages. Seldom were there even typos or spelling errors.

Ennis acknowledged a gradual shift in his attitude toward Guy as they worked together. They had started out much friendlier, but "somewhere along the way there I reached the point where I couldn't rely on Ray's discretion."

> At times he was difficult. There were times, especially in the beginning, when he and I would disagree. Being a regular columnist was new to him and having to deal with a satirical columnist like Ray was new to me.

With Guy's evolution from reporter to feature writer to columnist came new challenges. Ennis seldom took up any matters with the Herders, but Guy believed the opposite, that the Herders, especially

Steve, were constantly involved, and that Ennis was caught in the middle.

One flashpoint occurred when Guy wrote a series of columns about the apartment building where he was living at the time. Ennis recalled that some of them were funny, but there were a few too many.

> Any one of them on its own was fair comment and probably not libelous, and we let him run with it. Like everyone else I was getting a kick out of it. But one day, I don't recall why, I had referred another matter to our lawyer. While the lawyer had my attention, he pointed out to me that it looked as if Ray was using The Telegram as his weapon in a fight with his landlord and collectively his articles could be libelous ... So, I basically put it to Ray that if he had nothing new to say, he should just move on.

Guy began referring to Ennis as "the genteel parlour editor." That label did not fit Ennis, and he resented it. Other forces amplified the tension. For Guy, as Ennis acknowledged, it was the stress of a daily deadline, the daunting 20,000 or so words a month, the equivalent of a small book. As well, Guy—rain or shine, melancholy or buoyant—was always expected to be funny. Ennis understood. "On more than one occasion I remember him lamenting the expectation that we wanted him to be funny was the heaviest of all burdens."

For Ennis, part of the struggle was the daily tension of vetting a columnist who was brilliant and funny, but who also could be cruel and, in Ennis's opinion, sometimes careless with the facts. He liked to handle Guy's copy personally, but there was little time to do so each day before the late morning roll of the presses. Guy was rarely on deck for consultation before 11 a.m. Ennis worried about the column, but he also was aware he had a thoroughbred on his hands. The result was that Guy was edited sparingly.

Other and more complex roots to tensions between Ennis and Guy are harder to calibrate. They related to an unfortunate dynamic between them, of which they were both aware. Guy spoke of it only in veiled innuendo. Ennis hoped to ignore it. It had to do with religion.

Going back to around 1968, Ennis used to host occasional weekend get-togethers with a cluster of *Telegram* reporters, usually including Guy, Associate Editor Wick Collins, Canadian Press man Dave Butler, and others, including spouses. One regular guest was Father Patrick Kennedy, a local priest and communications person for The Roman Catholic Archdiocese of St. John's.

"Discussions were often rambunctious," Ennis recalled, "especially with Wick and Father Pat. Ray occasionally interjected, but usually sat back and let others do the arguing."

Kennedy was Ennis's friend. There could hardly be any reason why a friend who happened to be a priest should not be asked over for a drink. Moreover, Kennedy was a communications man, interested in the media and engaged in the affairs of both church and state. Guy saw it differently. The evenings at Ennis's house with Kennedy made Guy uncomfortable.

With justification in 1960s Newfoundland, Guy regarded the Catholic Church and indeed all local church hierarchies as political entities, partisan players in the public affairs of the province. That certainly was the case in major government policy matters such as education and health care.

Partying with Kennedy was for Guy a bit like partying with Smallwood Cabinet ministers. Guy, along with most *Telegram* reporters of his era, made it a firm rule not to associate with the Smallwood people on anything approximating a personal or social basis.

There may be danger of overstating the business of sectarian influences at the *Telegram* and other Newfoundland media in the late 1960s and on into the 1970s. There would be much greater risk in ignoring them altogether.

It was from the mid-1970s into the 1980s, after both Ennis's watch and Guy's tenure, that religious influences on the *Telegram* and other St. John's media had profoundly negative consequences.

The sexual predation scandals at the Mount Cashel Orphanage were well known in certain St. John's circles long before they became public knowledge. By the mid- to late 1970s, scores if not hundreds of powerful people knew of those scandals, and remained silent. At various points, that knowledge was suppressed by most public institutions in Newfoundland, the Provincial Justice Department and all major media outlets among them.

At the *Telegram* in 1976, publisher Steve Herder killed a Mount Cashel story generated by two of his top reporters, Bill Kelly and Bob Wakeham, which had the potential to explode scandal a decade and a half before that happened. Kelly had an impeccable source for his information inside the Catholic Church hierarchy itself. His information was vague about the actual nature and magnitude of the scandal, but solid in that it included the fact that three Irish Christian Brothers who had been teaching at the orphanage had been sent out of the province for their involvement.

Kelly's source was Gabriel McHugh, a powerful Irish Christian Brother who was investigating the matter on behalf of the Catholic Archdiocese of St. John's, ultimately for the Vatican. McHugh admitted a problem to Kelly but tried to downplay its severity with terms such as "fondling" and "corporal punishment." He also attempted to persuade Kelly that the story should not be published.

Both Kelly and Wakeham, who had firm but incomplete corroborating information from unidentified police sources, felt they had enough material, soundly sourced, to merit the newspaper's front page.

Herder concluded, ignominiously, that the story in that form would do more harm than good, a phrase that seemed to echo the words of McHugh himself. The story was spiked. Fourteen years later the raw details of the extreme sexual abuse of young boys by the Brothers at Mount Cashel finally saw the light of day in a newspaper. That paper was the weekly *Sunday Express*, whose publisher was Michael Harris, and one of whose star columnists was Ray Guy.[58]

As for his own religious views, Guy ultimately would have wished a plague on all their houses—basilicas, mosques, synagogues, and cathedrals alike.

But it is also true Guy also could be offhandedly cryptic and cynical in his comments about religion, occasionally fuelling accusations of bigotry. Anyone highly tuned to religious or political slights sooner or later would find one, or at least imagine one, in Guy's writing. Persons of the Roman Catholic persuasion in 1960s St. John's, by far the province's most cohesive and focused denominational force, might detect them more readily than others, just as Liberal Party loyalists would have in the political realm. Guy, culturally Church of England but theologically indistinct, was certainly not a bigot. He was, however, a notorious provocateur. The more sacred the cow, the more Guy saw it as steak.

Ray Guy tiptoed back into the *Telegram*'s pages in 1971, finally showing up in print on Monday, January 12.

The external political temperature was unusually low. Inside the newspaper, with the new owners in place, the Davey report still casting a shadow, and with his own generous dollop of paranoia, the new year did not strike Guy as welcoming. But he arrived back in print in a whimsical frame of mind. His January 12 topic was olfactory sensitivities, a treatise on odours, on which matters he waxed both amusing and insightful.

He declared the smell of earth to be male, and the smell of salt water to be female. He then moved to somewhat firmer ground by recalling the odour of church on Sunday as experienced by an outharbour juvenile:

> A bell in a steeple will give him a mental whiff of that bottle of scent known as "Evening in Church." It was the ruddy boredom that makes the churchy smell linger in memory.
>
> Smelling was about the only diversion left open to him. He could get away for only a minute or two fluttering his palms on his ears to make the hymns sound like acid rock music. An unobtrusive but telling clout to the short ribs cut that off in a hurry.
>
> He couldn't look around to see how people were putting their mouths in all shapes singing while the rest of their face remained deadly serious. He could only sit there and smell.
>
> Dust and dilapidated cobwebs. Sun-warmed varnish. Mothballs off people's Sunday suits. Musty prayer books. Puffs of sharp coal smoke from the backfiring stoves. Aluminum paint or "Black Dazzle" on the stove pipes burning. A sniff of chilled blood from the coppers for the plate. Liniment and Friars Balsam and oil of wintergreen with which the old anointed themselves continuously. That's what the sound of a church bell smells like.

Whimsy pursued Guy into the following day's column. The result was a localized version of *The Devil's Dictionary*, a satirical dictionary written in 1911 by American journalist and soldier Ambrose

Bierce. In it, Bierce defined egotist as, "(noun) a person of low taste, more interested in himself than in me." He defined a lawyer as, "(noun) one skilled in circumvention of the law." And he defined marriage as; "(noun) a household consisting of a master, a mistress, and two slaves, making in all, two."

Guy launched his own devilish dictionary with some localized and competitive constructs:

> Executive Assistants (Cabinet) ... Six $10,000 a year scrub nurses to be recruited from among the local press—the news of which has got one half the corps trembling with anticipation under their ragged garments and the other half holding out for a 99-year lease on the Funks.
>
> University ... A Young People's Home; a social welfare institution in which those facing young age may rest happy and content and want for nothing in their sunrise years.
>
> The Hit Parade ... The nasal screams of jungle savages in heat alternating with the mewlings of tubercular Victorian spinsters.
>
> Genteel-Parlor Editors ... The sort who will change a certain phrase in a column to "Charts" and Vulture Centre and who have to look up the weather reports to see which way the wind blows.

This latter entry touched raw nerves. Guy the satirist usually referred to the city's foremost theatre, the Arts and Culture Centre, as "The Tarts and Vulture Centre." Obviously, some vandal on the news desk had deemed "tarts" too tart for the *Telegram* in the 1970s. The parlour editor entry, meanwhile, was a shot across Ennis's bow—an unsubtle shot, and unnecessarily bitter.

Guy's devilish dictionary would reappear from time to time. He regarded it as a quick and easy fix on days when the news was uninspiring or a rare occasion when Guy found something more interesting than work to do on a weekday evening.

Ray Guy's misgivings about the *Telegram*, about his own future, and about Newfoundland's, were not constant obsessions in 1971. Along the way, he continued to write some of the best satire of his career.

Guy enjoyed and generally worked with a strain of Newfoundland humour that involved satirical sendups of activities or events that seemed absurd to him, requiring little embellishment. The late 1960s and early 1970s brought a flowering of artistic endeavours that were not exactly native to Newfoundland—locally written stage plays, filmmaking, and rock and roll music among them. All encountered potholes on the road to many successes. Guy tended to give all such cultural manifestations shorter shrift than many of them deserved.

Films such as *The Rowdyman* drove Guy crazy with every swagger of every outport macho thug and every lovely-tell-your-mudder Newfie cliché. Ironically, the film was written by and starred Gordon Pinsent, one of the province's best actors, who years later would become a Guy friend and collaborator.

Guy lampooned certain supposedly authentic local dramas, including the stage play *The Head, Guts and Sound Bone Dance*, written by fellow *Telegram* columnist, Michael Cook. In Cook's play, authentication efforts included an actor playing a fisherman urinating into a bucket onstage at Guy's Tarts and Vulture Centre. The play was about fishermen, and the fisherman, after all, stood on a stage. Guy joked that he would write his own play in the *Head*,

Guts vein, which he proposed to call *The Head, Guts, Sound Bone, Slub, Gurry, and Manure Dance.*

Guy also loathed the very name of a good local rock band of the time, The Philadelphia Cream Cheese. The band later evolved into the justly famous traditional folk band Figgy Duff, more acceptably renamed for a soggy Newfoundland pudding with the texture of a sponge cushion.

It was in this take-no-artistic-prisoners frame of mind that Guy penned a memorable column of February 23, 1971, proposing his own Newfoundland feature film.

> Here is but a rough outline of the pivotal film of the early 1970s, which will no doubt have Pauline Kael groping for fresh adjectives and will, for once, leave Dwight MacDonald without a word in his cheek [Kael and MacDonald were celebrated mid-20th century US writers and film critics for magazines such as the *New Yorker* and the *Partisan Review*].
>
> Remy Martin, our hero, is washed ashore at an early age in an otherwise-empty wooden crate of the same name on a beach near the picturesque fishing village of Little Scummy Cove on the south coast of Newfoundland. His origin remains a mystery for there is nothing to tell from whence the infant came save a scrap of battleship linoleum clutched tightly in his left fist and inscribed with the enigmatic words, "Mangez de la merde."
>
> Through a fortuitous circumstance, this water-borne waif is discovered before the gulls could get at him by Wish and Abby Puddester, simple fisherfolk who with wordless gratitude accept this gift from the sea and take the child to raise as their own.

Our story, then, is the Pinteresque—some would say Dali-esque, most would say nothing at all—tale of Remy as he grows to childhood, boyhood, adulthood and lumhood, for in the end he becomes the elemental hoodlum with overtones of Gertrude Stein.

Played out among the exquisite and eternal realities of Little Scummy Cove with that aqueous pixie, the North Atlantic, lending spumy counterpoint to the drama, this motion picture will ask nothing of either "Citizen Kane" or "Ryan's Daughter," lacking, as it will, the existential dearth of the former and the chauvinistic sexist rip-off of the latter.

As with much of Guy's writing, this fine piece of nonsense is full of associations, obscurities, curiosities, and unique coinages. Readers of sufficient age and interest who can recall the great British comedian Ronnie Corbett may well hear echoes. Many references would baffle a modern reader. A few would have baffled a contemporary Ray Guy fan. One, however, had a distinct ring of political currency: mangez de la merde.

Only a few days earlier, on February 17, Guy had written about an occurrence in the House of Commons in Ottawa where Prime Minister Pierre Trudeau (Papa) had lost patience with persistent questions from John Lundrigan, a bold and disputatious Newfoundland Tory MP. Trudeau told the nagging Lundrigan, *sotto voce*, but unmistakably, to fuck off. Trudeau later explained that he had merely said something like "fuddle duddle."

When Guy first wrote about the incident, he recalled that Trudeau a week earlier had rolled down the window of his limousine and told some protesting truckers to *mangez de la merde*. Guy was amused by the fact that while the Trudeau phrase was reported verbatim in the French media, the English Canadian Press reported only that the Trudeau comment was the equivalent of "go to hell," which does not carry the same dismissive freight.

Guy also lamented that Parliamentary decorum prevented Lundrigan from answering Trudeau with a volley of fine Newfoundland cursing which he said should include "the classic introductory 'be the lard liftin' ... followed by a riddle of adjectival clauses chasing a tumble of improper nouns all mixed together with Biblical exhortations of the most inspiring sort."

As for certain obscurities in his movie column: who today will know that the name "Wish" is short for Aloysius, a common Newfoundland male name of the era, pronounced allah-wishes?"

"Lumhood?" This would appear to be an original Guy coinage: hoodlum inverted.

Meanwhile, the expression "most people would say nothing at all" is either homage to, or plagiarism of, the early 1960s British satirical *Beyond the Fringe* stage reviews. The *Fringe* troupe included Dudley Moore, Peter Cook, Jonathan Miller, and Alan Bennett. Guy had his own vinyl recordings of their stage shows and had heard them first in his early 20s. Their impact could be detected often in his work.

Until October of 1971, Ray Guy remained productive and punctual, his work at times outstanding. The Thomson newsroom was doing business more or less as usual. In other corners of the Duckworth Street building, however, there were mounting tensions.

Mutinies on ships usually start below deck, well away from the officers on the bridge. At the *Telegram*, the first wave of rebellion against the paper's new owners started in the basement composing room in response to two Thomson initiatives directly adverse to the interests of the compositors and a threat to all hands, on deck and below.

The new owners had moved the paper to six-day-a-week publication. The traditional fat Friday weekend edition was bolstered by syndicated comics, meat-and-potatoes feature reports by "Telegram Staff Writers," and the "bush notes"—homely dispatches from outport stringers. All were moved to Saturday, annoying both staff and many readers. Along with adding an extra publication day, the Thomson brass implemented an unstated policy of not filling vacant jobs. The policy was beginning to bite.

Bill Gillespie, a former *Telegram* reporter and subsequently a CBC national radio reporter and foreign correspondent, reported in the *Alternate Press* that between the Thomson purchase in June 1970 and the end of 1971, the paper's payroll dropped from more than 200 employees to 151, a 25 per cent smaller staff to produce a 20 per cent bigger product.

The rollback ended a four-year trend in which 15 new employees a year had been added to the payroll. Another trend also ended: circulation had risen since 1965 by 2,000 subscribers a year on weekdays and 1,500 a year on weekends. As Gillespie reported:

> By 1970 the paper had over 50 people gathering and compiling news, including one person whose time was completely devoted to doing features as well as a summer employment program which hired at least five students each summer in the newsroom alone, a system of high school correspondents and a university correspondent.
>
> And despite the expansion the paper was not coming anywhere close to losing money. In fact the position of *The Evening Telegram* had become so strong, partly due to the decline of the only rival, *The Daily News* and partly due to its continuing improvement, that it had a virtual monopoly on local ad revenues. As Bill Doody, now an MHA but then manager of Duff's

Supermarket, once said in a letter to *The Telegram* after they raised their ad rates 15 per cent, "Thank you for not raising them 30 per cent; we would still have to advertise with you in any case."[59]

Two other grievances were in play. The paper was moving away from hot metal type production and gradually toward a cold offset process in which columns are pasted onto paper backgrounds and replicated photographically. The jobs involved were fewer and less skilled.

Young Jim Herder watched the flow of events despairingly from his position as a Thomson executive in Toronto. His loyalty to his new employers, who treated him well, could not obscure the distressing reality in St. John's:

> The changes Thomson made to *The Evening Telegram* were like the changes they made elsewhere when they acquired a newspaper. While Roy Thomson assured my father that there would be "no editorial interference" from head office, he was right, but the elephant in the room was staffing. Roy was a man of his word, and never interfered with the editorial position of the newspaper. However, I think there were 58 people in the newsroom when Thomson Newspapers Limited bought *The Evening Telegram* in 1970. That number came under review almost immediately to reduce costs and increase profit.
>
> When reporters left they were not replaced. When columnists retired, they were likely not replaced.
>
> Investigative journalists of which *The Telegram* had the best in the province, if not the Atlantic provinces, moved elsewhere. They were "not replaced."
>
> It was insidious ...

A new and dangerous dynamic at the Thomson *Telegram* was that staff and management, traditionally functional allies if not close friends, were becoming hostile foes.

On October 20, 1971, 53 members of Local 441 of the St. John's Allied Printers Union walked out on a wildcat strike, in part because the paper was publishing six days a week instead of the traditional five. Ennis and Guy, both non-union staff members, were surprised that morning when they were confronted by pickets at the Duckworth Street main entrance to the newspaper. Ennis, arriving early, said good morning to his younger brother, Gerry, a photo engraver who was a member of the union's executive. He then crossed the picket line unobstructed and took the elevator to the third-floor newsroom where he prepared for a busy day.

Guy arrived much later, chatted with the boys on the line for a while, then climbed back into his Volvo and drove off. The strike lasted three days. Guy was gone three months.

Greg Davis, who wrote a master's thesis on Guy at Memorial University, reported that a sizeable public clamoured for the columnist's return through letters to the newspaper: "Approximately one letter a day was published in the Telegram until Guy returned eighty-six days later in January 1972."[60]

Guy softened his return to the *Telegram* on Tuesday, January 18, 1972, with light satire. His column occupied its once-customary page 3 slot. He decided to interview himself, in the process sending up some current Ottawa Unemployment Insurance jargon, while paying mock homage to a recent retirement speech by Smallwood. The UIC froth of the day included a designation of certain recipients as "unemployed employables."

Joey had allowed that he had felt like "a boy out of school" the day he retired. Guy picked up both themes:

"I feel like a boy out of school," remarked Ray Guy on Thursday after announcing his resignation as an unemployed employable living in his parents' house for almost six consecutive weeks thus becoming something of a legend in his own time.

"My career has now come full circle," said the personable pop-gutted former unemployed employable who started a daily column in the People's Paper on Tuesday. "I now am back to where I left off two months ago at my first love, Journalism."

Mr. Guy, who had announced in late October that he would put his legs under his father's table only until he could find another half-decent job, says the verdict now is clear and it is his plain and simply duty to resign.

Final judgment was handed down Jan. 5 when his mother said: "You have been lying around the house having a nice rest up for nearly six weeks and it is high time you got back to work." He says he took this as a clear mandate.

"I will now go on to my career or writing," he said. "It is the only trade I have. The crookedness and contrariness with which God blessed me will not henceforth be wasted but will be used by me in another field of service to Newfoundland."

Despite increasing insecurities about the future of the *Telegram* and his own, for much of 1971 and most of 1972 Guy was largely distracted by a relentless parade of bizarre political events.

January 1972 may have been the lowest point in Newfoundland's political affairs since 1934 when as "Britain's Oldest Colony" it forfeited responsible government and fell under the rule of a London-appointed commission.

Following an inconclusive October 1971 election, Smallwood had gathered his battered wagons in an ever-diminishing circle around the Confederation Building and blundered on. But by January the ping-ponging, one-or-two-person margins of power had shifted to Conservative Party leader Frank Moores. Smallwood at last resigned, an unemployed unemployable.

For Guy, these events portended great change, a significant fork in the road. Could he ever again be inspired to write as he had when Smallwood was the target that loomed larger than all others? As it turned out, Smallwood hung around the fringes of Newfoundland politics for a few more years, essentially getting in the way and hobbling his own former party. Guy too hung in, generally writing well, but his political satire was less consistent and less fearsome than in the past.

There had been just too many changes.

CHAPTER 15
The Long Goodbye

Rumours, false hopes, false promises, false charges, false
economic thinking ... must be cleansed from the body politic.
—*Frank Moores, January 30, 1970*

Rumours, false hopes, false promises, false charges, false
economic thinking, false teeth, false faces, and falsies ...
must be cleansed from the body politic.
—*Ray Guy, around the same time*

Divorce has two speeds: the Nevada-inspired, add-water-and-stir
version; and the interminable and tortuous kind. Decisive couples
might acknowledge incompatibility or infidelity on a Friday, have
moving vans at the door by Saturday at noon, and be on dating
sites by Monday. Others rag the puck forever, moving in and out,
sometimes dodging extortionist legal fees by the reliable expedient
of dying.

Though he lived to tell the tale, Ray Guy's divorce from Lord
Thomson's *Evening Telegram* was the tortuous type, commencing in
1971 and ending in 1974, when he left the paper awkwardly. There
were brief return flirtations in 1976 and in the 1980s and 1990s as
local *Telegram* management periodically changed and rediscovered
him for weekly or Sunday edition columns.

For Guy, the *Telegram* of his salad days had been much more than a job. There was a symbiotic relationship, one that entailed commitment, supported by bonds of affection and creative tension. By 1971, with the Thomson corporate culture fully at play and Smallwood teetering, much of the good had gone out of it. It was time, and Guy knew it. He expressed it to me and to other friends. But the break-up was easier to imagine than to achieve.

Quality peaks and valleys marked his early 1970s columns. In the early months of 1973, a valley, Guy wrote numerous columns that betrayed a distance from his work and general lack of enthusiasm. But even as his work grew less consistent, outstanding peaks could be found.

Guy could still flash sharp satirical teeth when the subject was politics and the new Moores government. To Guy, regime change looked more like regime continuity. His column of February 8, 1973, was headed "The Restructuring of Mr. Shaheen." It castigated the Moores and John Crosbie Tories for their reversal of attitude toward oil refinery promoter John Shaheen, one of the devils incarnate of Smallwood's industrial debacles.

> We recall some of the many endearments. "This is a piece of Shaheenery," cried Mr. Crosbie during the long but hot summer of 1968.
>
> "The only risk Shaheen is taking in this deal," he charged, "is the risk that the people of Newfoundland might change the government and stop this highway robbery."
>
> At one point while objecting to a clause in the Come by Chance deal, Mr. Crosbie decried the concessions and remarked that "Shaheen already has the premier by something I won't mention."

BREAKFAST AT CLARIDGE'S

Having been in receipt of such hard usage from the PCs in the past Mr. Shaheen seems to have found it in his heart to forgive them.

The whole kit and caboodle of them have been over in London ensconced in one of the most exclusive and expensive hotels in the world (poor Mr. Smallwood preferred the equally high-toned Savoy) with Shaheen in their midst ...

For his part, Mr. Moores has seen fit to severely chastise two members of the local press and it must be coincidental that those same two parties have recently been sued for libel by Mr. Shaheen.

It is all very cozy.

Guy's columns, and *Telegram* reporting generally, prompted one Moores Cabinet minister to label the newspaper "a cesspool of cynics," and another to declare that the paper appeared to want the province to have no government at all. Guy responded that he regarded cesspool of cynics as a delightful phrase. "If I had the means I would set up a social club for colleagues with that name on it. It has a certain 18th century London ring about it."

Other topics inspired him. Another February 1973 column was as insightful and biting as any that had gone before. His subject was the rise of a yuppified Newfoundland middle class.

Guy referred to an article he had read in the *Times of London* written by John Masters, a mid-century British writer best known for the novel *Bhowani Junction*. Guy knew this book, although he misspelled the title in his column. Such a glitch was an occupational hazard for a columnist who wrote late at night without the benefit of Google or even an encyclopedia; indeed, without even a roommate at home who might be called to search for the book on his own dishevelled bookshelves.

Masters, who looked askance at all colonial outposts, including his native India, had visited Newfoundland and written about it, lamenting the absence of a "stabilizing and energizing" middle class. Guy begged to differ, and he undertook to set the record straight. The column was more than just funny. It was one of his few statements about his own preferred rungs on the social and economic ladder.

Everyone to his fancy. Personally I have always thought that the only interesting people were the filthy rich or the filthy poor and that the classes in between are dishwater dull creatures who care about their clothes and tend to go on about Swedish crystalware and lawn-mowers with push-button start.

At any rate, the "deficiency" is rapidly being made good. There are manifestations of this on every hand. The vacuum is being filled by an influx of professors and doctors, lawyers and contractors, branch managers and top civil servants.

By their consumption ye shall know them. "Gourmet food" sections have appeared in the supermarkets. Glass and cedar houses in the $50,000–$100,000 class are springing up on meadows just outside the city ...

A new lighting fixture shop features $1,000 to $6,000 chandeliers in its window, there is much knowledgeable chatter about wines, it is bemoaned that Portugal has become cluttered with secretaries and teachers in the summer and that Florida is awash in outharbor shopkeepers and retired rural magistrates in winter ...

It takes a growing middle class to act as fertile ground for those trends because only they read *Time Magazine*, watch the *CBC National*, have some money and are easily bored.

The filthy rich read only the *National Geographic*
and the filthy poor read only the Eaton's catalogue.
Cheer up, though. Only you read Ray Guy.[61]

Other columns were barometers of Guy's disenchantment with the
new government and perhaps even with Newfoundland and Labrador as he found the place in 1973. A February 24 column about the
municipal government of St. John's betrayed a sense that Guy had
dashed it off in a hurry and mailed it in. It did include the clever
subhead, "His Worship, The Nightmare," in reference to the latest
developers' friend to wear the mayor's chain of office. Thereafter the
piece wobbled, ending with a perfunctory and patronizing apology
to the Townies for disparaging their realm:

> One thing I might say, perhaps, is don't get me wrong.
> I have nothing in the world against the poor St. John's
> people. Take them by and large and take them one at a
> time and there's no nicer people than you ever wish to
> meet.
>
> But if there's more than five or six in the same room
> at one time I still get a bit sticky in the armpits. Funny
> about that.

Winter and spring of 1973 were not cheerful for Guy. He lived
alone in Chamberlains, a short but tedious commute from downtown St. John's on the old Conception Bay Highway. He worked
disproportionately at night and slept away many precious daylight
hours that might have cheered him up. His workplace, despite good
friends there, was neither as comfortable nor as spirited as it had
been.

Guy had accepted finally that a change in government would
not mean a fundamental change in the political and economic ethos
that had prevailed in Smallwood's Newfoundland. The failed old

Newfoundland and Labrador nation was as indifferently governed by Moores as it had been paternalistically ruled by Smallwood.

The times were indeed changing, and not in ways that Guy admired. Inexorably, Newfoundland and Labrador was becoming an ordinary, federally powerless, tail-end province, a backwater in the increasingly assertive and confident Canada of Lester Pearson and then Pierre Trudeau. On both sides of the Gulf of St. Lawrence, the novelty of quaint Newfoundland, and of a Canadian nation now fully formed at least from east to west, had worn thin. In Toronto, mindless Newfie jokes abounded, usually adaptations of rusty Irish or Italian immigrant groaners.

Two Ray Guy columns in March 1973 betrayed a gnawing despair, manifested, as it often did, in a longing for the better Newfoundland spirits of his childhood days.

One column made a convincing case that Newfoundlanders of a certain status, the self-sufficient Guy family among them, had eaten better in the 1940s than they could in the 1970s. Another column was a sad and chilling lament for a bygone Arnold's Cove that could never exist again. Both columns reflected not only Guy's discomfort at work but his chronic vulnerability to the unbearable eastern Newfoundland winter. His melancholy was always more palpable during what old-time Newfoundlanders used to call "the long and hungry month of March"—March being a metaphor for that interminable slushy stretch between Christmas and late April.

The food column revealed a writer ahead of the curve regarding global food and agricultural trends that today's eat-local foodies would salute. Guy's nostalgic free-verse poem to outport grub of yesterday offered homage to small-planet production, organic and unprocessed edibles, and local self-sufficiency. Read on, McDonald's, and close your doors for good.

> In my time I have passed over my gums the following
> items that never saw the inside of a store:

Carrots, turnips, potatoes (red, white, and blue), cabbage, parsnip, beet, spinach, lettuce pumpkin, vegetable marrow, radish, dandelion, peas, beans, and even—one year—tomatoes.

Apples, crabapples, damson plums, gooseberries, currants (red, white, and black), cherries (sweet and sour), caraway, rhubarb, parsley, chives, mint, watercress, mustard, savory, hops.

Blackberries, blueberries, marshberries, strawberries, partridgeberries, dogberries (for wine), bakeapples, raspberries, wild gooseberries, dewberries, and maidenhair teaberries.

Trout (both sea and mud), lobster, mussels, clams, salmon (fresh, corned, or smoked), herring in all ways, cod cheeks, heads, tongues, sounds, and hearts, codfish fresh and salt, boiled, baked, stewed, and roasted, caplin fresh, dried, or smoked, mackerel, turbot and snails.

Turrs, rabbits, moose, venison, partridge, ducks, geese, shell-birds, tickleaces, pigeons, twillicks, and bull-birds.

Mutton and lamb (saddle, leg, chops, stewed, fried, roasted, boiled), beef, pork, hams, sweetbreads, tripe, blood puddings, brawn, kidneys, liver, heart, butter (salted or unsalted), fowl, domesticated goose and duck, goat, goats' milk, hens' eggs, ducks' eggs, gulls' eggs, terns' eggs, plovers' eggs.

The dogs ate what was left over.[62]

The food column lives up to Patrick O'Flaherty's characterization of Guy's best work as "a cranky, disconcerting, insistent reminder of a previous dignity, now violated."

An even clearer example came just four days later in a short dispatch that Guy called "Goodbye to Arnold's Cove." It was his saddest column. It also was one of the few pieces in which he did not mask heartache with levity, or rage with satire. Anger drove the piece. But in its clipped, near-poetic, near-desperate sentences, his Arnold's Cove column was a keening cry from the heart:

> I was born there.
>
> Two-thirds of my life so far has been lived there.
>
> My parents are there with their neighbors and friends and relatives.
>
> My grandparents and my two brothers and many other of my people are in the graveyard there ...
>
> ... In fact it is still the only real home I have ...
>
> ... Two or three times in the past when things got tough and I was a bit ground down I chucked everything up and bolted for Arnold's Cove until I got my wind back.
>
> It is nice to have some place to run to.
>
> But now I must leave home forever.
>
> The hardest thing will be to convince my parents to leave their home also.
>
> They are getting a bit up in years. It won't be easy. It may hurt them also.
>
> But I do not want them to live little more than three miles away from "the largest oil refinery in Canada."
>
> I don't want—nor do I want them—to go to sleep each night three miles away from a 300,000 barrel-a-day gasoline dump.
>
> Or where the sulphur dioxide fumes smear the sky across the harbor and turn the sun bloody in the evenings over Bordeaux.
>
> If I wanted to live in such a place as that, I would never have come back from Toronto ...
>
> ... I did not leave home. Home left me ...

Goodbye to Arnold's Cove, my home. Where in the world shall I find another?[63]

March finally ended in May, and the approaching summer cheered Guy up. Luckily, the great tradition of *Telegram* reporters and columnists hopping into the *Telegram* "staff car," or even into one of the Herder family's armoured personnel carriers, huge Buicks and Cadillacs, to hit the rural trail, had not yet been halted by the Thomson meddlers. Neither Ennis nor Steve Herder would have allowed that to happen.

In June, Guy toured the Bonavista Peninsula, where he praised the homes, gardens, churches, fences, and people, while slagging the accommodations and food.

> Anyone advising tourists to visit Bonavista and vicinity without some sort of a trailer, or even a tent, is guilty of criminal fraud.
>
> He should be sentenced to eternity at the sadistically-named O'Happy Sight Motel with an amplified band of the North Korean brainwash type crashing away two feet below his room until the wee hours.[64]

Guy visited Clarenville, a town he always admired, and the nearby Random Island communities. He enjoyed and celebrated them all, while shaming the local eateries without mercy.

> Yesterday we stopped at a roadside place and had some damnable fried chicken (the only food, so-called, available along many of our roads) and so suffered the consequences.
>
> Within six hours our guts were pitched completely out of order. While these roadside gastronomical assas-

sins do not actually poison their unsuspecting victims, they put them into some hellishly nasty crumps.[65]

In his June 30, 1973, column, Guy listed no fewer than 45 communities he and his unnamed photographer had visited on their four-day road trip. He loved every possible aspect of the journey, save those involving cutlery.

He rhapsodized about the town of Trinity, on the north side of Trinity Bay: "I say here and now that Trinity, T.B., is the best and most remarkable place in Newfoundland that I have ever seen. Trinity is surely the most precious community jewel in Newfoundland's crown."

Trinity's economic and cultural history is one of entrepreneurship and individual achievement, rooted in the salt fish trade requiring a fleet of schooners to deliver the cured fish to St. John's or to foreign markets. Along with its lovely houses and commercial rooms, Trinity's spirit of self-sufficiency sat very well with Guy.

Nearby Port Union, however, was a different story. Port Union was purpose-built in the early 20th century as an operating base for the Fishermen's Protective Union led by the dynamic and enigmatic William Ford Coaker. His was a three-decade quest to wrest control of the fish export and fisheries supply trade from the oligopoly of brokerage merchants of St. John's and their satellite buyers in major fishing towns such as Trinity.

To that elusive end, the FPU recruited thousands of northeast coast fishermen and through their Fishermen's Union Trading Company went into the fish export business itself. It built its own schooners and row housing for union members. It even ran its own newspaper, the *Fishermen's Advocate*.

As a committed foe of all movements involving charismatic leaders and seemingly servile followers, Ray Guy saw Port Union and Coaker through a limiting lens. The FPU and the FU Trading Company had elements of both. Those elements had always been enough to eclipse in the minds of many, Guy included, the union's undeniable achievements for the betterment of fishing families.

In his June 30 piece, Guy concluded his review of Trinity very deliberately, wearing his disregard for Coaker and Port Union like a hair shirt:

> His memorial at Port Union is one of the ugliest things of the kind I have ever seen. At the top of a grandiose flight of concrete steps is a hulking and sullen bronze head, not unlike the bust of Mussolini, and set on a squat hour-glass-shaped pedestal like an old-fashioned lady's corset in white marble.
>
> In death, he has turned his back on Port Union. What loathing, bitterness, and hatred seem to be evident in that lumpen bronze head. These emotions seem to leave not the slightest room for a trace of pity, or even sorrow.
>
> All the relics of Coaker's material works at Port Union are ugly in their physical appearance—the very gateway to the now-abandoned farm, the squat, lumpy concrete fence around his personal monument, the joyless rows of duplex houses for the workers.
>
> It all has the ugliness and brutish, sullen heavy-handedness of a man with a gross heavy chin. Indeed, you can sense in these relics the basic style in miniature of a totalitarian state.

In the midst of this excessive rant, Guy paused to include the remarkable confession that his observations are from one "who knows as much about the history of that character as I know about the workings of a space rocket."

This confession seemed to give Guy licence to simply witness the relics and report his gut reaction. The confession, of course, was disingenuous. Guy was not a historian, but he was a voracious reader, most notably of Newfoundland books, newspapers, magazines, poetry, just about anything committed to paper.

One of the most nuanced and even-handed portrayals of the FPU and Coaker's impressive achievements is included in S.J.R. Noel's *Politics in Newfoundland*, published in 1971. Guy had read Noel's book, and had written appreciatively about it long before his visit to Port Union.

Most disconcerting for me, Guy had read and commented favourably on a series of feature pieces I had written for the paper on Coaker and the FPU a year earlier. I read Guy's Coaker column in the waning months of my own time at the *Telegram*. I was taken aback. His views of Coaker and the FPU, which I felt were churlish and driven by peevishness rather than good journalism, created tension between us.

During that long summer of 1973, Guy made efforts to remain amused and engaged. Then, abruptly, matters got worse.

Guy rarely tossed his hat high in the air, especially in praise of powerful people. He had had his differences with the Herders, and with Ennis. But when Ennis suddenly decided to leave the paper, Guy, by his standards, was more than generous in his recognition of Ennis's contribution and with his personal gratitude.

Under the large title "Ad Multos Annos, Ennis!" Guy lavished on Ennis the kind of personal praise seldom found in his writing. His column of September 8, 1973 took his readers inside the *Telegram's* newsroom, divulging both feelings and facts:

> The light has, as they say, gone out.
>
> For the past week or so we here at the People's Paper have been dashing to and fro and crying "woe, woe" because "Little Father"—as the Russian peasantry would put it—has gone away.

The loss to us of Robert J. Ennis, former managing editor, is unsettling if not grievous.

Keep a sharp eye on the People's Paper in weeks to come and any changes you may spot in it—for better or for worse—will be a manifestation of Mr. Ennis' passage.

Such was the nature of his position that perhaps 99 per cent of Telegram readers didn't know he existed.

Us lesser fry—Colleagues Crocker, Benson, Collins, Benedict, Devine, et al—constantly had our names and mugs in the papers yet Mr. Ennis, the leader of the pack, was rarely publicized during his tenure.

But for upwards of 10 years Robert J. was more or less the kingpin of the news end of The Evening Telegram.

As with so many of his columns, and with the same gaping space to fill every day, Guy hijacked his own Ennis testimonial to make a few broader observations about local journalism and the folks behind it.

This recent departure of Mr. Ennis points up an odd thing about newspapers and the news media in general. You know so very little about the persons who are actually responsible for bringing you the news on which you must depend.

All you get is the bare bones biography at the time of their appointment and the time of their departure— age, if married, address, previous position, number of children (if married), parents' names and that's it.

News directors or managing editors or whatever are a somewhat mysterious and secretive race.

News director F. White of CJON, for instance. Hails from Comfort Cove, drives an old Cadillac, abides at Elizabeth Towers and was once given an autographed reproduction of the Mona Lisa by poor Mr. Smallwood.

Or Mr. Callahan of the *Daily News*. Once of the *Western Star* at Corner Brook, once of the CJON newsroom, once head of the ministry of mines and resources, average height, slightly balding, no recorded scars or tattoos.

As to the CBC, most of the populace think Aubrey Mack runs it. For the Corporation is such an intricate labyrinth of positions and offices it would be a hard day's work just to find out who was responsible for washroom maintenance.

None of the names mentioned by Guy's Ennis tribute would have needed elaboration to a Newfoundland audience in 1973. The paragraphs above were thematic of his disregard for the local media competition, especially those components of it that he felt were politically bent during Smallwood's years as premier. Guy once described the Newfoundland political and media scene of the 1960s as a teeter-totter with the entire government and all media except the *Telegram* crowded onto one side. He said he felt an obligation to sit at the upper end.

Guy often reminded his readers of the CJON (Guy's CJRS) ownership team made up of prominent Smallwood Liberals Don Jamieson and Geoff Stirling. CJON News Director Freeman White did little during his career to disguise his high esteem for Smallwood. William R. Callahan had moved directly in 1972 from the Smallwood Cabinet to the *Daily News* as publisher, taking with him James R. Thoms, former editor of the Smallwood propaganda rag, the *Newfoundland Bulletin*.

The late Aubrey "Mack" (MacDonald), meanwhile, was an eccentric and endearing CBC radio announcer and St. John's character who would not have gone astray in James Joyce's *Dubliners*. Mack was given to colourful jackets, equally colourful hats and ties, and on-air bloopers. He always insisted on the plural when introducing newscasts: "Here ARE the news." He told borderline jokes on air. When he married a much younger woman, he said she complained of "old age creeping up on her."

CBC Television became a strong journalistic force in Newfoundland in the early 1970s. As TV news gained prominence, "current affairs," nose-to-nose accountability interviews, commentary, and documentaries became staples of CBC's local supper-time news program, *Here & Now*. CBC Television was still relatively new, having been kept out of Newfoundland and Labrador for more than a decade after Confederation by the combined lobbying forces of CJON, led by Jamieson and Stirling, with Smallwood himself as their most reliable lobbyist in Ottawa.

Never reluctant to burn a bridge in front of him, Ray Guy used the same "Ad Multos Annos, Ennis!" column to take an oblique swipe at the *Telegram*'s newly appointed managing editor, Maurice Finn. Finny, as he was inevitably known in a newsroom obsessed with nicknames and diminutives, had been a straightforward and hardworking desk editor who made his best contribution to the paper under Ennis's steady direction.

> If I was younger and had my health and strength I would look forward with a happier countenance to breaking in a new managing editor—Mr. M. Finn, married, three children, et cetera.
>
> But I almost think I'm past my labor in that regard. When the edge goes off your teeth every knot you strike is a strain. I struck one yesterday, for instance,

when they cut our "Chrissy's Dick" reference to native chicken dishes.

Not to disparage the new Mr. Editor one jot or one tittle but I like to think that his predecessor would have recognized it instantly as one of our fine old, though lesser known, Newfoundland folksongs of an entirely harmless nature ...

... That "dick" is the traditional Newfoundland term for rooster, that Mary Ann wanted the loan of Christopher's rooster so as to set some hens, that the song has been heard many times at church suppers and on so decorous a medium as CBC radio and that if "Ryan's Fancy" made a recording of it they would have a hit on their hands.

Perseverance is, I suppose, the only answer. In any event, all that remains for me is to sincerely—if a hired fool can ever be sincere—say thanks and goodbye to Mr. Ennis and wish Mr. Finn success and good luck.[66]

Ennis's departure from the paper reflected his own frustration at the Thomson regime. He seized a corporate career opportunity that grew directly out of his success at the paper.

Several big cheeses from Brinco, the British Newfoundland Corporation, attended a *Telegram* editorial board in 1973. Brinco was the parent company of the Churchill Falls (Labrador) Corporation which had just completed the massive hydroelectric power project on the Upper Churchill River in Labrador and was now embarking on a smaller project downriver at Gull Island.

Ennis, who knew a lot about the Churchill Falls development, gave the Brinco gentlemen a rough time at the editorial board, mainly about a notorious Churchill transmission contract with Québec. According to Ennis, the Brinco mucks "appeared to like it," and invited him to Montreal, by corporate jet, for a chat. An attractive offer soon followed. Ennis's success with Brinco led to international sales with SNC-Lavelin, and to a comfortable retirement in Oakville, Ontario.

Ennis left behind a newspaper much stronger than the one he had joined a decade earlier. He left behind as well several young journalists much better equipped to advance their own careers. And he left Ray Guy. With Ennis gone, and despite their differences, Guy had lost his most effective defender and champion. The ultimate consequence was inevitable. Yet Guy's dreary journey to the door took nearly another full year.

In 1974, during the final six months that Ray Guy worked full-time for the paper, his columns were not noticeably worse or better than they had been the previous year. Content overall had been a shade more pedestrian for a while. Still fine writing was displayed in all his pieces and excellence marked more than a few.

On January 4, he wrote about the perils of being stuck on Duckworth Street with a flat tire on a freezing and miserable winter evening. "It was a night to freeze the 'ears', as they don't say, off a brass monkey." He apologized for the quotidian thinness of the column with the explanation that he needed to make it to the "bond" store—an old Newfoundland term for a government liquor outlet—before it closed. Somehow, with a borrowed lug wrench, the wretched tire got fixed.

> Off now, with 20 minutes to spare, to pick up a crock of much-needed antifreeze. I go in doubt and trepidation. Knowing this man's town, the booze shops have probably closed early on a night they were never needed more. St. John's—still beyond the pale of civilization.

Guy's most important column of 1974 appeared in the *Telegram* on February 12. In a sense, this single column and its subject matter marked the end of his lonely vigil as Lear's Fool, as the local jester-in-chief, and as the self-appointed guardian of the good in Newfoundland and Labrador affairs. Reinforcements were about to arrive.

The night before, he had gone to see a show at a St. John's theatre. If Guy was initially cynical about the so-called Newfoundland Cultural Renaissance of the 1970, he checked his bile at the door the night he attended an early *Codco* comedy show. He was, by any standard he had previously revealed, rhapsodic in his approval.

The importance of the next day's page 3 review cannot be overestimated. Guy was the first to introduce to a wide Newfoundland public a new and different genre of Newfoundland satire. He did not name them in his column, but nearly all the actors he saw that night were destined to become local and eventually national celebrities, famous as television satirists—more famous even than he.

The column, read in retrospect, displayed prescience approaching prophecy of what was about to happen on the Newfoundland and Canadian comedy front:

> It may seem rather pointless to comment on a stage show which has already ended its week's run and which, in any case, was seen only by about 150 people a night and that in St. John's.
>
> But in the case of the entertainment called "Cod on a Stick" it is safe to say that it will be recalled by popular demand and that many other shows like it will be seen in Newfoundland from now on.
>
> It is a gate-opener. It is sure to become something of a rage.

In 2017, the CBC Television satirical review program *This Hour Has 22 Minutes* celebrated its 25th season. The same year, the Newfoundland comic and rantsman Rick Mercer announced the end to his successful CBC show *The Mercer Report* after 14 successful seasons. Both shows can trace their roots directly and indirectly to *Cod on a Stick*, as can literally dozens of other stage, television, and radio programs and Canadian comedy personalities.

Mary Walsh and Cathy Jones, *22 Minutes* charter members and veterans, both appeared in the version of *Cod on a Stick* that so impressed Ray Guy that evening in 1974. Greg Malone, Andy Jones, and Bob Joy all would have performed. Long since, those latter three have become—in Malone's and Jones's cases—iconic Newfoundland and Canadian drama and comedy stars, and, in Joy's, a stellar career as a Hollywood character actor. Rick Mercer and *22 Minutes* stars such as Mark Critch and Greg Thomey, all Codco disciples, are always the first to acknowledge that it was the Codco phenomenon that opened their eyes to the dreams that were possible, and that stoked their confidence to pursue them.

Guy knew intrinsically what that satirical genre was and where it was going. He spotted its essential comedic components: authentic dialect and language, inherently comic situations exaggerated only slightly, superior writing and acting, and irreverence, irreverence, irreverence. He traded heavily in those commodities himself. Few had a truer ear than his for the indigenous brand of Newfoundland levity that has become a Canadian comedy staple.

During his remaining few months as a daily *Telegram* columnist, Ray Guy exhibited flashes of the wit and wisdom that had made him what he was. It was not consistent. He wrote, perhaps too frequently, of what he considered the questionable Confederation bargain, against a growing generational current increasingly inclined to respect it. He reprised lists of old Smallwood industrial initiatives, not always wholeheartedly, to compare them to ongoing atrocities under the Moores regime.

On April 25, 1974, Guy produced a frail column declaring the Newfoundland fisherman to be extinct, like the Beothuk. He recalled Smallwood's forecast that "the cowboy looms larger in Newfoundland history than the fisherman." He had been present in 1965 when Smallwood made that prediction during a cattle-drive down the Burin Peninsula Highway to launch his foolishly bally-hooed Newfoundland era of saddles, chaps, and 40-litre hats. By 1974, there was little risk of stepping in cow manure on what he had dubbed the Marystown Trail. In his April 25 piece, Guy wondered whether fishermen had taken the same trail out of town by which the cowboys were supposed to arrive.

> It was only five or ten years ago that you could be fairly certain there were still some fishermen left in the country and holding their own against the cowboys.
>
> You knew there were some still around because every time a batch of them drowned there'd be an item in the papers and a bit on the radio.
>
> Even this slight indication that Newfoundland still had fishermen seems to have disappeared these late years.

In June 1974, as Guy worked his way through what would be his final full month as a daily *Telegram* columnist, there were new hints of his disposition and displeasure regarding his chosen career as a newspaperman. As often happened in his columns, especially in this period, he started out on one tack and ended on another.

His tone was droll at the outset of his June 14 piece, bemoaning the lack of variety in newspaper columns in small cities such as St. John's, compared to those in New York or London. He lamented the dearth of good gossip columns, which he considered an important indirect conduit for real news. He declared that coverage of what was then called Magistrate's Court in Newfoundland and Labrador was the closest the media ever got to ordinary people coping with the dilemmas of ordinary life.

If he was bemused at the start of this piece, it soon became obvious that he had a more serious message. His readers were about to witness another incautious chomp by Guy at the chilly hand that continued to feed him.

Guy was echoing, and localizing, complaints that had been identified three years earlier by the Davey report on Canadian media. It was all about the impact of media ownership concentration, of precisely the Thomson Newspaper kind:

> Sometimes you get the feeling that the newsrooms of the city are as divorced from reality as the earth is distant from the sun.
>
> Their almost exclusive stock in trade has become reports of speeches, seminars, election campaigns, council meetings, legislative shenanigans, endless press releases ...
>
> There is only one virtue in that sort of news. It is cheap ...
>
> It is cheaper for a newspaper to turn its reporters into two-legged tape recorders than to hire enough people to dig another bit into the political dung hill.

There is little doubt which newspaper "a newspaper" was. Guy could see the decline with his own eyes as he walked around the *Telegram*'s Duckworth Street building. Former *Telegram* reporter Bill Gillespie had documented much of it two years earlier for the edgy but short-lived St. John's periodical the *Alternate Press.*

The local media, Guy argued, had allowed the lines between the public and Confederation Building and City Hall "to become blocked by verbatim reports and official press releases."

> The line to the University (a town of 10,000 with an annual revenue of more than $25 million and an influence supposedly immeasurable) appears to have been ripped out altogether.
> Even the old-fashioned "beats," which gave at least a glimpse of reality, have fallen.
> Funny that when everything else under the sun has become so dear the news media have become so cheap.

The reference to beats was unmistakeable. At the *Evening Telegram*, "beats" had been an innovation in local journalism introduced by Bob Ennis. Beats are a basic news gathering strategy to enable reporters to gain expertise in select coverage areas. All reporters at the newspaper in the late 1960s and early 1970s benefited from beat journalism. The system provided modest opportunities to do research, develop contacts, and to become generally better informed about discrete areas of social and economic policy and political activity.

The Thomson owners of the *Telegram* were committed to filling even more news columns than the old owners. The difference was that the Thomson owners had no real interest in what those columns contained as long as they defamed no one and alienated no advertisers.

At times during the early summer of 1974, Guy appeared to be chronicling his own journey toward the side door of 294 Duckworth Street, the usual staff entrance which gave onto Solomon's Lane. The lane joins Duckworth and Water Streets, in those days offering a minor shortcut to several nearby pubs.

On July 4, 1974, apparently running short of topical material, Guy commented on an alleged story he said he had read in the November 17, 1971, edition of the *Telegram*. The article concerned a bird. The entire story contained precisely 13 words: "The chitwhurphy of New Zealand is nearing extinction according to leading ornithologists there."

Guy noted that the item seemed similar to those tiny bulletins used to fill small spaces in newspaper columns in the days when print was made from lines of lead that were not amendable to last-minute stretching or compressing. Those little gems were called fillers, rarely more than a few words long.

Guy cited, as an example, an item under a headline such as "Ceylon's Tea Crop Poor." The entire story might read, "The tea crop in Ceylon is said to be poor this year." He then revealed the dark truth behind the chitwhurphy's extinction. Close to deadline, he had been asked by an agitated copy editor if he could quickly find a filler as the normal supply was missing or had run out. Three years after the fact, Guy decided to make a clean breast of it:

> God may see the little sparrow fall, but it is only *The Telegram* that keeps an eye on the N.Z. chitwhurphy (deceased).
>
> You won't find the little thing mentioned in any dictionary, encyclopedia, or reference book either. For truth to tell, I made him up myself.
>
> It is much the same procedure as the springing, fully fledged, of Pallas Athene from the head of Zeus.

On Saturday, July 13, Guy published a mysterious column announcing that he was heading west for a while. He said he hoped to see the west coast again, the west coast of Newfoundland that was. "Or Cape Freels or St. Alban's or Merasheen or Cape St. Mary's or maybe even Labrador."

The piece was a quarter of his normal column length.

> ... In the excitement of hitting the trail for points west of old Sin John's, I find it difficult to concentrate on making this piece much longer.
>
> Perhaps, under the circumstances, Mr. Editor will let me get away with a shorter piece than usual.
>
> Always an understanding bloke, is Mr. Editor.
>
> That's it, then. Tally ho and away we go. Three cheers for God, Queen and Country and the devil take the hindmost.

There is no telling what he was up to with that enigmatic tease. Normally his best work would appear in the weekend editions of the paper, aimed at the larger circulation that came with the paper's extensive rural reach.

Conjecture is the best that can be offered. Guy was finished as a daily columnist, and he knew it. He was weary and he was discouraged. He was like Amos the Sheep: feeling old and feeling cold and tired of giving his wool away.

Guy did not resign from the newspaper, nor was he fired. No one knew what was happening, perhaps least of all Guy himself. He would write for the *Telegram* sporadically in subsequent years, but never again would he be its star columnist, its go-to-first daily attraction, the rapier-sharp terror of page 3.

Guy could not return to the comfortable enclave of his past. It was no longer there. For more than a decade he had basked in creative comfort at the *Telegram*. There he had enjoyed many important friendships. There he had gained fame. There he had polished his craft as a satirist and columnist to a high sheen. He had become, warts and all, a writer of standing and influence. He knew and appreciated all of that. But everything about the *Telegram* had become more bitter than sweet. The newspaper had burned him out and it had not compensated him well.

In an autobiographical sketch written in 1982 for the Resource Centre for the Arts, Guy lanced a boil. He recalled being paid $45 a week when he joined the paper permanently in 1963. He was not so unhappy six years later when he was earning $85 a week until he learned that several Carleton journalism graduates were hired at starting salaries of $100 to $120 a week.

Despite his disappointments, Guy's post-mortem on his tumultuous *Telegram* years could not ignore irrevocable and precious truths.

> What *The Telegram* did for me was knock some of the cursed shyness out of me, gave me a broad smattering of background knowledge on just about everything that goes on in the Happy Province and MOST OF ALL, it forced me to write.

It had ended. Guy had nowhere to go, and no one with whom he could travel. His commitment to his craft, to his newspaper, and to Newfoundland and Labrador had eaten up his younger adult years.

Ray Guy was 34. Perhaps the daily columnist chapter of his life, should have ended more ceremonially, at 30, like any good newspaper story.

Ray Guy by R.D. Wilson, 1968.
This sketch was retrieved from Guy's wastepaper basket.

Alice Adams, c. 1930.

Baby "Rae," c.1941.

Iris and Ray Guy, c. 1943.

Ray as "father-giver"
at Iris's wedding, 1963.

High school drama on Bell Island, 1956. Guy as Charlie McCarthy.

Photo: Iris Brett

School friends, Sylvia Wadman (left) and Daphne Guy, July 1957.

Photo: Iris Brett

Ray Guy at 16, Arnold's Cove.
Photo: Iris Brett

The Guy house in 2021, with former shop attached.

Ray Guy,
Ryerson graduation, 1963.

Michael J. Harrington,
Telegram editor 1959–1982.

Photo: Bill Croke

Gary Callahan, 1968.

Photo: Bill Croke

Ray Guy at work, 1968.

Photo: Bill Croke

Bob Ennis (left with pencil behind his ear) and, clockwise,
Tom Power, Maurice Finn, Pat Doyle, and Carolyn James.
Photo: Bill Croke

Ron Crocker,
Telegram reporter, 1968.
Photo: Bill Croke

Bob Ennis and Hubert Herder,
1968. Hubert Herder became
publisher after the 1971 sale of the
Telegram to Thomson Newspapers.
Photo: Bill Croke

Ray Guy, hamming it up at home, 1969.
Photo: Ron Crocker

Steve Herder.

Family, mid-1980s: Alice, Ray, Iris, George;
daughter Rachel peeking out behind chair.

Ray and Kathie, 1976 or 1977.

Guy as playwright, 1988. His play at the
LSPU hall that year was *Frog Pond*.
Photo: Steve Payne

Guy and Mary Walsh, LSPU Hall, St. John's, 1988.
Photo: Steve Payne

Ray Guy was awarded an honourary doctorate from Memorial University in 2001. From left: Kathie Housser, Ray Guy, Annie Guy, Herb Brett, Iris Brett, Rosemary House, Johnny Housser, Kay Benson, Bob Benson.

Iris Brett and Dr. Guy, 2001.

Clockwise from back left: Larry Kelly, Karl Wells,
Sheilagh Guy Murphy, and John J. Murphy, 2010.
Photo: Randy Dawe

W.J. ("Young Jim") Herder, August, 2021.
Photo: Newfoundland Camera

Writer at Large

PART II

WITHOUT LIES

CHAPTER 16
Bi-Coastal Affair

If Kathie hadn't married him, Ray would have died from loneliness.

—Alice Guy

Aunt Cissy Roach, Ray Guy's wickedest alter-ego, seemed to share Alice Guy's despairing prognosis of Guy's fate had he not found love. As early as 1970, Aunt Cissy provided her own dark perspective, which is to say Guy's, on his prospects for finding a mate.

Guy had mentioned to Aunt Cissy that he was about to return to "the House." He meant the House of Assembly, of course. Aunt Cissy misinterpreted House to mean the House of the Rising Sun.

> You got your handicaps, we know; but surely God you're not driven to visitin' a House yet. Laziness! Run a rake through your hair now and then. Put on a bit of talcum powder and blacken your boots.

There's lots of young maids on the loose, blind as bats but too much vanity to wear eyeglasses. I'd say that's your only hope ... if you got one at all. When they gets close enough to see what they're up against, it'll be too late—if you're on your toes. 'Pride goeth before a fall.'"

"My dear woman," I said, put out. "When a person gets to this age they have more elevating things on their mind than ..."[67]

A pivotal chapter in Guy's life closed on that summer day in 1974 when he headed "west" from his Duckworth Street *Evening Telegram* encampment.

An uncertain transitional year followed in which Guy, hanging out alternately in Chamberlains and Arnold's Cove, faced the vagaries of freelance journalism for the first time in his life. The transition was far from complete when a very different journey began on a summer day in 1975, the day Guy encountered Katharine Kennedy Housser.

Kathie Housser was born in Port Alberni, British Columbia, on September 22, 1946, into a pair of high-achieving blue-blood clans, the Houssers on her father's side and the Farrises on her mother's.

Housser's father, Harry Cron Kennedy Housser, was born in Vancouver in 1915. He married Martha Louise Farris in 1941 in Kingston, Ontario, where he was serving with the Royal Air Force. Louise Hadley Farris was born in Bellingham, Washington, also in 1915. She died in Victoria at 85 in 2001. That same year, Alice Louisa Guy, Ray Guy's mother, died in Arnold's Cove at the age of 101.

After high school in Vancouver, Kathie Housser headed for McGill University in Montreal on a scholarship. She studied German, Latin, and English, maintaining an A-minus average that, she said, slipped in her final year. By then Housser wanted to get on with it. She had grown tired of school and was smitten by the excitement of Expo 67 and the 1960s political surge that affected many reflective young people of that time. Going into her final year, she told her mother she was "worn out." Louise's advice was direct: "Do nothing and say nothing for a while." Housser survived her final year at McGill, but she did not remember it fondly.

Housser's first radio job was with station CJOH in Ottawa. She soon moved to CFCF in Montreal, "a horrible British enclave," as she described it. At CFCF, "not a single f'ing word of French was spoken among the management ranks." Only the station's technicians conversed in their native language to help Housser advance her own bilingual aspirations.

Comfortable with left-leaning and union politics, Housser also worked for the American Newspaper Guild, a union for reporters, which in 1972 was just establishing its offices in Ottawa, to begin its successful March toward dominance in the newsrooms of the nation as the Canadian Newspaper Guild.

Housser described it as a perfect job at that point in her life. But not forever. She began to fear she would be a secretary all her life.

To alter course, Housser decided to take a year off. Unemployment Insurance (Employment Insurance today) enabled a perfunctory back-packing tour of Europe, a rite of passage in the 1970s for smart and privileged young Canadians, their Maple Leafs stitched to their backpacks to distinguish themselves from reviled Americans abroad.

The Grand Tour behind her, Housser enrolled at Carleton University to study journalism. Unlike Guy's three-year program at Ryerson, hers was a one-year Bachelor's (honours) degree, a journalism crash course built on her foundation of a good undergraduate degree from McGill. Armed with the Carleton credential, her course was pretty much set: journalism, and probably radio in which she already had a grounding.

At Carleton, Housser was once more an ace student. But she was not among the journalism graduates most in demand. All the "lovelies," as she called them, were recruited avidly for television, especially by the CBC. Housser chuckled at the notion that she found herself numbered among the less telegenic. The matter did not keep her awake.

Housser was flattered anyway to be invited to Toronto by a legendary CBC Radio guru of the day, Margaret Lyons, to chat with some regional CBC Radio people. The so-called CBC Radio Revolution of the 1970s at CBC was well under way. Programming wizards such as Alex Frame, Mark Starowicz, and Doug Ward were inventing or reinventing iconic radio shows—*Radio Free Friday*, *This Country in the Morning*, and As *It Happens*—and launching or burnishing the careers of superstars such as Peter Gzowski, Barbara Frum, and Newfoundland's Harry Brown.

Housser passed on an opportunity to work at the local CBC radio shop in Toronto. She was looking for something more pioneering. One of the regional bosses she met was Des Brown, representing CBN, CBC's radio station in St. John's. "Des offered me a one-way ticket to St. John's," Housser recalled. The job was to produce and vitalize *Newfoundland Today*, the CBC St. John's morning radio show.

As Guy languished in Arnold's Cove in the fall of 1974, trying to figure out his next move but not bothering the UIC fund, a couple of local CBC people got wind of his availability. CBC St. John's announcer Doug Laite and News Director Bob Ross decided to drive to Arnold's Cove. One of their proposals, that Guy write commentaries for *Newfoundland Today* and read them on the radio himself, was summarily ruled out by Guy. "Well," Laite suggested, "you write them and I'll read them."

Guy began writing weekly pieces for *Newfoundland Today*. Laite, an actor as well as a radio announcer, read them effectively, and they were instantly popular. Along with Guy's contribution, the morning show needed other improvements. It needed more substantive content, meat-and-potatoes journalism, and a new producer to see to it. It needed Kathie Housser.

When Housser arrived in the late spring of 1975, Guy's pieces already were part of the show. Housser loved the writing and appreciated the political edge. However, she thought it passing strange that such an important contributor to the show reputedly refused to darken the door of the CBC Radio building, then located on Duckworth Street, a short block from the *Evening Telegram*.

With Laite's encouragement, Guy also wrote skits for the local CBC television variety show, *All Around the Circle*. Guy created a character, Uncle Eli, one of several outharbour wiseacres and sages he would invent for radio and television. Those characters also were performed by actors, tricked out in what CBC producers imagined was a fisherman's only garb: guernsey, salt-and-pepper cap, and knee rubbers, all worn about as comfortably as a fisherman would wear a tuxedo to the squid-jigging ground.

Guy would drop off his television and radio scripts weekly at the CBC Television building located on the northern fringe of the city, on the edge of the Memorial University campus. The radio commentary would be couriered to the Radio building downtown.

Housser thought it was all too weird. She insisted on meeting Guy, with whom she had spoken only by telephone. "I told him I couldn't work with the f'ing Phantom of the Opera."

They met professionally, at least once, probably twice, in St. John's. There was chemistry. A first date was agreed to, over lunch. It was overtaken by events.

The night before the date, Housser and Rosemary House, a young researcher at CBC Radio, attended a "Screech-in," a Newfoundland tourism ritual in which innocent codfish are obliged to kiss rum-sodden strangers. Around 5 a.m. the following morning, Housser, hung over and heading for work, fell and cracked her elbow.

"She was navigating the metal stairs over the cliff side at the back door of CBC on Henry Street," House recalled. "She was trying to open a pack of Tic-tacs. She fell on the steps, busted her elbow and was carted off to hospital and her arm put in a cast." House taped an apology note to the office door for Guy, explaining why Housser could not make the lunch date.

Nothing at all was heard from Guy. A maddening silence ensued. As House related it: "he wouldn't answer his phone. Kath was in an agony. She had missed her chance! He had gone to ground!"

By then, Housser had confided in House, the only other woman in the *Newfoundland Today* program unit. In House's words, Housser had a "huge crush" on Ray Guy. "She told me she was crazy about Ray. And I couldn't imagine it. Kathie was this brassy mainlander and Guy was this Newfoundlander to the core. Anyway, lo and behold ... there was something going on between them ... Thus I knew that perhaps Kathie's huge crush was apparently reciprocated when that 'script' arrived."

Ah—the Script. It arrived in what looked like the usual delivery package for Guy's weekly commentary. But this script was not for broadcast.

> I only have two things to say this week. One is that I would like to return to work at *The Evening Telegram* and the other is I would like to marry Katharine Housser of Port Alberni, B.C. Signed, Ray Guy.

What the eff? "Those two lines made up the script in its entirety. Not another word," House remembered. "I can still see it in my mind's eye. The boys—this was a deeply male dominated space and Kathie was carefully navigating—all thought the script was Ray having a nervous breakdown. It was Ray's 'swan-song' as Doug (Laite) put it. He knew nothing of Kathie's feelings."

The two-line script arrived on a Thursday, House recalled. "What should she do? It seemed that Ray might be in love with her too! I kept encouraging her to just drive down to Arnold's Cove to confront Ray. What did she have to lose? So she drove to Arnold's Cove with her arm in a cast in her rickety old blue station wagon, 'the Rocket.'"

There was no heads-up for Guy. "She went to confront him on his intentions ... She called me when I was getting home at 2 a.m. and asked me to do the Monday show for her. I asked her if everything was alright. She said it was great. She and Ray Guy were getting married. She came back to town and told me they were getting married the following week. And all was wonderful."

House finally met Guy in person for the first time two days before the wedding. "It was at Bob Benson's. Bob was the best man and I was the best lady, or maid or whatever it was. We were figuring out how the ceremony would go. It was the first time I met Ray and I was surprised how young he was. I always thought he was immensely old. Like I was 22, but because I had grown up with him, I thought he was a much older man. He was 36, which was old ... but not an old man. Quite handsome. Obviously intensely shy."

Just six weeks after they had met, Kathie Housser and Ray Guy were married. The ceremony was performed on September 25, 1975, at the Anglican Cathedral in St. John's, where Alice Adams and George H. Guy had wed more covertly 40 years before.

In Guy's large body of subsequent writing, there appears to be only one reference to that auspicious day. In the summer of 1985, he wrote and narrated a television documentary for a CBC network series called *Cityscapes*. He led his viewers on tours of both the magnificent Basilica of St. John the Baptist, the Catholic fortress high on the hill, and the worthy Anglican Cathedral, 300 metres and a ritual or two below. As he informed his national television audience:

This is the Anglican Cathedral. It was started in 1843. It's a neo-gothic design by Sir Gilbert Scott. The cathedral was badly damaged of course by the great fires of the last century. And the building of it is still in progress ... I was married right here and I remember the wedding rehearsal well.

Directly above where you'll be standing, says the minister, are four huge boulders and they each weigh more than a ton. They're not fixed there, he said, or mortared in any way. They just lean against each other like that and it's only the force of gravity that keeps them up. Well I think he might have been pulling my leg. But the next day when he popped the question for real, what I said, as far as I remember was, I will, I will.

A reception at the Hotel Newfoundland rounded out the wedding festivities, and Ray and Kathie left for their honeymoon, "out around the bay," as her brother, Johnny Housser, recalled.

Out of the flurry of events surrounding their efficient courtship and marriage came a flurry of Guy-Housser family stories.

On the day of the wedding, House was riding a creaking elevator at the old Newfoundland Hotel, heading for the pre-nuptial get-together where the Housser and Guy kin, still virtual strangers, would continue to size each other up.

In the lift with her was a young gentleman—"very handsome, very hip, and distinctly uptown," as House recalled her first impression. "I had no way of knowing that Kathie's young brother had turned up on the day of the wedding as a big surprise (flying all night long from Fort Mac). But he knew, considering my formal dress and bouquet, that I must be the bridesmaid!"

It all seemed foreordained. Rosemary House and Johnny Housser have been married for more than 40 years and have raised two daughters.

The Housser parents, meanwhile, had arrived in Newfoundland a few days earlier. The day after their arrival they took the two-hour drive to Arnold's Cove to meet George and Alice Guy.

"My parents were rather cosmopolitan and very Vancouver," Johnny Housser recalled. "They were taken into the parlour in Arnold's Cove to have tea and biscuits and what-not. My mom said it was very disconcerting, because in the hour and a half or two hours that they were there several people came into the kitchen and sat down, looked at them for a while and then got up and left."

The Vancouver Houssers were strangers to outport culture and mores, and especially to the dynamic of the Guy residence, which also housed a post office and a small general store. The Guy residence was a very public place.

Guy and Housser had a short outport honeymoon, returning to a quasi-outport, Chamberlains, to set up housekeeping. Their first child, Rachel Housser Guy, was born in 1977. Their second daughter, Annie Guy, was born less than two years later. By then, with help from George H., the couple had purchased an older "character" house on Hamilton Avenue in St. John's, where they lived until the mid-1980s.

After living in BC for several years, where Johnny attended law school, he and Rosemary moved back to St. John's in 1984 with Sally and Emma, their daughters, then aged four and two. With Rachel and Annie, there then were four little cousins, aged two, four, six, and eight. The kids and couples bonded, becoming fast family friends.

On many levels, Ray Guy and Kathie Housser experienced a marriage like any other. "It was pretty straightforward," House said. "They were like every day normal people having kids, doing jobs and all the rest of it; but then when they were drinking it was terrible."

Hamilton Avenue was when the heavy drinking became daily, House recalled.

By the mid-1970s, Guy was already a heavy imbiber, a habit easily acquired in the St. John's news racket of the 1960s and 1970s, where boozing was fashionable and almost ritualistic. During most of their 38 years together, Guy and Housser both suffered frequently from severe drinking problems and the related nightmares of fatigue, anxiety, and stress. Guy's bipolar diagnosis, the scariest of the couple's various illnesses, came when he was already past middle age. Treatments of that profound and baffling condition, while improving, remain far from adequate.

Work and financial worries came early and often. The joys and frustrations of parenting had arrived very quickly. Not only kids, but dogs and cats that were equally non-compliant. Their elderly parents, always important to them, were gradually winding down.

If conventional in many ways, the Guy-Housser marriage was in other important ways unusual. Housser was the principal breadwinner, still not that common in the 1970s. Guy's work, despite his talents and achievements as a journalist and satirist, was more scattered, not always in demand, and rarely earned what it should have.

On the work front, Guy had burned some bridges behind him, and one or two ahead. But at least one bridge seemed fireproof. In 1976, Steve Herder, then publisher of the Thomson *Telegram*, took him back at the newspaper, only a year after Guy had referred to Herder, unfairly and with some cruelty, as "heavily timbered in the attic."[68]

Guy may have been attempting an apology to Herder years later, in 2011, when his 1976 book, *That Far Greater Bay,* was reissued. He wrote:

> Most books have a "Dedications" stuck in the front. I was going to do it with the first one but then it seemed to be a little on the grand side. Harking back to the

times when the stuff in this book was first written, here it is: To my father, who never saw me stuck for a roof over my ahead, and to Steve Herder, who never saw me stuck for a job of work.[69]

Annie Guy, who was interviewed for this book, is forthcoming about her father. Her affection for him and her appreciation for her childhood with him are striking. Annie remembers her father with warmth, and with her own flashes of Guy-Housser humour.

What she misses most about her father are his compassion and his diverse talents. "He was a caring person, and he had all kinds of artistic skills. He could draw. He could paint. He was a great photographer." Annie said her father could be totally trusted to select a piece of jewellery for her mother, his eye spot-on and totally attuned to her taste.

Annie's memories of her father were at their most graphic when she talked of his love of gardening, especially his love of flowers, their colours, and their fragrances. "He liked growing herbs and vegetables, but it was flowers he loved best. He had demands for his flowers. They must be pretty, or they must have a lovely scent."

The second house owned by the Guy-Houssers was on Holbrook Avenue in the west end of older St. John's. It was near two city landmarks. One is Bowring Park, a public space based on 50 acres donated by the Bowring family and expanded over decades to nearly 200 acres. The other local landmark, just around the corner from Holbrook Avenue, was the Hospital for Mental and Nervous Diseases. The hospital was known to all simply as "the Mental." Guy joked that as far as he could see excellent people hung out at both locations.

Holbrook Avenue featured their first major garden, a Ray and Kathie joint venture that became a showpiece. They worked on it relentlessly each spring and summer for 15 years or more. It engaged the interest and participation of the girls. Annie says she never regarded it as work. She loved digging holes. Like her father, she appreciated the challenge of gardening in Newfoundland, with its 2-inch layer of acidic soil.

Annie remembers an attempt to create a garden for herself only to discover that under the thin layer of topsoil she had chosen resided a huge rock. Her father suggested planting all around the rock. He informed Annie that the heat from rock would benefit the plants. It worked great, she said, with flowers blooming everywhere—begonias, roses, icebergs, irises.

Guy's skill as a gardener was countervailed by his ineptitude as a handyman. Annie said her mother had her own modest set of tools which Guy was not permitted to touch. Housser would carry out minor household repairs herself. Once back from the garden, Guy was more or less useless. Comedian Steve Smith (a.k.a. Red Green) thought it best if women found men handy rather than handsome. Housser found Guy handsome enough, but exceedingly unhandy. Guy once said that whenever he walked by a shelf of hammers at Canadian Tire, his thumbs would swell up spontaneously.

Annie Guy said she was aware from an early age that her father was a popular writer but was unaware of anything unusual about it until elementary school. There she and Rachel would occasionally hear rude comments from kids who had heard them from their parents in response to something their father had written.

Annie was in elementary school in the early 1980s when Guy was writing monthly for *Atlantic Insight* magazine and in a variety of local publications. She was a teenager when, after 1986, he wrote weekly for the *Sunday Express* newspaper in St. John's. In the 1980s, Guy also was a frequent CBC Radio commentator. In short, by local standards, he was famous. Annie said a typical schoolyard slight would be, "You're Ray Guy's daughter. My dad says your dad is full of ... whatever."

Annie remembers her father "banging away at his old Royal typewriter" at all hours, and, most disconcertingly, talking in funny voices. In the 1980s, Guy also became a local television actor, playing the role of Jack House, "the star boarder," in the CBC Newfoundland comedy series *Up at Ours*. He also wrote for the show, voicing the lines for other characters as he wrote them. "He'd be talking like a little old lady," Annie said. "Except he'd be the only one there. He was practicing his lines."

As a family, the Guys and Houssers would visit Arnold's Cove in summer. Occasionally, they would get out to the old Adams homestead at Bordeaux for picnics. Annie remembers Bordeaux only as a muddy and grassy area. She was made aware of gravesites there, now unmarked, that could have been those of her Adams ancestors, or even of French occupiers from the late 1700s.

Through 38 years of marriage, with both common and unusual headwinds, Guy and Housser were devoted to each other and they were devoted to their daughters. The couple had their children and much more to help sustain them. They loved books. They appreciated irony and edgy humour. They were not opposed to gossip. Their mutual gifts for language and athletic turns of phrase provided free and priceless entertainment. Their collective talents made it easier to weather the storms. In the artful words of Percy Bysshe Shelley, Guy's favourite poet, it helped them "beacon the rocks ... On which high hearts are wrecked."

CHAPTER 17

Where the Need Is Great

Shelley, of course, had much more to say about love and marriage, not all of it encouraging. He described wedlock, or at least monogamy, as "the longest journey," endured "with one chained friend, perhaps a jealous foe."[70]

Despite such poetic caution—Guy would have read Shelley's—and despite the burdens, marriage for Guy was emancipating. A family of his own focused and settled him in a pod of affection, responsibility, and purpose. It provided him with new and different subject matter for his writing. The new material often was on a different plane, more intricate than his Juvenile Outharbour Delights, and relieved of the endless scurrility of Newfoundland and Labrador politics. Marriage and children ended the twin curses of his early adulthood: solitude and frequent loneliness.

The late 1970s was also a time of professional satisfaction. Beginning in 1976 and for the remainder of the 1970s and most of the 1980s, Guy had one of his most durable and stimulating gigs.

For four of those years, he wrote for a Halifax-based regional magazine called *Axiom*. That publication was succeeded by *Atlantic Insight*, a glossy, well-produced monthly, also Halifax-based, distributed widely in the Maritimes although sparsely in Newfoundland. Taking over a space previously occupied by the sagacious Dalton Camp, Guy owned the back page of *Atlantic Insight* every month for almost a decade. It was his most extensive foray into a non-Newfoundland market. A book titled *Ray Guy's Best,* a compilation of his *Insight* columns, sold as well on the Mainland as it did in Newfoundland.

The challenge of writing for non-Newfoundland readers was good for Guy. The arcane intricacies of Newfoundland and Labrador politics, post-Smallwood, were of marginal interest to Mainlanders.

The changes reflected grounding and contentment, and sporadically successful attempts to drink less. In part, it reflected his determination to appeal to a new readership on the other side of the Gulf of St. Lawrence, which he believed—Kathie Housser was certain of this—would be key to his financial success as a freelance writer. Mostly it reflected his new status as husband, father, and breadwinner, although the latter role continued to be ancillary to Housser's more stable and consistent CBC career.

Atlantic Insight forced Guy to find new inspiration, and he did. Guy endeared himself to his new Mainland readership with a formula. The columns offered an inviting mix: children and pets, self-effacing wit; wry, but never demeaning, observations about Newfoundland and Labrador life; and, always, stellar prose that rings as rich today as it did in 1980. An early *Insight* piece entitled "Our Climate Condemned Us to Canada," featured Guy at the top of his whimsical game.

In other free Christian democracies you can set your calendar by the seasons. White Christmases are guaranteed. Promptly on the first day of spring the trees explode into leaf with a soft vegetable thunk. On midsummer's day, a heatwave arrives on time and at six minutes past four, September 21, every leaf unhitches itself simultaneously. Even in Newfoundland that's the sort of climate still taught in the schools ...

Here, however, the trees are just as bare on Coronation Day as they are on the Feast of the Circumcision while, on the other hand, there are shirtsleeve days in February and icebergs in July. Incest and poor diet have long been put forward to explain Newfoundland politics and Newfoundland politicians but, to my own mind at least, not enough weight has been given to climate. It's hard to be a warm, meaningful, sincere, relevant human being like they have in the States when, for nine months of the year, you may step out the door on green grass in the morning and come back to supper with the snow halfway up to the window ledges.

Guy carries on to explain that Newfoundland has polka-dot, brown and white rabbits due to pathetic but inevitable indecision as to which season they are in, and to explain the habit of Newfoundland weather forecasters of speaking in riddles and circumlocutions.

On TV, they go at their maps like windmills in a force 10 gale, interspersing all sorts of swoops and arrows with pregnant lice representing the sun and when they're finished I'll challenge anyone to repeat what they've just said. It saves them from being kicked to death in public. High-speed gibberish is their only method of self-defense in a place where a balmy and tranquil sunset can give way to a night like that on which Lucy Grey was lost.[71]

Guy explains the influence of weather on Newfoundland's new status as a province with a much-told anecdote about the signing of the Terms of Union with Canada in 1948.

A leading member of the Newfoundland and Labrador delegation to Ottawa allegedly followed his usual practice, a prudent one back home, of wearing his fleece-lined long johns to Ottawa in May. Sweltering in a microwave on the Rideau, he allegedly was prepared to sign anything so long as he could board the next eastbound train.

"It was the custom among the older folk for the women to sew their men into these long-johns about the latter part of September and to cut them free again in early July," Guy joked. The politician in question was Gordon Bradley, who became Newfoundland's first Canadian senator.

In a column describing the Newfoundland and Labrador obsession with spending time in the woods or aboard pleasure boats, or almost anywhere they can be more miserable than they would be at home, Guy sought to identify with more urbane Maritimers who, like Guy himself, preferred the comforts of the Great Indoors.

Guy observed that Newfoundlanders and Labradorians have never had "cottages" the way so many other Canadians do. If wealthy, they may have had what they called summer places, full-size or even grand houses, a half-hour from home at Topsail or Manuals for St. John's folks, or at George's Lake for the Corner Brook gentry.

Today the trend is toward "bay houses," century-old outport homes, often derelict. Further down the torture chain there are countless two- or three-room plumbed retreats called cabins, also known as shacks if amenities are sparse. Still in evidence today is that most baffling Newfoundland escape phenomenon of the latter half of the last century—campers or mobile homes parked permanently in gravel pits, usually within feet of the Trans-Canada or some other major highway.

In Guy's assessment, Newfoundlanders retreat to such double-bunk cells to "expose themselves to all the rustic horrors. Backfiring septic tanks, stinking camp stoves, attic wasps' nests, frothy-muzzled bulls with blood-stained horns."

Guy contrasted those sorts of long-weekend, back-to-nature adventures with what he understood to be a more committed back-to-the-land movement more common in the Maritime provinces.

> The Maritimes is, I understand, chock-a-block with persons who've fled the hideous complications of urban living for double-shell houses, solar heating, airtight wood stoves, hydroponic gardens, windmill generators, ram-jets, composting crappers, airlocks, R-48, goat husbandry, hydraulic yogurt-makers and half-finished submissions to Harrowsmith.
>
> Most, I'll venture, come from Boston or Montreal rather than Moncton or Halifax. Your Haligonian, I daresay, is like your St. John's man, a true urban philosopher able to see eternity in a grain of sand, recapture the thrill of the chase in side-walk doggie-do or the Great North Woods in a potted geranium.[72]

In Guy's post-*Telegram* writings are scores, possibly hundreds, of references and allusions to Kathie and the kids. All are affectionate and bemused. One minor public criticism of Housser in print was a reference to the impact on her "otherwise fine mind" of reading certain books that Dr. O'Flaherty might have considered beneath the ranks of literature.

Atlantic Insight in the early 1980s featured some of Guy's least political and least acerbic writing. The girls were young. His obvious comfort with fatherhood found its way into many of his *Insight* essays. The kids, a cat named Hodge, and various other pets all made appearances, indicative of a period in a parent's life when children are at a perfect age and pets are part of a well-rounded family.

The children and their animals inspired Guy's most endearing stories. Daughter Rachel, around five at the time, was reported by her father to have forsaken her early Christian faith upon the untimely death, squished by a car, of the family cat, Hodge, named for one of Dr. Johnson's beloved felines.

> Trouble is, our older child was told that Hodge had gone to live with Baby Jesus. So finely tuned is her sense of property that for the two years past she has not forgiven the aforementioned Infant. By what right did Baby Jesus take away daddy's Hodge, her Hodge?

Guy records, rather sadly, that yet another Christmas had come and gone and there had been little or no progress made in returning the doubting daughter to the garden of Jesusly grace. Frustrated, he decides to take the matter up directly with the Petkiller-in-Chief:

> Due to his [Hodge's] absence—pay strict attention, God—you suffer the loss of one child's prayers. So, clean up Your act, Old Man. You know and I know that Hodge went to the Robin Hood Bay dump in the Glad bag and that I'm not so good at explaining these things. But You did hear me say at the time, didn't You, "God help me," and You didn't.
>
> Anyway, I forgive You. You have Your troubles, God knows.[73]

In an earlier *Atlantic Insight* piece in a similar vein, Guy featured his younger daughter, Annie, three Guy household cats, and, dangerously, his mother-in-law, Louise, visiting from BC.

Guy offered a brief description of an outsized cat named Cecil, who weighed in at an intimidating 22.5 pounds, but who was relatively peaceable: "Cecil doesn't do much. Blood sports interest him not at all. This may be because mice look to him like sow bugs and sparrows like house flies."

He expended a sentence or two on the cat Turpin, named for Dick Turpin, the 18th-century English highwayman.

> Turpin, also known as "Rough Trade," is constantly pouncing on Cecil and on his sister with what sometimes seems to be lascivious intent. Since we paid the vet good money to circumvent Nature, I asked his doctor about this. He allowed as there might be "some residual testicular matter."

As the column unfolds, the main players are the cat Penny, named for her copper colour, and Penny's custodial handler, Annie, aged six.

> Penny, the Half-a-Mew, keeps much to herself, but one day Anne decided Penny had the flu and should be put to bed.
>
> Anne has a remarkably high pain threshold and the determination of a salmon headed upstream. James Bond would crack under interrogation and deliver the House of Windsor to the KGB before Anne would say what happened to that whole package of fig bars.
>
> She's been trying, perhaps for 15 minutes, to get dolly's flannel nightie on Penny. The struggle was ferocious but near silent. By the time the fray was discovered, the

nightie was in shreds and so was Anne—just this side of needing a transfusion.

It was in that column that cat Hodge made his first appearance, elaborately described.

> He [Hodge] was as small and scrawny as the young Sinatra and had bat ears like the Prince of Wales. He was named after Dr. Samuel Johnson's pet whose master went out to fetch oysters for pussy's dish himself lest the servant be irked by the chore and mistreat the cat.
>
> Hodge never enjoyed good health. The vet gave us something called "bitch's supplement." It's used to build up dogs after they've pupped, but the doctor figured it might help cats, too.
>
> My mother-in-law had just come to visit. That morning from the kitchen I called out to my wife: "Precieuse! Have you made up the bitch's supplement yet?"
>
> M.-in Law claims she thought she was about to get her breakfast in bed.

When Guy wrote about animals, or of certain humans such as the elderly or the otherwise vulnerable, he displayed an uncanny capacity to view the world through their eyes. To a cat, he observes, adults must be rather scary:

> Consider. Suppose you're lying on the carpet reading this tasteful organ and, suddenly, you are grabbed and swooped up into the air, 20 feet high or more.
>
> A huge red face with teeth is thrust up against yours. The giant's breath is hot and it makes growling idiotic noises and cluck clucks at you. You'd probably grab its eyeglasses and pee all over it, too.[74]

Along the way, Guy had noted that after the many cats of his childhood, he had been without them for years. "The hiatus ended when at last I entered into Holy Acrimony." Holy Acrimony wrought changes in Ray Guy and in his writing. The satirist was reinventing himself, as a husband, as a father, and as a writer of greater breadth and of a different sensitivity and insight.

For more than half of the 1980s, Guy's *Atlantic Insight* monthly column was his most revealing and defining work. From those reflective pieces, produced at the rate of only a dozen a year, we learn much of what is publicly available about his career and domestic joys and tribulations.

What was never directly mentioned in print was his perpetual struggle to remain on an even keel. "You never really knew," Housser said. "Sometimes it was whether he looked out the window in the morning at fog or sunshine." There is little doubt that Guy's bipolar disorder and his battles with booze were connected.

Working from home and writing for a monthly publication and intermittently for local publications and the CBC enabled Guy to live with those demons, meet deadlines, and maintain quality. Housser was his most reliable editor and proofreader and his essential business manager.

While he still wrote for smaller publications at home, his local contributions had no reliable home. Most of his local print outlets of the 1980s, such as the *Newfoundland Quarterly*, *Newfoundland Lifestyle*, and a short-run magazine called *This Week*, had modest circulations.

Guy began writing for *Atlantic Insight* in April 1979, its first issue. In a letter to the magazine's editor, Sharon Fraser, he wrote that *Insight* had always been important to him because "it allows me to proselytize on the other side of the Cabot Strait where the need is great."

Fraser offered her own credible assessment of Guy's work as an introduction to the 1987 collection of his *Insight* columns:

The column has, likewise, been of special importance to readers of *Atlantic Insight*—not as much for the proselytizing as for the humour. Ray Guy's name is, of course, synonymous with humour but what makes his humour special is its edge of skepticism, its tempered cynicism, its remarkable compassion. He understands how the world works and how he and his fellow Newfoundlanders fit into it.

Fraser observed that Guy's writing changed over the years in both style and substance:

The change reflects both the changing times and a reluctant maturity. Ray Guy still sees injustice and exploitation all around him but he sees them today with the satisfying attitude of one who can have an effect, of one who has a listening and respectful audience.[75]

"Tempered cynicism" and "remarkable compassion" are adept phrases that capture important truths about Guy's evolution as a writer in the 1980s. Fraser could not, however, anticipate all the consequences of his increasing exposure beyond Newfoundland and Labrador, or of his imperative to earn a living.

Despite only scattered print exposure in Newfoundland and Labrador, Ray Guy was far from idle on the home front during the 1980s. Throughout the decade, he wrote commentaries for CBC Radio in Newfoundland and occasional scripts for CBC Television. He wrote a successful play, *Young Triffie's Been Made Away With*, and he became a television actor. He also cultivated an adjunct trade as a kind of journalistic tour guide, a squire for the always curious Mainland press corps.

Partly through his work for *Atlantic Insight*, but also because of his reputation as the satirical giant-killer of the Smallwood era, Guy had developed a reputation among Mainland reporters as Newfoundland's go-to quipster. The bigger newspapers and other media with decent travel budgets regularly sent their people to Newfoundland, the newish and seemingly exotic province, for perfunctory political survey pieces and quirky television news kickers. Guy excelled at aiding and abetting their efforts, but it gave him little pleasure.

As every writer with gifts of wit and satire knows, it is one thing to come up with deadly lines and deft commentary while sitting reflectively at a desk, driving on a deserted country road, or, as Guy sometimes did, strolling on a lonely beach. It is a much greater challenge to come up with the perfect sound bite or witticism on cue, a command performance, with a reporter scribbling feverishly at your knee or a TV camera winking 6 feet from your chair.

Guy joked about his role as the unofficial, add-water-and-stir Newfoundland and Labrador clipster. In fact, the role troubled him, adding to other stresses he encountered while trying to cobble together a decent freelance living.

Guy's popularity with offshore reporters had an early and auspicious beginning in 1971 when he was noticed by *Time Magazine*, which then maintained a bureau in Montreal, headed by James Wilde, a seasoned foreign correspondent. Wilde flew to St. John's to meet Guy, lured by the compelling tale of a local satirist in defiant opposition to a powerful premier. The two writers got along. Guy had long admired *Time*'s crisp and high-velocity prose, and Guy's subtle wordplay pleased Wilde. His report, "Jester in the Kingdom of Joe," cast the unkempt Guy as a witty and subversive force, insulated by jokes and a kind of poetic licence, while gradually but surely undermining the monarch:

To anyone passing him on the stairs, he could be the janitor, casually toying with a cigarette, impatiently waiting to mop up. Usually dressed in faded khaki trousers and a worn shirt. If he is wearing socks, they are unlikely to match. But in Newfoundland, Premiers do not read janitors and socks are not the measure of a man. Throughout the quiet nighttime hours, Ray Guy will agonize over a typewriter and in the morning, nervous men will search out his words. In Memorial University's English classes, where he is recommended reading, students will study his driving excellence of language: somewhere in the Witless Bay Barrens, Aunt Cissy Roach will cackle malevolently.

In 1971, every Canadian journalist read *Time Magazine*, especially its *Time Canada* section. Wilde did more than any other to introduce Guy as a fruitful contact in Newfoundland. Wilde left behind precisely the kind of Guy quotes those visiting reporters sought when making their rounds in the Happy Province. Their Newfoundland assignments were rarely about news. They were about colour, the brighter and more variegated the better. For television reports, even on the CBC, outport accents requiring on-screen text translation were especially prized.

Wilde asked Guy to describe Newfoundland's politicians. Guy complied:

> Decent, upright, honest persons whose mothers always count the silverware after having them to tea.

And Newfoundland's civil service:

> It is organized along the lines of the Mexican army— not much pay but unlimited licence to plunder.

With the majesty of *Time* as his calling card, Wilde was among the few reporters ever to get Smallwood to comment on Guy. Smallwood told Wilde he read Guy "only occasionally" and found him "very witty." Wilde conveys the sense that Smallwood was keen to change the subject to one closer to his heart. Wilde soon quotes Smallwood on his favourite subject, in perfect pitch:

> All my days are busy. Each one more busy than the last. I'm never not busy. I don't know what it is not to be busy. If I am not busy at this, then I'm busy at something else. You know how it is when you're busy.[76]

The Mainland media traffic to Guy's door intensified after he became a freelance journalist in 1974. One notable performance was offered in 1975 when he was still describing himself as an Unemployed Employable.

Writer Silver Donald Cameron called on Guy at Chamberlains in the summer of 1975. Silver Donald, so named to distinguish him from the main herd of Nova Scotia Donald Camerons who were not prematurely grey, was then and remained an author and an academic of substance. He had moved from Ontario to Cape Breton to pursue a writing and teaching career. Silver Donald's piece appeared in the November 1, 1975, edition of *Weekend Magazine* under the title "Fool's Laughter—Ray Guy's Satire Turns to Sorrow." It telegraphed the challenges Guy would encounter as a journalist without a journal.

Then 36, Guy was more than a year into his post-*Telegram* life. His tongue was loosened by a beer or two and there were plenty of cigarettes at hand. An accompanying photo in the magazine shows him hove off in his comfortable recliner, moderately untidy, which was not uncommon. If Guy put on a new suit, he tended to look like he had slept in it. Silver Donald also found him in the mood to be provocative and quotable.

Three years into the Moores premiership, Guy was woefully aware that the new Newfoundland politics looked remarkably like the old. Cameron wanted to hear from him on the subject. Guy did his best. If anything was missing, it may have been a more worthy target than Premier Frank Moores—a Smallwood perhaps, at whom Guy could aim his more acidic darts. As Cameron discovered, Guy still had the words. He seemed to be seeking a place to land them.

There were many memorable lines:

> It hasn't taken him [Moores] long to find where Mr. Smallwood hid his book of operating instructions ... while poor Mr. Smallwood in full flight always reminded us of a little cock-sparrow Napoleon, the cut of Mr. Moores when top-notch recalls nothing so much as one of those gross slope-headed Fishing Admirals who made things so merry for us so long ago ...

Anger and attitude were on display:

> There's 10,000 or 12,000 a year ... headed to T'ronto to work in construction or down the sewers or whatnot—10,000 or 12,000—and meanwhile planes are landing at Torbay with 10 or 20 people a month, comin' down here to run the banks and chain stores and take top civil service posts. I s'pose they're qualified—why shouldn't they have jobs?—but their influence is so far out of proportion to their numbers because they automatically go to top positions.

And raw emotion surged:

How much would it take to force us all out of Newfoundland? How much did it take to force people off
smaller islands? How much did it take to force people
off Bell Island?

The same tears but more of them. The same heart-
break but more of it. The same pain deeper than words
but multiplied.

It is a strange, illogical and perhaps primitive feeling
to feel at home here and only here. But it is a real feeling. If it is not, then where does the pain come from?[77]

Cameron, who died in 2020, visited Newfoundland often and had
an empathetic awareness of such Newfoundland angst. He found
Guy quotable enough, and typically outrageous. But there was
something disconcerting about Guy's performance which Cameron did not flag. A Ray Guy caricature was now taking the stage,
in apparent rehearsal for a role that would become important to
his future as a freelancer. Guy was aware that this new brand as a
mercenary pundit could redefine him. He also knew his cheaper
wisecracks could be marketed. By his own account, the conflict
made him uncomfortable, even a little embarrassed.

Guy usually treated such discomfort with satire. For *Atlantic
Insight* in 1987, he described a fictional encounter with a fellow
from CBC's *The National* during a local election campaign. "They
tell me you're the funny guy around here," he quotes Mr. CBC as
saying. "So all I want from you is a short, snappy comment on each
of three political leaders."

Guy noted, with slightly veiled admiration, the efficiency and
confidence of those Mainland reporters. They seemed to know exactly what they wanted and how to get it. He wrote that he would
become even more helpful by creating a "get" list for the perfectly
rounded eight-minute takeout on a program such as *The Journal*,
CBC Television's illustrious current affairs show of the 1980s. His

advice to the CBC person was to cast the following characters for the piece:

1) An up-and-coming young leftish person destined to loom large in Newfoundland's future;

2) An up-and-coming young rightish person, likewise destined;

3) Horny-handed fisherfolk in a picturesque village no more than 20 miles from St. John's airport;

4) A woman sociologist from the university, preferably one who rears goats and operates an airtight, cast-iron, wood-burning apparatus;

5) A populist buffoon who, with the fisherfolk, counterbalances the profundities and the two up-and-comings and the goat lady.

Obligingly, Guy not only provided the categories, he offered names or at least the coordinates for local performers totally suited to fill them. He explained that each such person holds office under each heading for a term of five years.

Richard Cashin, the fisherman's union chap, occupies category Number One while Miller Ayre, a businessman and St. John's city councilor, fills Number Two. Number Three is staffed by three or four fishermen from Petty Harbour, a village conveniently near St. John's but which looks like Peggy's Cove N.S. did when Peggy was still a maiden. In the fourth category, there are actually two women sociologists. They divide the burden, depending on whose goat herd is due to freshen. I have the honour to hold down the fifth posting myself with my term still a year and a half to run.

Walking an appropriately hazy line between satire and the way things really were, Guy confessed that it was all becoming too much. Certain of the office holders he appointed had become parodies of themselves, and he feared a similar fate.

> The CBC chap confided that those horny-handed fisherfolk in Petty Harbour have become so professional they're almost useless ... "The very gulls have learned to swoop past on cue. I was tempted to tell them," sighed the CBC chap, "to drop their phony Newfie act and show us something of their souls."

Guy acknowledged defeat. It was time to give it up.

> I couldn't come through. It was a poor excuse that I had a broken leg still a-mending, a six-month-old upstairs with a rising temperature, a Block man at the kitchen table shaking his head over my income-tax returns and the upshot of a recent breathalyzer test still pending. The CBC was welcome to my blood but you couldn't see my merry old soul for bandages.[78]

Satire aside, greater and lesser versions of all the calamities listed above, and many others, befell Guy during his challenging years as a writer too talented to be struggling but constantly facing demeaning invitations to act the fool for profit.

In short, and despite such touchstones as *Atlantic Insight* and CBC Radio, Guy's road from secure and salaried employee of the *Telegram* to "populist buffoon" was often rocky. He needed to earn a living to augment, if not match, Housser's CBC salary. With a few notable spikes, his post-*Telegram* years would always be low-earning years. Magazines such as *Atlantic Insight* would have paid in the low hundreds of dollars for each column. Too often, media folks both locally and from away expected the celebrated local fool to work for fool's gold. It was Housser who put a definitive stop to Guy's good-natured tendency to do just that.

Nor did passing years and perpetual stresses contribute to better health. As the 1980s rolled on, Guy was bedevilled by financial matters, by the routine pressures of family life, and by his private demons. He was in his 40s when he realized—Housser may have realized it first—that he would have to diversify, to cultivate and market his auxiliary talents as a playwright, an actor, a television commentator, even as a writer of books for children.

Guy also realized a cold fact that many other Newfoundland journalists had absorbed in the 1970s and 1980s and since. If skilled local journalists wished to remain in Newfoundland and Labrador and earn anything approximating professional incomes, they would have to shill for government or private enterprise, or, if incapable in the gut of doing either of those, seek work at the CBC.

CHAPTER 18
Radio Waves and Raves

Until the early 2000s, CBC Radio and Television, despite common management at the top, functioned as silos both regionally and nationally, a house divided, as it were, by a common purpose.

The English Radio and Television networks gave each other a wide berth, Radio resenting TV's greater resources and commercialism, TV snickering disdainfully at Radio's above-the-fray self-satisfaction. The Francophone service, Radio-Canada, was a separate solitude altogether, essentially replicating all English services for a much smaller geographical and linguistic reach. Resentments crossed the language lines as well as those of the internecine media services.

Despite such distemper, the twin worlds of CBC and Radio-Canada, most notably on the radio side, remain beacons of quality and useful public service when compared to most of their private broadcasting competitors. Over the decades, they also have presented boundless creative and financially stable career opportunities for ambitious young and talented Canadians. Aspirants have had both Radio and Television and two languages in which to seek success. By 1990, they had CBC *Newsworld* and its Francophone sister service. Today, CBC talent finds new outlets on multiple digital platforms.

In the 1970s and 1980s, CBC jobs were abundant, especially in thriving regional centres such as Newfoundland and Labrador. Many technical, production, and administrative support jobs could still be won by persons with high-school level education. All editorial, production, and even senior management jobs were reachable by people with undergraduate university degrees in almost any discipline.

Both Ray Guy and Katharine Housser benefited from the largely autonomous leadership at the programming level in local CBC Radio and TV. At various times, each enjoyed opportunities in both. Housser was a career public broadcaster in radio and television. Guy found opportunities as a versatile freelance contributor who had discovered that there could be more to journalism than newspapers, and more than one way to package his prose.

Years before, from his safe *Telegram* seat a block or so east of the CBC Radio building on Duckworth Street, Guy had often ridiculed the public broadcaster, deriding its apparent multitudes of staffers as "the sandal-shod minions of the CBC." In so doing, he was cheered gleefully by his newspaper colleagues and occasionally by CBC's own managers, especially when the Corporation's powerful unions were defamed. When the wheel finally turned, and Guy needed the CBC, minor exhibitions of humility and compromise might have been expected. But Guy was Guy. Neither would be offered, but a few would be forced upon him.

At the newspaper, even under the proprietorship of Lord Thomson of Fleet, Guy generally wrote whatever he felt like writing, enjoying a nearly unfettered licence that he occasionally misused. At the CBC, programing is the domain of producers, an elite and powerful college of cardinals who make the content decisions. In news and current affairs, producers are generally treated with some deference even by management. At the CBC, writers, whether staff or freelance, work for producers.

Guy rarely did exactly what he was told in any previous role, and few editors dared suggest what he should do. While hardly a sweat shop, the CBC expected him to do what he was asked to, at least in broad strokes. The smarter producers were collaborative. But overall, the Guy wine was watered more at the CBC than it had been at the *Telegram.*

Inherent differences existed in the interests and approaches of those media. To oversimplify an important one, the 1960s and 1970s *Telegram* was "into" Newfoundland politics. The local CBC, on balance, and especially CBC Radio, was more engaged with Newfoundland culture, music, and the arts. It covered the basic news, but it disproportionately reflected the arts, usually attempting to tidy them up. At Memorial University in the 1960s, a professor adapted and improved upon a quote from C.P. Snow. The role of Memorial, it was said, was to "humanize the sciences and Simonize the arts." Local CBC Radio appeared to have a similar mission. The arts, of course, included comedy, and Guy was funny.

Beginning in the mid-1970s, CBC Radio and TV producers encouraged Guy to play to one of his proven but gentler comedic strengths, the creation of old geezer wise guys from the outports. That programming tendency, a very CBC and, frankly, a very Townie thing, sought stereotypes: exaggerated versions of old bay-farts who were rarely as clever in real life as their fictional caricatures might suggest, even those created by Guy.

Among Guy's late 1970s characters, first created for the TV music program *All Around the Circle*, was one called "Skipper Eph." Eph was short for Ephraim, one of a long list of Old Testament names given to Newfoundland men, baymen mainly, around the turn of the 20th century.

Newfoundland writers of the era could not seem to get beyond the Old Testament for names, and CBC producers picked up the habit. The hero of Harold Horwood's 1966 novel *Tomorrow Will Be Sunday* is Eli Pallisher. The father of Newfoundland novelist Percy Janes was named Eli too, and the leading character of Janes's 1970 novel *House of Hate* was Saul Stone. Ted Russell's radio scripts of the 1950s were *The Chronicles of Uncle Mose*. In the *Chronicles*, even Jethro Noddy's billy goat had an Old Testament name, King David.

Male names such as Israel, Joshua, Hezekiah, Aaron, Eleazar, and Abraham were common, especially in Protestant outports. Outport Newfoundland women born between 1900 and 1940 disproportionately were named Sarah, but many were given lovely, less common biblical names such as Leah, Delilah, Miriam, and Tamar.

Less common again was the name of a woman from Glenwood in Central Newfoundland who wrote an admiring letter to Ray Guy on October 1, 1973. It was signed "sincerely, (Miss) Zipporah Steele," to which Ms. Steele added: "how's that for a Bible name—Moses's wife." Ms. Steele pointed out that she was "not a recluse like Aunt Cissy Roche or Roach," but despite five heart attacks and surgery for a slipped disc, she never had to buy a vegetable and still grew enough potatoes for her own use and to give her friends. Postscript, Zipporah noted that "I make my own bread and Black Current Liquor ... good too."

Another old-skipper series, again created by Guy at the behest of CBC Radio producers, featured an Uncle Eph-type character reincarnated as Skipper Abraham Boggs of Bung Hole Tickle. One Skipper Abe piece, which Guy once read at an authors' evening in St. John's, was titled "Kicking against the Pricks," paraphrasing a favourite Guy quote from his Bible studies days. Coupled with "Giggle the Bastards to Death," the titles might constitute Guy's own mission statement.

In the "Pricks" piece, Skipper Abe reported that little Agnes Peabody of Bung Hole Tickle had competed in and won the All-Newfoundland Kick-The-Rock Hopscotch Playoffs at a competition in Port aux Basques.

Abe was put in charge of an initiative to assure that little Aggie received a suitable welcome home and proper recognition for, well, her feat. "Welcome Home Aggie" in big block letters sewed to six white sheets did not quite do the trick.

> ... We wanted something else ... the schoolteacher was no help at all. He went through his book on, wassaname, Shakespeare, but there was nothing there, he said ...
>
> So we went to the clergy. He got together with the Salvation Army Officer and the assistant priest down there in Bung Hole Tickle East and the three of them mauled over the scriptures for the best part of the evening.
>
> Finally, they come up with just the ticket. Deuteronomy, I think it was, Third Chapter, Seventh Verse— "Thou canst not kick against the pricks."
>
> See, back in them days pricks is what they used to call stinging nettles and bushes with thorns on them. And way in them times they used to run around in their bare feet. So, naturally enough, somebody had to tell them not to go kicking stinging nettles with their stark naked toes.
>
> Anyhow, it had a wonderful nice ring to it. We chopped out the word "not" and wacked it down on the victory banners in block letters; "Welcome Home Aggie! Thou canst kick against the pricks."
>
> And by golly, can't she ever![79]

Both Eph and Abe were among several awkward commissions offered Guy by the CBC. Those imperfect castings reflected no reluctance by the Corporation to hire him. Many producers were keen to do so. Instead, they reflected a misreading of Guy's core satirical strengths, which at their best were spiky, scolding, substantive, and much closer to current social and political matters than to some quaint and illusory pastoral outport past. By contrast with the Abes and Ephs, Aunt Cissy Roach, created for the *Telegram*, was always on top of actual public affairs and frequently in full rant against real-world perfidy and malfeasance.

During the 1970s and 1980s when Guy's more questionable CBC assignments were made, colliding forces were at play. One was an inherent difference between his advanced ability to create lyrical prose for print, aimed at the human eye, and a simpler, less-nuanced style of writing better suited to radio and the human ear. A listener to a radio reading does not have the same luxury to pause and grasp a simile or a subtlety as a newspaper reader does.

More worrisome, CBC management and occasionally producers had a tendency to declaw and debark Guy. Skippers Eph and Abe could be droll and entertaining, but neither did much in their time to afflict the comfortable or comfort the afflicted, as a good satirist, or a good journalist, should.

For such real and sometimes perceived CBC management meddling, Guy and Housser often blamed John O'Mara, a senior manager in radio, and his boss, John Power, who was director of the Newfoundland and Labrador region at the time. Neither manager was as hostile to Guy as Guy and Housser believed him to be. But both managers were highly sensitive to public sensitivity and to criticism.

The Skipper Abe pieces are well written, and many of them are funny. The handling of dialect and outport turns of phrase are true and on-target. But those touches did not represent Guy at his satirical best. The smaller number of first-rate pieces were offset by too many rustic Little Aggie tales that felt force-fed and contrived.

The CBC producers of such material may have had Charlie Farquharson in mind. Farquharson was Don Herron's deliberately cornball hayseed punster of the 1960s and 1970s who entertained Canadians over a mock CBC service called "KORN Radio." Farquharson's CBC Radio and TV performances made hundreds of Canadians howl with laughter, and surely thousands more wince and squirm with embarrassment.

Guy's heart was not really in this work. One result was that he occasionally slipped into a clumsy recycling of previous works, old Guy chestnuts that were fresh in the late 1960s but belaboured by the 1980s.

An example was one recurring Guy character, a stuffed-shirt, university pollster or researcher touring outharbours to capture public opinion as close to the stagehead as possible. In the nicely titled "Litres of Baccalieu" piece from the Skipper Abe series, the urban visitor is carrying a valise full of information about the metric system, seeking input, rather belatedly it seemed, as the metric system was introduced in Canada in 1970.

Skipper Abe:

> There was a feller come out tormenting me about it the other day. All dressed up in a suit of clothes, chin whisker on his face, one of them small satchels in his hand ...[80]

A decade and a half earlier, this character had pre-appeared, in a better guise in fact, out from the university to probe the impact of resettlement on village intelligence.

In that early piece, Uncle Anchorite Codpiece (pre-Eph, pre-Abe) and his grandson Sylvester Codpiece were cutting fish when a rap came to the stage-house door.

Sylvester answered it. "Uncle Rite! Chap here from Sin John's, tam on his head, pimple on the top of it, chinwhisker on his jaws, wants to see you."

> The visitor came carrying a tape recorder, a briefcase and a notepad.
> "Well, my good man," he said. "I'm Professor William Scrod from the university and we will shortly be launching another important study into resettlement."
> "... now tell me in your own words whether or not the Darwinian notion behind theories of intelligence that intelligence is adaptable and even that adaptation is the essence of intelligence applies in your case."
> "Lot of that on the go," said Uncle Rite. "Got a touch of it meself this week. Loose one day, seized up the next ..."
> "Deaf as a haddock," explained young Sylvester.[81]

Guy knew what he wanted to do at the CBC, as he always knew at the *Telegram*. He was happy to deliver satire and he loved to make people laugh. But he was also a serious journalist. He needed a public purpose. In the 1980s, Guy wanted to hunt bigger game than the CBC wanted hunted. Perhaps for him the CBC itself was big game.

In May 1980, CBC host and news announcer Doug Laite, always a loyal Guy fan and promoter, sat the writer down for a half-hour television interview, part of a network series on Canadian writers. It was slow going at first, but Laite pecked away, eventually drawing Guy out, getting as close to him as any interviewer ever had.

Laite introduced him as Canada's best columnist, noted Guy's description of himself as "a short, fat slob with a Mickey Mouse voice," and reminded viewers of Guy's status as a winner of the Stephen Leacock Memorial Medal for Humour.

Guy referred to his interest in journalism as his "call to holy orders." He told Laite that as a child he had listened to the Superman radio series but "identified with the nerd, Clark Kent."

Guy's characteristic self-deprecation came through in the interview. Laite asked him about the Leacock Prize, which Guy won in 1977 for *That Far Greater Bay*, his second book of newspaper columns, and about his National Newspaper Award. He had won the latter prize a decade earlier for his *Telegram* feature on the sad state of the Newfie Bullet passenger train.

Guy told Laite he had spoken to the judges of the Bullet piece after the decision and concluded that the piece had won "not entirely on its merits. They got a lot of weighty pieces, sociological stuff about the citizens' protest of the Spadina Expressway in Toronto and so on. The Bullet piece was comic relief."

If Guy had been a Toronto writer, his reports on the Spadina Expressway would have been weighty and funny. By then, he had his own advanced theory about the importance of comic relief in political commentary. It reflected his previously stated resolve of the Smallwood era to "giggle the bastards to death." He shared his theory with Laite:

> I discovered early that people wouldn't take a steady diet of righteous indignation and frothing at the mouth; preachifying about the defects of politicians. I also discovered that humour and satire could be very effective weapons, and practically the only ones available at the time of Smallwood's heyday.

Guy suggested that extensive government control of, or influence on, the Newfoundland media made reporters lazy. Most local media of the era were either compromised by various degrees of government advertising dependency or unduly impressed with Smallwood, who spoon-fed and charmed them. Guy discovered a new way to commit challenging journalism.

> He [Smallwood] was so flamboyant and colourful and bizarre, you didn't have to decorate much. You could take any speech of his and give it a little twist and it was Joey-in-Wonderland stuff—such an obvious target.

Doug Laite's mid-1970s encouragement of Guy as a radio commentator helped Guy's transition to freelance survival. The transition was never perfected, but in the 1980s Guy's CBC Radio commentaries did include one superior series. It lasted one season.

That series was a unique and biting weekly satire called *His Worship*, which skewered, and at times backhandedly praised, then St. John's Mayor John J. Murphy. Arguably, Murphy, a former broadcaster, was the city's most eccentric and interesting mayor of the late 20th century. Murphy had married into a successful Water Street department store business called The Arcade, known for clothing and dry goods at affordable prices. Whatever the quality of Arcade clothing, Murphy became popularly known as "Rags." Rags was a Townie in full, a leading retailer, president of the Board of Trade, and a Rotarian for 50 years.

Murphy as mayor was a constant St. John's presence. He was all over the local media. He could be seen almost daily perambulating along the city's streets and walking trails, often hunched below an umbrella or holding a quiff hat in place against a gale of wind, always exuding an affection for the old city that made him a popular and recurring choice at the municipal polls.

Murphy had a few personal affectations and quirks that made him attractive to a satirist. He pronounced certain favourite words in unusual ways. "Tremendous" always became "tremendjus." He affected patrician comportment. One story, not to be told under oath, but often told by Guy, was that Murphy, while campaigning provincially for the Liberal Party in a St. John's by-election, donned white silk gloves for his handshakes with working-class voters.

Guy's mischievous collaborator on *His Worship* was Karl Wells, then the popular daily weatherman for the CBC television news program *Here & Now*.

Wells, an accomplished broadcaster now retired, is also an actor with a gift for voice impressions. He soon had John Murphy's distinctive shrill pitch down so perfectly that members of Murphy's own family complained to the CBC about confusion in the community. People sometimes heard the voice on the radio without having heard the setup or realizing it was satire. They wondered why the Mayor's comments sounded extreme, even by his usual exuberant standards.

A classic early edition of *His Worship* opens with sound effects— the roar of waves on a beach and seagulls squawking loudly. The Mayor is supposedly strolling on a Florida strand in early spring, Newfoundland's most reprehensible season, encountering along the way just about every St. John's patrician and outharbour mayor with the time and money to get out of Newfoundland in March or April. The year would have been 1980. Brian Peckford was the premier, having recently replaced the rakish and much-married Frank Moores. The wave noise fades out, replaced by the unmistakable Murphy chirp:

Well. Well. Good morning to you Mrs. Smallwood. Morning Ank. Lovely morning. Now there's a sight you won't see every day of the week. Mrs. Smallwood and the Honourable Anthony J. (Ank) Murphy busy as nailers with their little buckets and shovels building a sand castle together just above the high-water mark.

Yes, I must say that at this time of the year St. Pete's Beach beats the absolute heck out of Northern Bay Sands. Yes indeed. I mean here it is not quite breakfast time and here one is walking alone in one's sandals and one's navy blue bathing suit and already one's chain of office is almost hot to the touch. Really amazing. Really amazing.

Grayshus me. Here's an absolutely top-notch conch shell. Councillor Pumphrey will be so pleased with this I'm sure, and I mustn't forget that bag of grapefruit for Deputy Mayor Shannie Duff ...

Morning Doctor Collins. Canon Babb. Lovely Morning. I mean where else but St. Pete's beach would you see a scene like that. The Minister of Finance for Newfoundland and the Right Reverend Canon R.R. Babb sharing the same bottle of Coppertone suntan lotion ...

Yes, a little home away from home is what one can truly call Florida. I mean within five hundred yards on any beach you're bound to run into ever so many ... Good morning Mrs. Moores ... Newfoundlanders taking advantage of the tremendjus travel bargains available after the 15th of April.

Morning Mrs. Moores! Lovely morning, yes indeed. A lovely, lovely lady, that Mrs. Moores is too.[82]

Karl Wells's ability to mimic John Murphy's voice perfectly complemented Guy's ability to capture Murphy's exuberant phrasing.

Wells was a teenager when Guy was at the height of his *Telegram* fame in the late 1960s. He recalls becoming aware of Guy as a key voice among a growing movement of Smallwood detractors, a camp with which Wells identified.

"We were always a family that received *The Telegram* every day, and dad was a news junkie," Wells notes. "So I started reading Ray. I thought he was brilliant. I thought he was a genius. I'd never read anything so funny and so well-written before. I read him religiously then. He was so far above everything else that was in *The Telegram* at the time. That's what it seemed like to me anyway."

Karl Wells also recalled his first meeting with Guy, which he thinks was in 1977. It took place at the old CBC Radio building on Duckworth Street, which had its main entrance on Duckworth and a rear entrance that gave onto Henry Street next to what was then the Capital movie theatre.

"Kathie had brought her baby to work. And I remember she let me hold the baby ... it was her first child." Karl said Housser and daughter, Rachel, had left by the front door and he was on his way out the back door when Guy was coming in. They had not previously met but each recognized the other from photos and from Karl's TV role.

"He asked, 'is Kathie here?' And I said no, she just left about 10 minutes ago. And he said, 'Jesus Christ.' And I said she took a cab. And he said, 'she took a cab! We can't afford cabs!'"

Wells worked for Kathie Housser when she was producing the local afternoon show *On the Go* for CBC Radio. He respected her as a journalist and they became friends. "I was terrified of her at first. She had this reputation for being ornery and difficult to work with and demanding ... I suppose I was intimidated by her. And I had heard that she had graduated top of her class from Carleton and that she used to correct student papers when she was still a student."

Wells was also aware that Housser had triggers. "She became really angry when, after she got married to Guy, some fool at CBC decided they were going to change her name for her. They started sending her packages, transmittable envelopes and so on, with 'Kathie Guy' written on them. She would cross it out and put in 'Housser.'"

Wells discovered his talent for impersonating Mayor Murphy quite by accident. In one election campaign, Murphy ran armchair ads on CJON television in which he talked directly to the camera about municipal matters. Wells started aping him for fun. Someone remarked on the uncanny resemblance and Wells kept practicing. Next thing, he would become Murphy in the CBC television studio as he was warming up to do his weather forecast. The crew would be in stitches.

Radio producer John Furlong got wind of it. Furlong suggested that Wells simply get on the radio and talk like Murphy, making it up as he went. Wells declined, insisting he would need a script. Furlong asked Wells what he thought of having Guy write it. Wells was thrilled. "Yes, absolutely. He'd be perfect." Wells said he was not sure Guy knew what he was getting into.

"He called me and wanted to hear me. He wanted to be sure that what he was hearing about my impersonation was true." Wells channelled Murphy and began to tell Guy, by telephone, of his (Murphy's) concern that there might not be adequate bunting, with Union Jacks, on the windows of Water Street business premises for an upcoming royal visit. Wells says Murphy had promised publicly that he would have his entire staff standing on the roof of the Arcade waving Union Jacks when the Royal personages passed by.

"Guy asked me to think about words and phrases that John would say that I thought I could do well. When you do an impersonation of somebody, it's like when you do a drawing of somebody, a caricature, you focus on some feature, like Trump's tie, and when you're doing the voice it's the same kind of thing. And I had a few words, like tremendjus ..."

A CBC colleague of Wells was a close friend of the Murphy family. Through that colleague, Wells learned that when the *His Worship* pieces started to roll out, the family, especially Marjorie Murphy, John's wife, was not pleased.

"Not necessarily Murphy himself, but members of his family were not happy. And I do remember at her father's [John's] funeral, Trish Murphy, John's daughter, came up to me and said, 'dad loved your impressions.' She said, 'one of these days when all this is passed, I'd like you to do it for me.'"

Meanwhile, true to the local CBC ethos of the time, someone at the TV station made rogue copies of the broadcasts and gave them all to Murphy. Murphy's second wife, actor Sheilagh Guy Murphy (no relation to Ray), later informed Wells that Murphy had the entire collection at home. "He probably had better quality tapes than I had," Wells noted.

Internally at CBC and externally in the community, the response to *His Worship* was overwhelmingly positive. Wells saw the pieces as reflecting a well-established genre of CBC radio dramatic-comedic programming, in the Max Ferguson tradition. When Ferguson impersonated Pierre Trudeau in a mock setting such as having tea with the queen, a listener would hear the soft clink-clink of superior china.

Wells said he would have liked to have included additional voices and more sound effects in the pieces. He found CBC Radio management of the era a little gun-shy of such Toronto trappings.

Producer Furlong found other enhancements. On one notable occasion, Guy's script called for the voice of Bas Jamieson, a hugely popular CJON open-line radio host and brother of federal Liberal politician Don Jamieson. Bas, in an admirably sporting gesture, came to the CBC studio and recorded his own voice. For several golden radio moments, Bas Jamieson, Mr. CJON, could be heard on the CBC asking "Y'r War-ship" a list of fictional questions written by Guy.

As radio entertainment, *His Worship* had success baked into it. It had Murphy, the Townie on steroids who had the ability to be both mocked and admired, often by the same people. It had Guy, in a largely anonymous role that properly played to his strengths. And it had Wells, who had earned his own celebrity status on CBC Television.

Despite his high CBC profile, Wells strived to salvage as much of his own privacy as he could in the fishbowl of small-city broadcasting. A mark of Wells's conservative social caution was his stipulation, accepted by both Guy and CBC, that if there was anything in Guy's scripts that he was uncomfortable reading, he reserved the right to drop it. Another reason for this rule, in the context of *His Worship*, is that Wells had always liked John Murphy, even before he met him. Eventually they became friends. When Wells married his long-time partner, Larry Kelly, Murphy and Sheilagh Guy Murphy attended the wedding.

But the kudos for *His Worship* were not universal. As time went on, top CBC managers in St. John's became less comfortable with the broadcast and more attuned to members of the mayor's family and other detractors. While Wells and Guy were both credited in the introductions to each episode, perils remained. Wells shared the concern that "there might be someone out there who might think it actually was him."

His Worship debuted during the 1982–83 programming season. At the end of season 1, there was a strange silence inside CBC Radio about what would happen next. Wells wanted to know if there would be a second season.

> Furlong was non-committal. I was thinking, why non-committal? It was a bona fide hit. Ray was concerned as well because that was a big part of his income. At the time it may have been his only income.

Finally, I went down to radio—maybe I was summoned, I don't know—and I went into Furlong's office. He didn't say a word. He just reached into his drawer and took out this piece of paper and laid it in front of me. I just took it up and read it. It was from Marjorie Murphy to [CBC regional director] John Power.

She was saying this is all very well for Ray Guy and Karl Wells. "I'm sure they're having a great time. But it's not very much fun for me. People are saying to me, 'I heard John on the radio this morning. Is he well?' John, they actually think it's John! They actually think it's him! Please take this off or get rid of it!"

And, Wells recalled, that was that. "I remember running into Peter Miller, who was hosting the show at the time. And I remember saying to Peter, 'I can't believe that they're getting rid of this segment. It's so popular.' And Peter said, 'well you know, when you've got the Regional Director basically giving it the thumbs down, there's not much you can do about it.'"

Wells and Guy were disappointed. "I was especially disappointed for Ray. I always regarded him as this institution, this great Newfoundland artist. And he had to eke out, scratch out, a living. And I just felt it was wrong. I just felt he had been let down by the CBC."

Much later, in 1986 or 1987, Furlong called Wells and asked if he would do a John Murphy voice for a radio program. "I asked him if they were going to bring the series back, and he said no, it was just a one-off. I said forget it."

Murphy was elected mayor of St. John's three times. He served two terms in the 1980s, 1981 to 1990, and was elected again in 1993 before losing and retiring in 1997.

By the time Murphy returned as mayor in 1993, there had been extensive personnel changes at CBC Newfoundland and Labrador, in management and elsewhere. A door opened for a return of *His Worship*. It should have remained shut.

Wells and Guy both accepted the challenge. "The writing was as good as it ever was," Wells recalled. "But I was nervous because I had not done the voice in so many years. And by this time his voice had changed ... he didn't sound like he used to. He was older."

Wells said the new, older Mayor Murphy was harder to do. "I did the new voice on the first episode and didn't like it. Decided to go back to the old way." The series was short-lived. Wells had assessed the situation correctly. *His Worship* had had its day.

His Worship frequently featured sharp satire and savvy political commentary. It was not Skipper Abe. Murphy was a public figure, and the municipal government of St. John's was second only to the provincial government in Newfoundland and Labrador's governing power structure. The politician and the politics were fair game. Both Guy and Wells were comfortable with the format. The writer wrote it with precision and the actor performed it with panache.

During the 30 or so *His Worship* episodes, Wells never once invoked his editing prerogative. "I loved doing them. And I was getting a lot of kudos from people I respected. I remember Andy Jones saying how much he liked them. And I thought Andy Jones was a god." Jones is a Codco charter member, comedian and playwright, fairly regarded by many as Newfoundland's finest actor.

His Worship was an example of CBC Newfoundland and Labrador at its best. Its premature demise was not.

In the late 1980s, the Ray Guy radio problem, or challenge, spilled briefly into television. Guy's earliest column series for CBC-TV's *Here & Now* news show featured a 1950s costumed Karl Wells playing outharbour shopkeeper P. Michael Hynes. While the series was designed to have political edge, ultimately it swam in a similar stream to the outport uncles and old skippers material. It was a disaster.

Guy's television producer at the time was Bob Wakeham. "I was trying to figure out how to exploit his talents on a television news show, without having to put him in front of the camera," Wakeham recalled.

"So we came up with the character P. Michael Hynes, who owned a convenience store somewhere out around the bay. Ray wrote the script, and Karl Wells did Hynes. We built a small set, with a counter-top and shelves full of stuff you'd find in one of those ubiquitous stores, and Hynes [Wells] would pontificate on everything under the sun going on in Newfoundland. Ultimately, there seemed to be a consensus that it didn't work as well as we would have liked."

A minor irony was that both Guy's and Wells's parents were shopkeepers. Both artists were on comfortable turf with the idea of a P. Michael Hynes. The problem was neither the acting nor the writing. More likely it was that P. Michael Hynes, outport shop-keeper, like Abraham Boggs, ancient sage of Bung Hole Tickle, was a mummer, a dress-up—unrecognizable and surreal.

By contrast, *His Worship* had been a credible and only margin-ally exaggerated impression of a well-known public figure. Ray Guy fans appeared to want solid content delivered by an actual person. They wanted Guy unplugged.

Eventually they got him, on television. The P. Michael Hynes experiment was redeemed in the 1990s in another piece of experi-mental programming devised by Wakeham for *Here & Now*.

"I killed P. Michael," Wakeham said, "and then decided to just have Ray sit in a comfortable chair and talk once a week about anything that crossed his mind. As it turned out, he was a natural in that setting."

Despite Wakeham's commitment to it, and Guy's too, the series, while popular, was uneven and sometimes awkward. Some viewers complained that Guy looked and sounded uncomfortable, which was his natural mode in groups larger than two or three. Overcompensating, Guy sometimes seemed to be spitting through his teeth even when saying something innocuous. Occasionally, his tone lacked irony where it was needed most.

But a key component of this series worked. Guy was Guy, a real person commenting on real life. And based on viewer feedback, the series sat well with a large segment of the *Here & Now* news audience.

Azzo Rezori, a former CBC reporter and a close friend of both Wakeham and Guy, may have identified the dynamic that allowed Guy on television to be both awkward and appreciated: "He was an icon. He was like a prophet pounding away at his topics. He was an anachronism. But his self-consciousness was somehow endearing. Viewers may have felt for him ... were willing to walk with him."

One reason why the series defied the odds and survived for nearly a decade was that Wakeham gave Guy what he needed most, which was carte blanche to write and read whatever he wished. Finally, Guy was unleashed for CBC-TV's substantial local news audience as a satirist and a commentator with his powder dry, no longer square-pegged as an amusing but harmless misfit.

The series had brilliant moments. Guy's Denominational Fire Department piece, quoted in Chapter 2, remains a classic, much needed during the denominational education debates and brawls of 1992. His mad notion that firefighters would henceforth fight a fire only if the homeowner adhered to the same faith as the firefighter perfectly matched an education system in which you would be taught to read only if you attended the church that owned the school.

But carte blanche has its perils. Guy was less than a year into his *Here & Now* armchair series when he talked himself into trouble. In June 1991, he delivered a routine piece about vandalism in St. John's, making passing reference to some neighbourhoods in the city where such misconduct was thought to be more common.

The column was pre-Twitter and pre-Facebook, but the response to it would have set them both on fire. The notorious local radio open-line shows were swarmed with angry callers from those corners of town, their cries amplified by a chorus of political opportunists and echoed by Guy and CBC detractors.

The matter could not be ignored. In his next column, on June 19, 1991, Guy faced the vexed crowd with a curious blend of contrition and defiance. It tamped down the flames a bit, while remaining cleverly true to Guy's first principle as a columnist: short of defamation, he could say what he damned well felt like saying.

Last week, right here, I suggested, I intimated, OK I said, that there are probably some people in St. John's who think that all the punks in town are located in certain areas.

I don't believe that. I don't think that, and I didn't say that. There are some people who still do. Now that's hardly a hanging matter is it? Hardly a wild and outrageous comment? Hardly a big deal?

Look what happened. For a whole week now. CBC got some news out of that. And lots left over for NTV. And the newspapers have mulled it over. And the radio open line shows have certainly got their pickings out of it too. And what is this big news? What's all this twitter about?

"OOOh. Something scandalous my dear. I heard that she heard that someone heard that Ray Goy, Ray Goy, said that all the punks in town are up there in Shea Heights, and Buckmaster's and Humpty Hill Pond. I didn't hear it meself. No. But I heard that she heard that he heard that he really said it. Tut tut tut. He should be shot! The head tore right off 'en. And what's the gov'ment going to do about it?"

... Well my time is about up here. But let me say
this. Let me just say this. If some people in places like
Shea Heights and Buckmaster's Circle and Mundy
Pond [were offended] ... I've been at this racket in the
newspapers and whatever for nearly 30 years. And if
you don't know by now who's side I'm on and who's
side I've always tried to be on, I'm sorry. I can't help you.
That's your problem.

Everything short of defamation, of course.

Later in the decade, Guy was holding forth as usual from his
Here & Now armchair. Suddenly he painted himself into a more
serious corner. A 1998 piece was under-scrutinized by CBC editors, perhaps because it sounded like vintage Guy in both tone
and content. It focused on an old Smallwood era target, former
Cabinet minister William R. Callahan, whom Guy disliked and
disrespected.

Callahan was a journalist who had held leadership positions
in the Corner Brook *Western Star*, the *Evening Telegram*, and the
Daily News. He held those latter two jobs following his many years
as a Smallwood confidant and minister. Post-politics in the 1990s,
Callahan ran a small private journalism school in St. John's.

As a member of Joey's Cabinet in the late 1960s, Callahan was
Newfoundland's point person in negotiations with Ottawa for the
development of Gros Morne National Park on the Great Northern
Peninsula. In those years, Guy and other critics suspected Callahan
of delaying the park for dubious reasons, including the possibility
of a silica mine within its proposed boundaries where "glass-grade"
silica had been detected. In the 1970s, Guy had written a dozen or
more *Telegram* columns on the subject, encouraging his west coast
readers to write letters of protest, which many of them did.

In his *Here & Now* commentary of April 28, 1998, Guy suggested that Callahan not only had delayed the park, threatening

its existence, but had had nefarious motives for doing so. He ridiculed Callahan in every possible way, as a journalist, as a journalism teacher, and as a devout Catholic. Callahan and his lawyer isolated a total of eight accusations in Guy's column, asserting that none of them was true.

Under Canada's reverse-onus defamation laws, the accused bears the burden of proof. Outcomes are crapshoots. A British Columbia Supreme Court judge once ruled that "son of a bitch" is not libellous, but "sick son of a bitch" is. CBC's lawyers and managers—I was one of the managers at the time—concluded that Guy and the Corporation had neither the ultimate defence of truth nor the arguable but less reliable defence of fair comment based on facts. The CBC concluded that several of Guy's defamatory statements simply could not be proved.

During an entertaining discovery hearing, Guy contended that all right-thinking Newfoundlanders knew the column was true, and implied the whole proceeding was a storm in a teapot. Following the discovery, a trial appeared quite possible.

Instead, the Corporation settled, paying Callahan an amount that remains hidden behind a confidentiality agreement. In an interview for this book in 2015, Callahan, the only person ever to successfully sue Ray Guy, said the award had taken care of his mortgage. Guy, prudently, made no public comment.

I saw Guy only a few times after the Callahan case. He remained, as always, friendly and funny. He exhibited no resentment to the CBC or to me personally. Housser, however, later indicated that Guy had felt betrayed by the CBC. Guy believed that his satirist's licence and local renown would have taken him to victory in a defamation trial. He also may have felt that a trial itself, win or lose, would have been an important statement in the interest of press freedom. I cannot say he was wrong.

Guy's armchair essays on *Here & Now* ran weekly for several years in the early to mid-1990s and sporadically thereafter. Among his best CBC work, they warrant a reprise, perhaps a published collection.

Amid the vagaries of freelance journalism and his battles with depression and alcohol, Guy led an engaged and productive life during the 1980s and 1990s. He continued to make light of his role as a go-to jokester, "a fool for fun and profit." His reputation beyond Newfoundland and Labrador grew apace, but sadly it never flourished.

His *Atlantic Insight* work had been consistent and welcomed by readers. It stretched him as a writer. His local presence on radio or TV was regular. His byline too was pervasive, not only in *Insight* but in a new St. John's weekly, the *Sunday Express*, and scattered among a multitude of smaller local publications.

In the 1980s, the daughters moved into their teen years. Housser left CBC Radio to join CBC Television as a producer with CBC's new *Newsworld* channel, becoming the Newfoundland and Labrador go-to guru for much of the national CBC news coverage from the province. Her reputation at *Newsworld*, now called *CBC News Network*, was as a solid and seasoned producer.

Journalism and satire got Guy in the door at the CBC. Once there, however, he discovered and developed a rewarding relationship with another of the Corporation's many mansions, the entertainment division of local television, where music and dramatic comedy reigned. This significant development in Guy's CBC career ran on a parallel track with his contributions on the information side.

As a writer and pundit for radio and TV, Ray Guy had played his Queen and his Ace of Hearts. He might as well play his Jack. With a little help from his friends, Guy became an actor. His single but significant television character was the sanguine boarding house bachelor, Jack House.

CHAPTER 19

Acting the Fool

Mary Walsh, scourge of politicians, "the bitch goddess of Canadian political satire," as *Maclean's Magazine* writer Brian D. Johnson once called her, does not usually hesitate when asked a straightforward question.

Could Ray Guy act?

"Er ... ah ... he could play himself."

Walsh was one of Guy's closest and most loyal friends. She grew up reading Guy and savouring what she read. She eulogized him warmly at his memorial service in 2013.

Walsh read Guy's *Telegram* column daily during her high-school years, and she read whatever she could find written by him until the day he died. Years before they met, Walsh felt she had known Guy forever.

"I was in Grade 9 and pretty much against everything that I could possibly be against," Walsh said. "And yet every day when I came home from school I read Ray's column. People don't think about how influenced young people were by it."

If Walsh was predisposed to admire him, after February 12, 1974, Guy could do no wrong. On that date, Guy's review of *Cod on a Stick* appeared in the *Telegram*, following one of its earliest performances at the Arts and Culture Centre. The show was an instant hit despite significant criticism from sensitive quarters.

The Cod Company, soon known as Codco, was founded in 1973. Their first show, *Cod on a Stick*, premiered that year at Theatre Passe Muraille in Toronto. Almost instantly, Codco became the unofficial custodians of Newfoundland humour—whatever the ingredients of that secret sauce—and the first to successfully export it. Whether conceived to do so or not, the troupe was destined to change the tone and temperature of Newfoundland and Canadian humour. Guy was one of the first to notice.

When Guy heralded Codco's arrival, Walsh was over the moon. "I remember we were so amazed," she recalled. "Ray said we were the children of Johnny Burke ... that was such a fabulous review, I guess that would have been 1974 ... and we were all in awe of him of course because we all read him."[83]

While there was churn in Codco membership over the years, the early core writers and performers were Walsh, Greg Malone, Tommy Sexton, Dyan Olsen, Cathy Jones, her brother Andy Jones, and Robert Joy.

Walsh noted that Guy's review was surprising because Guy, with his long-standing daily newspaper column, "seemed like an establishment figure ... although later on I realized that he wasn't establishment at all. Anyway, we revered him."

Malone had a similar response. "Ray was properly worshipped by the young population of the new Memorial University where my friends and I had lately settled," he wrote in his introduction to *Ray Guy: The Revolutionary Years.*

"So it was a great surprise when my friends and I found ourselves discussed in his popular column ... Our little show was enjoyed by all, even, and most importantly, by Guy ... and we were vastly pleased with his recognition."

Toronto audiences had gushed over *Cod on a Stick.* In St. John's, however, Codco ran into some fierce opponents. A defining theme of Codco comedy was its relentless unmasking of the hypocrisy of religion, especially that of the Catholic Church in which most members of the troupe had grown up.

The Church pushed back. Father James Hickey, then a spokesman for the archbishop of St. John's, stood on the steps of the Basilica of St. John the Baptist and told a reporter he didn't think much of Codco's efforts. He condemned the troupe for "belittling Newfoundlanders."

Subsequent events showed, dramatically, that Hickey, a recognized aspirant to power in the Newfoundland Catholic establishment, was not ideally suited to judge. In September 1988, Hickey pleaded guilty to 20 charges of sexual assault, gross indecency, and indecent assault involving teenage boys while he was a parish priest on the Burin Peninsula. He spent five years in prison.

"At least we weren't molesting children," Walsh commented sardonically.

But there were other and more credible public foes. The witty contrarian Rex Murphy, a major Guy fan who in 1974 enjoyed in Newfoundland the celebrity-commentator status he would later achieve nationally, went on television to pass judgment on Codco in his own caustic way. A new sewer project had just been announced for The Battery, a cliffy and traditionally ill-treated adjunct community east of downtown St. John's. Murphy said the development was a good thing and could have a bonus benefit as a repository for Codco scripts.

With Rex Murphy and the Catholic Church in one camp, Guy's endorsement of Codco was indeed more anti-establishment than not. Fortunately, as a local opinion leader, Guy ruled, especially among the post-Smallwood generation. His unqualified applause was important to Codco. It helped open a door to a wider audience for a new brand of irreverent Newfoundland humour, a brand not so different from his own.

Walsh and Guy finally got to know each other in 1978, the year they were both cast in the CBC Newfoundland and Labrador situation comedy series, *Up at Ours*, developed by Gordon Pinsent.

Acting for television was the most bizarre incarnation of Guy's post-*Telegram* career. Walsh, who played the lead role in *Up at Ours* as the boarding-house mistress, Mrs. Verna Ball, was in Guy's corner throughout, as a friend, performance coach, and as a frequent drinking buddy. Walsh's early collaborations with Guy were rooted in both work and play, the latter reflecting the fact that for many years they both were over-the-top consumers of the old powerful and dangerous.

They came together to help get *Up at Ours* going. Conceived by Pinsent, who Walsh calls everybody's favourite Newfoundlander, and realized for television by skilled local CBC producer Kevin O'Connell, the series was a milestone of homegrown television achievement.

CBC Television did not sign on in Newfoundland and Labrador until 1964, 15 years after both Confederation and CBC Radio had arrived simultaneously. This outrageous delay was engineered by Newfoundland and national Liberal Party grandees, pressured to protect the private interests of CJON-TV, the Newfoundland television monopoly owned by Liberals Geoff Stirling and Don Jamieson.

Despite the delay, perhaps due to it, CBC Television in Newfoundland and Labrador in the 1970s and 1980s became the most productive and successful of the Corporation's regional TV bases.

Its local audience acceptance was rivalled only by Winnipeg's long-established production centre and by intermittent flashes of similar success in Halifax.

"I started to work with Ray when he was Jack, the star boarder," Walsh said, referring to Guy's role in *Up at Ours*. "At that point Ray was so shy that his chin was always on his chest. He just never looked up at all. You could hear him say the odd really funny thing now and then."

In its first year of production, *Up at Ours* achieved reasonable audience support in Newfoundland and Labrador, despite weak scripts and some painful overacting by several members of a mainly amateur cast. It fared less well in other Canadian markets, where it played through a regional exchange structure then common in CBC-TV.

Notable exceptions to overwrought performances included Walsh, who had had significant stage experience with Codco, and who was well cast as the boarding-house proprietress, and Guy himself, whose modest "acting" role seemed to consist of occasional grunts and a know-it-all arching of his bushy eyebrows. Other strong performers in the large cast included Kevin Noble and Janice Spence.

The Newfoundland and Labrador television audience usually embraces locally rooted programming, and *Up at Ours* survived its first season despite an unevenness that reflected too many writers with different styles and talents. Neither Guy nor Walsh was among those first-season script writers. By the show's third and final season, and with the help of writer David Ross, Guy and Walsh wrote all six episodes, imposing a more consistent standard and generally smarter dialogue. Coupled with his acting earnings, Guy's writing fees were a welcome boost to the family income.

Following its third season, *Up at Ours* became a casualty of several forces, including the notoriously shifting underpinnings and mandates of CBC Television entertainment shows, budget restraints, and out-of-Toronto productions. Quality reasons also contributed to its demise. Too many cast members were inexperienced actors. And despite improved writing, scripts were so thin on plot that sporadic funny lines and able performances could not redeem them.

At the same time, certain cast members, Walsh and Guy foremost among them, drank too much. "I'm not sure what really happened," Walsh said. "I was drinking heavily then. We all were, except for Kevin O'Connell who was sober as a judge ... Perhaps if he was drunk it would have been OK."

Looking back at it all, Walsh also laments poor communications inside the CBC, never knowing from one episode to the next where the project stood. "When you're not in on the decision-making you often don't know what's going on in the CBC. So you don't know what secret things they are doing. I mean you could kill a bird and study its entrails ..."

Amid the chaos, Guy and Walsh bonded. "We became friends ... from acting together and being bored silly together and then writing together in the last year. I was only 28, playing a much older woman, but Ray had much more the look of Jack the boarder."

As carousing pals, Walsh and Guy attended a swell party at Edythe Goodridge's house in St. John's one winter night in the early 1980s. Goodridge, a forceful member of the Canada Council for the Arts, was the province's angel bureaucrat in Ottawa, an indispensable broker for federal arts funding.

"Edythe had people from the Mainland she was impressing," Walsh said. How impressed they were may be open to question, especially if they heard about Guy's and Walsh's adventure late that night on a snowy St. John's hill. Considering the circumstances, Walsh recalled the occasion with some clarity.

"Michael Cook [a playwright and *Telegram* columnist, and husband of Janice Spence] was passed out under a table. Ray and I were drunk, and then [after the party] we went out looking for more booze and we couldn't find any. Somehow or other I knocked Ray down and as it turned out broke his leg. But we didn't know his leg was broken, so myself and Richard Cashin and Roseann [a CBC journalist, married to Richard] kept picking Ray up and, tiresomely enough, he kept falling down."

In sober daylight, it was discovered that Guy had broken his leg in four places. Walsh was mortified. "Once I called and Annie [Guy] answered the phone and she said, 'mommy it's the lady who broke daddy's leg.'"

In *Up at Ours*, Walsh and Guy both looked their parts, neither of which called for glamour. Neither Walsh nor Guy ever boasted much about their physical attributes. In one unduly modest moment, the best Guy could say about his physical appearance was that he had no visible scars or tattoos. Walsh, meanwhile, equally self-deprecating and endearingly disingenuous, explained to Maclean's Brian D. Johnson that "all of my features are squat in the middle of my face ... I look like years and years of longshoremen and ironworkers."

The question regarding Guy's acting was worth asking twice: Could he act? The second time around, Walsh was less equivocal:

> Well Ray had a very specific style. He wasn't what you would call an actor ... It's a very specific thing that you are attracted to. It's like can Russell Peters act? No. But can he deliver a line? Can he tell a story? Yes.
>
> Because when Ray wrote he always wrote in a voice, and he did the voices out loud. So he was always acting in a way. As a columnist he would be acting. And the children, he said, would often be a little alarmed as he was doing the voices ... I write that way too, and you really have to have an empty house to do it. Because otherwise you feel really foolish.

While it lasted, CBC Television's commitment to big-ticket Newfoundland music and drama production proved to be a minor bonanza for many local talents, Walsh and Guy among them. Among the positive by-products of *Up at Ours* were their subsequent collaborations.

After *Up at Ours*, Walsh moved on in television. She contributed to the *Wonderful Grand Band* show, CBC Newfoundland's most popular and best produced music and sketch comedy series.

The 1970s success of Codco and the 1980s success of *WGB* helped set Walsh on a path that in 1992 spawned *This Hour Has 22 Minutes* for CBC network television. *This Hour*, which celebrated its 25th season in 2017, launched with four Newfoundlanders as hosts: Walsh, Greg Thomey, Cathy Jones, and Rick Mercer.

"Comedy requires a passion for detached observation," Johnson wrote in his profile of Walsh. "And no part of the country is more detached than the island of Newfoundland—which the entire cast of *22 Minutes* calls home."

Johnson's notion of "detached observation" would have fitted Guy just as well, especially in the 1960s and 1970s: a bayman pounding relentlessly at power structures bunkered in St. John's and Ottawa.

Up at Ours was the foundation of Walsh's and Guy's professional relationship, but their alliance evolved and matured well beyond that time. Guy wrote three full-length plays in his career. Walsh produced all three for the stage. She helped write and produce a feature film version of one of them, the dark and tangled murder mystery *Young Triffie's Been Made Away With*. Without Walsh, those intriguing and complex plays might never have been noticed.

In 1982, Walsh was directing plays and serving as chair of Resource Centre for the Arts. RCA is the community collective that was set up in 1979 to purchase and run the Longshoreman's Protective Union Hall on Victoria Street in downtown St. John's. For more than four decades, the LSPU Hall has been the nerve centre of emerging art and artists in Newfoundland. If there really was a Newfoundland Arts and Literary Renaissance in the 1970s and 1980s, as the writer Sandra Gwyn suggested, the LSPU Hall was its Left Bank.

In 1983, Walsh assumed a new position at the Hall, that of animateur, defined by the Oxford Dictionary as "a person who enlivens or encourages something, especially a promoter of artistic projects." The animateur is the content guru for the LSPU Hall. Through that office, Walsh could spend money on productions that interested her. It was an easy decision for her to spend some of the Hall's meagre war chest to encourage and support her friend Ray Guy.

Based on her enthusiasm for Guy's writing, Walsh first conceived of a work originally known as *The Ray Guy Show*, but which eventually became *Stunned, Stung, Bitter and Twisted: The Ray Guy Review and Capelin Supper.* The review was a series of skits based on Guy's columns, with continuity and music supplied by a cast that included Codco alumnae Walsh and Cathy Jones, along with actors Greg Thomey, Kay Anonsen, Rick Boland, and Ed Kavanaugh.

According to Walsh, no script of *Capelin Supper* survives. "We wrote some new stuff for it, but Ray didn't. He and Kathie were gone somewhere. He left us a box of paper and took off."

The box, disorganized and dropped off one night on Walsh's front step, contained clipped columns, dated and stapled on white paper, along with a cluster of miscellaneous materials obviously tossed in the box by accident. Some was "private stuff," Walsh said, "such as letters to Kathie from her mother encouraging her to do her Kegel exercises and so on ... OOO-K!"

While Walsh has no copy of the *Capelin Supper* script, she could quote a few lyrics from the revue, including a thematic song written by Thomey:

> Am I a Townie or a Bayman I can't tell.
> When I go to Folk Night it's a living hell.

The revue played for two weeks and toured the province. "Ray liked it and he liked us. But Kathie [Housser] was scathing about it." Mary does not remember why. "She hated it." Walsh added pensively: "But she loved Ray and he loved her. I think she must have run protection for Ray in some kind of way."

Walsh next asked Guy to write a play for production by the Resource Center for the Arts. She provided no topic and no parameters. The commission for Guy had three words: "write a play." Walsh wrote the cheque, and Guy wrote *Young Triffie's Been Made Away With*—in the fullness of time.

> It was really late coming in, and then it came in on those six sheets of carbon paper ... he'd send them all to us ... so I guess there was never a copy of Triffie that he had ... but there was no ending and we were already in rehearsal, and he kept saying "it's coming it's coming. The bodies are piling up like seal pelts here."

The play received mixed reviews. Fortunately, the LSPU Hall in 1983 had a large and loyal support group. They wanted productions to succeed; they were then, as they remain, supportive of all Hall efforts.

Noreen Golfman, a professor at Memorial University who has promoted Newfoundland arts with a zeal usually achieved only by CFAs, described *Young Triffie* in language that reflected the play's ambition, but which also admitted its obscurity. The main themes of *Young Triffie*, Golfman wrote, were "incest, pedophilia, mutilation, trespassing, alcoholism and pornography ... and Pastor Pottle being nailed, comically, to a table."

Anything else? Apparently yes. In 1996, Memorial graduate student Michael Fralic wrote a thesis on Ray Guy's plays for his Master of Arts degree. The title: "Marginalization and the Active Margins in the Plays of Ray Guy." In it, Fralic declared that *Triffie* "focuses on a history of ethnocentric and egotistic missionary activity in Newfoundland." Turning to Guy's other two plays, *Frog Pond* and *The Swinton Massacre*, Fralic—admittedly writing for a different audience—seems to find an endless freight of obscurity:

> His second play, *Frog Pond*, addresses a psychological dependency among many Newfoundlanders on exogenous cultures as the sources of cures to Newfoundland's economic and political ills; and his third play, focuses on the residue of colonial attitudes in the new regime, and on marginalization practices among Newfoundlanders.
>
> Guy also emphasizes the multifarious responses to processes of marginalization among marginalized people, drawing attention to the active margin as a site of struggle and change.

Despite opaque beginnings, Fralic's thesis is a helpful guide to all three plays, as well as an early academic salute to Guy's most complex literary achievements. Fralic clearly demonstrates that he knew what the plays were about:

> Guy's first play *Young Triffie's Been Made Away With* is set in 1947 in the fictional outport of Swyers Harbour. In *Triffie*, Guy depicts a community dealing with some of the last in a long line of religious and secular missionaries in Newfoundland, and interrogates the motives and the effects of many of those who came with heroic notions of helping out a poor marginal society.[84]

In its opening-night performance at the LSPU Hall, *Young Triffie* received a standing ovation after the first act. Walsh's recollection of opening night was that it then proceeded to bore audiences to tears in the second act.

"The first act was brilliant ... and then we had to do the f'ing second act and that's the killer for everyone including Shakespeare ... in the opening scene of the second act we almost lost everybody all the time because it was just two men sitting down and giving out information."

Act 3 apparently rescued the show and standing ovations and curtain calls were the order of events in all productions, including at least one outside Newfoundland. *Triffie* played in Parrsboro, Nova Scotia, where the stage was the deck of an ancient ferryboat called the *Kipawa*. The old ferry once ran between Portugal Cove and Bell Island in Conception Bay. Guy would have taken it often as a high-school student on the island.

Did the play have a structure? On that topic, Walsh became defensive, for herself and for her friend. "Well, I thought it did," she said. "But the reviews we got from people who were drama-y said it was about structure, and I'm so bad with structure myself that perhaps I didn't recognize it, and perhaps the structure was off."

Perhaps it was not. Those "drama-y" types, whoever they were, irk Mary Walsh to this day. "I'm not an expert on anything like that," she reflected. "But I have done a lot of work that's pleased a lot of people over time ... and this show was an extraordinary crowd-pleaser, just like Ray Guy. Maybe somebody could break down a [Ray Guy] column who knows how columns should be written."

As Walsh relates it, there is an intriguing dimension to *Young Triffie* of which few people, including most audiences for the play, were ever aware.

The play was written almost a decade before the Mount Cashel sexual abuse crimes by Irish Christian Brothers and others by local Catholic priests were publicly exposed. However, it was written well after rumours were rife in St. John's about such crimes, rumours subsequently proved to have been covered up by church apologists in both government and the media.

"Ray had been at *The Telegram*, and people at *The Telegram* knew," Walsh said. "Remember, when the Mount Cashel boys came out ... they went to the police and they went to *The Telegram*. It [*Triffie*] was almost prescient, it was prescient because Ray was there."

Consistent with Walsh's analogy between *Triffie* and Mount Cashel, it turned out to be none other than Doctor Melrose, a pillar of the Swyers Harbour establishment when he wasn't busy molesting boys, who inflicted the multiple stab wounds to Triffie's teenaged back. The knife was wielded post-mortem. The good doctor had killed Triffie accidentally in a botched abortion following her illicit impregnation by one Billy Head. Billy turns out to be Triffie's own half-brother, sired by her father, Pastor Pottle. Guy always enjoyed such twists of gossip and intrigue. The play had it all—insult, injury, and incest.

If the links between Mount Cashel and *Triffie* were a theme, the script did little to connect the dots. Nor did Guy himself when, years later, he offered his own enigmatic comment, referring to the play, as he usually did, as "Triff the Stiff."

> Triff the Stiff sometimes frightens me. Nearly a quarter of a century ago she introduced some gruesome pedophilia in a fictitious religious orphanage. A decade later something similar, involving a completely different religious denomination, did occur. Coincidence ... or ...?[85]

Despite Hickey's criminal conviction in 1988, the Catholic Church fought his victims' claims for compensation for more than a decade. It was not until February 2009 that the Supreme Court of Canada ruled that the Roman Catholic Archdiocese in St. John's was "vicariously liable" for the sexual abuse of eight former altar boys by Hickey. Even then, the full magnitude of the Mount Cashel scandals remained to be revealed.

In Walsh's view, "*Young Triffie* was basically about a pedophile." The pedophile was a fundamentalist preacher, Rev. Pottle, in a socially pinched pre-Confederation Newfoundland outport.

"Rev. Pottle received pornography though the local post office. The contents of the brown porn packages were known only to Pastor Pottle and to the post mistress, Aunt Millie, who did not speak of it until long after young Triffie's death."

The play, Walsh contends, is about pinched villages, large or small, and how they hang together and circle the wagons when under scrutiny.

"Aunt Millie [the post mistress] even though she talked about everything, kept that to herself [the porn in the mail]."

In the play itself, xenophobic villagers in Swyers Harbour are much more inclined to speculate that it must have been the village's only CFA, an oddball elderly English gentleman named Washburne, who did young Triffie in.

The Mount Cashel sexual abuse scandal was not just a story of priests and brothers assaulting children. It was a story of a bigger village called St. John's, where powerful players of the clerical and business establishments, along with sympathizers in the media and the provincial bureaucracy, did everything they could to keep the crimes hidden. It was a nefarious cover-up enterprise which succeeded for almost a decade.

Years later Guy commented savagely: "It takes a village to raise welts on a child."

A lesser layer of intrigue in *Triffie*, sufficient perhaps to sustain another complete drama, is the news that the busy Pastor Pottle can find time for incest only on evenings when he is not mutilating sheep while preaching fanatically about the "blood of the lamb," or hanging out at nearby Whitbourne abusing children at a local orphanage: Incest, Mondays, Wednesdays, and Fridays. Pedophilia, Tuesdays, Thursdays, and Saturdays.

Despite its acknowledged lumpiness, the stage version of *Triffie* was an overall critical and audience success. The subsequent film version of the play, entitled simply *Young Triffie*, was another matter altogether. Handsomely shot in a 2006 co-production between companies based in Québec and Newfoundland, it was badly and inappropriately played for slapstick laughs.

The film flopped. "We were the only film that ever got NO stars in the *Globe and Mail*. NO STARS," Walsh declared, still crabby after all these years. "Every piece of shit that comes out of Hollywood gets half a star. We got no stars."

The *Globe*'s starless review by critic Liam Lacey was published on February 6, 2007. Wrote Lacey: "Fans of veteran comic writer and actress Mary Walsh will be expecting something considerably wittier than the Newfoundland-based black comedy *Young Triffie*, a shrill heavy-handed farce more to be endured than enjoyed."

Lacey's review noted in passing that a 1986 *Globe and Mail* assessment of the stage show at the LSPU Hall in St. John's had celebrated the production as "howlingly funny." But the film? "There's a contrived happy ending," Lacey noted, "though, strictly speaking, in a movie as painfully unfunny as YT, almost any ending is a happy one."

Walsh is analytical about why the film version was such a roaring failure, once again in Guy's posthumous defence as much as in her own.

> So it was an unfortunate thing, and I should have … I could have … you know in many ways … I didn't know how to deal with Denise (the film's producer, Denise Robert) and I didn't know when to fight and when not … and you know I never even made a small film, and here I was with four million dollars and a bunch of stars … making my favorite person in the whole world's play into a movie … something I always wanted to do …

Some of the problem was that I was working with a French crew and a French producer ... and they have a certain sense of humour and we have a certain sense of humour and Ray Guy and Denise don't share a sense of humour and neither do I and so every decision I made in the editing suite, she changed. And she said "I've made 29 films and I have an Academy Award ... and (implicitly) you have made no films and you have no Academy Awards ..."

A recipe for division to be sure. The tension became a daily grind, relieved only by moments of accidental levity. The film was shot in Newfoundland. When the soundtrack for one scene included crickets chirping in the background, dubbed over, Walsh attempted to explain that Newfoundland does not have crickets, a truth unwisely questioned by a technician. "Even if there were crickets," she quotes herself as saying, "there is no way you'd hear them over the f'ing wind."

It is reasonable to conclude that only the irrepressible Mary Walsh, even when enabled by Canadian filmmaking incentive programs and interprovincial production funds, would have ventured into such potential turmoil.

It was no small challenge for anyone to transform a Ray Guy drama, set in Newfoundland in the 1940s and riddled with Newfoundland dialect and lore, into a feature film by a Québec company and a Francophone crew, their cinematic abilities notwithstanding. It is equally fair to conclude that Walsh did so in large measure out of her regard and affection for Guy.

"I loved Ray. I really wanted to say something about what fills my heart about him. Ray was the kindest person ever in the history of the world." As for the *Globe*'s zero-stars assessment of *Young Triffie*, "Ray would have made that into something good ... he would have celebrated it."

CHAPTER 20

Boy Reporter

Nothing extenuate, nor aught set down in malice.
—*Henry Winton, Motto of the* Public Ledger,
St. John's, 1820

Treat with respect the power you have to form an opinion.
—*Marcus Aurelius, Motto of the* Sunday Express,
St. John's, 1986

By training at Ryerson University and by formative experience at the *Evening Telegram*, Ray Guy became an accomplished reporter and newspaper feature writer. He was a satirist, of course, but those are born, not trained. Satire was the gift that set Guy apart as a journalist, but his love of everyday reporting remained with him throughout his career.

Guy's early years as a reporter and feature writer at the *Evening Telegram* were years of constantly reinforced achievement, an upward career path, and considerable fun.

It was hardly surprising, then, when in 1986 he was offered an actual salaried job as a reporter, columnist, and feature writer for a new weekly newspaper with a barrel of money behind it, Guy thought he had gone to heaven without the inconvenience of dying.

In its day, the *Sunday Express* bid fair to become the best newspaper ever published in Newfoundland and Labrador. It was indisputably the province's best weekly ever. Behind the enterprise was the long pocket of Newfoundland's most interesting entrepreneur of his day, Harry Steele of Musgrave Harbour.

Steele had been a Canadian Navy man on an upward career path. He was a 39-year-old lieutenant commander when Liberal Defence minister Paul Hellyer's 1960s integration of the Canadian armed forces arrived. The new normal included the grunt-green camouflage costume that replaced the distinctive sailor's blue. The disruption drove Steele out of the military and into his second career as a full-time capitalist.

As an entrepreneur, Steele was both rich and tough. An early major venture was a failing airline, the former Eastern Provincial Airways. He whipped the airline into shape and sold it at a handsome gain. When his EPA pilots struck his airline in the mid-1970s, grounding his expensive fleet of Boeing 737s, Steele mocked them as "overpaid, oversexed bus drivers."[86]

Steele had a genuine affection for Newfoundland and Labrador, where in advanced age he still lives in 2021, and a healthy disregard for political and commercial power structures, his own naturally excepted.

Steele liked newspapers. In 1985, he bought the Halifax *Daily News*, a tabloid with editorial merit and edge. He already owned the Robinson-Blackmore printing company in St. John's, which published a string of weekly newspapers in Newfoundland, but no newspaper in St. John's and no provincial paper.

Steele had witnessed the decline of the *Telegram* after the Thomson takeover, and the death of the *Daily News* in 1983. He believed the cash-cow *Telegram* had grown journalistically unambitious and was vulnerable. He decided to start small, with a well-funded weekly broadsheet on Sundays, and nurture it toward daily production, with the rotund and sluggish Thomson daily squarely in its crosshairs.

In 1985, Michael Harris was one of Canada's most ambitious and able young journalists and authors. Napoleonic in stature and nearly so in confidence, Harris was well established as a former CBC Television host and documentarian. By then he was reporting from the Ottawa Bureau of the *Globe and Mail*, following a stint as the paper's Atlantic correspondent, based in Halifax.

Harris's personal career plan at the *Globe and Mail* had a focused goal. He sought what is known in the business as an ex-posting, an overseas bureau job. Specifically, he wanted Beijing, there to succeed a long string of superior correspondents at the *Globe*'s most prestigious foreign bureau, one of whom, John A. Fraser, had cut his teeth at the *Evening Telegram* in the Guy era. In 1986, the Beijing bureau opened up. Harris made his bid, but it was not to be.

Harris did not take the rejection well, nor was he kind to his successful rival for the job, veteran correspondent James Rusk. "I remember Geoff Stevens, the managing editor of *The Globe and Mail*, calling me in and saying James Rusk is going to China. 'We have to give it to the old soldier.' The joke in the newsroom was, 'now he can bore a billion people.'"

Harris had covered Steele and his Newfoundland Capital Corporation for CBC in Newfoundland and Labrador and in Halifax for both CBC and the *Globe*. The two got to know each other and they got along. At his meeting with Stevens, Harris already had a job offer from Steele in his pocket, to become the editor and publisher of a new weekly newspaper in St. John's.

Harris told Stevens that Steele wanted to give him the money to start a new newspaper. A skeptical Stevens asked to see the offer. Harris hauled it out. Stevens had a look and said, "I'd advise you to take that offer." Painfully aware that his primary ambition, the China job, was now perhaps five years away, and probably forever lost, Harris took Stevens's advice.

"The offer was $75,000 as editor-in-chief and publisher," Harris said. That may have been the most generous salary ever paid a journalist in Newfoundland to that point, and more money than Guy earned for a year's journalism for too many years during his long career.

Guy and Steele did not know each other personally, but Steele was a Guy fan. "They were both baymen," Kathie Housser said. "That was enough."

The timing for the *Sunday Express* seemed perfect. Budget cuts were already chipping at local CBC television news by 1986. Meanwhile, the *Telegram* had fully evolved as an everyday Thomson money-spinner, offering routine news coverage but with no more than a passing interest in substantial journalism. The *Daily News* was long gone.

With Steele as the angel investor, Harris as an adventurous and inspirational editorial spark, and veteran writers such as Guy complementing a small platoon of promising youngsters, the *Sunday Express* launched. It was a welcome Sunday treat for St. John's readers who consumed it in rapidly increasing numbers.

The launch was on September 28, 1986. Deep into that busy first edition, at page 22, was Guy's first *Express* column. It was a big day both for Guy and for journalism in Newfoundland and Labrador. Unfortunately, on that day, Guy was forced to turn adversity into a virtue. His first piece for the *Express* began this way:

> It was the notorious curse of Lord Roy that struck me down. Because the natural bad luck of man could never equal this for damnability.
>
> There we were on the eve of launching the *The Sunday Express*, a newspaper brilliantly conceived and, as you can see, marvelously executed. It was like the daddy's room off the obstetrics ward where everyone lights the filter end of his cigarette. Tremulous but hot to trot like everyone else was R. Guy, Boy Reporter yet again.

A serious but mysterious illness had overtaken Guy and the run-up to *Express* day found him confined to hospital making the best of a bad job.

> My own magnum opus for the first edition was all but finished. Last thing before I went to bed I tucked a card with the word "Press" on it inside the hat band of my brand new fedora. But later, in the wee hours, I rolled off the bed and flopped around the carpet like a beached halibut because someone had driven a red-hot knife through my head.

Despite the affliction, Guy found the resilience to offer wry observations on the state of medical care at the grandly named St. John's Health Sciences Complex:

> It's a great hospital, the Health Sciences Complex. As I mentioned, my own room is so spectacular that I keep the door closed to avoid being pestered by line-ups demanding guided tours. But if this is what's called a private room, I shudder at the thought of a public one.
>
> Mine is like the Arcade at the grand opening of the 64th and three-quarters Anniversary Sale. It is a never-ending parade of angels of mercy, great physicians, spotty interns, spiritual pastors of your choice, the lady about the liquids, maintenance personnel, strayed visitors to other private rooms and the occasional person wanting to know where the University Bursar's office is. The only private part is the toilet since it has a lock but after three or four hours in there you tend to get Demerol flashback.

For chain smokers such as Guy, hospitals imposed an auxiliary torture approximating cold-turkey nicotine withdrawal. In the interest of addicts who might find themselves so confined, the patient Guy offered useful advice. "Put your face against the ventilation panel of any staff washroom and inhale deeply."

Meanwhile, the *Sunday Express*, volume 1, number 1, had hit the streets. Among its curiosities was an unusual full-page ad. It contained five words, set boldly against an otherwise snow-white background. "Good Luck Harry" appeared in 60-point type in the middle of the page. Lower in the page and to the right were two words: "Craig Dobbin." Newfoundland's leading entrepreneur and sometime business rival was rooting for the paper and for Harry, as were countless other Steele and Harris admirers.

As early as its second edition, on October 6, 1986, the *Express* was demonstrating the superior news judgment and editorial strength that would define it.

The lead story was a scoop by Harris that Fishery Products International, Newfoundland's largest fish company, then controlled by the Newfoundland and federal governments, would be privatized and go public. Russell Wangersky, a solid reporter still training for his stellar future as a columnist, managing editor, and author, reported news of a potential buyer for the idle Come by Chance oil refinery. Barbara Yaffe, a former CBC reporter for the *National* who took up residence in St. John's following a CBC ex-posting there, added an inside piece on what veteran politician Jim McGrath hoped to achieve in his new role as lieutenant-governor, following a quarter of a century as the warhorse Tory MP for St. John's East.

Regina McBride, an *Evening Telegram* alumna, was given her own column. McBride was a unique social events reporter who would have been comfortable in the world of *The Great Gatsby*. At the *Telegram*, she had been a crowd pleaser, especially among the charmed and gilded upper stratum of St. John's society. Guy was a Regina McBride fan, not so much for her subject matter—although the columns sometimes offered coded gossipy political tidbits—as for her meticulous and detailed reporting.

Guy's own substantial contribution to the second edition was a full-page feature report on the bones of the Newfoundland Railway. The Newfie Bullet, the passenger train, was long gone, dead since 1974 when Guy had eulogized it after travelling on its final trans-island trip. What remained of the Bullet in 1986 was not exactly the Wabash Cannonball. It had become a sad and arthritic freight train, possibly the slowest train on earth.

Guy's report was reminiscent of his Leacock Prize-winning *Telegram* features about the old train two decades earlier. It began with historical context:

> "Claptrap and nonsense," growled Stephen Rendell, manager of the doughty Water Street firm of Job Brothers, "calculated to lead the people astray, make them discontented with their present lot, unsettle their minds and make them worse off than before."
>
> Since Mr. Rendell's diatribe against the new-fangled railway in 1880 to the present the "Newfoundland Railway" has been a hot potato tossed back and forth between management, politicians and laity alike, been the cause of rampant discontent and has littered the railway with "unsettled minds" like discarded railway ties.

Rendell's historical ravings foreshadowed the great railway debate of a century later. By 1986, the end of the heavily subsidized railfreight service in Newfoundland had been identified as a potential bonanza for trucking companies. Those companies and their lobbyists, elected and otherwise, argued that asphalt rather than steel was the answer for trans-island freighting. The old narrow-gauge railroad was the problem. Guy retained historical perspective in his description of the battle:

Mr. Rendell and his mercantile pals were perhaps less concerned with the tranquility and mental stability of the lower orders than they were with the spectre of the new railway snatching away their lucrative coastal boat trade and driving wages up to the crucifying level of $1 a day.

Today it is the truckers who are the most adamantly anti-railway, outfits like Atlantic Container Express Inc who with their super-lobbyist, former Premier Frank Moores, want rail out and trucks in.

The romance of the Newfie Bullet passenger train was well behind Guy. His reporting on the freight train matter was all business and politics. Researching the story, he perused government documents and quoted advocates on both sides, including rat-pack MP and future Newfoundland and Labrador premier Brian Tobin.[87]

Tobin and others argued that Newfoundland was being offered a Hobson's choice between a good railroad or a decent highway, when the Terms of Union between Newfoundland and Canada clearly called for both. Ultimately it became a choice between big bucks in the pockets of trucking companies or a slightly lower cost for imported food items in St. John's. No contest.

On that October day in 1986, the *Sunday Express* had offered a solid menu of stories. After only two editions, the *Sunday Express* was on a roll, the nature and quality of its journalism already taking shape.

Still to come in the same edition was the irrepressible McBride, reporting on a socially important, blueblood wedding in St. John's.

The Matron of Honor and the attendants wore identical ankle length dusty rose chiffon dresses, draped to the side and held with large bows of satin. Their headdresses were of baby roses and their bouquets were dusty rose carnations, pale pink fresia and baby's breath. The flower girl was dressed in white dotted Swiss over silk taffeta with puffed sleeves, a fully gathered skirt with deep ruffled hem and a rose sash tied at the waist. She wore a tiny crown of roses and baby's breath and carried a basket of carnations, baby roses, and baby's breath.

As McBride swanned across the social pages, Guy occasionally wrote signed editorials. One such contribution on October 12, 1986, offered a different view of high society in St. John's, or at least of one of its most established members. Reporters, especially Guy, rarely needed to write much about "His Worship" John Murphy. Usually, it was enough to merely quote him.

The subject was "sewerage." His Worship, Guy reported, was well aware "that there are 140,000 people flushing into the harbor of what is sometimes called Babylon Upon Cesspool each and every day but, no, there are no plans to organize snowshoe races across it on Regatta Day …"

Guy ascribed to Murphy the unconventional opinion that with two high tides a day and the flushing effect of the Waterford River, the St. John's harbour was kept in pretty good shape. Guy then quotes Murphy directly: "You wouldn't want to swim in it … you wouldn't want to swim in any man's harbor these days."

Guy reminded his readers of the Mayor's longer-term vision for sewage disposal in the city which involved a tunnel under the Southside Hills and out into Freshwater Bay, a large saltwater cove just south of the city. "The name … will obviously have to be changed," Guy quotes the Mayor as saying. He then reveals the Mayor's idea of the cleansing effect of salt water on sewage.

"Did you ever think of the amount of fish and whales that pollute the ocean? I mean, they go to the bathroom in the ocean, if you want to be crude about it. And the ocean, Providence, or whatever, cleanses it."

The journalistic and editorial pace of the *Sunday Express* proved sustainable through its first year, through 1987 and well into 1988.

A Guy column of April 17, 1988 was promoted on page 1 in hyped but incomprehensible language. "In Florida, they're still asking 'Who was that Guy?' Having fled clock-shock in the sunny south, Ray is back with a measure of citric acid for the men who ran him out of town."

When the "clock-shock" code was deciphered, it turned out that Guy had just returned from a Florida family vacation which, apart from a brief encounter with a pit bull, seemed to have produced little of interest. Even in Florida, however, he encountered curiosity regarding two bizarre initiatives of Premier Brian Peckford's government back in Newfoundland.

One was a cucumber farm in Mount Pearl which had become a laughable white elephant. The other, even more intriguing, was Newfoundland's experiment with Double Daylight Savings Time. Under DDST, children ran in the streets and took to the outport hills until an hour before midnight. Bleary-eyed working parents would turn in at 1 a.m., craving their four or five desperate hours of sleep, only to haul out again at 6 or so to snort sustaining coffee.

Sadly, with such delicious fare, Guy's DDST column was indifferently written. Its quality might have been a by-product of its subject matter. Even without DDST, Guy was a frequent insomniac.

An interesting sidebar in Guy's column had nothing to do with daylight. It was a more personal matter. The newspaper that day carried an amusing column by Alan Fotheringham, the popular Southam News and syndicated columnist who was Canada's best-known newspaper satirist. Although less recognized nationally, Guy was sometimes favourably compared to Fotheringham. In any case, the comparison was not a useful one, and it was surprising that Guy decided to make it himself, even in half-hearted jest, or in the fog of DDST.

Guy's regular column in the *Sunday Express* usually appeared at the top of page 7, the opposite-the-editorial or "op-ed" page, a location almost as choice as his old page 3 berth in the *Telegram*. In the previous week's *Express*, Fotheringham's column had appeared on page 7 with the explanation that he was replacing the vacationing Guy. On April 17, with Guy back in his regular place, Fotheringham showed up on page 6, the editorial page itself.

Fotheringham's presence was sticking in Guy's craw. Only a page away, Fotheringham chronicled the ineptitude of US president Ronald Reagan. A former screen actor and charmer, Reagan was considered to have been the modern US president most lacking in gravitas before Donald Trump came along in 2016 to claim the title forever.

Guy, his tongue not so firmly in his cheek, offered an entertaining comparative assessment of "the Foth," as he was commonly known, as an interloper and rival.

> We are both short, fat persons trying hard to be funny without letting the cracks show too much but there the resemblance ends.
>
> Whereas, Mr. F. can bolt about the continent like a demented water strider dogging Can-Yank politicians of every description, the best your humble have-not provincial scrivener can do is to take modest jaunts and hope to stumble over, say, His Ragship of St. John's in his subtropical habitat on a Florida beach.
>
> Had God seen fit, though, it would have been a marvelous stroke of luck to have encountered His Worship stretched full length on a St. Peter's Beach in tasteful bathing drawers (a mere $9.99 while supplies last) and to have conveyed his thoughts to eager Sunday Express readers under an exotic foreign dateline ...

Guy's feature writing had won him recognition and awards at the *Evening Telegram*. As part of his deal with Harris, he continued to write well-researched features as the born-again boy reporter at the *Sunday Express*.

With an additional decade and a half of life under his belt, Guy had more than ever to write about. He also could bring a long-game perspective to some older subjects. There are few better examples of this appealing brand of journalism than a Guy feature report in the October 26, 1988, edition. Well researched and written with élan, the subject was none other than Guy's ancient antagonist, Joseph R. Smallwood.

In retirement, Smallwood had launched a capstone literary project, a five-volume encyclopedia of Newfoundland and Labrador. Two volumes had been completed by 1988, largely underwritten by aged cronies and supporters, many of whom Smallwood in his heyday had helped make comfortable. By 1988, Smallwood, born on Christmas Eve 1900, was hobbled by the ravages of age. He had suffered a debilitating stroke. His closest contemporary friends were, literally, a dying breed. His personal publishing company fell into bankruptcy and the great encyclopedia project sputtered to a stop. In his feature piece of October 26, Guy picked up the threads of the story, writing with convincing, but not boundless, empathy.

Has the one possible grand and lasting thing of J.R. Smallwood's long and astonishing career been snuffed out forever or is there still a spark among the ashes?

"The Encyclopedia of Newfoundland," hovering on the edge of economic disaster almost since the day it was conceived, finally collapsed into bankruptcy last week ...

Two main factors seem to have put this outrageously ambitious project into a coma if not a coffin—the infamous Smallwoodian ineptness with money and a lingering and ugly political prejudice against a frail and ailing old man who in so many ways earned it.

Smallwood had promised that the Encyclopedia would be a complete record of Newfoundland and Labrador. M.O. Morgan, a former president of Memorial University, and Paul J. Johnson, a well-off St. John's insurance man, were two of the benefactors who eventually saved the project. In their foreword to Volume 5, Morgan and Johnson quoted Smallwood as having declared that "every theme belongs in the Encyclopedia. Every person, every event, every location, every institution, every development, every industry, every intellectual activity, every religious movement in Newfoundland belongs there."

Guy reported that no other Canadian province had attempted anything like Smallwood's Encyclopedia. Its only Canadian rival, he wrote, was "the universally acclaimed three-volume 'Encyclopedia of Canada,' tackled in the days of Alberta's oil boom and heavily funded by industry and by provincial and federal governments."

Guy quoted St. John's publisher Clyde Rose, founder and then head of Breakwater Books, as saying that the Canadian project, promoted by Mel Hurtig, had been sold before it was published. Rose suggested that the Smallwood project was beyond the reach of a poor province such as Newfoundland. "There's no market here to justify it."

Guy believed factors other than economics were at play in the widespread cynicism about Joey's great project. The aging and feeble ex-premier still had his share of bitter foes. Guy quotes Rose as declaring that he "didn't give a minute's thought to lending support to the project. I have absolutely no interest in keeping anything to do with Smallwood alive." In such remarks, Guy detected an attitude in 1989 as unseemly as he had found Smallwood's own dysphoria of 1969.

Guy's report was evenhanded, a disciplined treatment considering his own disregard for Smallwood. Tellingly, he gave the last word in the piece to Rob Pitt, who had edited Volume 1 of the Encyclopedia. Pitt amplified Guy's understated theme, declaring that the real obstacle to the Encyclopedia's success was "enduring political vindictiveness, deserved or otherwise." If Guy was no great fan of Smallwood, he appeared to approve even less of vindictive political loathing.

As it turned out, and perhaps stimulated by Guy's report, a cavalry of prominent scholars and corporate worthies soon appeared on the horizon, heading Smallwood's way.

The highest priest of Newfoundland literary scholarship in the 1980s, Dr. George Story, stepped forward to chair a new editorial board. The Joseph R. Smallwood Heritage Foundation was formed. The Foundation's 20-member board of directors brought promotional savvy, scholarship, and money, and not necessarily in that order. The modest $2.5 million required to complete the five volumes was raised in dollops, including a $5 contribution from a Bonavista school child.

The Foundation presented Volume 3 of the Encyclopedia to Smallwood shortly before his death in December 1991. By 1994, it had fulfilled its promise to Smallwood to complete all five volumes. Today, a complete five-volume set, if you can find one, sells for a bundle, commonly $1,000 or more.

The *Sunday Express* and Boy Reporter soldiered on, stalwart and valuable, to the end of the 1980s. Gradually, cracks appeared in the mortar. If Guy's reports and columns retained their quality, his early boyish enthusiasm for the paper had worn thin. Then came a dramatic workplace policy shift that literally gave Guy tremors. It further damaged his relationship with Harris which already had shown some fissures.

Harris said the change came more than halfway into the life of the *Express*, possibly in late 1988 or early 1989, when he personally decided to get ahead of the curve and address the proven health risks of first- and second-hand cigarette smoke in a work room. "I made the fatal mistake of being the first business in Newfoundland to bring in a smoking ban."

Guy, who had spent nine or 10 hours a day, multiplied by more than a decade, in a smoke-clouded *Telegram* newsroom, enjoyed the *Sunday Express* workplace, where he interacted well with the younger editorial team. With the ban, Harris sentenced Guy to a soggy sweater and a snowbank whenever he needed a smoke, which was about every 20 minutes.

Guy responded desperately but unwisely. As Harris tells it, "Ray was caught in the bathroom ... he had put masking tape around the door ... he thought he was going to get away with having a few ciggies ... and the females were coming to me and saying, 'we can't get into the bathroom. Ray has taped the door shut.'"

"He knew it was a childish prank ... and that's when he left us as a daily presence in the office." Harris rationalized the change. "I don't think that was a bad thing. His creative ritual was that of a loner, not in an open newsroom. So he started filing from home."

Harris also knew working from home would be a mixed blessing for Guy. "I think he enjoyed the camaraderie of the younger people. I think it reminded him of earlier times. And he was idolized by them. They knew we had a legend working with us."

The smoking ban was a fork in the road, but there were other currents of disharmony between Harris and Guy. Guy exhibited a high regard for Harris at times, at least for his skills and courage in journalism. At other times, he would damn him with faint praise. A case study in their relationship, and in the arcane ethics of their trade, played out in April of 1990, the same month Harris decided to leave the *Sunday Express* to work for Geoff Stirling at NTV.

In response to a singular public event, the two most ambitious news entities in the province, the *Sunday Express* and CBC News, made opposing decisions on the same difficult issue, each saluting high ethical principles.

A well-known and much-admired St. John's ophthalmologist and politician, Dr. Patrick McNicholas, had died, amid speculation that it had been by his own hand. Within days of his passing, CBC News reported that his death had occurred only a day or so before he was to appear in court on a charge of sexual assault against a 14-year-old girl. Prior to that shocking revelation, local media had reported McNicholas's death as "sudden," with no further elaboration.

That approach to reporting such deaths has always been a dubious practice, usually giving rise to rumours of suicide, especially when the victim had demonstrated no obvious health issues and the obituary reveals no cause of death. Most mainstream media outlets have a policy, written or unwritten, not to publicize suicides unless there is a compelling public interest for doing so. Public interest in such a context does not mean exactly what it says. It is not about interest as idle Facebook curiosity, but rather something approximating a genuine public need or a public right to know.

CBC reported the McNicholas sudden death, implying but not saying suicide, in the context of the charge against him and the impending court appearance.

In the McNicholas case, the suicide question became almost incidental to the debate that ensued. The harder issue was whether the charge of sexual assault should be revealed to the public in circumstances where the accused could never have his day in court, could never be found to have been innocent or guilty.

The conundrum is profound. Despite the inclination to draw a seemingly logical conclusion, the sudden death of McNicholas, even if it were proved to have been suicide, could never constitute conclusive proof of his guilt in the alleged sexual offence. Among other ethical knots, a suicide can be as consistent with innocence and the shame and helplessness of facing such a charge as it can be with guilt and the dread of conviction and a hostile prison.

The *Sunday Express*'s unwritten code of ethics usually amounted to a judgment call by Harris. His inclinations perhaps would have been informed by his history at the CBC, where every journalist has a policy handbook at hand. With Harris just out the door, the interim *Express* editorial group initially elected not to report the charge against McNicholas. Then, licking their chops all the while, they decided to thrash the CBC for having done so, donning robes of ethical propriety while revealing the charges against McNicholas in the process.

In its edition of April 22, 1990, the *Express* carried a didactic commentary signed by Phillip Lee, one of the paper's senior journalists. Lee denounced the CBC's decision, ignoring the irony of reporting the charge against "Paddy" for no better reason than that the CBC already had done so.

> Early last week, CBC television news reported that Dr. McNicholas was scheduled to appear in court on a sexual assault charge the day after his sudden death over the weekend.
>
> The good name of Dr. McNicholas has been unnecessarily smeared, Paddy's friends said. And they argued that the story implied that the doctor had killed himself to avoid facing the charge ...
>
> But there are two acid tests of a valid news story, however sensitive it might be. The story must both be true, and in the public interest.
>
> There is no doubt that the CBC's story was true. But the decision to air the fact that an information had been sworn out against Dr. McNicholas fails the public interest test.

How can a story that merely stated that Dr. McNicholas was to appear in court on charges be in the public interest? The man, innocent until proven guilty, was dead. Moreover, his criminal case, which was never even set over for trial, will never be resolved.

In its next edition, on April 29, the *Express* carried a long letter from Bob Wakeham, CBC Newfoundland's executive producer of news, criticizing the *Express* for criticizing the CBC.

Wakeham, rather too cavalierly, cast the McNicholas decision as an easy one:

> Relative to the soul-searching that journalists sometimes employ prior to airing or publishing a story, the debate on the McNicholas story was minimal.
>
> You contend, for example, that the story should never have seen the light of day because the information it contained was of no interest to the public.
>
> Wrong. It was entirely in the public interest to know that a prominent and influential member of the community has been charged with a very serious crime.

Into this smouldering cauldron rushed Guy, who believed the CBC had made the correct call and his own newspaper the wrong one. Guy seized the moment to provide his perspective on the issue and to offer his own ambivalent assessment of Michael Harris. Harris had just left the *Express*. Guy invoked his spirit, at the same time taking his measure.

In a fierce satirical take on the McNicholas matter, Guy advanced an argument for publication that was more sophisticated than either of the competing arguments by his *Express* colleague, Lee, or his once and future CBC colleague, Wakeham.

Guy's unusual perspective might more readily be applauded in the age of Me Too than it was in 1990. Guy implied that he had his own inside information about the matter, information that, with McNicholas's death, could never emerge through the legal system. On a matter of such importance, Guy's assertion that he had other information could be believed.

Guy approached his column of April 29, 1990, acidly and loaded for bear. It is possible that neither Mount Cashel nor *Young Triffie* was far from his mind:

> Once upon a time, long ago and far away in a land that never existed, there occurred the sudden death of a Prominent Citizen.
>
> So prominent was the citizen, indeed, that he got a big state funeral. All the big shots in the land turned out. And they all said the usual ritual and good things about the departed.
>
> Yet there hung over the proceedings a certain pall. For it was revealed in the public that the Prominent Citizen had been facing a charge in the courts, a charge of sexually molesting a 14-year-old girl.
>
> When this was reported some citizens of the land (that never was) were shaken by paroxysms of outrage and attacked the reporter. It was just not done to report such deaths about a dead Prominent Citizen. Or perhaps a live one either.
>
> Loud was the outrage and great the condemnation.
>
> But there was also in that same land (that never was) certain women who heard the reports with feelings that were very different. With profound relief did they hear as each one said to herself at that moment: "I was not alone."

For fear and shame and hatred had been the solitary burden of each one of them through decades. Too often they had been young girls again and battened in a doctor's chair and grabbed and groped and mauled ... and no one to listen and no one to tell.

Honor, Worship and Grace heaped praise on the Prominent Citizen, now dead. Opprobrium and scorn were heaped upon the reporter. But four, at least, of the women who remembered sought out the Reporter to say, what more, but "Thank-you."

The Wrong Call?

Irony of ironies in the land that never was.

His pulse clearly quickened by the McNicholas affair, and now with inside information regarding four other probable victims who demanded anonymity, Guy pushed on, to reveal what he could, and to sideswipe Harris in the process. If a certain respect for Harris was to be part of Guy's final message, it was much tempered along the way with slights regarding hubris and searing ambition. As he had done before with Horwood, Mowat, and others, Guys cut his way to his conclusion through a thicket of considerations and caveats.

SO ... YOU HAVE LEFT US, MR. HARRIS

See what happens, Michael, the moment you are out the door?

Harris is a funny stick. An odd chill emanates from his ventricles. You mistrust that when he's used you up you will go the way of all empty toothpaste tubes.

But, by golly, what he does well he does damned well.

Not the least of his accomplishments is The Sunday Express.

Harris traces tensions between himself and Guy back to years before the *Express*. The pair first crossed paths on the set of *Up at
Ours*. As Harris tells it:

> Here's the thing about Ray, and about me ...
>
> I wrote a number of the screenplays for Gordon
> Pinsent's *Up at Ours*. Six or seven of them. That's when
> I first met Ray Guy. Gordon Pinsent came down to
> give us a pep talk just before the series began. So all the
> people lined up to shake hands with each other. And
> I go to shake hands with Ray and he takes his hand
> back. And about a year later we met at CBC, and we
> were walking down a corridor and he said something
> to me which was not very kind ... and I said something
> back like, "I really liked your last column." And he said,
> "didn't you hear what I just said, 'I don't like you.'" And
> I said, "don't worry Ray, I like you enough for the both
> of us."

In subsequent years, Guy continued to cast Harris as vaguely satan-
ic, while occasionally giving the devil his due. Harris, meanwhile,
sees the glass as two-thirds full.

Rare Ambition is Harris's 1992 biography of John Crosbie and
the entire Crosbie clan. "In the end when I finished *Rare Ambition*,
the best review I ever had ... was by Ray Guy. And he, Guy, doesn't
gush." Harris said the book was "mindlessly thrashed" by the late
Jay Scott, then a powerful critic at the *Globe and Mail*." It also had
been unwelcomed by Rex Murphy.

Guy reviewed *Rare Ambition* for the *Montreal Gazette*, describing it as "a rollicking good read ... *Rare Ambition* deserves a place on
a short shelf of great Canadian biographies." In so praising it, Guy
joined a chorus of applause for Harris, led by such luminaries as

Peter C. Newman and Peter Gzowski. The chorus more than offset Jay Scott's or anyone else's condemnation.

As the 1980s wound down, the too-good-to-be-true *Sunday Express* proved to be just that. Initially, Steele was a journalists' publisher. Harris noted that when the business side of the operation asked questions, Steele would always support the editorial side. "He'd say, 'you know accountants never started a business.'"

The *Express* thrived editorially as a weekly, but as a business it could not break through even to twice-weekly publication. The Robinson-Blackmore bean-counters became increasingly irritable.

"They were on our case every month," Harris said, "because editorial costs were something they had never incurred before. They would read the paper backwards and count the ads and I would say, yes. But 'look what's in it?' And they would say 'who cares?'" Harris admitted that it also was a challenge for the small staff to come up with original stories every week.

When the paper was launched, Harris had been given a target of 12,000 paid subscribers. The target was easily reached. Circulation peaked at an estimated 20,000 readers. But the cost proved too high. Steele, despite his enthusiasm for the project, ultimately was a businessman.

Harris still gives Steele full credit for his effort to bring newspaper competition and quality back to Newfoundland. "Steele wanted something better and something more combative. What we were trying to do was take out *The Telegram* because they had fallen so low, they had gotten so used to not having to compete."

Harris left the *Sunday Express* before the *Express* left him. Feuding with the Robinson-Blackmore brass, sniffing slippage in Steele's commitment, and always a main chance player, in April 1990 he took over Stirling's NTV as News Director and co-anchor of its daily television newscast.

As was the case with the feud between Guy and O'Flaherty, Guy's discomfort with Harris reflected deeper animus on Guy's part than it did on Harris's. For Harris, Guy's commitment to fairness and good writing trumped all disaffection. For Guy, Harris's *Sunday Express* achievements were not to be denied, but they could not fully eclipse the personal disdain.

Guy's judgment of Harris in his *Express* column of April 29, 1990, may be read as faint praise today. In the circumstances, and from Guy, it was testimonial.

CHAPTER 21

This Guy, That Guy

Ray Guy's freelance writing did not make him wealthy. Nor did it make him more famous than he had made himself in the 1960s and 1970s when he and Joey Smallwood were each other's nightmares.

Writers with regular salaries or inherited wealth can relax and write only words to live by. Less fortunate freelance writers such as Guy produce most of their writing to keep the wolf from the door: words to live on.

To make a living, Guy was forced to write for any and everybody; to write in modes and genres that he had to learn on the fly and for publications with readerships ranging from the low hundreds to a few thousands at best. His early pursuit of a decent freelance income took him to unusual places. For about a year in the late 1970s, he wrote pieces for a publication called the *Bowlog*, a house organ of the Bowater's Pulp and Paper Company in Corner Brook.

If "the market" made uncomfortable demands, or forced Guy to scribble a few substandard screeds, his talent ultimately triumphed. He produced some of his finest writing during his long freelance career. Much of that writing remains underexposed.

Among many examples of Guy's achievements are two slender books that he wrote for and about children. Newfoundland does not boast vast numbers of successful children's writers, although exceptions such as the late poet Al Pittman and the prolific Kevin Major come to mind.

Guy wrote sparingly in the official children's and youth genre. But from his earliest reporting days, much of his work could easily be read and enjoyed by high schoolers, as it was during his *Telegram* years. Scattered throughout his work are many essays—notably his *Atlantic Insight* pieces about his own children and pets—that would resonate with children of 10 or 12. Guy's two children's books were accidental, written first as columns and expanded and packaged as books only after readers noted their distinct appeal to young people.

Sammy and the Miracles of Christmas, a slender hardcover book, is an illustrated reprise of two earlier Christmas columns. The book is illustrated by Boyd W. Chubbs with macabre pencil drawings of Sammy, members of his grim family, and of assorted sculpins and crows. One of the stories, "The Tale of Sammy and the Miracle Christmas Crow," is described by Guy as "a true and inspirational story" and "a seasonal tale for younger folk." Guy credited Mary Walsh with helping bring Sammy to life.

The *Sammy* stories are both distinguished and hobbled by unapologetic outport references and lingo rooted in Guy's 1940s and 1950s childhood. The stories are what they are: at times incorrect politically by today's codes, but faithful to their time and place. Guy, as usual, is in the corner of the less powerful people, and of animals, birds, and fish. In the Sammy stories, abused crows and sculpins avenge human tormentors.

In "The Tale of Sammy and the Miracle Christmas Crow," Sammy has a pet crow named Jack. Sammy believes crows can talk. There may be ornithologists who claim that crows would score well on law school standard admission tests.

For a crow, Jack appears to be a slower learner. On Christmas Eve, a window in Sammy's house is accidentally shattered. Sammy's father, unhandy as a killick, battles the wind and sleet to try and fix it, anxious to get it done and get back at the Christmas rum. When Sammy looks on indifferently, his father turns to him with what Guy would have his readers accept as an affectionate paternal admonishment:

> "Don't say a word," he remarked to Sammy who was standing there chewing the snow off his mitts. "Not one word, look, or I'll put this hammer right between your two eyes."

Sammy has hoped Jack would learn to sing the hymn "Jesus Loves Me This I Know" before school reopens so he can charge the local children a few cents to hear it. Sammy's father, meanwhile, has done his best to encourage the crow to become verbal, gruesomely, by splitting its tongue.

Unfortunately, Jack shows little progress until that fateful Christmas Eve. Frustrated, freezing, and cursing his fate, Sammy's father is apoplectic with rage when Jack flies over to him and utters with total clarity the only word he ever would:

> ... Jack spoke but one word, plain as day, clear as crystal, as plain and clear as ever came from any pulpit. "Arse-hole," he remarked to Sammy's father.

Sammy's father laughed until he wept. He then nailed a piece of Tentest over the window, went indoors and opened his Christmas bottle.[88]

"The Miracle of Sammy and the Christmas Sculpin" has many of the attributes of the Christmas Crow yarn. Sammy catches a sculpin on Christmas Eve. The sculpin requires no surgery and talks perfectly from the start, introducing itself to Sammy as "the Magic Christmas Sculpin." Confronted by an outharbour juvenile, the sculpin's pathetic plea for its life does not help one bit. For Sammy has in mind the normal fate of all sculpins that take the hook when an outharbour juvenile is fishing for a tomcod or a conner:

> "I don't care if you're Mr. Joey Smallwood," said Sammy. "You're going to get your guts jumped out."

It so happens. But the sculpin gets revenge:

> ... On the third stomp a pizen thorn on the sculpin's back went right up through the sole of Sammy's long rubber into the heart of his foot.

Sometime later at the cottage hospital, an attending physician is Job's Comforter:

> "Had a case like this once in Twillingate," said the doctor. "It don't look good at all. If that boy don't have to lose that leg it'll be a miracle."

At the risk of ruining the story for readers, a miracle it is.

> By Easter, the boys were still calling him Old Hopalong Cassidy and the girls wanted to see where his toenails

come off and turned their guts looking at it. But in the end, Sammy did not have to lose that leg at all.[89]

Guy's second children's book, *An Heroine for Our Time*, published in 1983, features 2,000-pound Baby Lala who smites bullies and generally wrecks elephantine havoc.

Like Sammy, the book originated as a newspaper column. It is illustrated by Sylvia Ficken. This time, Guy credits actor Rick Boland with the idea of turning it into a book.

Heroine is dedicated to two important women in Ray Guy's life—his mother, Alice Louisa, and his mother-in-law, Martha Louise. It probably owed just as much to two other important women in his life, daughters Annie and Rachel.

"This book ought not to be read to children over 95 years or under 10 months without parental guidance," Guy writes in a frontispiece.

Three short paragraphs at the beginning set the tone and the mood.

> Once upon a time there was a 2,000 pound baby.
> No, I tell a lie.
> Hardly 2,000 pound. A bit less. At the age of four months she weighed almost exactly a half a quintal under a short ton.

An Heroine for Our Time is 58 pages long. Take out Sylvia Fricken's great drawings of Little Baby Lala and her adventures, and Guy's text adds up to no more than 10 pages, about 2,000 words, the equivalent of two newspaper columns.

For Guy, even a kids' book can include political and social commentary. Medical expertise comes in for an elbow or two.

"It is really a blessing," said a specialist flown in from Montreal a-purpose, "that along with being largish she is able to rise and float in the air. Otherwise, I am very much afraid she would grow up bowlegged ..."

"Mars," said another. "I always said that if they landed foot on Mars, stuff like this was bound to happen."

Both Guy parents, Alice and George H., make cameo but anonymous appearances.

"It is God's will," declared one of her grandmothers who was of an exceeding patient and pious nature.

"To my way of looking at it," said one of her grandfathers, "in a twelvemonths time, yous'll have the makings of a damn fine wrestler."

The second grandmother then appears, clearly demonstrating her own practical and innovative approach from her home beyond the horizon and the mountains—British Columbia:

In a far distant land, another grandmother bought up half the wool the Hudson's Bay Company had in stock and, using two kitchen table legs as knitting needles, made her ever so many pairs of romper suits, soakers and bootees.

But even with such extended family support and admiration for "a far greater baby," Guy makes it clear that "it wasn't all beer and skittles" at home with Baba Lala:

Sometimes, at 2:23 o'clock in the night she'd rouse up and drift out of her crib to the loft and pound contentedly on the ceiling with her little rattle box which was made from two church bells welded to a truck axle.

Then, one eventful night, Little Baby Lala simply levitates out of the care and custody of her astonished parents. Lala goes about her business, doing good works, if mostly inadvertently.

Guy decides to have the rotund child attempt necessary reforms in keeping with his own sense of the public good. Accidently, while floating randomly around, Baba Lala crashes through a window of the Parliament building where a night sitting is in progress.

> The shock to the honourable gentlemen (mostly) was great.
>
> Them as had heads of hair turned grey upon the instant, them as were already grey moulted and went bald, and them as were already bald dropped down in their tracks with minor heart attacks.
>
> It would be a happy thing to say that they repented right then and there and achieved salvation but, alas, they were sunk too far into wickedness for that.[90]

An Heroine for Our Time ends happily, involving a special Newfoundland dynamic that readers will have to discover for themselves. The book is an endearing little tale, exuding parental affection. When it was published, Rachel was seven years old, Annie five. Annie recalled that when she attended St. Mary's Elementary School in St. John's in 1983 and 1984, *An Heroine for Our Time* was checked out of the school library more often than any other book.

Throughout his freelance career, Ray Guy made frequent but irregular contributions to the *Newfoundland Quarterly*, the venerable

Newfoundland arts and culture testament founded in 1901. If his only writing had been his pieces for the *Quarterly*, he would have made a notable contribution to Newfoundland letters and satire. His contributions reach back into the 1980s and forward until shortly before his death in 2013.

There is no thematic thread in Guy's *Quarterly* articles and few are driven by either political or contemporary events. A quarterly magazine can hardly be first with the news. Many of his articles, especially those written in his later years, rely heavily on memory and experience, but with flashes of original research.

In 2006, its 105th year of publication, the *Quarterly* devoted its summer number to northern gardening, one of Guy's favourite subjects. Editor Linda Whelan promised that "among the delights that await you: Ray Guy, who is almost as famous for his gardening advice as for his stringent political satire, manages to combine both voices in his latest offering."

In the piece, Guy harkened back to his teenaged enthusiasm for trying to make things grow.

> That year I was probably 16 ... part of my duty was to mow, with a scythe, three or four of the small hay-meadows we owned ... and no money in that at all.
>
> But that same year they started to build a federal government wharf. Great amounts of ballast were needed. My friend, Cyril, had his father's motorboat and dory and I went with him as helper.
>
> The rate per ton for those slippery, treacherous spine-tearing beach boulders was $10. My share per ton was $4. It was the first money I ever earned.
>
> Cyril bought a new church-and-dance suit for himself. I sent off to the mainland for four hybrid tea rose bushes—pink, white, yellow and red. Dame Edith Helen ... I forget the white ... Eclipse, and Crimson

Glory. They bloomed enough to give me whatever in the dickens I was craving for but they all perished over winter.

Guy then digressed to expose a little-known fact about horticulture in Newfoundland, a persistent reliance on plants with hallucinatory properties, and their implications for law and order.

> I remember Granny Guy hobbling around her little plot admiring her fine stand of opium poppies and, being a Salvationist, singing "What a Friend We Have in Jesus" while poking at weeds with her walking stick.
>
> Many years later I did some investigative journalism on the cultivation of opium poppies in Newfoundland. Devilment was part of my motivation. It seemed amusing to me that the "authorities" were in a fine old sweat about marijuana while thousands of Newfoundlanders grew (and always had) that pesky poppy, Papaver somniferem, from which can be extracted opium, morphine, heroin and codeine.
>
> The fact that pimply youths were being jailed for growing pot while my Granny sang praises to the Lord while nurturing her opium tickled my warped fancy.

Guy decided—more devilment—to present his research into the opium poppy phenomenon to a member of the Newfoundland Constabulary for comment. The response from the officer at the other end of the telephone soon shut down the discussion.

What, Guy asked, was the Constabulary doing about the fact that "opium-morphine-heroin-codeine poppies were nearly as prolific around the City as dandelions?"

There was a pause of the sort known as "pregnant." Then: What did you say your name was? Ah yes. Go on, boy, sure everyone knows you're cracked!

... My fragile pyche bled. Had I really ruined my image by acting the fool in print for too long?[91]

Guy feared and hated hospitals, which made his depictions of medical carnage especially horrific. In the Spring 2008 *Quarterly*, his unlikely topic was kidney stones, by most accounts the excruciating pinnacle of human torture, just short of waterboarding. He had first experienced the dreaded boulders many years earlier in a lonely room at the old Grenfell Inn in Wabush, Labrador:

> At about 2 in the morning in a hotel room I was struck in the side by a pain that doubled me into the shape of a worm on a hook.
>
> I was trundled to a clinic and the doctor said kidney stones, my first encounter. All the glory, all the vastness, all the enterprise and beauty of western Labrador is unfortunately for me suffocated beneath the clanging pain from hell. Much later a doctor assured me I wasn't exaggerating—one of his patients had twins, extra large, and at another time kidney stones and she would "take them twins any day of the week."[92]

Iris says Ray suffered often from the stones' affliction. After the Labrador episode came several trips to St. Clare's Hospital in St. John's. He was terrified of hospitals. "On one of his first visits," Iris recalled, "he went berserk. Cops were called. He threw quite a punch at one poor fellow. On subsequent visits, he was met at the door with a knockout needle."

In Winter 2009, the *Quarterly* dabbled in the challenging subject of Newfoundland architecture. The topic brought out the best in Guy, who always took an interest in buildings and building styles. He admired the architecture of the grand old stone structures of St. John's such as the Anglican Cathedral and the Basilica of St. John the Baptist. He felt those grand structures transcended sectarian smallness. He had celebrated both the Basilica and the Cathedral in his 1985 documentary profile of St. John's for the CBC-TV's "Cityscapes" series.

In his contribution to the *Quarterly*'s architecture edition, Guy was equally impressed by more modest Newfoundland structures, writing in celebration of the classic outharbour saltbox, especially its all-important porch:

> At the risk of falling, yet again, into my anecdotage, there existed, decades ago, in a village of only 200 with only three miles of road leading nowhere but to the railroad station, a different porch.
>
> There and then saltbox houses were the most prevalent. You see them now largely on post cards or in tourist TV commercials. Little two-storey houses with quite steep roofs and a one storey slope-roofed piece running along the "back" side ... the side facing away from the road.
>
> Back there was the main and usual entrance. The "front" door was hardly ever opened except to carry out a corpse and for ventilation on rare hot days in summer. The long, low dark porch on the back carried the most traffic. People who went to the clothesline or came to visit all passed through.
>
> Much other business went on in the porch. There was a large stack of firewood and a coal-pound containing the winter's allowance. There was a water barrel kept full by buckets brought from the village well and a cup or a ladle handy to drink from. There was a large

hooked mat for the depository of wet, muddy or snow-caked boots and hooks on the wall for rubber jackets and oil lanterns ...

At the back-end of the porch was a sort of bulk pantry containing a sack of flour, sugar, rolled oats, some gallons of molasses and whatever homemade jams and pickles that would likely freeze at 32°F. Small meats like a leg of lamb or a cow's head hung there also.

Partially hidden, somewhere between the door and the edibles, was a large enamel pail with a lid. Here the female visitors and household inhabitants of that gender went to relieve themselves. For the males there was, at some distance, an outhouse, below the seating holes of which large rodents flashed their glowing red eyes, either in expectation or indignation.[93]

Outhouses. There is no Ray Guy work more revealing of his wit, his talent for subtlety and brevity, and his love of pure fun, than the slim hardcover volume *Outhouses of the East.*

Guy came late to that 1975 project, after Nova Scotia photographer Sherman Hines had taken photos seemingly of every Canadian privy east of Montreal. The photos were mainly of exteriors—interiors requiring vacant possession, and posteriors out of the question.

The book giant Barnes and Noble describes *Outhouses* as "the international classic celebrating outdoor conveniences ... accented with humourous captions by Ray Guy." It could just as readily have been touted as "accented with excellent photographs by Sherman Hines." For Guy's mini essays lift this book to the plateau of advanced potty-humour, creating, as it were, an enduring virtue out of temporary necessity.

Guy's introduction to *Outhouses of the East* establishes his approach:

> The installation of the first two or three porcelain flushables in a community suddenly swung a spotlight of ridicule on the old faithful, now old-fashioned biffies, for miles around.
>
> A rustic stigma settled over them. The very concept of an outhouse prompted a faint smile, just as ducks do by their mere existence, or signs with the "Rs" printed backwards, or a prolonged prelude to a sneeze or words like "comatose ..."
>
> Outhouses, like poor puns, fell out of odor.
>
> But that's all behind us now. The appropriate interval has passed and an affectionate glow of nostalgia has replaced the more unkind spotlight generated by the first flush of indoor china.

Thirty-five or so of the privies captured by Hines appear in the book. Each offers unique features ranging from heart-shaped and half-moon ventilation cut-outs to tiny windows strategically placed at eye level from the seated position.

The *privy de résistance* is featured both inside the book and as an illustration on the dust jacket. It has shingles for cladding but is rundown, with a strip of felt missing from the roof and the door askew and draughty. The highlight of the photo, however, is not the architecture but a massive bull lying lazily directly in front of the door.

Guy:

> Here is what you call your classic approach-avoidance conflict. Many minutes—which seem like hours—are spent in psychological turmoil in the face of such a

situation. But finally, the need to approach can so over-whelm the tendency to avoid that the bull is taken by the horns.[94]

Literary criticism, usually in the form of book reviews, was not central to Ray Guy's stock in trade as a freelance journalist, any more than outhouse captions were. But literary evaluation was a challenge to which he always rose. His appraisals of Mowat's *The Boat Who Wouldn't Float* and Harris's *Rare Ambition* demonstrated that the role of critic was a comfortable zone.

Guy's positive evaluations of those books and his praise for others such as Richard Gwyn's *Smallwood* and S.J.R. Noel's *Politics in Newfoundland*, should not have left writers complacent about a Ray Guy review.

In 1989, the *Daily News Sunday Magazine* of Halifax asked Guy to assess two related books. The books were published by Formac Publishing of Halifax. Formac, in an alliance with Newfoundland's Breakwater Books, had just put out *Ray Guy's Best*, a collection of his *Atlantic Insight* columns. Formac also published *Atlantic Insight* itself, for which he was still writing in 1989.

Whether Guy was annoyed by the fee offered for the reviews, or by what he considered the inferior quality of the books, or both, the writers of both works might have wished Ray Guy had never been born.

The books were *The Channel Shore*, a novel by Charles Bruce, and *Charles Bruce: A Literary Biography*, by Andrew Wainwright, a professor of English at Dalhousie University. In his *Daily News* reviews on January 22, 1989, Guy spares neither book, nor their publisher: "A two-in-one pack is the apparent commercial aim of Formac Publishing." He records Formac's promotional claims for one of the books and juxtaposes his own.

Formac:

> Charles Bruce is one of the most distinguished Canadian writers of all time. His most noted work, *The Channel Shore*, is one of the best Canadian novels of the 20th century.

Ray Guy:

> If a hardware store attempted to get away with that sort of stratospheric hype, the Better Business Bureau would be down on it like a ton of bricks.

Guy then moves on to examine the books themselves.

In 1951, Guy reports, a collection of Charles Bruce's poems won the Governor General's Award for Poetry. Guy suggests that such unalloyed success could be expected to lead to similar recognition of his 1954 novel, *The Channel Shore*. It did not. There should be no shame in that, of course. But Guy, with a severe and misanthropic edge, uses it as a stick with which to beat Bruce's poetry as well as Bruce's biographer, Professor Wainwright. Guy first takes a run at the poetry, which Wainwright obviously adores.

> Much of the poetry is a sort of imitation Wordsworth. Salt in the blood, gales in the spirit, kelp-twisted sinews … that sort of thing. Wainwright is wistful about the poet's dogged determination to let fresher forms and more adventurous concepts pass him by.
>
> Wainwright achieves sputtering indignation. He goes far beyond any evidence he offers by his claim that Charles Bruce, son of Nova Scotia, is a rightful giant of Canadian literature and was done out of his due by (here it comes, yet again) some mysterious Upper Canada cabal.

As if to out-Guy Guy, the *Daily News* of January 22, 1989, head-lined the review of *Channel* with its own indelicate words: "Bruce's novel tedious, better left on the shelf."

By the time he gets to the novel, Guy is wielding a machete. He targets the plot:

> Anse and Hazel copulate, Hazel conceives and Anse leaves. Grant and Anna spark, Anna dies, Grant mar-ries Hazel and Alan is born. Hazel dies. After 27 years and 300 pages, Anse returns and a punch in the nose occurs. Such are the barest bones of Charles Bruce's 1954 Chedabucto roman-a-clef ...
>
> The book takes place in a fictionalized Chedabucto in the years between 1919 and 1945. It is shown as a tight little empire with a piece of shoreline which is, by turn, properly "sunshimmered" and "wind-blasted." The shore is peopled by gospel-grim Methodists and chop-py Roman Catholics who are forced to turn, since the heyday of the fishery, to woodcutting and hardscrabble farming.
>
> Enter Anse Gordon, the bold seducer of Shore maidens, "wild, no good" and a Papist with a broad streak of malice. How he got that way is uncertain. Maybe it was a whiff of mustard gas in the Great War, maybe his pregnant mother was startled by a Lutheran ...

Has the novel been adequately condemned by that point? Not in Guy's judgment.

> You don't find books like this anymore except, possibly, arranged two or three to a night table in rural bed-and-breakfast places. Dated ... stilted ... eminently perish-able ... like eating a box of cornflakes, one by one, to get

to the prize at the bottom ... which turns out to be three more cornflakes wrapped in cellophane.

It is possible to imagine Guy finishing that piece, then slumping back in his armchair exhausted and sated. It is hard to fathom what drove him to his unbridled thrashing of both the novel and the biography. There are ample samples in the review to justify a negative review of the novel, but too few to support the blizzard of scorn Guy heaped upon it.

In any case, Wainwright simply wasn't having it. On February 2, 1989, he parried, with a short, sharp missive, Guyesque in its snottiness. His letter to the *Daily News* editor ran under the headline "Delicious Parody."

> It was a learning experience to read Ray Guy's parody of how an ignorant and virtually illiterate person might approach the complexities of Charles Bruce's novel, *The Channel Shore* (*Sunday Magazine*, Jan. 22, 1989). The sheer terror of anything intelligent is conveyed so clearly, and the deathless yahoo prose style is without flaw in Mr. Guy's piece. His skillful satire reminds me of the Rambo reviewer's plot summary approach to complicated texts: "Adam and Eve eat apple. Leave garden. Life goes on." It amazes me that Mr. Guy can emulate so well those who use literature to wipe something other than a kerosene lamp chimney.

As noted, Formac was *Atlantic Insight*, which had been good to Guy for a decade. The *Daily News Sunday Magazine* was popular in the late 1980s, read by thousands of Nova Scotians whose sensibilities certainly would have been ruffled by Guy's condemnation of Nova Scotia's homegrown literary works.

As he had demonstrated elsewhere, including during his *Telegram* and *Sunday Express* years, Ray Guy could be just as fearsome when writing about sensitive matters closer to home. A good example was in 2000 when he contracted with *Canadian Geographic* magazine for $3,400 to write a piece on the seal hunt, then a fen of bloody controversy.

International celebrity-strutting and domestic political grandstanding had been features of the hunt for years. Those predictable rituals may have been the only aspects of the hunt more disturbing than the worldwide images of blood spurting from the snouts of seals in the unlucky path of a sealer's lethal gaff.

Guy was 61 at the time and not in robust health. Field research for the article involved choppering from St. Anthony on the northeastern tip of Newfoundland to the offshore ice floes in the company of bellicose anti-hunt politicians. Among that group was Gary Lunn, an MP from British Columbia who was the Reform Party's Fisheries critic, and Newfoundland's own seal-averse Fisheries minister, John Efford.

Guy's response to the seal hunt and the histrionic protests was predictably unpredictable, exhibiting no more support for the bloody spectacle on the ice than for the privileged legion of celebrities, expense-account animal rights crusaders, and politicians on the make. The fact that too many journalists who covered the hunt marched under one flag or the other in a highly divisive feud offended Guy still further.

Guy's freelance fee for that assignment was respectable and the Canadian Geographic Society which commissioned it got its money's worth. His understanding of the place of seals in Newfoundland's cultural and economic history was profound:

> In the communal consciousness sealing is relegated to folk song and story of a bleak and tragic cast. Newfoundlander Cassie Brown wrote her masterpiece,

Death on the Ice, about a sealing disaster in which the sealers' frozen corpses were stacked on a St. John's pier like winter firewood. E.J. Pratt's poetry was taught in the schools. His doleful lines on sealing tragedy—"ring out the toll for a hundred dead, who tried to lower the price of bread"—were to be memorized. In local legend, at least, the Pope had once declared the seal to be a fish, so that during Lent and on meatless Fridays, starving Roman Catholics had a little better chance to preserve both body and soul. The only virtue salvaged from a couple of centuries of seal killing was stoicism in the face of misery and calamity.

Guy also researched and grasped the economic value of the seal hunt to Canada at the turn of the 21st century. When a German reporter asked the question, Guy overstated confidently that it was "about the same as cuckoo clocks are to the main economy of Germany." The hunt, he reported, was valued at between $20 million and $25 million a year back then. The hunt's best-organized and richest detractor, the International Fund for Animal Welfare, was using the figure of $2 million after subsidies to the hunt were netted out.

Guy demonstrated a realistic grasp of the industry's true place in modern history and its status in the latter third of the 20th century:

> By the 1970s, sealing in Atlantic Canada had taken a sudden turn. What followed has been called many things: the March madness, the 30-year war, the dueling helicopters, the annual ice follies and the new Crusades. One form of cynical zealotry seemed to spawn another and so began the three-decade devil's dance over an industry whose value to Canada's gross national product

has been equated to two McDonald's hamburger outlets. What once seemed to be a perishing relic instead
split into three: the original European sealing industry
with headquarters in Bergen; the pro-sealing industry
subsidized by the Canadian taxpayer; and the anti-seal-
ing industry dominated by the International Fund for
Animal Welfare (IFAW).

It is not the function of personal journalism to conceal the writer's
point of view. It is, rather, to reveal and explain the subject, and to
find and assess competing views. Guy's seal hunt piece is one of his
best journalistic essays. He gives the colliding positions fair and
reasonable shrift. In doing so, he earns the right to offer his own
fix on the annual circus, which emerges in two short passages in his
report.

Arriving in St. Anthony on the return trip from the "Front"
off Prince Edward Island, Guy encountered Efford at the airport,
hosting a press conference. He also encountered the traditionally
compliant, pro-hunt Atlantic Canada press core. He would not become one of them. Guy was not running with the foxes, nor would
he hunt with the hounds.

> Wearying of what seemed to be many toadying ques-
> tions, I ask: "Minister, has Viagra cut into the market
> for seal penises?" Efford lasers me with a frightful glare,
> pivots 180 degrees on his heel toward another camera
> and later implies that I am a traitor to Newfoundland.

A lifelong lover of animals, Guy described a grim scene on the ice
that he had recently witnessed:

From my prudent perch, I hear the soft, melon-smash-
ing thumps of the bats as the sealers give the young
harps the regulation one-two killing blows.

Several seals hump slowly past me and I have the
fanciful notion of warning the poor brutes telepathi-
cally: "Duck down that hole in the ice, you fool, and be
quick about it." None do.[95]

Ray Guy's $3,400 fee for the seal hunt piece may have been his best
single payday as a magazine writer.

There are few records of Guy's actual earnings as a freelance
writer and commentator. Those earnings inevitably were erratic and
unpredictable, with spikes but more often with droughts for weeks
or months.

His varied and frequent CBC contributions were reasonable
for the times, ranging between $100 and $400 in the 1980s for various kinds of radio and television commentaries, which for several
years were weekly.

His acting gig paid much more, with writing credits on top of
performance fees for several *Up at Ours* episodes. As both a writer
and actor in the final season, each series may have earned Guy at
least $25,000.

Guy made other contributions to the CBC. His writing and
hosting roles for the St. John's episode of a network television series
on Canadian cities may have paid between $1,000 to $1,500. But
his script consultation fee for *The Gullages*, a local comedy series
in the early 1990s, paid no more than a few hundred dollars per
occasion.

In other genres, Guy made more money on *Young Triffie's Been
Made Away With* than on any other single piece he ever penned.
Walsh says his various writing fees from the film, and for a script

much amended by subsequent writers, including Walsh herself, earned him at least $50,000. He had realized income from *Triffie* stage productions as well. In 2003, the Stephenville Theatre Festival featured *Triffie* as their Newfoundland piece for their 25th anniversary. Guy collected the usual 10 per cent of the box office receipts, one of the many tricks *Triffie* had turned for him.

Writing in the *Newfoundland Quarterly* in 2005, Guy estimated even greater returns from *Triffie*, acknowledging Walsh's role in its overall success.

> Triff the Stiff has had a sporadic but steady life. This is largely because Mary Walsh took a shine to her. Triff has done summer theatre in Nova Scotia, the Neptune Theatre in Halifax, the Donna Butt show in Trinity, made it into a scholarly tome of Newfoundland plays ... In the 20 or so years since I so vilely did her in she's returned me, good for evil, about $80,000.[96]

Much of Guy's freelance journalism is safely contained in books and major periodicals such as *Atlantic Insight* and the *Sunday Express*. While most of his writing can be located readily, some eludes detection. There are contributions to obscure anthologies and one-off articles that may or may not loom up in library indices. A few unpublished partial or complete articles exist in draft form among his private papers at Memorial University's Centre for Newfoundland Studies. Online merchandising can be a good guide to his book-form collections of columns, which usually are still available, sometimes used, from private sellers.

Guy was not a good self-promoter. The closest he ever came to working with an agent was the constant and savvy advice of his wife, Kathie Housser. Guy was and is still recognized as a major writer in Newfoundland and Labrador. Beyond Newfoundland's shores, he has had a significant following only in the Maritime

Provinces, based mainly on his *Axiom* and *Atlantic Insight* columns, which were well established and regular for a decade.

Otherwise, Guy is known primarily to a small national community of academics and scholars, a smattering of Canada's literary elite from coast to coast, and a related but important community of indeterminant size—the Newfoundland and Labrador cultural diaspora in Upper Canada, the Newfoundlanders of 416 and 613.

CHAPTER 22

Views from Windswept Hills

Ray Guy's large body of writing remains underexposed, under-examined, underappreciated. Only a few academics have assessed his writing in depth. Journalists and reviewers have developed popular but narrow themes and his surviving admirers continue to admire. A thorough academic assessment of his contribution to Newfoundland literature and society awaits its doctoral scholar.

Along the way, and most notably around the time of his death in 2013, there has been extensive media commentary on his work and his impact. It has come mostly from his fans, hagiographic tributes; notable exceptions being insightful obituaries by Rex Murphy and Joan Sullivan. A year later, a group of St. John's artists organized a "Ray Day" anniversary event where Guy's writing was read at a downtown pub. It ran for only two years. In the summer of 2021, the Arnold's Cove Heritage Foundation unveiled a heavy steel outdoor bench bearing Guy's name as part of a larger exhibit to celebrate and re-claim the town's most famous son.

Along with the more predictable salutes at that time were testimonials from individuals who in the past might have had good reason to detest Guy. In a few notable cases, their hostility of old had faded in the glare of Guy's talent or had moderated in the collective sense of loss at his passing.

William R. Callahan, the former Smallwood minister and journalist who successfully sued Guy for defamation in 1998, had been ridiculed savagely by Guy in the late 1960s, mainly for his alleged role in delaying the start of the Gros Morne National Park. Guy mocked the minister's reports of possible commercial silica deposits within the designated park boundaries. He lampooned Callahan as Silica Bill and the Rocky Harbour Rooster. A satirical letter once appeared in a Guy column purporting to be from Callahan's wife. It was signed "Willica."

Callahan had moved to St. John's from Corner Brook in the mid-1960s after he won his Port au Port riding in the provincial election of 1966. In a 2016 interview for this book, Callahan said he never felt Guy had mistreated him, except for the column on which his lawsuit was based.

"Of course I knew about this reclusive, curmudgeonly character at *The Telegram*, but I didn't pay much attention. Joey used to get upset. But Guy didn't come after me personally, and I had no reason to think he would do me any wrong." If Callahan stopped just short of praising Ray Guy, he exhibited, in the circumstances, surprisingly little malice.

Ed Roberts, Smallwood's strongest Cabinet minister during the late 1960s, and a former Newfoundland and Labrador lieutenant-governor, also was pilloried and probably defamed by Guy in the 1960s and 1970s. Interviewed extensively at the time of Guy's death, and subsequently for this book, Roberts was generous and respectful of Guy's work, and insightful on the Guy versus Small-wood battles.

Roberts brings an elder-statesman perspective to those old battles, acknowledging both Smallwood and Guy as titanic New-foundlanders. Roberts observed that Guy posed a genuine threat to Smallwood because they both spoke persuasively to the same constituency, Smallwood's ragged-arsed artillery in the outports. Among other nuggets, Roberts confirmed the late 1960s daily practice of dispatching a car from the premier's office to fetch cop-ies of the *Telegram* hot off the press so that Smallwood and his ministers could get a jump on both the news and the latest Ray Guy irreverence.

Roberts's notion that Guy and Smallwood appealed to many of the same Newfoundlanders and Labradorians is persuasive. But Guy had other constituencies. By the time Smallwood's stature began to wane in the late 1960s, Guy's had waxed substantially. Guy spoke not only to Smallwood's Confederation artillery, most of them by then middle-aged or older, but increasingly to Small-wood's emerging younger critics. Those included academics at the university, education-reform advocates around the province, and the city's small but energetic counterculture and its overlapping arts community.

Guy also enjoyed an unlikely rapport, and one that Smallwood lacked, with the St. John's old-money and anti-Confederation crowd. Many of them detested Smallwood and licked their chops whenever Guy savaged him. A few of them, traditional Tories mostly, were recurring sources of information and dirt for Guy's columns.

Immediately following his death, much of the commentary about Ray Guy took the form of respectful platitudes. More bal-anced perspectives during his lifetime, and a few since, have iden-tified thematic threads and insights in Guy's writing, or marked its liberating impact on the struggling new Canadian province in the 1960s.

Despite their feud, Patrick O'Flaherty, one of Newfoundland's leading scholars of the era, was first to flag Guy's writing as soaring beyond quotidian journalism, attaining, in O'Flaherty's phrase, the ranks of literature. Writing in 1974 and with only the decade of Guy's *Evening Telegram* career to draw on, O'Flaherty identified the sources of Guy's inspiration and the nature of his muse:

> His values are deeply rooted in the outport life he knew in his childhood, and his language is rich with the idiom of old Newfoundland ...
>
> He resents the prostitution of the island by the horror of tourism, and the invasion of the people's privacy by the tormenting hordes of photographers, journalists, sociologists, and con men of all varieties who arrive annually to "study" and patronize them. When he sees the obscenity of industrial pollution and the danger posed by such pollution to Placentia Bay, he verbalizes the visceral response of the people, who like him retain a memory of cleaner, pastoral mode of living.[97]

Accolades from Mainlanders came more slowly.

"Canada's best columnist wasn't Canadian." That cheeky headline introduced an August 15, 2015, *Toronto Star* article on Guy by columnist Rick Salutin.

"I had the honour of participating last weekend in a tribute to Canada's greatest columnist," Salutin wrote, "except he wasn't Canadian. He was Ray Guy and he was a Newfoundlander." In Salutin's assessment, Guy as a writer took advantage of a still vibrant oral tradition in the outports. Salutin also noted well-known Ray Guy causes:

Newfoundland's denominational (Catholics, Pentecostals, etc.) school system drove him to fury. Fury is the moment of truth for a columnist. Do you just fulminate or do you control your rage? He was relentless describing the sadism of teachers in those crude schools.

Salutin recognized an important aspect of Guy's outport reminiscences:

His Encyclopedia of Juvenile Outharbour Delights columns ("Leave no tern unstoned") weren't sentimental.

He saw Guy's relationship with his readers as impassioned—"they were one community–and when he occasionally tried to transfer his work to the mainland (us) it didn't quite take."

In the academic world, an early and enigmatic appreciation of Guy's work was called "On Laughing at Ray Guy's Cats." Written by Dr. Cyril Poole, a Newfoundland scholar and writer who served for many years as principal of Grenfell College, Memorial University's Corner Brook campus, this essay assessed two collections of Guy columns, *You May Know Them as Sea Urchins Ma'am* and *That Far Greater Bay.*[98]

Poole appreciated Guy. He singled out several columns as classic and defining, including "A Christmas Story (Land Beyond the Blue)." Poole's prose can be obscure, at times leaving a reader feeling that only Poole understands Guy's writing, or else everyone else but Poole does. At times it is hard to tell if he is being serious or subtle. He finds offensive content in "A Christmas Story" where there is none. He concludes that the grandfather and grandson "angels" in this signature Guy story are "always pining for home in Placentia Bay." The opposite is closer to the truth.

Other observations in "Cats" are oblique but interesting. Poole cites a funny piece called "A Changed Person" in which Guy, in Old

Testament prophet mode, alludes to an incident in the biblical book of Numbers where Balaam's ass is reported to have spoken to him.

With some poetic licence, Guy quotes the ass as saying, "Why smackest thou me, Balaam?" Dr. Poole insists on setting the record straight. "The text does not bear this out. What the ass actually said was, 'What have I done unto thee, that thou hath smitten me these three times.'"

Lord only knows what Balaam's ass said. There are 60 or more versions of Holy Writ available on the internet in English alone. Balaam's ass, his donkey, of course, in today's sanitized testaments, may be misquoted in all of them. Guy enjoyed the same licence to invent dialogue for his columns as the Old Testament scribes did for theirs.

Despite its quirks, Poole's essay commands attention as an early scholarly work devoted exclusively to Guy and as an assessment based on a reflective read of two important Guy compilations. Poole's purpose, which he may well have achieved, was to make Guy's writing better known.

If Mainland recognition came slowly, CFA academics, less bruised perhaps by the storms of Newfoundland politics and culture, have provided some of the most cogent assessments of Guy's writing. The late Stuart Pierson, a Memorial University historian with a sweeping literary range, was a perceptive Guy fan, writing about his work with energy and flair.

Two essays on Guy appear in a collection of Pierson's writings called *Hard-Headed and Big-Hearted: Writing Newfoundland*. The book was edited by Stan Dragland, an author and student of Newfoundland writing, and introduced by J.K. Hiller, another Memorial historian and writer.[99]

It is not surprising that the names Dragland and Hiller show up in the Pierson collection. Hiller, CFA, also has written effectively and in depth about Ray Guy, while Dragland, CFA, has included generous praise for Guy in his more recent essays about Newfoundland writers and artists.

Hiller and Dragland shared with Pierson the dynamic of having adopted their Newfoundland and Labrador home with passion and commitment. Hiller, from England, has made Memorial University his base and St. John's his home since 1965. In fact, he was instrumental in recruiting Stuart Pierson to MUN. Pierson came from Washington State via the United States Army and Yale University, arriving in 1970.

Stan Dragland arrived three decades later, in 1999, directly from Ontario but originally from Alberta. In the eternity required for outsiders to melt into the Newfoundland culture, two decades are like a long weekend. But Dragland has made Newfoundland his literary obsession, researching and writing persuasively about Newfoundland and Labrador literature, music, society, and politics.

Pierson argued persuasively that Guy "belongs to a long tradition of funny journalists going back at least to Mark Twain." One local critic echoed that theme. Ed Riche, a top Newfoundland writer himself, once referred to Mark Twain as "America's Ray Guy."

Pierson includes Guy in a line of journalists such as Twain who, he suggests, emerged from small conservative towns. They came from all over the English-speaking world to go newspapering in big cities, only to learn quickly that "the world is run from on high by liars and hypocrites. In the face of such contrasts between what one grew up believing and what one found on the streets, one laughed or went bonkers, or maybe a little of each."

The gallery of satirists and humorists in which Pierson positions Guy includes Flann O'Brien, E.B. White, Will Rogers, Ambrose Bierce, Damon Runyan, and Ring Lardner.

"These writers are a bit leery of the modern world, by which I mean industrial capitalism and the bureaucratic state, or what Ray Guy calls 'The real bull-shit they got on the mainland.'"

Pierson attributes "a deep conservatism" to those writers, Guy included. He asks himself a key question: "What does this brand of conservatism want to conserve?" Pierson offers a useful answer:

> Something I think its proponents would call a human sense of proportion, a consciousness of being all in it together. There is a pervasive feeling that the most characteristic innovations of the twentieth century— advertising, mass propaganda, the technocratic state, weaponry capable of vaporizing cities—commit the sin of pride.

Years later, in 1991, Pierson reviewed *Ray Guy's Best*, a collection of more than half of the 90 or so columns Guy wrote for *Atlantic Insight* between 1979 and 1989. The *Insight* columns had been written nearly a decade later than those of *This Dear and Fine Country*, which is a collection based on Guy's Skipper Abe series for CBC Radio.

Pierson tracked Guy's evolution as a writer:

> The same funny moralist is at work in this new one as in the earlier collections. The same unerring eye for the ludicrous, the same skewers into pomp, the same wry outrage of life's, politics', history's constant stream of silliness. He's got, over the years, surer of himself and of his craft, and, though he still speaks of demented editors and their "pathological fixation on a silly little thing called a deadline" (p. 144) I sense a facility in these pieces, a confidence absent from some of the earlier columns in The Telegram, especially where he padded shamelessly with the (one) short sentence paragraphs and agonized and chewed the corner of his handkerchief."

Pierson complained that the editors of the new book included only about half of all of Guy's *Insight* columns. Pierson repaired to a library and read the 40 or more that were omitted, concluding that "in the columns left out, I count only one so bad as to deserve oblivion."

Allusions to Guy's work show up sporadically in Dragland's work. For a latecomer, he has made an informed contribution. In *Strangers and Others*, Dragland quotes a blurb Guy wrote for the cover of a collection of Codco plays.

> Self-confidence and self-mockery need each other. Both were blighted by the diktats of the Commission (of Government), the Juicy Fruit dollars and the cock-sure teeth of the Yanks and the witch's tit charity and Newfie jokes of Confederation. It was a long season we endured between Johnny Burke and *Cod on a Stick*.

For Dragland, those words alone inspired empathy and admiration for Guy. By quoting them, he offers an outsider's awareness of what it must have been like for Newfoundland and Labrador artists and writers of earlier eras—the Johnny Burke years, even the Ray Guy years. With notable exceptions, creativity and opposition were much less vibrant in those days than they were when Dragland first saw St. John's at the end of the 20th century. He concludes:

> Ray Guy's point in the blurb is that when a place has found its voice, or even a voice, visions of the place other than those purveyed by officialdom will be advanced. It's no wonder Ray Guy welcomed Codco. His was for years almost the lone satiric voice to be heard in Newfoundland. Calling the Smallwood government on its bullshit, as he so often did in his newspaper columns, his sense of smell acute and his courage high,

must have been like crying in the wilderness. He left a literary legacy that will last, though, and he has worthy inheritors.[100]

In 2009, Hiller reviewed *Ray Guy: The Smallwood Years*, a collection of Guy columns published by Boulder Publications in 2008. This was 17 years after Pierson had reviewed *Ray Guy's Best*.

Echoing his late friend, but in a milder tenor, Hiller criticized the collection as lacking context about the times and circumstances of Guy's writing. His review expressed appropriate respect for the value of such collections to the public. Equally welcome was Hiller's blown-away-Brit understanding of some of the sources of Guy's inspiration and of his impact. He had seen their like before:

> I arrived in Newfoundland in 1965, fresh from the English satire boom—"That was the Week That Was" on television, "Beyond the Fringe" in London's West End, and the clever, witty criticism of the establishment which appeared in the early issues of Private Eye magazine. Students joined in, and politicians became fair game—especially after such delicious incidents as the Profumo affair with all its ramifications. This is also where "Monty Python" took root.

Guy's satire did have roots in the satirical Brit irreverence described by Hiller. Guy was a major *Private Eye* fan, and, of course, he had his own collection of *Beyond the Fringe* LPs, which he prized and played often.

Hiller found Newfoundland society of 1965 closed and compliant, diminished in the long shadow of Smallwood's confidence and swagger. Before Guy, Hiller writes, there seemed to be little open political debate.

Once his columns started appearing in The Evening Telegram, I recall people wondering whether there could actually be a real person called Ray Guy—who would dare say such things? How could this stuff appear in public print?

Hiller was well positioned to monitor the impact of Guy's work, especially the ways in which it both complemented and was influenced by the growing dissent at the university and beyond.

> Guy questioned the government's insistence on "modernization," praised the traditional outport way of life ("Juvenile Out-harbour Delights"), and excoriated bureaucrats and politicians for the damage done to individual lives and communities ... The jury is still out on the resettlement programme, but Guy and others— Harold Horwood, for instance—did much to challenge the Smallwoodian gospel that 1949 was Year One of the New Dispensation, and that "Uncle Ottawa" was the source of all good things.[101]

Like other observers, including Ed Roberts, Hiller grasped the importance of Guy's entertainingly serious celebrations of pre-Confederation life in Newfoundland. The connection Guy created with his readers through humour and nostalgia helped build his credibility and his platform. Richard Gwyn called Smallwood a deadly serious clown. He could have applied that designation to Guy.

Other academics have attributed to Guy's writing a level of social and political substance rising well above routine newspaper writing. A few have deemed his work influential enough to have altered the course of Newfoundland and Labrador history.

Excerpts from Greg Davis's master's thesis on Guy's political influence in the Smallwood years were published in 2009 in the

Newfoundland Quarterly. Davis reinforces the widely held view that Guy played a direct role in Smallwood's political demise in the early 1970s:

> His [Guy's] columns were one of the few ways in which Smallwood's government received persistent criticism from the media ... The response that Guy's work received indicates that his columns were widely read, could articulate and influence public opinion, and were acknowledged by others, including Smallwood and his ministers. Ray Guy's work therefore contributed significantly to the growing dissatisfaction with and ultimate defeat of Smallwood's government.[102]

While several senior academics have assessed Guy's work well, an undergraduate student of English at Memorial University made her own compelling contribution in the early 1980s. Janet Kazmi's essay for her English 3155 course, "An Analysis of *That Far Greater Bay* by Ray Guy," found its way into the MUN's Centre for Newfoundland Studies in 1982. The essay, written in cursive, in the days when long-hand college essays would still get read, is direct and unpretentious.

> Keen discernment and appreciation for human nature make his work universal, although set in a Newfoundland context.
>
> By its own nature, the subject matter must be both topical and contemporaneous, but Ray Guy endows it with lasting value. His sense of humour gives life to the topic; his sensitivity gives it soul. At his best, Ray Guy fulfills the role of any great writer—to enable his readers to view their surroundings in a fresh, new way, and to see themselves as they are ...

For Kazmi, Guy's writing has a variety of flavours. She illustrates several with convincing examples from *That Far Greater Bay*. Guy, Kazmi writes, can be flamboyant and fanciful:

> Berserk! And he with the bitter roars coming out of him and swinging a two-edged sword around his head and a helmet with those cow horns sticking out of it and his light color hair strung out behind.

He can be smooth and polished:

> Lamplight is warm and mellow like candlelight and on stormy winter nights with a gale of wind drifting the snow outside and the window panes frosted up, the effect of lamplight and flickering firelight was very easy indeed.

Sarcastic:

> The same pity you'd have for any unfortunate victim of a gang rape. Newfoundland—the good time had by a bloated few. What does she do now? Tumble downstairs in hopes of a miscarriage?

And elliptical:

> Dust and dilapidated cobwebs. Sun-warmed varnish. Mothballs off people's Sunday suits. Musty prayer books. Puffs of sharp coal smoke from the backfiring stoves.[103]

The professor who assessed Kazmi's essay awarded a check mark of approval at a paragraph in which Kazmi describes Guy's broader importance.

Ray Guy is a voice of conscience for all Newfoundlanders. He is a chronicler, an entertainer. He is a journalist of considerable political acumen, aware, alert, and active, skilled at wielding an acid-dipped pen in the cause of Justice and fair play.

The approval was warranted.

As he practiced his highly personalized journalism, Ray Guy inspired other journalists, especially young Newfoundlanders in the 1970s and beyond.

Marie Wadden is a journalist and author whose career as a CBC reporter began in 1977 when women, as Kathie Housser discovered, were fighting their way into newsrooms where they were treated with insolent inequality by too many of the men. "I knew I was in trouble," Wadden reflected, "when I was introduced around the virtually all-male newsroom in a mocking kind of way as the 'best looking news reporter we've hired in a long time.'"

Guy's daily *Telegram* column inspired Wadden. In the mid-1970s, she was young enough to have picked up the Ray Guy habit from her father:

I was living at home, where my father, who hated Joey Smallwood, read Ray Guy assiduously. Joey was trying to make his comeback in 1975. I rarely read newspapers but found myself reading Guy, because dad enjoyed him so much ...

... I liked what he was doing to ridicule the current political situation, not just Smallwood, but the smarmy Frank Moores too. That's when I started looking into the possibility of doing journalism. Guy showed that it could be done in a new way, with original writing, not the usual "rip and read" teletype approach that seemed to be the style of the day.

Guy's influence on writers has not been limited to journalists. A well-known beneficiary is Wayne Johnston, widely regarded as Newfoundland and Labrador's most accomplished novelist of the last quarter century.

Johnston has published 10 books of fiction. In three of his novels, a central character is a newspaper columnist, Sheilagh Fielding. Johnston fans have long been aware of a connection between Fielding and Guy, a connection Johnston has acknowledged.

The only Newfoundland writer more complex than the real Ray Guy may be the fictional Sheilagh Fielding. Johnston said he created Fielding for his *Colony of Unrequited Dreams* as a foil for Smallwood, with whom she would be linked for a lifetime. "It had to be a woman," Johnston said. "A man would have had to play on the same field as Smallwood, and Smallwood would have destroyed him."

Fielding is influenced by several people. "My father's voice is there. Fielding includes some of the Confederation non-conformists, like Grace Sparkes ... journalists, like [Harold] Horwood. Myself of course."

Grace Sparkes, well known in Newfoundland for three post-Confederation decades, was a stalwart anti-Confederate non-conformist who did it all: teacher, scholar, reporter, anti-Smallwood political activist and opposition candidate, actor, and musician. In her spare time, Sparkes was an avid curler.

In *The Custodian of Paradise*, Fielding interrupts her St. John's newspaper career to write a book. She exiles herself to an uninhabited south coast island that Johnston calls Loreburn.

Harold Horwood quit his job as a senior and salaried editorial writer at the *Evening Telegram* to move to Beachy Cove, a nook just north of St. John's where there were more foxes than people. There he launched a major writing career, living for many years largely on the fat of the land.

Unlike Sparkes, Guy was not a curler, although he did joke once that he planned to take up calisthenics to try and shrink his beer gut. But Guy would have had much to discuss with Sparkes. Hers and his blended contributions to Sheilagh Fielding feel totally believable.

Johnston noted the irony that his father, Arthur, an anti-Confederate to the bone, worked for much of his life as a federal public servant, inspecting fish plants in Newfoundland. When he retired from his government job, Arthur took up farming full time, and, in Johnston's recounting, remained happy and self-sufficient for the remainder of his days.

Johnston identified just that self-sufficiency as common among a certain breed of Newfoundlander, and shared by individualists such as Guy, Horwood, Sparkes, and Arthur Johnston. "They all had this streak like Fielding," Johnston said. "They didn't need anybody on their side. Guy had it. Determined. He seemed to have an almost American belief in self-reliance."

In Johnston's *First Snow, Last Light*, Sheilagh Fielding summarizes her relationship with Smallwood in a way that both Sparkes and Guy would have admired.

> In New York in 1920, I had a steamy affair with Smallwood that almost boiled over into holding hands. He proposed. I said nothing. He stormed out. Back in St. John's he proposed again. I was no longer indecisive. Nor was the woman he proposed to, whose name was Clara.

"Fielding had nothing," Johnston said. "She was an oddball. An erudite oddball. She didn't hang around with powerful people, but she knew a lot about them. It was like Guy seemed to be. Shyness was a survival mechanism. Don't let anyone in but it all came out in the writing."

Johnston's fictional Fielding wrote for the fictional *Evening Telegram* in the 1930s. Ray Guy wrote for the real *Evening Telegram* in the 1960s and 1970s. Wayne Johnston wrote for the real St. John's *Daily News* just before its collapse in the early 1980s.

As chronicled in the novel *First Snow, Last Light*, Fielding's *Telegram* column of August 12, 1931, was based on an interview with the colony's then prime minister, the slippery and diabolical Sir Richard Squires. Squires of course was a real person, a hero and mentor to Smallwood in the 1930s.

In her opening paragraph, Fielding makes Squires regret ever sitting down with her, savagely mocking his moribund clichés.

> At his invitation, I interviewed Sir Richard, who said he wanted the Newfoundland people to know that he could not afford to have a black cloud hanging over the skeletons in his closet while waiting for another shoe to drop ...

The column ends:

> Sir Richard has nothing else in mind than the curtailment of our gluttony. He had decreed that belts must be tightened notch after notch until they go twice around our waist. Told by me that they already do, he asserted that they must be tightened until they go thrice round. Thus must be ushered in the era of wasp-waistedness and minimal ingestion ...[104]

Ray Guy would have loved that column. Indeed, he could have written something very much like it himself. Inspired by so many Newfoundland spirits, Guy's included, Johnston was well equipped to share those attributes with Sheilagh Fielding, in whom they will live for as long as there are books.

Much has been revealed about Ray Guy by academics and critics who have studied his work closely. Guy's own writing, as has been emphasized, is itself a book of revelations.

For those reasons and others, it was an intriguing and welcome experience to encounter a perspective on Guy by a journalist I have always admired. Azzo Rezori and Guy were close friends for more than 20 years. Curiously, Rezori to this day has read little of Guy's writing.

Rezori was a reporter in St. John's from the mid-1980s until his retirement in 2016. He came to St. John's from Toronto in 1985 to work at the *Telegram*. Over three subsequent decades, he became best known as a reporter with CBC's *Here & Now*, his lyrical prose and accented delivery evocative of the great CBC foreign correspondent Joe Schlesinger.

Rezori's parents were Austrian. He described them as colonials. "They had a superior attitude, like the Brits in India. Superior to everybody." Rezori grew up in Rothenburg ob der Tauber, a town of 10,000 in the middle of old West Germany. By all accounts, including Rezori's, it is one of the best-preserved medieval townscapes in Europe.

Biographical facts about Azzo Rezori make his comments about Ray Guy the more intriguing and welcome. His father, Gregor von Rezzori, was a satirist, novelist, screenwriter, and occasional actor. He wrote in three languages, achieving European celebrity and significant North American notice in the 1970s and 1980s.

When Gregor died in April of 1998, at 83, Michael T. Kaufman's obituary in the *New York Times* described him as "Gregor von Rezzori, born Gregor Arnulph Hilarius d'Arezzo ... an Austrian-born, Romanian, German-language novelist, memoirist, screenwriter and author of radio plays, as well as an actor, journalist, visual artist, art critic and art collector."

To Azzo Rezori (one *z*), Gregor von Rezzori (two *z*'s) was something less impressive—a narcissistic, controlling, and deadbeat father. "He left me out to dry, on my own, unparented, in Paris, when I was in grade 12."

Rezori said his father once forged a birth certificate to put the extra z in his son's name—a child of Gregor had to be a Rezzori. "He smuggled that extra z into my name!" Getting it removed, Rezori said, involved a legal process which Gregor resisted.

One night in 1986, the editor of the *Telegram*, Sean Finlay, invited Rezori to dinner at his house on Prescott Street in St. John's. Among the guests were Guy and Housser.

Liquor flowed freely. That night Rezori, a raconteur in his own right, realized he was in the company of a strikingly different and talented person, an enigmatic and bashful and outstanding teller of tales. He hoped he could befriend Guy, but on that first occasion it was Housser and Rezori who clicked. Housser had travelled extensively and was interested in European history. They found much to discuss. Rezori's rapport with Housser soon won him an invitation to the Guy-Housser residence on Holbrook Avenue, with its florid and fragrant garden.

Rezori recalls one large party at Holbrook where neither Guy nor Housser was the centre of attention. That honour went to Mary Walsh. Rezori says Guy hung out in a quieter room and drew a smaller audience. "Perhaps one room wasn't big enough for them both."

Rezori describes Guy as having a "responsive and quicksilver mind. He communicated by telling stories. When someone told a story, Ray could always come back effortlessly with a related one. Anecdotes were his version of small talk."

That same storyteller in small and friendly groups was also the Ray Guy of legendary reticence in crowds. Rezori found Guy's shyness endearing, so much so that he felt it sometimes gave him an aura of helplessness.

Daylight visits to Holbrook Avenue gave Rezori another lasting image of his new friend, Guy the gardener. "It was obvious right away that he had a great knowledge of and a great love of gardening. He would talk about it with sophistication, about importing special species of flowers from England and other places."

Rezori describes the Guy-Housser Holbrook Avenue garden in full dress as "structured and landscaped; set out in charming and pleasing levels. I think Ray tackled his garden the way he tackled his columns."

Rezori remembers sitting with Housser and Guy in their garden as an exceedingly pleasing experience. "I never really thought I would feel comfortable with him." It took some time. Rezori noted Guy's tendency to avoid intimate talk and at times to talk in riddles. He said it was very different from his own German cultural experience, "where conversations start with a question about the state of your soul."

Equally pleasant were Rezori's visits with Guy and Housser in the 1990s after they had moved to the Tolt Road in St. Philip's. But there were differences. While the view of Conception Bay was striking, Rezori was less impressed by the Tolt Road garden. "It was more rustic. Holbrook was a little garden paradise. But the Tolt was rougher. Perhaps they had not been there long enough to pour enough love into it to make it respond."

In their Tolt Road days, both Guy and Housser had largely sworn off alcohol, but a glass of wine was always on offer for guests. Rezori found their company as agreeable as ever, while detecting gradual shifts.

"Tolt Road was an isolating experience for them. Kathie mentioned that Ray had almost no friends at that point." Rezori said one exception always mentioned was Bob Benson, Guy's most important and durable companion from their *Telegram* years. Housser also acknowledged the friendship of new friends such as Jonathon Crowe, a former CBC *Here & Now* sportscaster and news anchor whom Housser knew from work. Rezori did his best to stay in touch and visit often. He never felt unwelcome.

Rezori's friendship with Guy was unusual because he had not been drawn to Ray by his writing. In a sense, he had gone out of his way to avoid it: "I was much more interested in Ray as a man, in his sphinx-like way of communicating. Behind what I knew was his acidic writing there was a kind and endearing man."

Early in their friendship, Rezori did read sample pieces of Guy's best-known writing from his *Telegram* and early freelance work. In doing so, and despite a command of the English language that Canadian university graduates might envy, Rezori ran into a problem. It was precisely the problem that ultimately sentenced Ray Guy to his status as Canada's least-known outstanding writer.

Rezori quickly realized he "did not have the upbringing, the cultural background, that would let his work resonate. I'm just not from here. When I read him, it was like rain falling on asphalt." He felt disconnected from Guy's political writing and the long hangover from the Smallwood years. "I felt much of it made him [Guy] sound like an anachronism."

Azzo Rezori, Kathie Housser, and Iris Brett are among the few people I have known who could talk about Guy endlessly and not rhapsodize about his writing and his literary triumphs. With Rezori and Housser especially, Guy's green thumb got at least as much attention as his carefully cultivated prose.

One of Housser's early comments in conversations about Guy has haunted me: "You can never fully understand Ray without understanding his love of gardening."

By that measure, I have never fully understood him. I knew about Guy's interest in gardening and had observed his regard for trees and flowers. His writing is, as it were, full of it—informed, funny, but to my taste idle in its tenor, signifying little. Gardening to Guy seemed like Horace Rumpole's interest in wine in the John Mortimer classics *Rumpole of the Bailey*. It had its place. Rumpole would refer to his favourite wine as "Chateau Thames Embankment." In the years when I knew Guy best, he would refer to February and March as his favourite gardening months in Newfoundland, and joke about his ability to "talk a good garden."

Chats with Housser and with Rezori made a difference. I had never fully grasped Guy's immersion in greenery as being, for him, a matter of the heart. It is a pleasure for me to report that others did, and to be convinced at last that it was true.

CHAPTER 23

Hail and Farewell

On May 30, 2001, the prophet Ray Guy suddenly found himself honoured, rather publicly, in his own land. Memorial University awarded him an honorary degree, Doctor of Letters. After all, as Guy noted in his convocation speech—with malice aforethought—Joey Smallwood and John C. Doyle each had one.

It was a big day for Guy. He wore the mortar board with aplomb, surely his weirdest piece of headgear since his pith helmet days. Memorial's Public Orator, Shane O'Dea, seemed to relish his role, which was to formally present Guy for the degree.

> Column by column, Guy chipped quietly away at the face of the idol, until, in 1971, that idol fell to be re-placed by a Tory party committed to the outport, to

Newfoundland and to good government—well, at least for a time. Ray Guy had the satisfaction of seeing the politicians he had condemned, put out, and what he had praised made promised. Few satirists can achieve a goal like that.

Dr. Guy accepted the praise with equanimity, apologizing for his free degree "to all of you who have worked for yours."

In the tradition of honourees, Guy offered a lament and advice to his fellow graduates, most of them a half-century younger than he. He alluded to his own place in the parade, an aging boomer, helping to swell the ranks of Newfoundland's grey-haired needy, with fewer and fewer younger people available to meet their needs:

> We are the pig that got swallowed by the python. That huge blob of so-called Baby Boomers who were once the Pepsi Generation and which is now moving down the digestive tract and is just reaching the 60-year-old mark.
>
> I dare say you do get some horrific emotional blackmail from my generation. "Who's going to buy us our walking frames and wheelchairs? Who's going to pay for our gin and Viagra and other medical necessities? If you all go, what are we going to do for potential kidney donors?" All that sort of subtle Newfoundland persuasion.
>
> Pay no heed and go. We'll get along somehow.

In his oration, O'Dea aptly noted the common threads between Guy and the great 18th-century Irish satirist Jonathan Swift.

> ... One is tempted to draw connections between Swift and the man before us for are they not both fathers

to their nation's penchant for satire? Are they not the breeders of bile, lacerators of corruption, lancers of the boil that suppurates on the body politic? Perhaps, but one has to tread warily here for Jonathan Swift was an urbane, sophisticated churchman; one who moved in the great circles of 18th century society. Mr. Guy, as he has so frequently told us, is only a bayman.

In the comparisons of Guy and Swift, there is no reason to tread as warily as O'Dea suggested. A Memorial graduate student of the future could do worse than explore the literary and political links between the two "laceraters of corruption."

There were differences, of course, as O'Dea observed. Swift saw his satire as an impediment to his rise to greater status. Like a lawyer too brilliant to be awarded silk, Swift, a clergyman, rose to become dean of a cathedral in Ireland but was thwarted in his ambitions to become a bishop or an abbot. He lamented the detrimental impact of having spoken too much truth to too much power.

> Had he but spar'd his Tongue and Pen,
> He might have rose like other Men:[105]

Guy, by contrast, truly did not give a damn about social or political status. He certainly had no hope of either church or state preferment, and fortunately no interest in either. Expecting little from society, he happily settled for less.

If a serious study of Swift and Guy were undertaken, it would find more common ground in less conventional places. Foremost would be their compassion for the less privileged and for the physically and intelligently damaged.

As noted, the Guy-Housser home on Holbrook Avenue was a stone's throw from the Waterford Hospital, the storied "Mental" of St. John's. Guy was always sanguine and often amused by having the old asylum as his neighbour. He may have been comforted by it. Plenty of artists, Guy among them, have been sufferers themselves.

Guy's empathetic credentials, his underdog advocacy, were well established throughout his career. They were obvious in a piece headlined "Peering through the Fence at the Waterford Hospital," written in the mid-1990s during one very brief and final fling as a weekly columnist for the *Telegram*.

> Up back of the Mental is where I've been living for the past dozen years or so.
>
> In other words, on the other side of the fence from the Waterford Hospital, formerly the Hospital for Mental and Nervous Diseases.
>
> I credit my mother-in-law with inadvertently giving me the distinguished address of "Up back of the Mental."
>
> The dear creature stepped off the plane at Torbay with 5,000 miles of jet lag behind her and 500 years of culture shock ahead of her and a St. John's taximan to greet her.
>
> "Whirrdo, missis?" she thought she heard the taximan say. Oh, oh ... where to? And she gave our address. "Ah ... righton. Up backa the Mental."
>
> ... Her darling daughter and hem hem "exotic" husband apparently lodged in the rearward cells of some mental institution.

Guy's choice of idiom for discussing the delicate topic of mental illness is not today's idiom. The modern delicate and carefully nondescript phrasing is infused with the language of inclusion, the differently abled, one's place on the spectrum, and similar obfuscations. Writing in the 1990s, Guy had barely caught up with lingo of the 1970s:

"Not In My Backyard," or NIMBY is a fad of recent years ...

When we first looked at the house the real estate agent volunteered that there was no need to worry about "the Mental Grounds behind you." He, himself, lived just up the street and had small children. Never the slightest bit of trouble.

I have taken a selfish gain from living over the fence from "the Mental Field."

Something about being in touch with and not apart from all of God's human mysteries, the frailty of the human mind, momento mori [sic], eternal childhood ... as per our teachings in "old" Newfoundland at granny's knee.

I would pass the scattered ciggy through the fence when asked or agree that, yes, it was so lovely here in Florida or that, by all reports, General Eisenhower had given the Hun another good punishing yesterday.

Better than that, our children grew up with the benefit of living "up back of the Mental." They neither stare, nor flinch nor make sanctimonious pitying faces, I hope, when they see people who are different.

Eventually the Mental Field, the large playground adjacent to the old hospital where patients and inmates played ball or simply hung around outdoors, became real estate too valuable for such ennobling purposes. The journalist Ray Guy duly reported the typical urban-progress outrage.

Gradually, the remaining Waterford Hospital patients have been pushed off "the Mental Field."

They used to come out for walks, helped along or by themselves, to have small picnics on the grass, to sit by the fence in the shade of the trees and bushes, sometimes to play informal ball games.

But, gradually, whoever owns the property started to rent it out to continuous replay of sports teams.[106]

Numerous couplets from Swift's poetry and many passages from his prose establish his similar identification with people who are different. Swift wished to be known for his compassion for such sufferers. He hoped to be recognized too for very concrete contributions to the welfare of the intellectually impaired. His "Verses" on his own death made his intentions clear:

> He gave the little wealth he had,
> To build a House for Fools and Mad:
> And shew'd with one satyric Touch,
> No Nation wanted it so much ...

Like Swift, Guy took the part of the halt and the lame and stuck up for the fragile. He felt he had been there. He understood the pathos of the displaced and forgotten elderly, Bob Dylan's "old men with broken teeth stranded without love." Guy found those broken old men and women among the victims of moving fever, often among the baymen, among St. John's corner-boys too, and inevitably at the Mental.

In 2004, when Ray Guy was 65, reporter Clare-Marie Grigg of the weekly *Independent* went to his house for a chat.

The *Independent*, for which Guy also wrote, was, like the *Sunday Express*, another upstart newspaper hoping to find a niche for quality journalism in St. John's. Founded by businessmen Ward Pike and Jon Drover, it survived four years, beating against the usual headwinds, including the *Telegram*'s hegemony in the local print advertising market.

Reporter Grigg started her story with a characteristic Guy-Housser anecdote.

> Hasty introductions are made as a big, hairy, panting dog plonks itself down in the middle of everything. His wife, CBC producer Kathie Housser, makes a quick exit:
>
> "Where are you going?" Guy hollers.
>
> "To meet my lover," his wife shouts back.
>
> "Which one, the fat one or the skinny one?"
>
> "The older one."
>
> "Ahh, the one with the money."

By the "20-aught" years, Guy had become famous for being famous. For the final edition of the *Independent*, on April Fool's Day, 2006, Grigg connected with him once again. Under the headline "No More 'Round the Mountain"—a reference to the headline of his Leacock Prize feature on the Bullet—Grigg reported that Guy had suffered a mild stroke a week earlier that had temporarily stopped him from writing. Grigg's story was a compact reprise of several Guy themes, a thumbnail portrait of the artist at 67, with seven years of his life remaining.

"Anything to do with your eyesight gives you a little thrill of horror," Grigg quotes Guy as saying, "I've gone from terrified to comatose to now I'm getting a bit cranky."

Guy had written monthly for the *Independent* for four years. The newspaper's demise was the collapse of one more redoubt in the retreat of quality print journalism in Newfoundland and Labrador. It was a retreat that so closely coincided with Guy's own career that his critics might have accused him of having caused it—instead of the truth, which is that he fought mightily to prevent it, almost literally to his dying day.

"I can't say I didn't expect it," Guy said, "but it's really too bad. It was a handsome paper and it provided a great service. Over the years I've had, I don't know, 10 or a dozen horses shot out from under me and ... I'd really like to offer some cheer to people at *The Independent* who figure all is lost and this is it. I know how they must be feeling. Who was it said? 'I feel your pain.'"

Inevitably, Guy's recounting of his career as a print journalist harkened back across the decades to his final days as a columnist in the employ of Lord Thomson of Fleet. Guy crossed the decades as if they were days, eerily remembering the many Thomson miseries:

> Once a month there were two survey creeps used to come down from headquarters, Tweedledum and Tweedledee, and you'd feel something nasty behind your back, looking over your shoulder ... these two Mafia types.
>
> I decided to quit that for good ... you know it was so much a part of my life, the way I lived, that I just got in the car and drove and found myself sitting on a wharf, the end of the wharf, here, in fact, in St. Phillips, looking across at Bell Island and I was possibly there for half a day, comatose and I had no realization of how I got there, but it was really, really devastating.[107]

Two years later, on July 6, 2008, approaching 70 and in declining heath, Guy showed up in yet another Sunday newspaper personality feature, in of all places, the *Telegram*. By then, the *Telegram* had handily won the two-decade war for Sunday newspaper dominance in St. John's, and Guy, with no competing Sunday paper available, had become a safe subject for the old paper's own celebrity brightener, *20 Questions*.

Reporter Everton McLean asked Guy the usual questions, but the answers were less predictable. As might be expected, most of them were amusing:

> McLean: Who would you least, or most, like to be stuck in an elevator with?
>> Guy: Least: Brian Tobin. Most: An elevator repairman.
> McLean: Do you have any hidden talents?
> Guy: I can talk a really great garden.

One exchange was poignantly revealing.

> McLean: What is your most treasured possession?
> Guy: My wedding ring.

"Holy Acrimony," as he called it, had been an essential state for Guy. The ring was by no means his only family and marital treasure.

As part of her large contribution to this book, Housser shared a thumb drive containing family photos. Inadvertently, as far as I am aware, it also contained several family emails, mostly on mundane and routine matters. Among those emails was a short note from Housser to Guy, written from Vancouver during a visit she had made alone to see her family there. I have no permission to quote that note. But I can say this: few on earth have received a sweeter and more affectionate message from a lover or a spouse.

It was not a surprise to me to hear from family sources that the daughters were devoted to their parents. Following Guy's death in 2013, Rachel reportedly waged an ongoing campaign to get her mother to move to Halifax to be near them. For much of that period, Housser was in and out of hospitals and rehabilitation facilities in St. John's, battling the pulmonary illness and recurring pneumonia that eventually led to her death on September 10, 2017, four years and four months after Guy's.

Ray Guy fans and students often cite or quote favourite articles that feel thematic of the writer's values and beliefs. None ever does so completely, but a few come close. One such, cited by Cyril Poole and others, and a personal favourite, is "A Christmas Story."

In it, the more worthy Christian teachings are given Guy's approval. Others fare less well. First written as a *Telegram* column and later published in *That Far Greater Bay*, the essay neatly frames the satirist's view of the world. It also reveals the depth to which Ray Guy in childhood had absorbed old-time Christian metaphors and the distinct mix of martial and gospel music of the Salvation Army in 1940s and 1950s outport Newfoundland.

Guy sets the stage for his heavenly allegory as poignantly as can be wished:

> A youngster angel by the name of Clarence—four foot, seven inches tall and no odds how many years old—was out for a walk along the Golden Strand one day in company with a grandfather angel.
>
> The weather was fair to middlin' as it generally always is in the Land Beyond the Blue.
>
> The grandfather angel dodged along puffing on an imaginary pipe stuffed with imaginary Beaver tobacco of the very best light-leaf plug.
>
> It was imaginary because this part of the Kingdom of Heaven is plastered fore and aft with "No Smoking" signs.[108]

The staid Church of England taught Guy mainstream biblical literacy. The Salvation Army, Granny Guy's church, seemed to imbue in him a sense of emotional mystery—not blind faith, but boundless fascination. At the barracks, uniformed Sally Ann officers hammered home their strict injunctions with rousing hymns, driven by brass wind instruments and bass drums. Many of those messages were charitable and humane. More than a few promised fearsome reckonings for backsliders and hell's flames for flat-out sinners.

In "A Christmas Story," Guy casts his grandfather angel as "a Salvationer in life although many times a backslider." In life "Below," the grandfather angel had feared that his backsliding might offset the notable contribution to worship that his willing penitence and powerful singing voice made each Sunday evening. Heaven, as Guy relates, did not change grandfather's tune.

> And now, up here at last in the Glory Land, as he dodged along the Celestial Landwash, anyone with half an ear could easily hear above the waves of the wide Ocean of Mercy as they rolled in on the Golden Strand.
>
> "Oh, we'll walk and talk on the Golden Strand,
> "We'll walk on the Golden Shore …"
>
> Horrk. Ptwew! Here he took out his imaginary pipe and launched an imaginary spit to leeward.
>
> "We'll sing of His love in the Realms Above,
> "And we won't come back anymore."

As Guy points out, it is always chancy to fault the Almighty, and the grandfather angel was truly impressed by the favourable tides of his new community, with its "hills behind with no dark valleys and from whence came the Light." Despite that, the grandfather remained very much a Placentia Bayman, and there was one feature he missed about the Far Greater Bay, even from the vantage point of Paradise:

> … and that was a bit of fog. Oh, not all the time, mind you. And not a cold, black troublesome fog with the wind southeast. But a white and luminous caplin-skull fog in a stark calm now and then for remembrance sake.

Guy takes pains to sculpt his grandfather angel, and he takes his time doing it. He has a purpose for creating this wise and venerable person. At heart, the story is about the learning relationship between Clarence, the boy angel, and his grandfather, a relationship much enhanced by their current favourable setting. Heaven, in Guy's vision, is a long teachable moment, sometimes called eternity.

Grandfather angel's important lessons include the sorry but enduring state of Newfoundland, the perniciousness of newspapers, the necessity for equality among peoples, and a surprisingly modern tutorial on ecological stewardship.

> "Hello, then! Hello, then! Hello, then!" sang out the youngster angel, Clarence, of a sudden.
>
> He snatched something out of the water and skipped backwards out of the lop so as not to get the tail of his robe of purest white wet or overrun the tops of his long rubbers.
>
> "What's this, granda?" he said. "What's this?"
>
> "That's what they calls paper down Below," said grandfather angel, for he was wonderful sagacious and had sailed on foreign-going vessels. "'Pears to be a newspaper of some description."

The words St. John's and Newfoundland could be discerned on the paper, which prompts Clarence to ask exactly the right questions to advance his general knowledge.

> "What's a newspaper, granda?" He asked. "What's St. John's? What's Newfoundland?"

At this point granda, who has brought several worldly habits with him from Placentia Bay, runs the risk of instructing at a level over the child's head, and at a volume designed for other angels or even archangels to hear, perhaps indulging a long-standing earthly tendency to suck up to his betters. Or perhaps he thinks that a Higher Power can alleviate Newfoundland's distress even where Confederation could not.

> "Newfoundland is a poor country badly used by traitors!" said the grandfather angel, suddenly rising to the rolling heights of oratory that he had achieved while giving his Testimony before the Penitent Form down Below. "But one which, by the Grace of He Who is Higher Than All, will always muddle along through the rough and the smooth and find a safe harbor at the last!"

And St. John's?

> "An untidy place, an unruly place, where much riotous living goes ahead and where you got to watch 'em like a hawk or they'll rob the coppers off your eyes ...
>
> "And a newspaper, Mr. Quiz-Box, is where they cuts down trees and squats them out flat for to make paper and then prints stuff on them. It is a sinful, sinful practice.
>
> "Them fellers what puts out the newspapers down Below should be on their knees night and day, beggin' forgiveness for destroyin the handiwork of Our Blessed Lord in the forests and turnin' it to such a low and useless purpose."

Clarence's next question is more challenging. He wants to know how things actually were, back down Below, where he had spent only a few short years. He wishes to compare affairs Below to his understanding, based on his recent school experience, of the goings-on Above.

"Granda? All hands is alike up here in the Glory Land and there is no difference with regards to race, country, color, religion, creed or politics. But do you remember ... do you think ... that me and you ... I mean to say, yourself and myself, mightn't be Newfoundland angels?"

"What," said grandfather angel, amazed, "in the devil put a notion like that into your head!"

"Well," said Clarence, "them two fellers sittin' back of me at the St. Stephen's Upgradin' School for Cherubim and Seraphim said the other day that I must be a Newfoundlander because I talks quare."

"You're old enough to know better," said the grandfather angel. When you comes through the Pearly Gate it is like joining on to another country. All hands is alike when they passes out the citizenship papers ...

"... We might or might not be Newfoundland angels. I can't clearly remember. But if you thinks so, keep it to yourself, as talk like that will only cause a fuss. And the Kingdom of Heaven is the last place in the world that we wants to stir up a fuss."

Clarence seemed satisfied at this point and skipped off to have a bit of a fly-around for himself.

But soon he is back, seeking clarification:

"Do even RCs and Church of Englanders get in through the Pearly Gates if their applications are in order?"

"Oh, yes, yes, indeed," said the grandfather angel in tones of awe, for the flexibility and stretch of the very outer boundaries of Salvation never ceased to amaze him.

Thereafter, discussions between granda and Clarence become more temporal. Granda tries flying himself, but he is not good at it. It frustrates him and makes him cranky. Reverting to worldly habits once more, he admonishes the boy:

> "Clarence!" he called out sharply. "Come down here and pick up that harp of yours. Lodge it up above high-water mark. The tide is risin.'"
>
> "Oh, shag that bloody harp," cried Clarence petulantly. "Harp, harp, harp is all I hears. I'm sick of harp practice. I can play by ear already but they says you got to play by note."

Inevitably, Ray Guy's Heaven has features in common with the ways of Christians Below. The immediate problem, Guy reveals, is that birthday celebrations for the Prince of Peace are approaching rapidly—this is, after all, a Christmas Story. Preparations for the celebrations are running behind schedule, as they commonly do on earth.

> Clarence knew that he would never get that bloody harp down pat in time. Playing by ear was all very well for informal occasions, but you really needed to be able to play by note at the birthday of the Fairest of Ten Thousand, the Lily of the Valley, the Bright and Morning Star.

Fortunately, granda is there, Heaven-sent as it were, to assuage the boy's anxiety,

> "Don't trouble yourself," said the grandfather angel, knowing Clarence's worry. "Don't trouble yourself so long as you always do the very best you can."

In a masterful column about Confederation, Ray Guy uses a similar device, an explanatory conversation across generations—this one more down to earth. The technique works to evoke the power of anti-Confederate sentiment that lingered in Newfoundland and Labrador throughout at least half of his lifetime and was intense during his childhood and youth.

Because he grew up in its shadow, Guy understood the emotional freight of the Confederation decision with its irreversible fact. The fictional essay "But You Said We Won" is one of the most poignant of his early career. In it, the Confederation surrender breaks an old man's heart.

Guy imagines a conversation with an older person who passed away in August 1943, "out Home." The younger man in the conversation is a Newfoundland Canadian not much engaged with the past. The older man is the ghost of an outport elder who died before the end of World War II but not before the distant rumblings of the Confederation battle were heard throughout Newfoundland.

A series of questions from the older spirit are met by polite and patient answers by the young man. But there is a disconnect. Unbeknownst to each other, the two are discussing different topics, one World War II, the other Confederation with Canada. The elderly gentleman asks:

> "Do England still stand?"
> "O, yes, sir. And our Sovereign sits yet—in her castle at Windsor ... as they say."
> "Well, we won then."
> "Oh, yes, sir, we won. It was a bit ticklish in spots but we made it."[109]

The skipper then asks about an old friend whom he recalled as having been ill when he was:

"Did Billy last long?"

"Oh, yes, sir. He rallied after that and he was great and smart and only passed away, I think it was, the year before ... no in the summer ... two years before Confederation. They put his pipe and a bottle of rum in the box along with him."

"Eh, my son?"

"His pipe, sir, and a bottle. They put it in with him. It was his wish."

"Confederation?"

"Yes, Confederation. Joined on to Canada. It was in 1949. April Fool's Day. You know, upalong. Canada. We were joined on."

"You said we won."

"But that was the war, sir. This was after. I can't mind too much about it. I was a boy then."

"The Commission done it."

"I don't think so, sir, altogether. I'm going by what I'm told. I believe we were more or less on our own again, then."

"Then how many was there killed?"

"So far as I know, sir, there was no one killed. There was only a lot of talk all the time, and swearing. When it came about they put the flag down to half-mast but there was no one killed."

"No one?"

"No, sir. No one ... so far as I know."

"No one."

The satirist's role is indeed to tell all the truth, but, as Emily Dickinson instructed, "to tell it slant." Ray Guy tried to live by the verities he promoted with his satirical gifts. In life, he was a kind of secular Salvationist himself, many times a backslider too.

Guy's pre-Confederation childhood left him not just with memories and stories, but with something more profound—something approximating touchstones for life.

In his half-century marathon of words, Guy was consistent in the major themes of his life and his literary art. To oversimplify those themes: He feared and abhorred demagoguery. He hated bullies. He felt Newfoundland and Labrador lost about as much as it had gained from Confederation with Canada. He felt an obligation to judge the world as he found it and to shout his verdict as loudly as he could.

Guy loved trees and plants and dogs, but he had no interest in hunting, fishing, or hiking. He believed formative education was mostly about good teachers. He disliked cheats of all kinds, including welfare cheats. But, characteristically, he did admire the candour of one outport acquaintance who, when asked what he was doing, replied, "b'y, they says I'm foolish ... anyway I'm gittin' a foolish pension."

Guy grew up in an anti-Confederate family in a pre-Confederation culture. Despite the positive memories of his childhood, and despite his sympathy for Major Cashin and the cause, he was not a militant anti-Confederate. Rarely in his writing is there any serious anti-Canadian sentiment.

He loved and married Kathie Housser, an arch-Canadian. He wrote glowingly of her home province, British Columbia. He was not cynical about Canada as a nation, and he acknowledged indisputable federal benefits. But he always resented the compulsion of many post-Confederation Newfoundlanders to condemn the pre-Canadian past as inferior and best forgotten.

On a friend-to-friend basis, Guy was not always an easy guy to love. But unless you were one of the many targets of his rapier pen, he was impossible to dislike. Guy knew his demons and afflictions.

He worked valiantly if not always successfully to wrestle them to the ground.

One long ago St. John's winter when Guy, Everett Bishop, and I lived together in an apartment built for two, Guy fell into a seasonal funk that astonished Bishop and scared the hell out of me. I had witnessed its like, but not its intensity, before. For days, then weeks, Guy moved ghostly around the apartment, up half the night, acknowledging nobody, deathly silent. His dark demeanour suggested that he had been offended in some fashion or was somehow owed redress for some mysterious slight.

On a morning in March, he and I were alone in the apartment. Ray was shuffling about in the kitchen, brooding and glum. He set a plate and cutlery on the table. He then placed a $5 bill on the plate, smothered it with ketchup, and commenced to cut it up with the fork and knife.

A door closed between us. Later that day, in confusion and despair, I packed books and bags and took a cab to Smith Avenue Extension, where an attic bed-sitter was available on short notice.

Presently, a sealed envelope was delivered.

"It was The Game, you see," Ray wrote. "One day I realized that I hadn't spoken to you for days. I thought, 'I'm One Up!' Now then, we'll see who could hold out the longest? Iris and I used to play The Game. Cheesies ... what Games Iris and I used to play!"

The letter carried on for pages, cheerfully bringing me abreast of latest gossip in the *Telegram*'s newsroom and defaming various Cabinet ministers, including William R. Callahan, who at the time was in particular Guy disfavour: "He's One Down."

A few weeks later Guy and I were headed for points south in his Datsun 510. We made early stops at Heart's Delight, where he told my father, "I'm here to shake your hand," and then at Arnold's Cove where Guy's father, George H., asked me, on the quiet, if he had "either" girlfriend in St. John's, while his mother, Alice, handed Guy an envelope with "a bit extra" for the trip.

Those vignettes are from the days when my view of Ray Guy was up close and personal. We had our days together, laughing days mainly. But for most of our busy lives we were in different places, different cities, experiencing radically different Canadian cultures. As a result, what I knew first-hand about Guy has been hugely and generously augmented by others who also knew him well. I also learned much from his writing over so many years and from the writing of others about him.

In recent years, reading every written word of his that I could locate, my conclusion is that I had gotten to know him reasonably well decades ago. Almost everywhere in his writing I found the footprints of his values and convictions, and of his wisdom. I realized too what an influence he had been, and how hard I had tried—and how difficult it was—to absorb a few of his ethical and journalistic strengths into own my life and work.

In Ray Guy's obituary, published in the *Telegram* on May 16, 2013, the family encouraged donations in Guy's memory to the Canadian Mental Health Society (bipolar). In the first of several interviews for this book, Kathie Housser made it clear that when it came to his psychological pain, "Ray wanted it all known."

When Kathie became too ill to comfortably talk about her husband, her brother, Johnny Housser, and his wife, Rosemary House, conveyed a special message from her to me. These words are Johnny Housser's:

> Kathie said she was concerned that some of Ray's more eccentric behavior might be reported on, commented on, without an overriding reference to the fact that he was a fairly significant sufferer of bi-polar disorder.
>
> She just asked me again to request that you keep that in mind when you are reporting on events that he may have been involved in.

I have kept that in mind.

It was a reasonable interval after her husband's death when I approached Kathie Housser with the idea for a book about Ray, and with an essential question: Would she co-operate? She was resting at the time, recovering from her latest battle with an acute chest cold. "Have at it," was her reply. "The hairs on my head are numbered."

The pervasive cancer that killed Ray Guy was diagnosed in the spring of 2013. It was not a surprise. Both Guy and Housser had been silently aware for months. They did not discuss it until there was no choice.

Iris Brett said Ray had looked ill for most of the year before his passing. He was emaciated, weak, and he appeared to be existing mainly on liquid nutritional supplements. Iris said it was obvious that he was losing interest and not working in the final two or three months. She attributed his condition to acute depression.

Azzo Rezori visited less frequently in the last months of Guy's life. He recalls occasions when "there was only half of him there. He was very heavily medicated."

Iris says it was a great shock when Housser called to tell her that Guy had been admitted to the Health Sciences Complex and had been diagnosed as terminal. She left the Cove immediately for St. John's.

"He could hardly speak. But he said, 'you are never far from my thoughts.'" They were his last words to her.

Rosemary House also recalled visiting him in hospital. She quoted him as saying only, "it is hard for people to know what to do ... you know, between now and then."

After a week at the hospital, Guy was transferred to a palliative care facility where he spent his final few days. Kathie, daughter

Annie, and Iris were there throughout. In the compressed time frame from diagnosis to death, daughter Rachel made it home from Nigeria barely in time to see him alive.

Guy's palliative pain treatment was the "butterfly," an injection device installed beneath the skin that provides relief from the severe pain of advanced cancer by continuous injection of opioid drugs. Housser thought the treatment was effective in sparing him intense pain.

Just two months earlier, Guy had said goodbye to some other people who mattered much to him, his remaining regular readers of the *Northeast Avalon Times*.

Of all the publications for which Guy had written, none was dearer to him than the *Northeast Avalon Times*. By his own account, no publisher was more accommodating and respectful of him than Kathryn Welbourn, who owns and runs the newspaper.

Guy wrote monthly for the *NEA Times* from 2003 until March 2013, two months before his death. Housser said that his association with the newspaper gave him dignity as he aged. Guy's final "30" was registered in the *Northeast Avalon Times*'s March 2013 edition.

"Hail and farewell," he wrote. "My thanks to you, and to one heck of a patient publisher. This is my last crack out of the box anywhere, at any time. No apologies and no silly excuses. I was born April 22, 1939. I began this journalizing racket in 1962. So, I have settled Mr. Hitler's hash, defrosted the Cold War and pensioned Joe Smallwood."

"Come Robin," Guy wrote definitively. "Our work here is done."

The last day of Ray Guy's life was a Tuesday. Iris was with him in the early evening. At 6:20 p.m. he left her alone, in the loneliest room of all.

ENDNOTES

1. Cited in Richard Gwyn, *Smallwood: The Unlikely Revolutionary*, rev. ed. (Toronto: McClelland and Stewart, 1972), 293.

2. Ken A. Tulk, *Arnold's Cove: A Community History* (Robinson-Blackmore Printing and Publishing, 1997), 24.

3. Ray Guy, *Evening Telegram*, January 20, 1970, 3.

4. Tulk, *Arnold's Cove*, 53.

5. Greg Malone, *Don't Tell the Newfoundlanders: The True Story of Newfoundland's Confederation with Canada* (Alfred A. Knopf Canada, 2012), 236.

6. The late Tommy Sexton sang "The Babylon Mall" as vocalist for The Wonderful Grand Band. The song was written by band member Jamie Snider.

7. Guy, "Water Street's Ebb and Flow," *Canadian Geographic* (Spring 1999), 59- 61.

8. Guy, *Evening Telegram*, September 10, 1968, 3.

9. Guy, *Evening Telegram*, September 11, 1968, 3.

10. Guy's own weakness in Mathematics did not deter him from ridiculing a dull-knife Newfoundland politician who, he said, had "graduated from Memorial, excelling in short division."

11. Peter Neary and Patrick O'Flaherty, *Part of the Main: An Illustrated History of Newfoundland & Labrador* (St. John's: Breakwater Books, 1983), 156.

12. "Dulce et Decorum Est" is Wilfred Owen's World War I poem. The quotation "Dulce et decorum est pro patria mori" translates as "It is sweet and fitting to die for one's country." From the poem:

    > My friend, you would not tell with such high zest
    > To children ardent for some desperate glory,
    >
    > …
    >
    > The old Lie: Dulce et decorum est
    > Pro patria mori.

13. The term "yarn" in Newfoundland has the general meaning of a story or tale, told with licence for exaggeration or outright fiction. A "cuffer" shares those connotations but has the more expansive meaning of "a friendly chat; an exchange of reminiscences; a gathering for this purpose." *Dictionary of Newfoundland English* (*DNE*), s.v. "cuffer."

14. Guy, "The Poor We Have with Us Always," in *You May Know Them As Sea Urchins, Ma'am*, ed. Eric Norman (Portugal Cove, NL: Breakwater Books, 1975), 89.

15. Guy, "Uncle John," in *That Far Greater Bay* (Flanker Press, 2011), 148. This collection of Guy columns was first published in 1976 by Breakwater Books and was the winner of the Stephen Leacock Memorial Medal for Humour.

16. Guy, "Tying Cans onto Sheep's Tails," in *That Far Greater Bay*, 93, 94.

17. Guy, *Here & Now*, CBC Television, NL, December 1, 1993.

18. This four-page "life" of Ray Guy, by Ray Guy, was written in support of a stage production revue of Guy's works called *Stunned, Stung, Bitter and Twisted*, which played at the Longshoremen's Protective Union Hall from September 14 to 26, 1982. It is not clear to whom Guy sent it, possibly to someone doing publicity for the show. Attached to the note was

a cheeky postscript: "Please send me a copy of your finished article. You lot pay even less than *The Telegram*."

19. *Newfoundland Herald*, November 6, 1999, 29.

20. Peter C. Newman, *Renegade in Power: The Diefenbaker Years* (Toronto/Montreal: McClelland and Stewart Limited, 1964).

21. In August 1969, Guy inscribed this volume, along with two other weighty drama textbooks, and gave them to Everett Bishop of Heart's Delight. Everett is my Heart's Delight childhood friend who shared an apartment with Guy and me during 1969/1970 when he and I both attended Memorial University. In 2014, when Bishop became ill, he sent the books to me. I am pleased to own them.

22. Ian Wiseman, "I's the B'y Who Meets Ray Guy," *Quill and Quire* (May 1985), 29. Wiseman, who became a CBC producer and executive producer, and later a professor of journalism at King's College, Halifax, was one of many Newfoundland and Labrador journalists of our generation who apprenticed at the *Evening Telegram* and was influenced by Guy.

23. Guy, "Stories," *Newfoundland Quarterly* 103 (Summer 2010), 34.

24. Excerpted with David Day's permission.

25. *Unsafe at Any Speed*, the title of Ralph Nader's 1965 book on the American automobile industry. Chapter 1 is devoted to "The Sporty Corvair." Nader faulted the Corvair for an unsafe suspension system, which made early 1960 models prone to dangerous oversteer.

26. James Boswell, *The Life of Samuel Johnson*, vol. 2 (1906; Dent: London, Everyman's Library, 1973), 291.

27. The opening verse of "Elegy Written in a Country Churchyard," by Thomas Gray:

> The curfew tolls the knell of parting day,
> The lowing herd winds slowly o'er the lea,
> The ploughman homeward plods his weary way,
> And leaves the world to darkness and to me.

28. Ray Guy, "A Landscape of Awe and Dread," *Newfoundland Quarterly* 100, no. 4 (Spring 2008), 27.

29. Jack Fitzgerald, *Crimes That Shocked Newfoundland* (St. John's, NL: Creative Publishers, 2008), 75, 76.

30. Guy, *Evening Telegram*, January 22, 1972, 1.
    Tommy Toe was a St. John's character of legend who went missing during a major harbourfront development in the early 1960s. According to St. John's archeologist Gerald Penney, "the legend is he is somehow encased down there in the concrete, but we didn't find him." Steve Bartlett, "What Lies Beneath," *Telegram*, March 13, 2010. Malcolm Hollett had been a staunch opponent of Smallwood during the Confederation referenda campaigns, and subsequently became leader of the Newfoundland Progressive Conservative Party.

31. Oliver L. Vardy, Smallwood's long-time confidant and deputy minister of Tourism, could not run for office, having previously been convicted as a young man of armed robbery in the United States. Eventually charged with fraud and breach of trust in Newfoundland and Labrador, he fled in old age to St. Petersburg in Florida, where he fought extradition and lived with illnesses until his death in 1980. Doyle, meanwhile, whose Canadian Javelin Company developed iron ore mines in Western Labrador, faced various US charges for stock fraud and manipulation, and, in Canada, for tax evasion. He exiled himself to Panama City, eluded extradition, and lived there in luxury until his death in May 2000.

32. Gwyn, *Smallwood*, 291, 300.

33. Joseph R. Smallwood, *The Time Has Come* (St. John's, NL: Newfoundland Book Publishers [1967] Ltd., 1967), 218, 219.

34. John C. Doyle was not a subtle crook. In 1979, as a producer for the CBC current affairs program *the fifth estate*, I tracked Doyle down in Panama City. He complained bitterly about being harassed by the Canadian tax authorities, and by Crosbie.

He played an electric organ for CBC's camera at his penthouse suite. He took us on a city tour in his Lincoln, parking at one point and inviting us into an up-market jewelry store. Staff there clearly knew Doyle and greeted him warmly. He appeared to own the place. "Pick up something nice for your wives, boys," he said quietly to members of our crew. "I'll look after it." There were, of course, no takers!

35. Guy, *Evening Telegram*, July 4, 1968, 3.
    Note Guy's spelling in this column, "Hoares egg." The common Newfoundland name for sea urchins is whores' eggs. Guy's first book, a collection of early *Telegram* columns, was *You May Know Them as Sea Urchins, Ma'am*. In the *Dictionary of Newfoundland English* entry for this word, a quarter of a page is devoted to the various spellings and names, including "Ose Eggs" and "Oar's Eggs." *DNE*, s.v. "ose egg." Guy's spelling here is unusual, and somewhat unlikely, inviting speculation that a *Telegram* desk editor was in a bowdlerizing mood that day, and was not having whores' eggs.

36. Guy, *Evening Telegram*, January 22, 1972, 3.

37. Guy, foreword to *Ray Guy: The Smallwood Years* (Portugal Cove, NL: Boulder Publications, 2008), v, vi.

38. Guy, introduction to *Ray Guy: Beneficial Vapors*, ed. Eric Norman (St. John's: Jesperson Printing Ltd., 1981), 1.

39. Arnold's Cove Board of Trustees, letter to the editor, *Evening Telegram*, February (date unclear), 1969, 28.

40. The quotation was attributed to William N. (Bill) Rowe, a Smallwood Cabinet minister and subsequently a well-known Newfoundland broadcaster and author. At the time when Guy was writing with confident authority about resettlement, he was 29. Rowe, the minister in charge of the program, who defended it with equal confidence, was 26.

41. Guy, introduction, *Beneficial Vapors*, 1, 2.

42. The lyrics for the song "The Government Game" were written by Al Pittman. Final verse:

> And when my soul leaves me for the heavens above,
> Take me back to St. Kyran's, the place that I love;
> And there on my gravestone right next to my name,
> Just say I died playing the government game.

43. Gwyn, *Smallwood: The Unlikely Revolutionary* (Toronto: Mc-Clelland and Stewart, 1968), 79, 133, 237.

44. Guy, *Evening Telegram*, April 28, 1971, 3.

45. Harold Horwood, "The Acid Is Shitty in Van," in *Voices Down East* (The Fourth Estate, c.1970), 30. (The actual publication date is not revealed in the magazine.)

46. Harold Horwood, *Among the Lions: A Lamb in the Literary Jungle* (St. John's, NL: Killick Press, 2000), 19–37.

47. James Overton, "Sparking a Cultural Revolution: Joey Smallwood, Harold Horwood and Newfoundland's Cultural Renaissance," *Newfoundland Studies* 16, no. 2 (Fall 2000), 166-204.

48. Guy, *Evening Telegram*, October 20, 1969, 3.

49. Quoted in Gordon Inglis, *More Than Just a Union: The Story of the NFFAWU* (St. John's: Jesperson Press, 1985), 87.

50. This observation is based on personal experience. As a student at Memorial University, I had the good fortune to study 18th-century English Literature with O'Flaherty, who celebrated the works of Swift, Johnson, Dryden et al. with infectious energy and humour.

51. Patrick O'Flaherty, "Newfoundland Writing, 1949–74: Comment," *Canadian Forum* (March 1974), 29.

52. Guy, *Evening Telegram*, July 3, 1969, 3.

53. Jonathan Swift, "Letters," in *Eighteenth Century English Literature*, ed. Geoffrey Tillotson, Paul Fussell, Jr., Marshall Waingrow, with Brewster Rogerson (New York: Harcourt, Brace & World, Inc., 1969), 458.

54. Horwood, *A Walk in Dreamtime: Growing Up in Old St. John's* (St. John's: Killick Press, 1997), 240.

55. "Podauger days," variously spelled as pod auger, pot auger, etc., is "a very remote period before modern inventions." *DNE*, s.v. "podauger days." Crunnick is "Small dry or withered timber, trunk, etc; ... the trunk or bole of a tree, also the roots with bark all gone and whitened by the sun or weather." *DNE*, s.v. "crunnick."

56. "Labor Lords" was a sly Guy reference to Stephen, Lord Taylor of Harlow. In 1967, J.R. Smallwood, usurping a power normally enjoyed by universities, appointed Taylor, a life peer, former Labour MP, and former Undersecretary of State for the Colonies, as president of Memorial University, where he served, by many accounts badly, until 1973. Lord Thomson, meanwhile, also handpicked by Smallwood, had been chancellor of Memorial from 1961 to 1968.

57. Until about 1700, fishermen in Newfoundland were forbidden by so-called fishing admirals—"lords" mainly—who ran the colony forbidding people from building homes with chimneys in them. The law was enforced rigorously as one of the means of preventing permanent settlement in Newfoundland. Such settlement was deemed to be a threat to the English West Country fishing interests who preferred a transient seasonal fishery and complete control of the fishermen. It also would have been a threat to the Admiralty, which supported the seasonal shipboard fishery as a training ground for sailors.

58. A thorough account of those events is found in Michael Harris's *Unholy Orders: Tragedy at Mount Cashel* (Markham, ON: Penguin Books, 1990). In references to Mount Cashel in this book, I have relied extensively on Harris's work, augmented by other sources and personal knowledge.

59. Bill Gillespie, *Alternate Press* 2, no. 1 (February 1972), 4.

60. Greg Davis, "Ray Guy: Journalist as Political Opposition during the Smallwood Years," *Newfoundland Quarterly* 102, no. 3 (2009), 42.

61. Guy, *Telegram*, February 16, 1973, 3.

62. Guy, *Telegram*, March 23, 1973, 3.

63. Guy, *Telegram*, March 27, 1973, 3.

64. Guy, *Telegram*, June 29, 1973, 3.

65. Guy, *Telegram*, June 30, 1973, 3.

66. Guy, *Telegram*, September 8, 1973, 3.

67. Guy, *Telegram*, February 23, 1970, 3.

68. Wiseman, "I's the B'y Who Meets Ray Guy," 29.

69. Guy, *That Far Greater Bay*, x.

70. Percy Bysshe Shelley, "Epipsychidion," in *Shelley: The Pursuit,* by Richard Holmes (London: Quartet Books, 1976), 633.

71. Guy, "Our Climate Condemned Us to Canada," in *Ray Guy's Best* (Breakwater Books, 1987), 2, 3. Originally published in *Atlantic Insight*.

72. Guy, "Country Comfort's a Penthouse in the City," in *Ray Guy's Best*, 7. Originally published in *Atlantic Insight*.

73. Guy, "A Christmas Lament for a Child's Loss of Faith," in *Ray Guy's Best*, 183, 184. Originally published in *Atlantic Insight*.

74. Guy, "The Hazards of Cats, Kids and Squishy Pussy-Treet," in *Ray Guy's Best*, 170, 171.

75. Sharon Fraser, introduction to *Ray Guy's Best* (Halifax: Formac Publishing, 1987). In an arrangement with *Atlantic Insight*, Breakwater Books, St. John's, published the same book with the same title in Newfoundland, also in 1987.

76. James Wilde, "Jester in the Kingdom of Joe," *Time*, August 23, 1971.

77. Silver Donald Cameron, "Fool's Laughter: Ray Guy's Satire Turns to Sorrow," *Weekend Magazine*, November 1, 1975, 16–19.

78. Guy, "Playing the Newf Goof for Mainland Media," in *Ray Guy's Best*, 19, 20.

79. Guy, "Kicking against the Pricks," in *This Dear and Fine Country*, ed. Eric Norman (Breakwater Books, 1985), 35, 36.

80. Guy, "Litres of Baccalieu," in *This Dear and Fine Country*, 15.

81. Guy, *Telegram*, August 13, 1970, 3.

82. Guy, *His Worship*, CBC Radio, St. John's, NL, 1984, voiced by Karl Wells.

83. A note written by Jamie Fitzpatrick in 2001 for the Newfoundland and Labrador Heritage Society described Johnny Burke (1851–1930):

> A St. John's balladeer. Several of his songs, such as *Cod Liver Oil*, *The Trinity Cake*, and *The Kelligrew's Soiree*, remain popular to this day ...
>
> The Bard of Prescott Street,' as he became known, was the son of a well-known sealing captain. He worked as a poet, actor, singer and playwright, but is best known for writing songs about contemporary events and personalities, songs that revealed Burke's sharp eye for detail and deft touch with wit and satire ... Burke marketed his songs on 'broadsheets,' printed pages of lyrics that sold for two to five cents a copy.

84. Michael Fralic, "Marginalization and the Active Margins in the Plays of Ray Guy" (master's thesis, Memorial University of Newfoundland, 1996), iii.

85. Guy, "Uncanny Connections," *Newfoundland Quarterly* 98, no. 1 (2005), 39.

86. Stephen Kimber, "Hard ... and Soft as Harry Steele," *Atlantic Business*, Steve Kimber.com, May 11, 2014. https://atlantic-businessmagazine.ca/article/hard-and-soft-as-steele/

87. The "rat pack," a posse of noisy Liberal MPs during Tory prime minister Mulroney's first term, 1984 onward, included Sheila Copps and her three mustachioed co-rats, Brian Tobin, Don Boudria, and John Nunziato. They were regularly denounced by the Conservatives as sleazy, slimy, and slick; and by John Crosbie as "rodent-like." They got on Mulroney's nerves.

88. Guy, "The Tale of Sammy and the Miracle Christmas Crow," in *Sammy and the Miracles of Christmas* illust. Boyd W. Chubbs (Portugal Cove: Boulder Publications, 2007), n.p.

89. Guy, "The Miracle of Sammy and the Christmas Sculpin." *Sammy and the Miracles of Christmas*. n.p.

90. Guy, *An Heroine for Our Times* (St. John's, NL: Harry Cuff Publications, 1983), 7, 47, 48.

91. Guy, "Gardening," *Newfoundland Quarterly* 99, no. 1 (2006), 54, 55.

92. Guy, "A Landscape of Awe and Dread," *Newfoundland Quarterly* 100, no. 4 (Spring 2008), 26.

93. Guy, "Architecture in Newfoundland," *Newfoundland Quarterly* 102, no. 1 (Winter 2009), 8.

94. Guy and Sherman Hines, *Outhouses of the East* (Nimbus Publishing Ltd., 1975), 5, 45.

95. Guy, "Seal Wars," *Canadian Geographic* (January/February 2000), 42, 43, 48.

96. Guy, "Uncanny Connections," *Newfoundland Quarterly* 98, no. 1 (2005), 39.

97. Patrick O'Flaherty, "Newfoundland Writing, 1949–74: Comment," *Canadian Forum* (March 1974), 29.

98. Cyril Poole, "Laughing at Ray Guy's Cats," in *In Search of the Newfoundland Soul* (St. John's, NL: Harry Cuff Publications, 1982), 30, 32.

99. Stuart Pierson, "Ray Guy's Journalism: A Humane Sense of Proportion," in *Hard-Headed and Big-Hearted: Writing Newfoundland* (St. John's: Pennywell Books, 2006), 81.

100. Stan Dragland, *Strangers and Others—Newfoundland Essays* (St. John's: Pedlar Press, 2015), 53, 54.

101. James K. Hiller, review of *Ray Guy: The Smallwood Years*, by Ray Guy, *Newfoundland and Labrador Studies* 24, no. 1 (2009), 155-56.

102. Greg Davis, "Ray Guy: Journalist as Political Opposition in the Smallwood Years," *Newfoundland Quarterly* 102, no. 3 (2009), 42.

103. Janet Kazmi's Ray Guy quotes, at pp. 2–11 of her essay, are from *That Far Greater Bay*.

104. Wayne Johnston, *First Snow, Last Light* (Alfred A. Knopf Canada, 2017), 384, 43.105.

105. Swift, "Verses on the Death of Dr. Swift," in Eighteenth Century English Literature, 386.

106. Guy, "Peering through the Fence at the Waterford Hospital," *Telegram*, April 6, 1995, 3.

107. Clare-Marie Grigg, Giggle the Bastards to Death—Ray Guy Chose a Career in Journalism Because—While Superman Was a Jerk—Clark Kent Was a Hero," *Sunday Independent* 2, no. 33 (2004).

108. Guy, "A Christmas Story," in *That Far Greater Bay*, ed. Eric Norman (Breakwater Books, 1976), 95–101. All quotations from this story are from this edition.

109. Guy, "But You Said We Won," in *You May Know Them as Sea Urchins, Ma'am*, ed. Eric Norman (Breakwater Books, 1975), 22, 23. All excerpts from this story are from this edition.

NOTE TO READERS

Ray Guy's large body of writing as surveyed for this book spans five decades, from the early 1960s, when he was a student at the Ryerson Institute of Technology, to 2013, when he wrote his final published words for the *Northeast Avalon Times*. Much, but not all of it, has been easy to locate.

Fortunately, large groupings of Guy's columns, essays, and reports have appeared in a small number of publications which are archived, in some cases digitized, and otherwise readily available to researchers.

Collections of Guy's *Evening Telegram* and other columns have appeared in eight different books, a few of them in multiple editions, many of them still available.

Listed here by their original editions and publishers, the books are: *You May Know Them as Sea Urchins, Ma'am*, edited by Eric Norman, Breakwater Books Ltd., 1975; *That Far Greater Bay*, edited by Eric Norman, Breakwater Books Ltd., 1976; *Beneficial Vapors*, edited by Eric Norman, Jesperson Printing Ltd., 1981; *This Dear and Fine Country*, edited by Eric Norman, Breakwater, 1985; *Ray Guy's Best*, Formac Publishing Company Ltd. and Breakwater

Books, 1987; *Ray Guy: The Smallwood Years,* edited by Kathryn Welbourn, Boulder Publications, 2008; *Ray Guy: the Revolutionary Years,* edited by Stephanie Porter, Boulder Publications, 2011; and *Ray Guy: The Final Columns, 2003–2013,* edited by Brian Jones, Creative Publishers, 2017.

Guy's *Evening Telegram* columns have not been digitized. However, Boulder Books, which has published two collections of his *Telegram* columns, made hard copies of nearly all of them. Those were available to me, a trove of solid material readily at hand.

Those collections cover as much as two-thirds of Guy's published works. The remainder, still hundreds of pieces, are scattered in a multitude of publications large and small. A search for them has included sources as diverse as the audio and video vaults of the CBC, several national newspapers such as the *Toronto Star*, magazines such as *Canadian Geographic*, and a plethora of narrow-circulation publications, including the *Newfoundland Herald, Newfoundland Lifestyle,* the *Bowlog* (a house organ of pulp and paper compamy Bowater Inc.), and *Decks Awash,* for several decades a respected publication of Memorial University's Extension Service.

Previously unpublished or private Ray Guy writing to which I had access and permission to quote has come largely from the Guy collection at the Centre for Newfoundland Studies at Memorial University and from materials made available to me by Ray's sister, Iris Brett, and his late wife, Kathie Housser. I am happy to possess a few notes of my own from Guy, to which I make occasional references in the book.

I have not read every word Ray Guy wrote. No one but Guy ever has. I am confident that I have sampled most of it; however, after working on this project sporadically for five years or more, I am still turning up articles of which I was unaware.

All excerpts from publications have been noted and attributed, wherever possible with publication dates and page numbers. Sources and notes appear either in the manuscript itself as the quotations are introduced, or as endnotes.

Kathie Housser supported this project from the beginning and in many ways, including permission to quote all but a few family-focused emails written by her husband or family members. Her ongoing illnesses and untimely passing on September 10, 2017, meant her involvement in the research could never be as thorough as both she and I would have wished.

Iris Brett has been equally generous and essential to this book—an endless font of Ray Guy stories, family history, photos, hospitality, funny emails, and good cheer.

The book relies heavily on personal interviews. Most major interviews were conducted face to face, intermittently over a period of about four years. Most were audio recorded and should constitute a useful recorded archive for Ray Guy students, which will be offered to the Centre for Newfoundland Studies at Memorial. A few key interviews were done through email exchanges.

My interview with author Wayne Johnston was the only substantial one conducted by telephone. It was unusual. When in full novel-writing mode, as he was at the time, Johnston's practice is to write at night and sleep by day. The telephone interview began around 8 p.m., Toronto time. Wayne was having his breakfast coffee, alert and cheerful.

Unless they are otherwise attributed or qualified, readers should assume that direct quotes in the book are from my personal interviews with the individual being quoted. Readers also should be aware that excerpts from Guy's writing adhere to his exact words, spelling choices (Canadian versus US) and style. A few words misspelt in both forms are noted with the designation *sic*.

Other contributions to this book have been made by individuals who knew Ray Guy and his writing well or were simply happy to help. That help came in many modes, from inspiration to accommodation, to such time-consuming tasks as reading and assessing manuscript drafts, to professional editing. There were countless important smaller contributions such as locating and lending photos and books to reliable family and friendship support.

I want to underscore for readers that this book is not the definitive biography of Ray Guy. Nor is it the ultimate work of scholarship or academic discipline that his body of writing merits. There is ample room for others to weigh in, and I sincerely hope they do.

All contributors to this book are hereby acknowledged and thanked profusely. They are listed here, alphabetically:

Carolyn Atkinson, Michael Benedict, Everett Bishop, Ted Blades, Iris Brett, Anne Budgell, Iona Bulgin, William (Bill) Callahan, Lesley Choyce, Diane Crocker, Robin Crocker, Christine Davis, David Day, Glenn Deir, Geoff D'Eon, Robert J. (Bob) Ennis, Eric Facey, John Fitzpatrick, Sheila Fitzpatrick, Jessica Grant, Annie Guy, Michael Harris, W.J. ("Young Jim") Herder, Jenny Higgins, Rosemary House, Johnny Housser, Katharine (Kathie) Housser, Wayne Johnston, James Lorimer, Susan Newhook, Patrick O'Flaherty, Steve Payne, Maxine Reccord Pinhorn, Norm Pinhorn, Stephanie Porter, Azzo Rezori, Edward Roberts, Cynthia Smith, Marie Wadden, Bob Wakeham, Mary Walsh, Kathryn Welbourn, Karl Wells, Gavin Will, and Debbie Youden.

INDEX

Ron Crocker grew up in Heart's Delight, Newfoundland and Labrador. His early education was at United Church schools in Heart's Delight and Green's Harbour. He is a graduate of Memorial University of Newfoundland and Osgoode Hall Law School in Toronto. After a print journalism back-  ground that included five years with the *Evening Telegram*, Ron worked for more than 30 years with the CBC as a journalist, producer, and executive. He lives in Glen Haven, Nova Scotia. Ron is currently a senior investigator with the Nova Scotia Office of the Ombudsman. His first book was *Forever Bluenose: A Future for a Schooner with a Past*, published by Nimbus Publishing of Halifax in 2013.